TING 50
DREAMS AND MY GIRLFRIEND 1

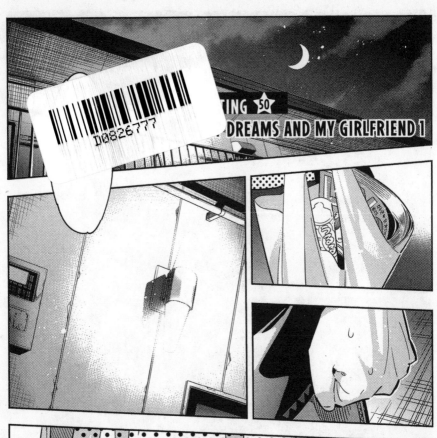

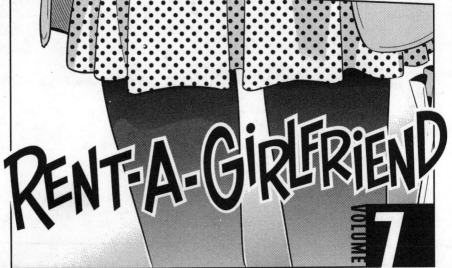

RENT-A-GIRLFRIEND

VOLUME 7

REIJI MIYAJIMA

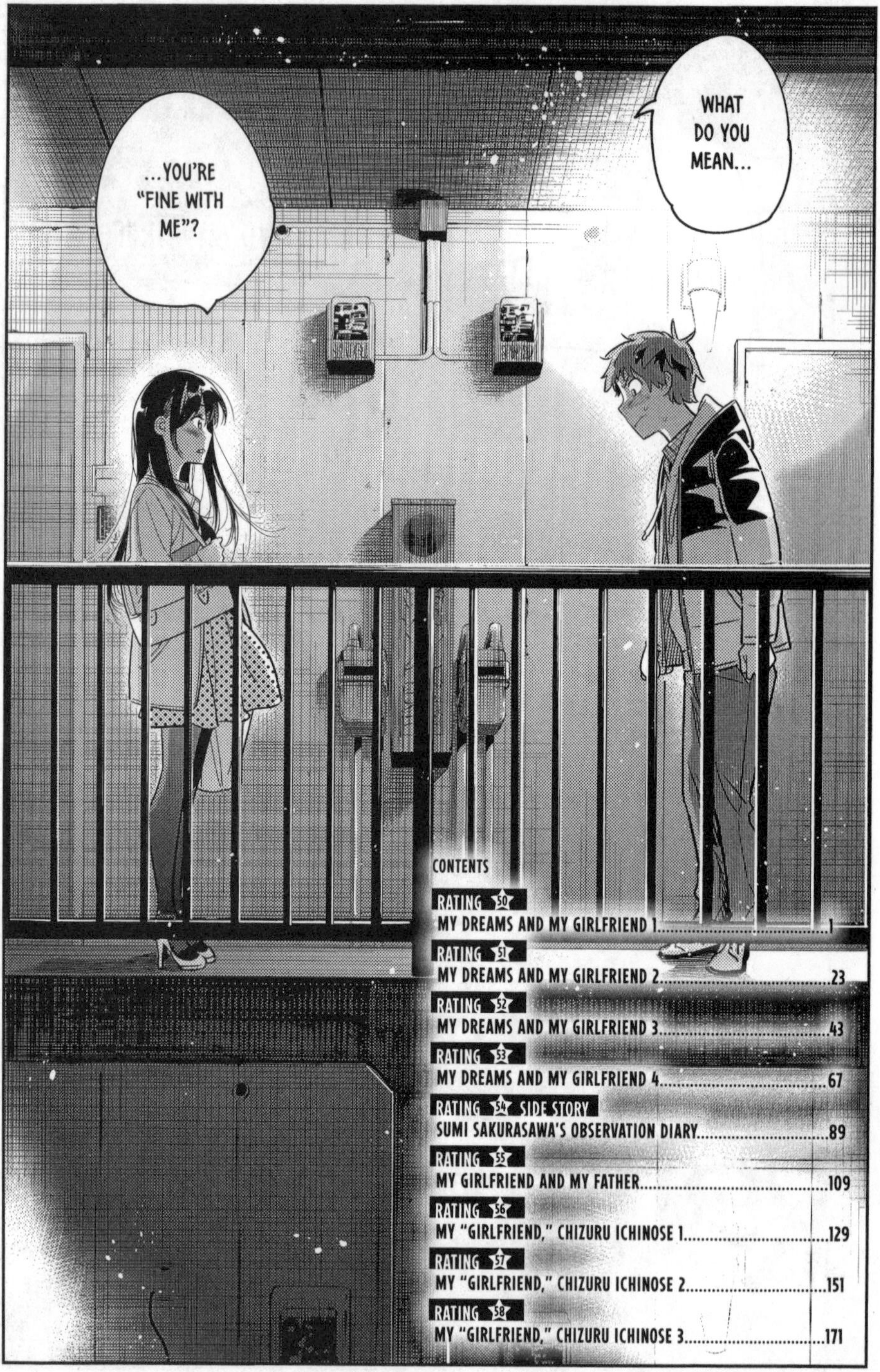
WHAT DO YOU MEAN...
...YOU'RE "FINE WITH ME"?

CONTENTS

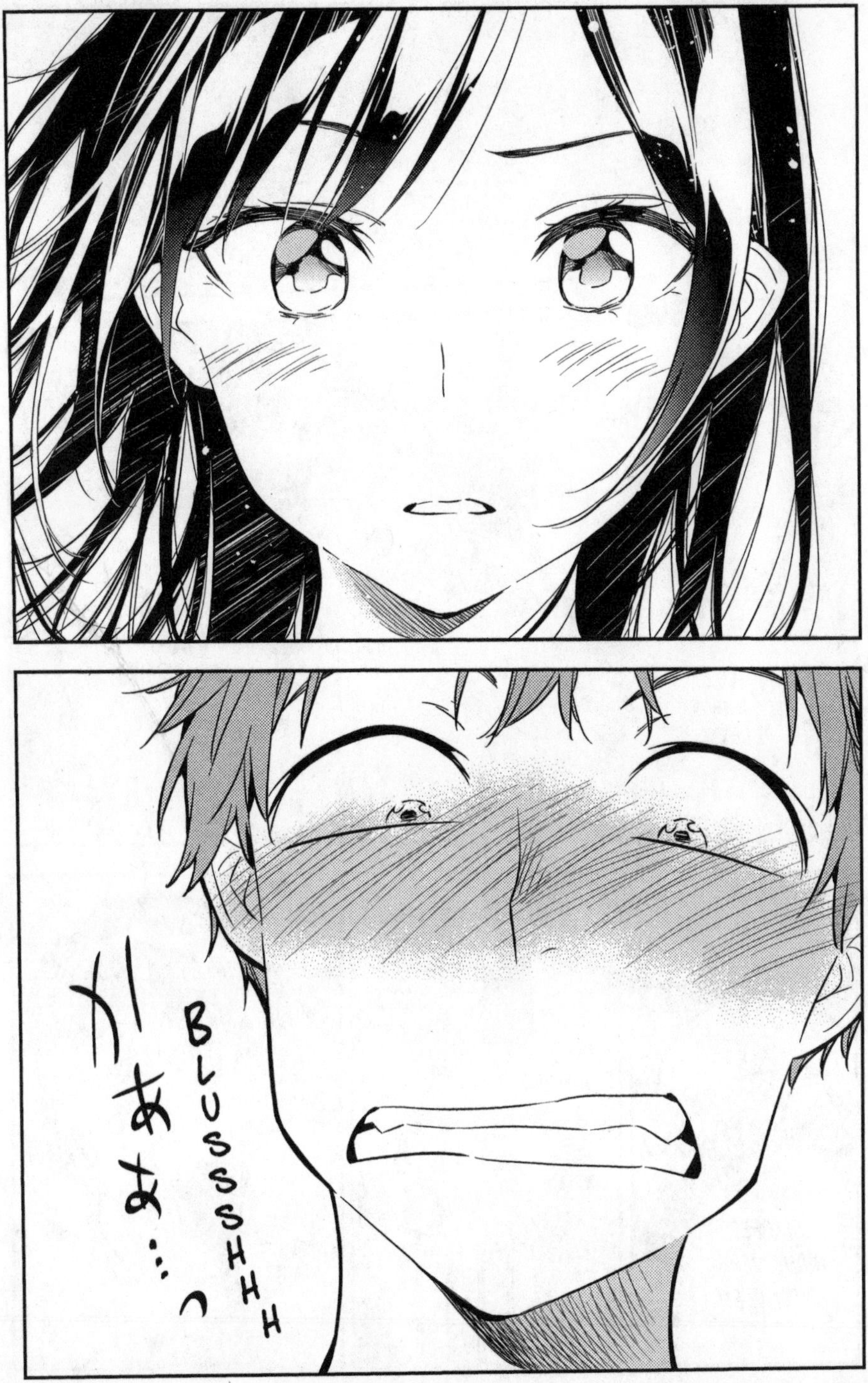
カあぁ…っ
BLUSSHHH

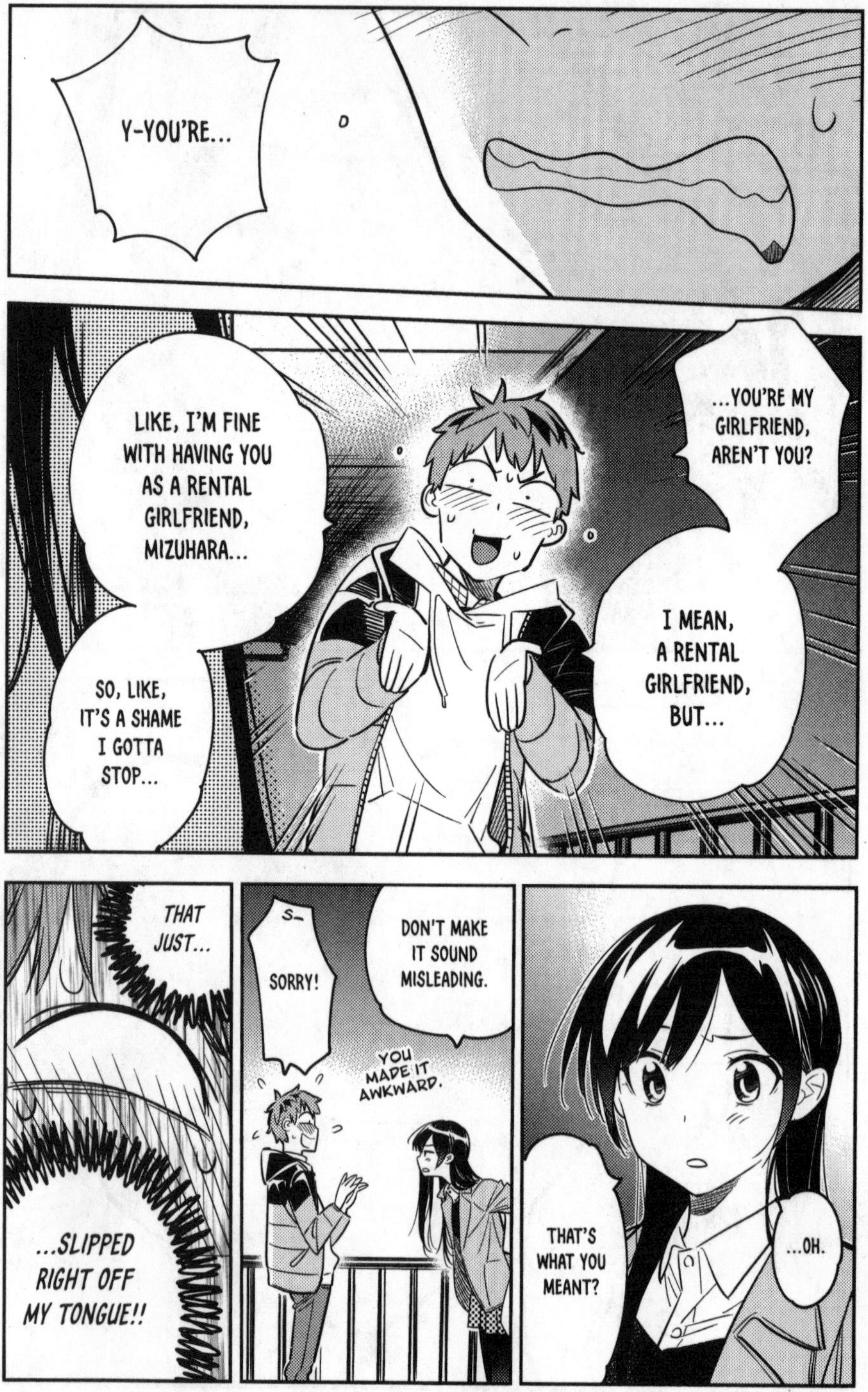
Y-YOU'RE...
...YOU'RE MY GIRLFRIEND, AREN'T YOU?
I MEAN, A RENTAL GIRLFRIEND, BUT...
LIKE, I'M FINE WITH HAVING YOU AS A RENTAL GIRLFRIEND, MIZUHARA...
SO, LIKE, IT'S A SHAME I GOTTA STOP...
...OH.
THAT'S WHAT YOU MEANT?
DON'T MAKE IT SOUND MISLEADING.
S— SORRY!
YOU MADE IT AWKWARD.
THAT JUST...
...SLIPPED RIGHT OFF MY TONGUE!!

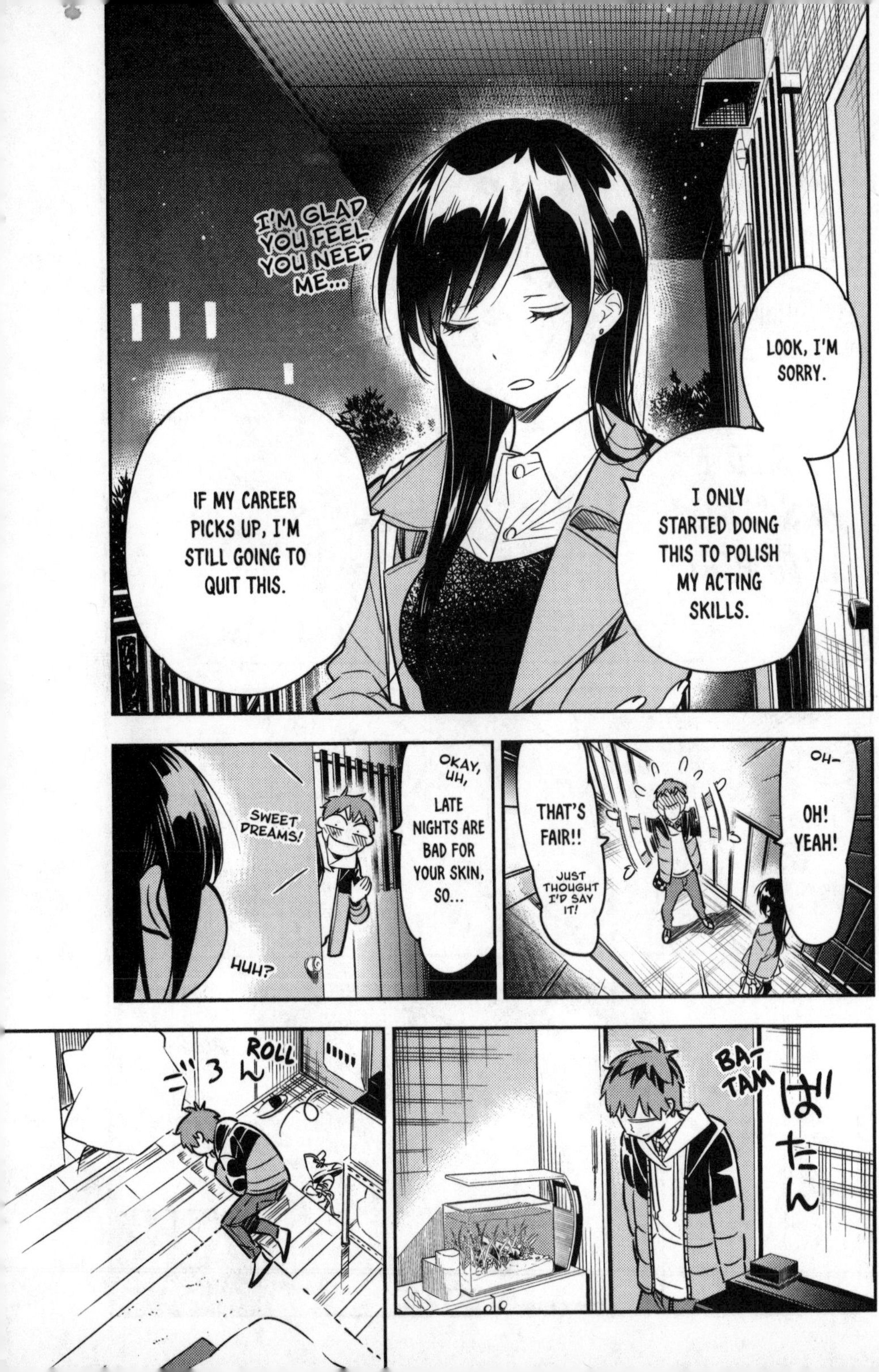
I'M GLAD YOU FEEL YOU NEED ME...
LOOK, I'M SORRY.
I ONLY STARTED DOING THIS TO POLISH MY ACTING SKILLS.
IF MY CAREER PICKS UP, I'M STILL GOING TO QUIT THIS.
OH—
OH! YEAH!
THAT'S FAIR!!
JUST THOUGHT I'D SAY IT!
OKAY, UH,
LATE NIGHTS ARE BAD FOR YOUR SKIN, SO...
SWEET DREAMS!
HUH?
BA-TAM
ばたん
ROLL
ごろん

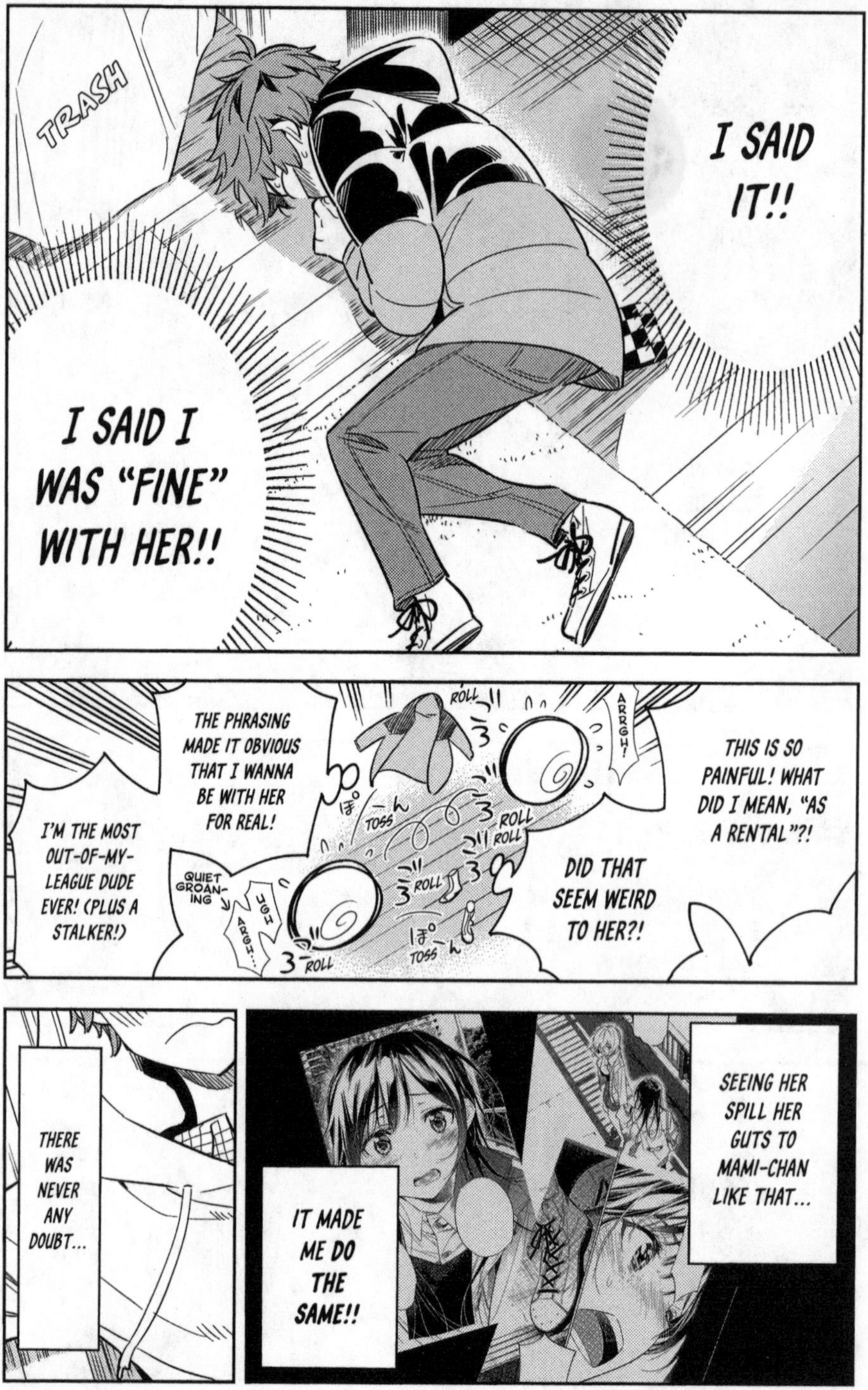
I SAID IT!!
TRASH
I SAID I WAS "FINE" WITH HER!!
THIS IS SO PAINFUL! WHAT DID I MEAN, "AS A RENTAL"?!
ARRGH!
ROLL
DID THAT SEEM WEIRD TO HER?!
ROLL ROLL
THE PHRASING MADE IT OBVIOUS THAT I WANNA BE WITH HER FOR REAL!
TOSS
ROLL
TOSS
I'M THE MOST OUT-OF-MY-LEAGUE DUDE EVER! (PLUS A STALKER!)
QUIET GROANING
UGH
ARGH...
ROLL
SEEING HER SPILL HER GUTS TO MAMI-CHAN LIKE THAT...
IT MADE ME DO THE SAME!!
THERE WAS NEVER ANY DOUBT...

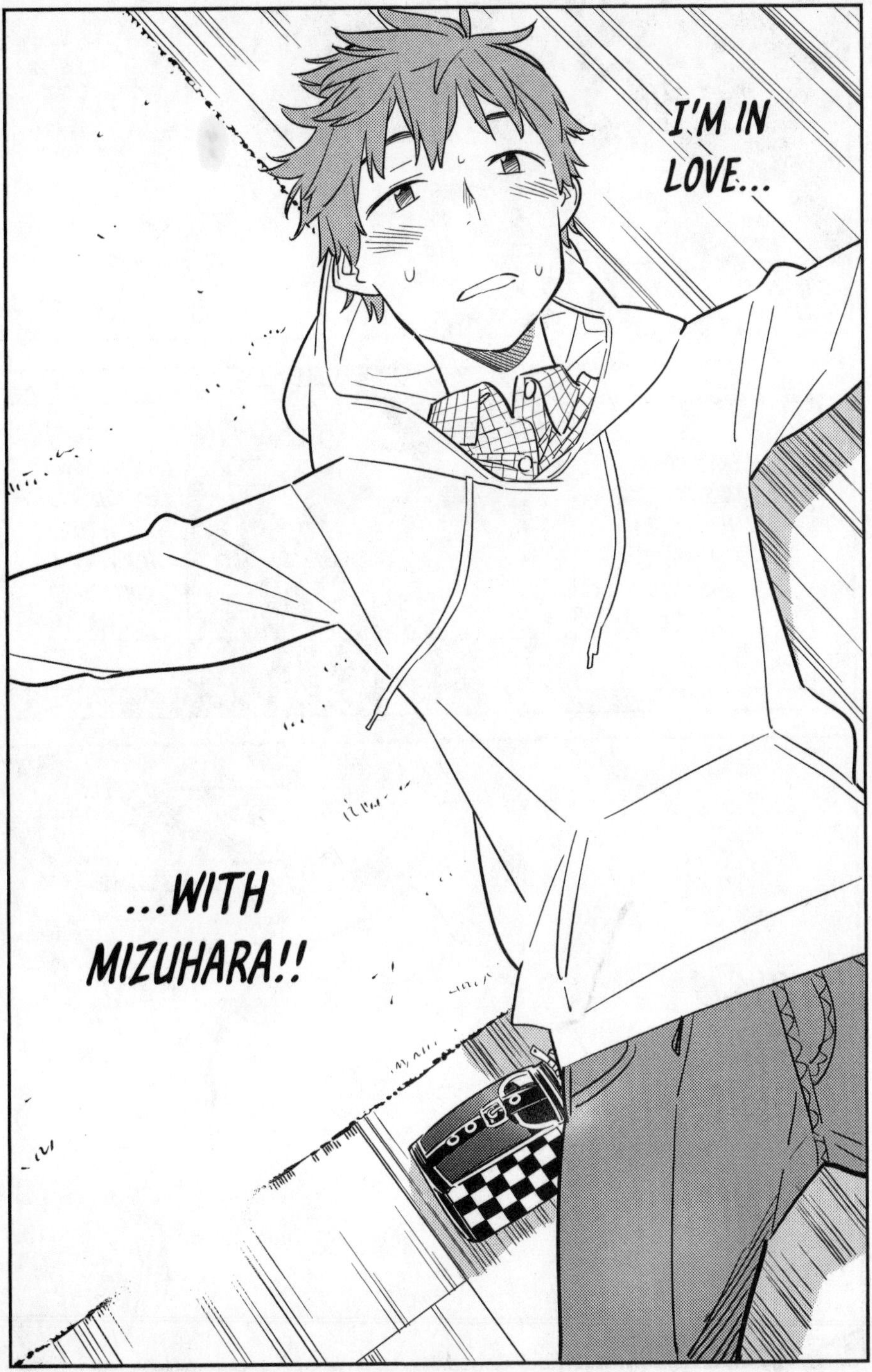
I'M IN LOVE...
...WITH MIZUHARA!!

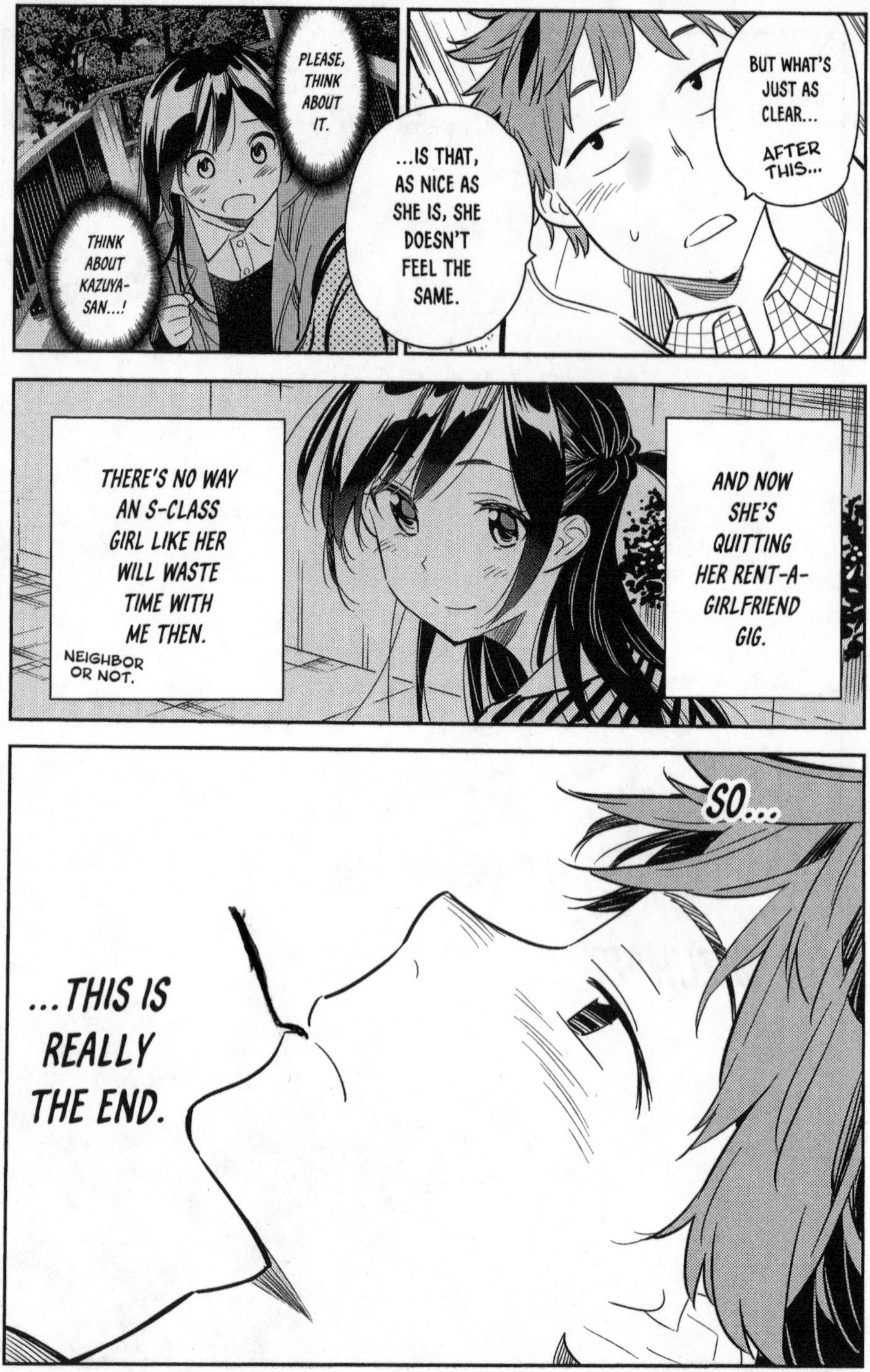
BUT WHAT'S JUST AS CLEAR...
AFTER THIS...
...IS THAT, AS NICE AS SHE IS, SHE DOESN'T FEEL THE SAME.
PLEASE, THINK ABOUT IT.
THINK ABOUT KAZUYA-SAN...!
AND NOW SHE'S QUITTING HER RENT-A-GIRLFRIEND GIG.
THERE'S NO WAY AN S-CLASS GIRL LIKE HER WILL WASTE TIME WITH ME THEN.
NEIGHBOR OR NOT.
SO...
...THIS IS REALLY THE END.

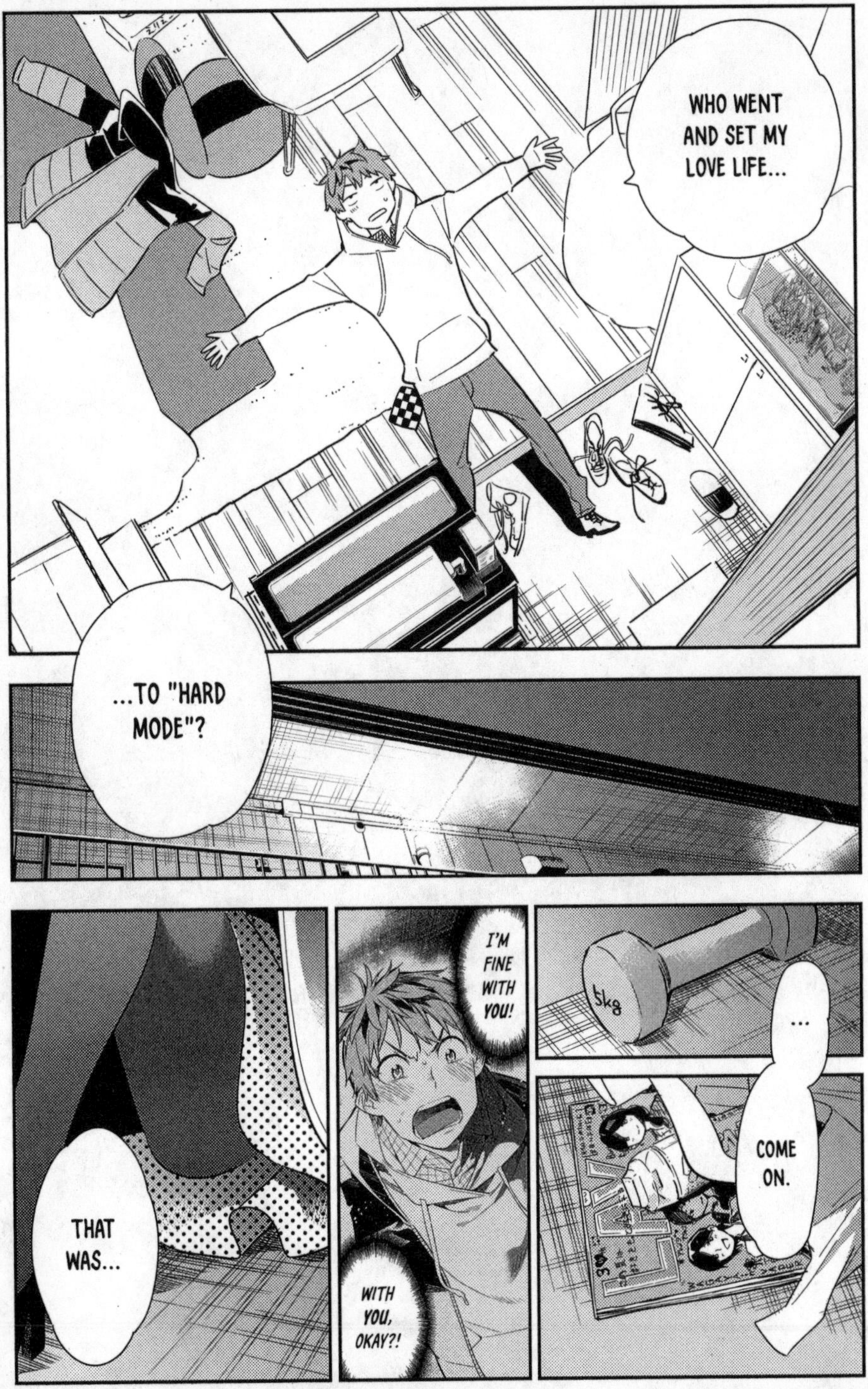
WHO WENT AND SET MY LOVE LIFE...
...TO "HARD MODE"?
5kg
...
COME ON.
I'M FINE WITH YOU!
WITH YOU, OKAY?!
THAT WAS...

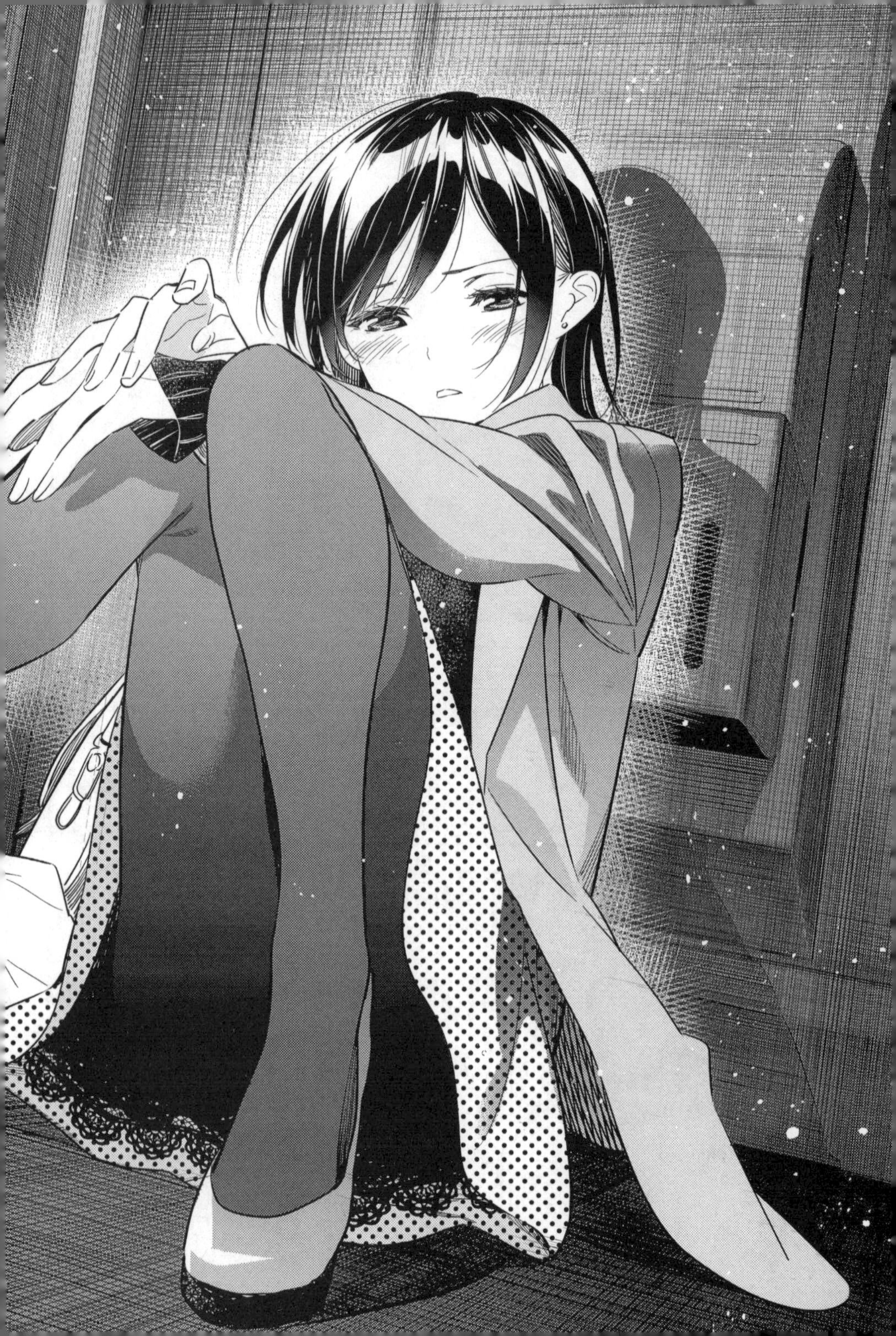

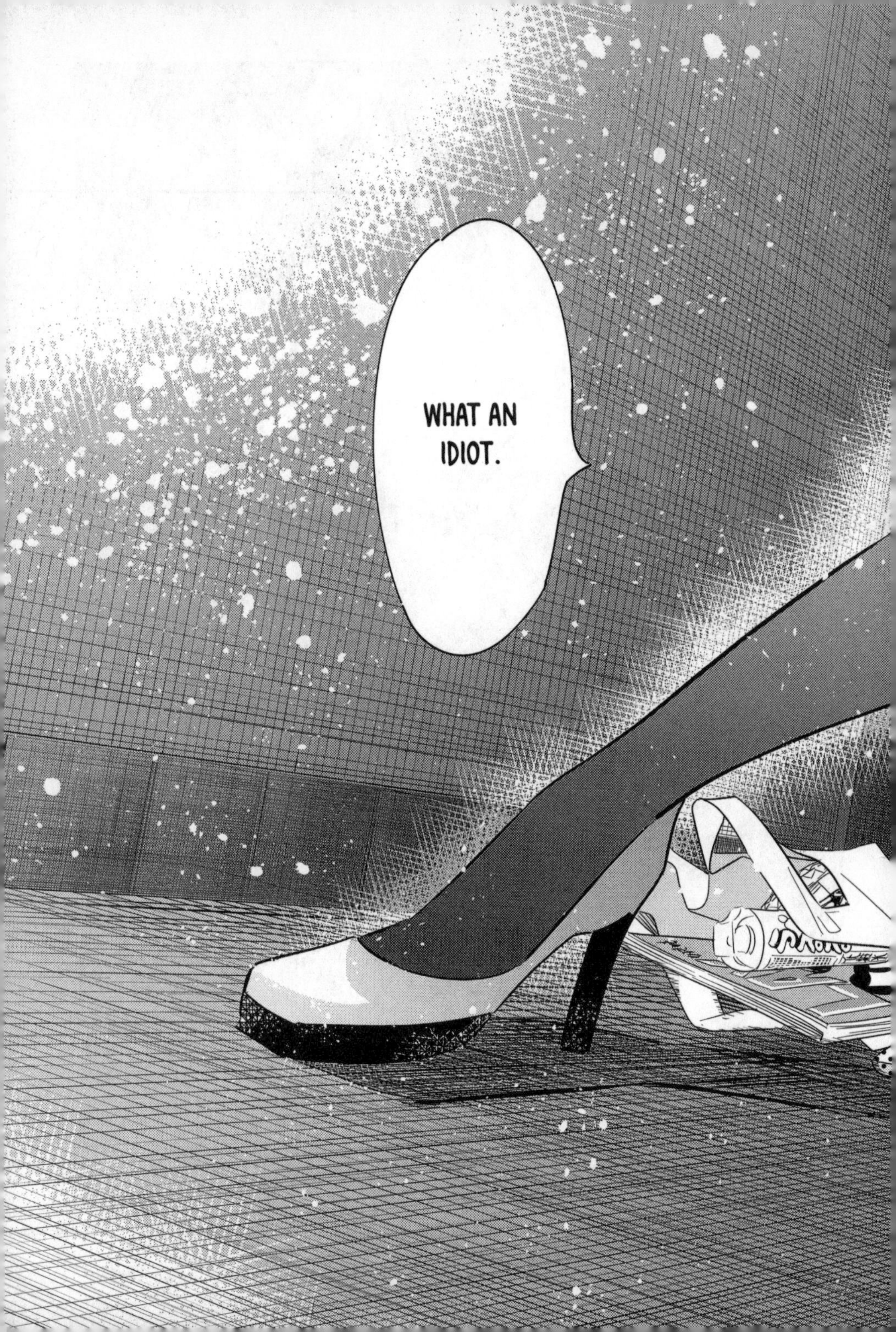
WHAT AN IDIOT.

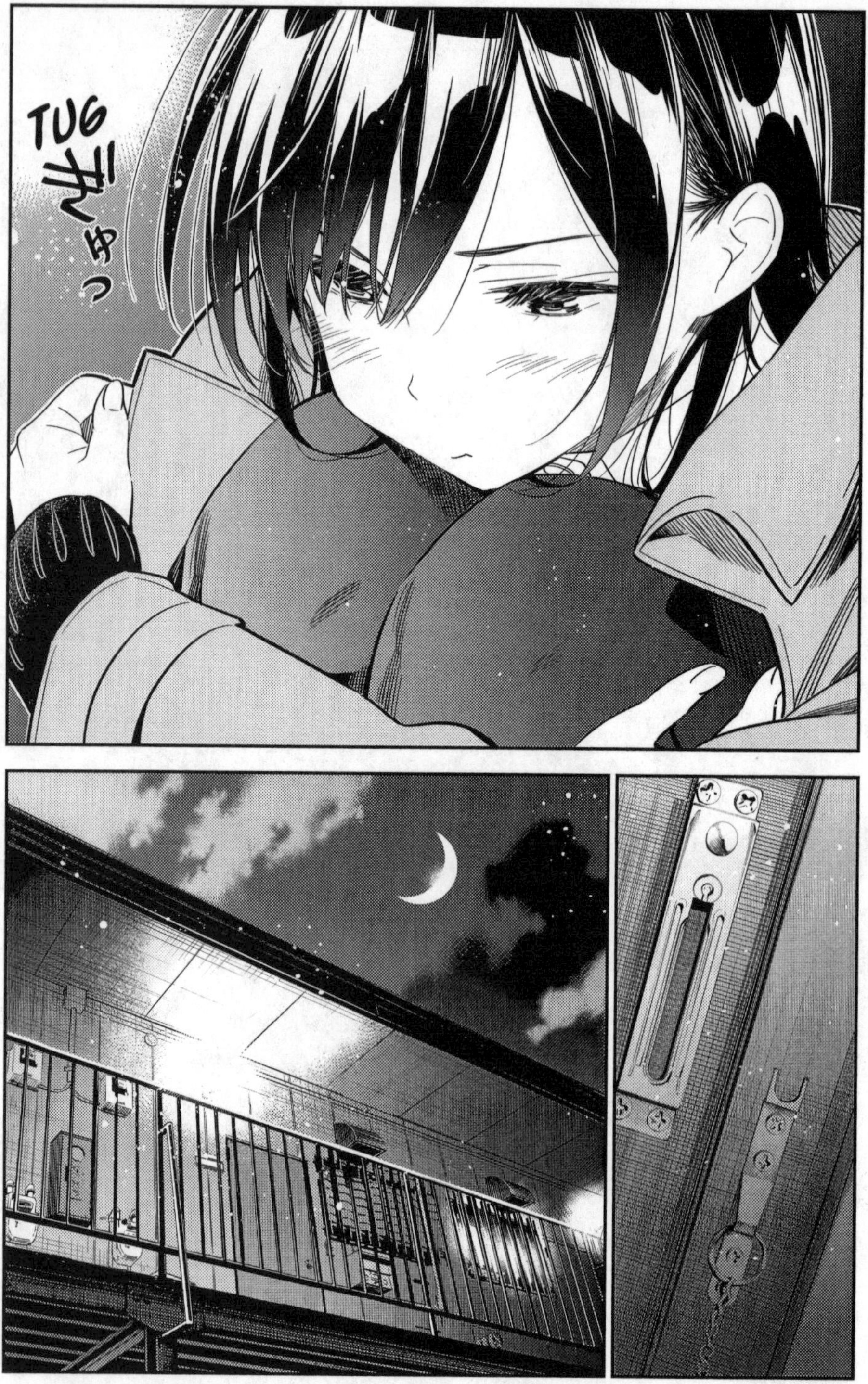
TUG
ぎゅっ

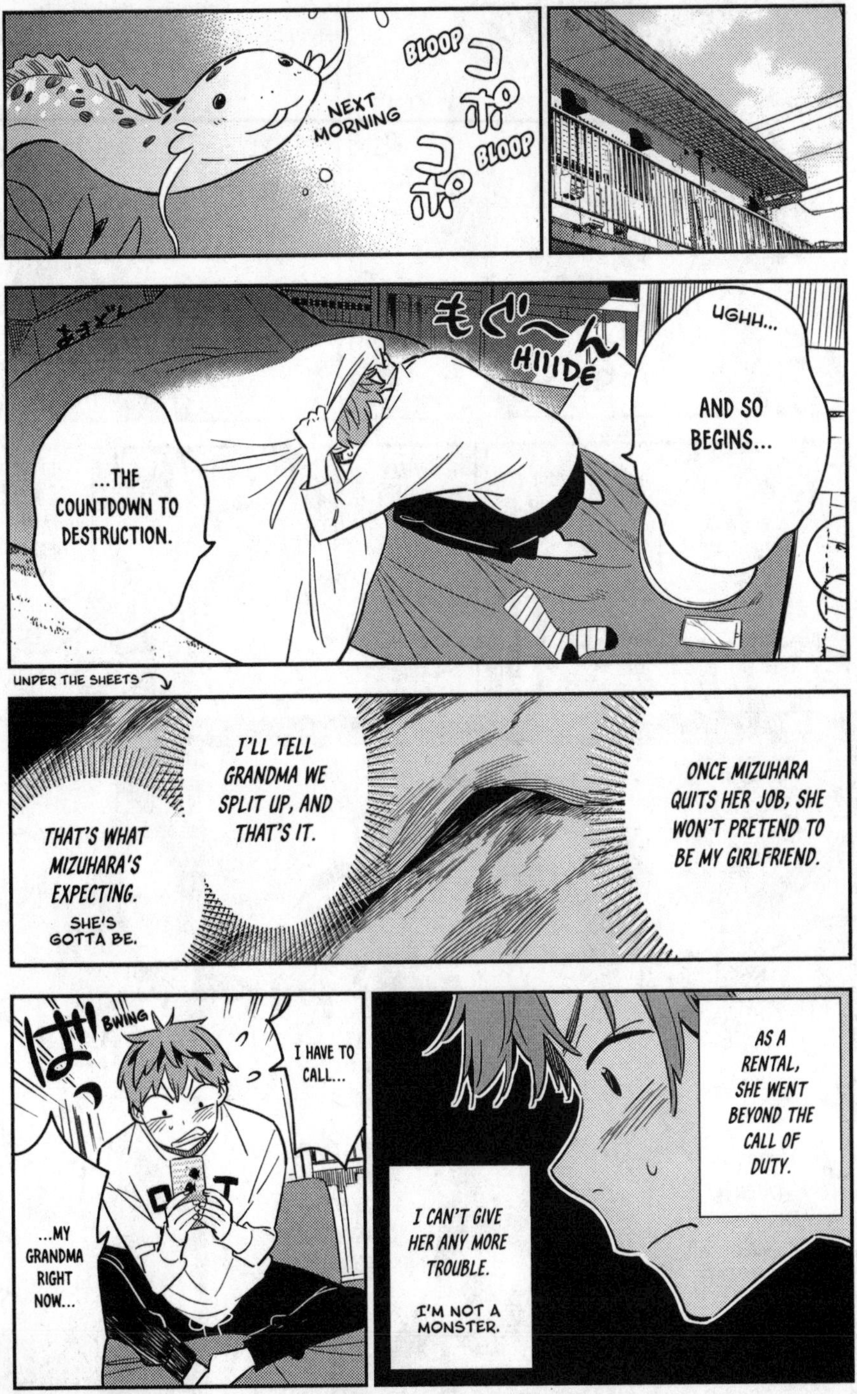
コポ
BLOOP
NEXT MORNING
コポ
BLOOP
UGHH...
AND SO BEGINS...
もぐ～ん
HIIIDE
...THE COUNTDOWN TO DESTRUCTION.
UNDER THE SHEETS
ONCE MIZUHARA QUITS HER JOB, SHE WON'T PRETEND TO BE MY GIRLFRIEND.
I'LL TELL GRANDMA WE SPLIT UP, AND THAT'S IT.
THAT'S WHAT MIZUHARA'S EXPECTING.
SHE'S GOTTA BE.
AS A RENTAL, SHE WENT BEYOND THE CALL OF DUTY.
I CAN'T GIVE HER ANY MORE TROUBLE.
I'M NOT A MONSTER.
ぱっ
BWING
I HAVE TO CALL...
...MY GRANDMA RIGHT NOW...

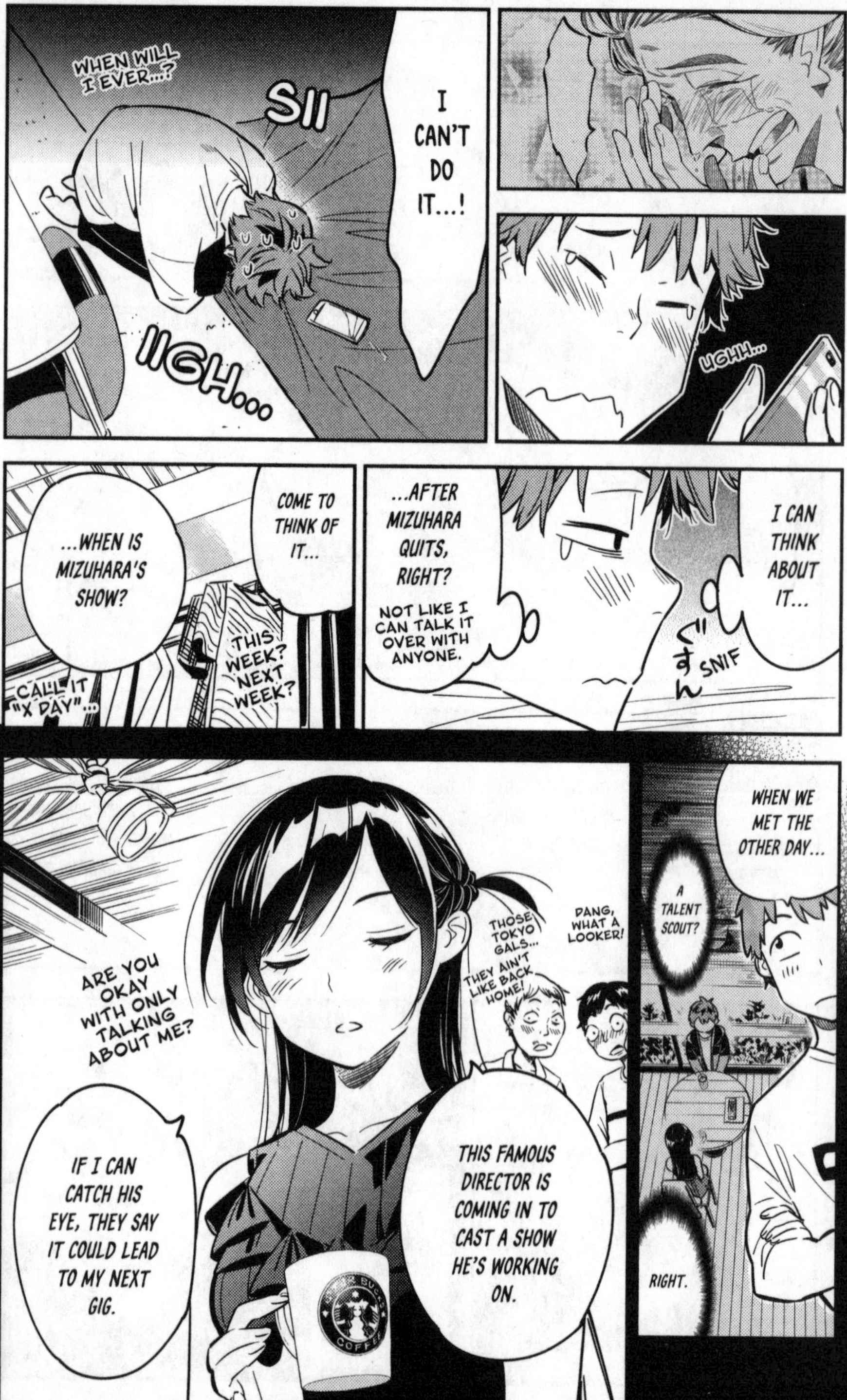
UGHH...
I CAN'T DO IT...!
WHEN WILL I EVER...?
SII
IIGH...
I CAN THINK ABOUT IT...
...AFTER MIZUHARA QUITS, RIGHT?
NOT LIKE I CAN TALK IT OVER WITH ANYONE.
ぐすん SNIF
COME TO THINK OF IT...
...WHEN IS MIZUHARA'S SHOW?
THIS WEEK? NEXT WEEK?
CALL IT "X DAY"...
WHEN WE MET THE OTHER DAY...
A TALENT SCOUT?
RIGHT.
DANG, WHAT A LOOKER!
THOSE TOKYO GALS... THEY AIN'T LIKE BACK HOME!
ARE YOU OKAY WITH ONLY TALKING ABOUT ME?
THIS FAMOUS DIRECTOR IS COMING IN TO CAST A SHOW HE'S WORKING ON.
IF I CAN CATCH HIS EYE, THEY SAY IT COULD LEAD TO MY NEXT GIG.

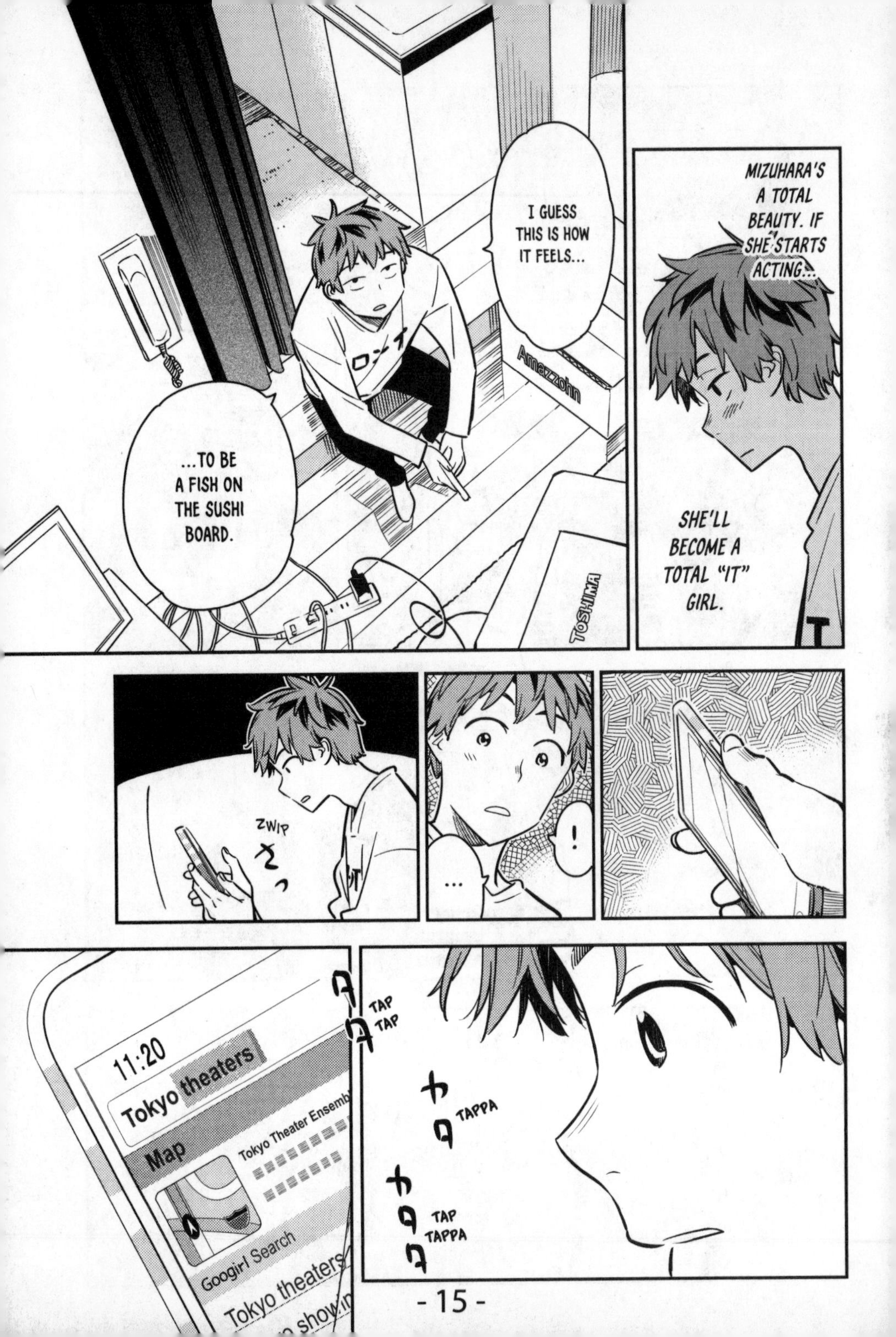
MIZUHARA'S A TOTAL BEAUTY. IF SHE STARTS ACTING...
SHE'LL BECOME A TOTAL "IT" GIRL.
I GUESS THIS IS HOW IT FEELS...
...TO BE A FISH ON THE SUSHI BOARD.
Amazzohn
TOSHIMA
!
...
ZWIP
TAP TAP
TAPPA
TAP TAPPA
11:20
Tokyo theaters
Tokyo Theater Ensemb
Map
Googirl Search
Tokyo theaters
Tokyo showi

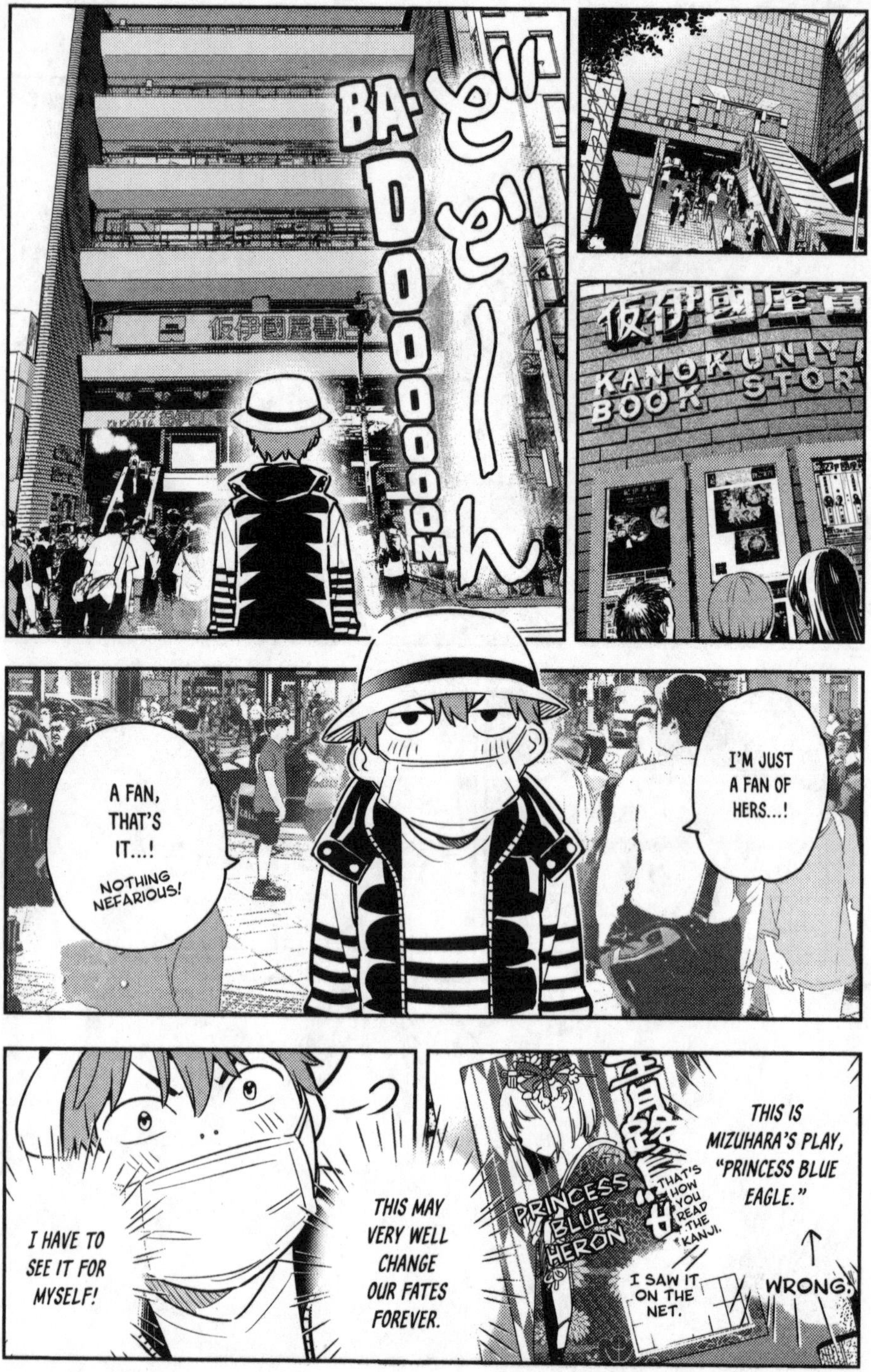
仮伊國屋書
KANOKUNIY
BOOK STOR
BA-DOOOOOOOM
どどーん
仮伊國屋書店
I'M JUST A FAN OF HERS...!
A FAN, THAT'S IT...!
NOTHING NEFARIOUS!
THIS IS MIZUHARA'S PLAY, "PRINCESS BLUE EAGLE."
WRONG.
PRINCESS BLUE HERON
THAT'S HOW YOU READ THE KANJI.
I SAW IT ON THE NET.
THIS MAY VERY WELL CHANGE OUR FATES FOREVER.
I HAVE TO SEE IT FOR MYSELF!

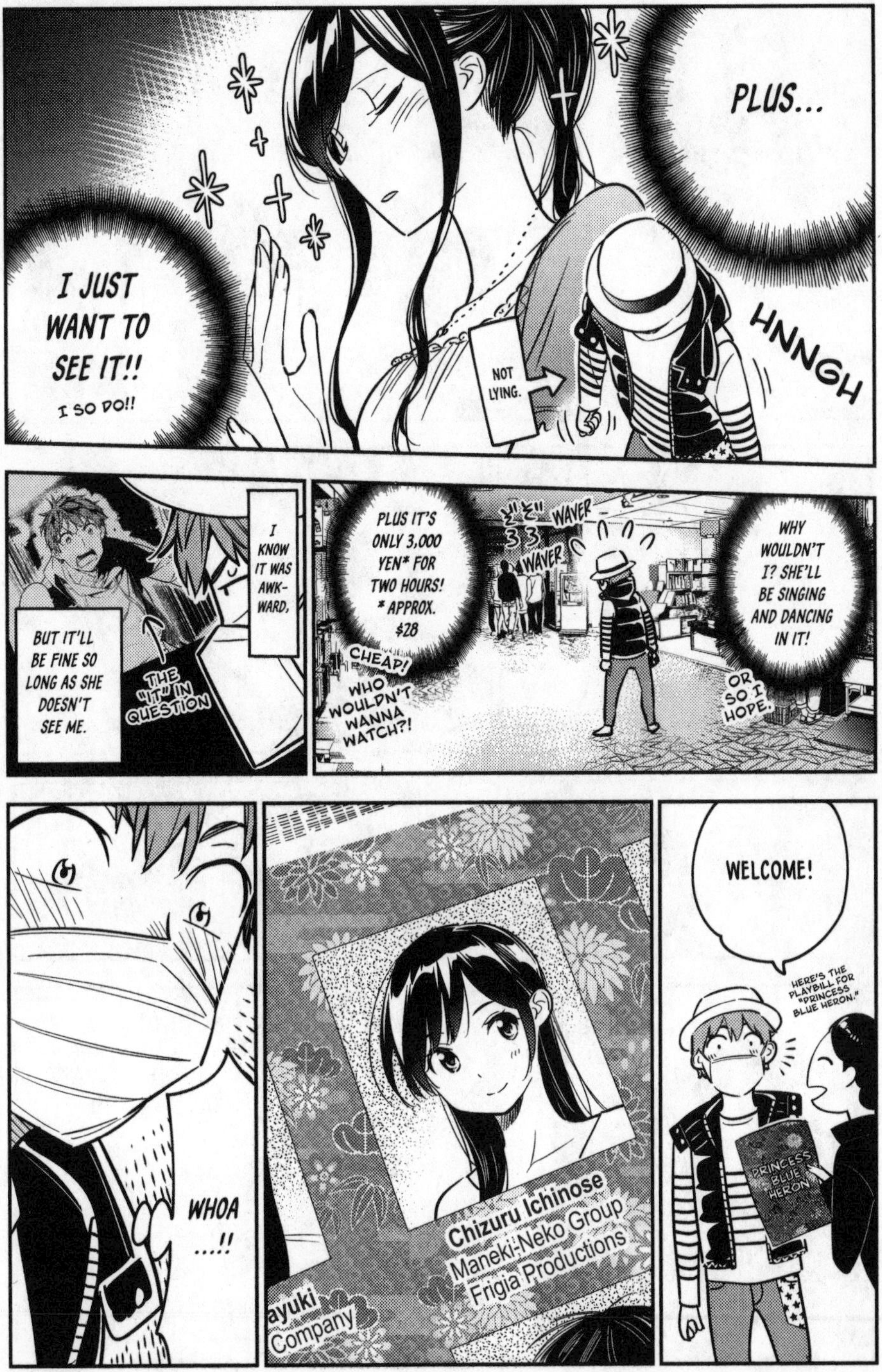
PLUS...
I JUST WANT TO SEE IT!!
I SO DO!!
HNNGH
NOT LYING.
I KNOW IT WAS AWK-WARD,
BUT IT'LL BE FINE SO LONG AS SHE DOESN'T SEE ME.
THE "IT" IN QUESTION
WHY WOULDN'T I? SHE'LL BE SINGING AND DANCING IN IT!
OR SO I HOPE.
WAVER
WAVER
PLUS IT'S ONLY 3,000 YEN* FOR TWO HOURS!
* APPROX. $28
CHEAP!
WHO WOULDN'T WANNA WATCH?!
WELCOME!
HERE'S THE PLAYBILL FOR "PRINCESS BLUE HERON."
PRINCESS BLUE HERON
Chizuru Ichinose
Maneki-Neko Group
Frigia Productions
ayuki
Company
WHOA ...!!

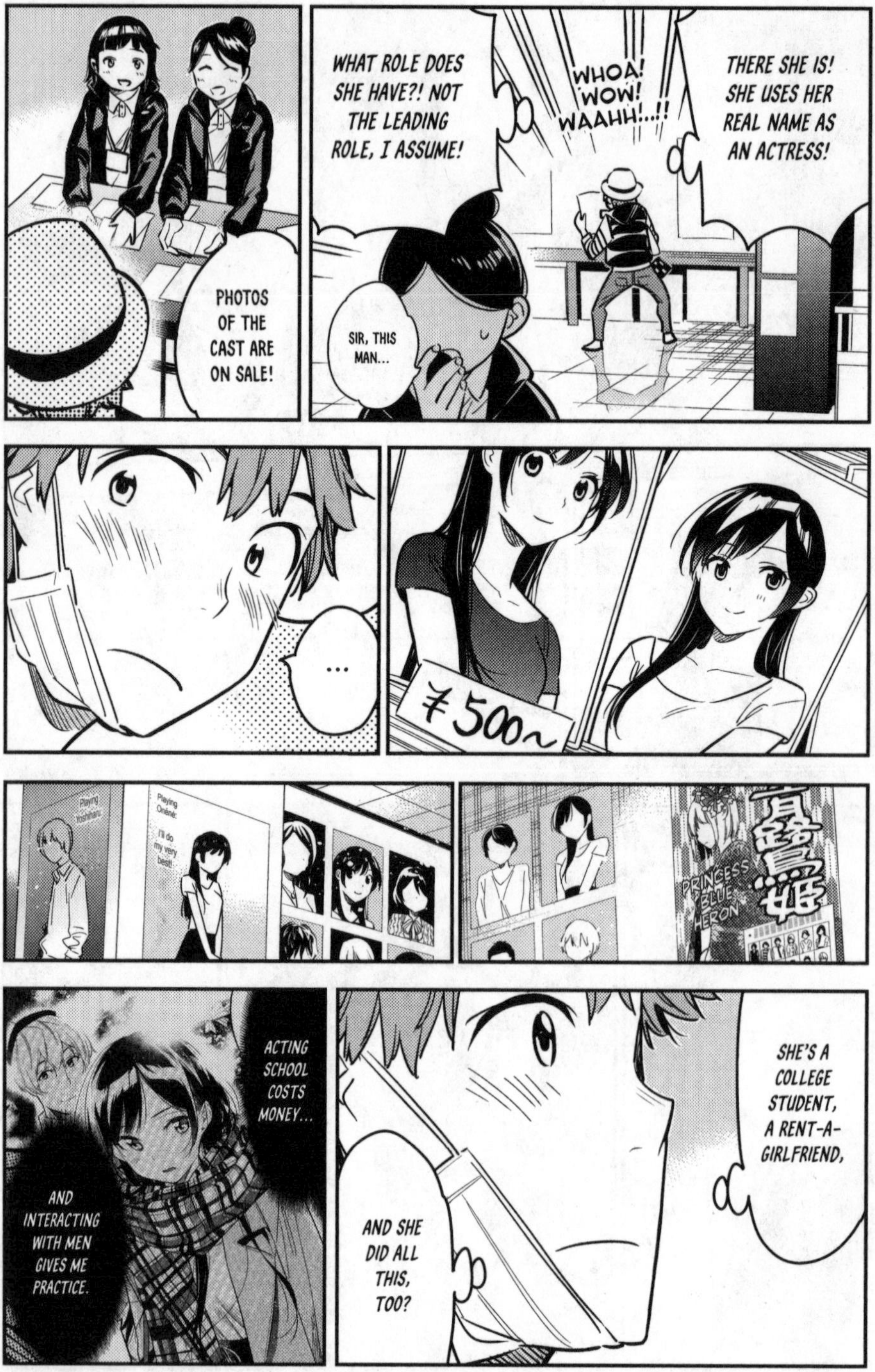
THERE SHE IS! SHE USES HER REAL NAME AS AN ACTRESS!
WHOA! WOW! WAAHH!...!!
WHAT ROLE DOES SHE HAVE?! NOT THE LEADING ROLE, I ASSUME!
SIR, THIS MAN...
PHOTOS OF THE CAST ARE ON SALE!
¥500~
...
PRINCESS BLUE HERON
Playing Onéné:
I'll do my very best!
Playing Yoshiharu:
SHE'S A COLLEGE STUDENT, A RENT-A-GIRLFRIEND,
AND SHE DID ALL THIS, TOO?
ACTING SCHOOL COSTS MONEY...
AND INTERACTING WITH MEN GIVES ME PRACTICE.

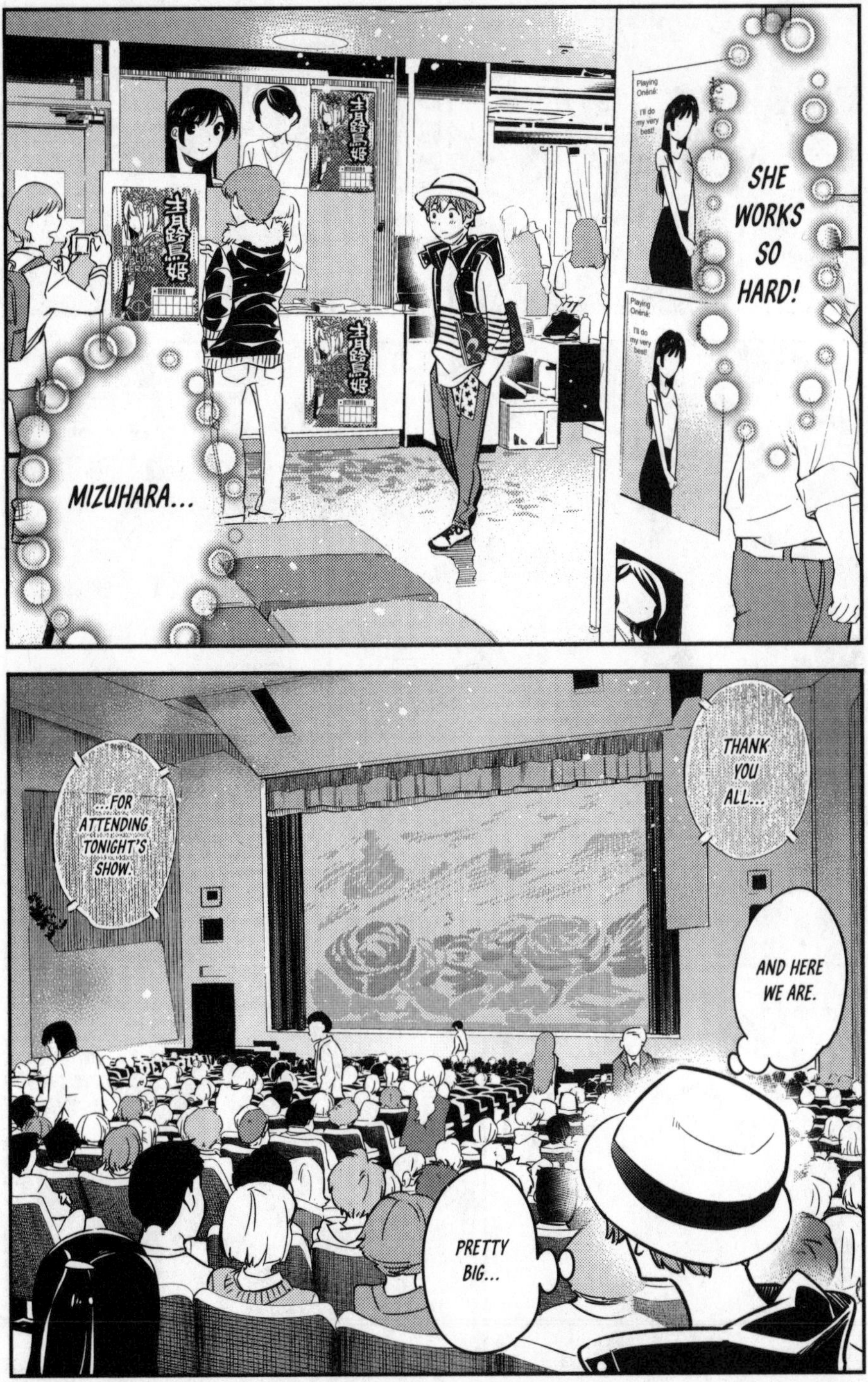
Playing Onéné:
I'll do my very best!
Playing Onéné:
I'll do my very best!
SHE WORKS SO HARD!
MIZUHARA...
THANK YOU ALL...
...FOR ATTENDING TONIGHT'S SHOW.
AND HERE WE ARE.
PRETTY BIG...

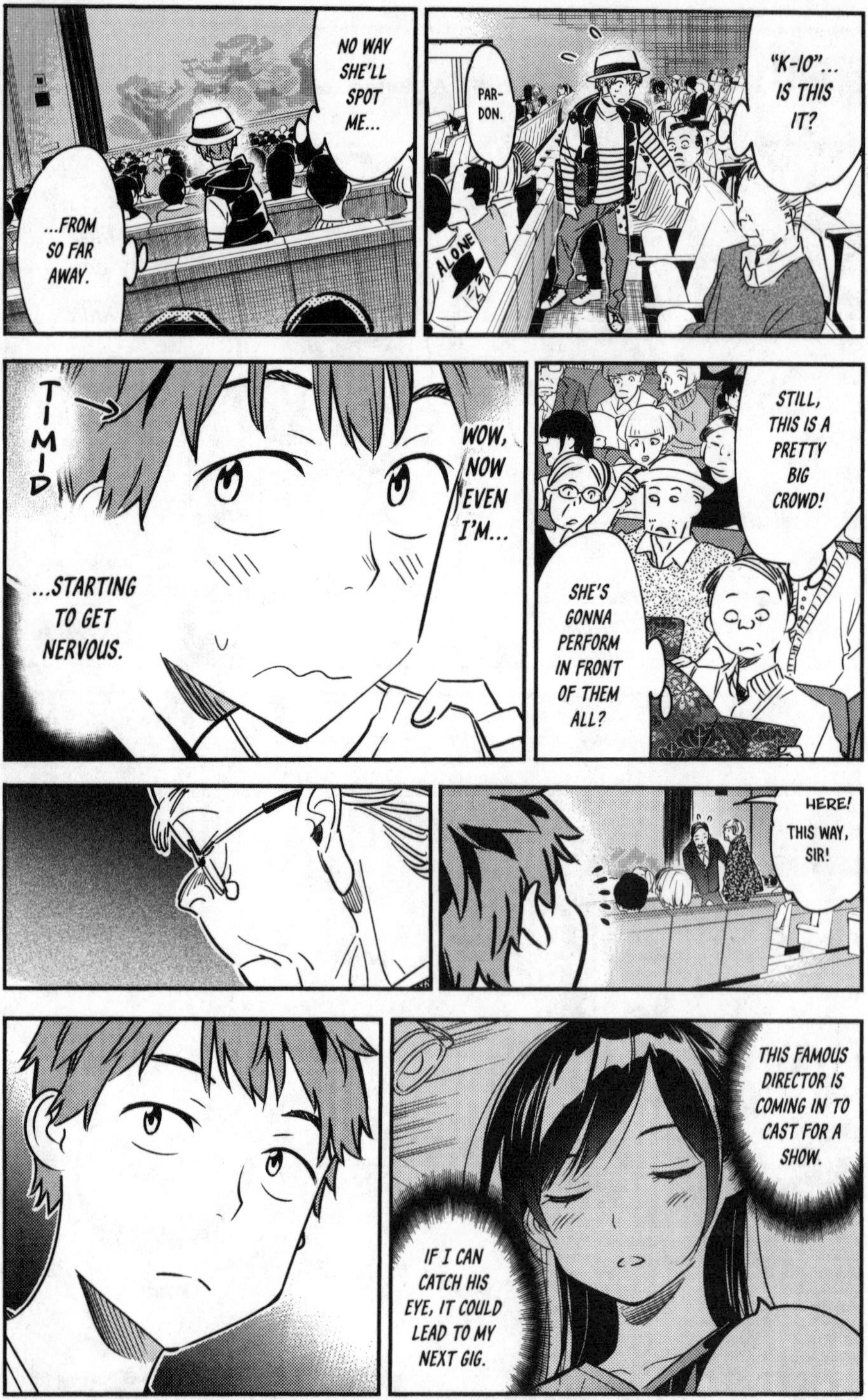
"K-IO"... IS THIS IT?
PAR-DON.
NO WAY SHE'LL SPOT ME...
...FROM SO FAR AWAY.
ALONE
STILL, THIS IS A PRETTY BIG CROWD!
SHE'S GONNA PERFORM IN FRONT OF THEM ALL?
WOW, NOW EVEN I'M...
TIMID
...STARTING TO GET NERVOUS.
HERE!
THIS WAY, SIR!
THIS FAMOUS DIRECTOR IS COMING IN TO CAST FOR A SHOW.
IF I CAN CATCH HIS EYE, IT COULD LEAD TO MY NEXT GIG.

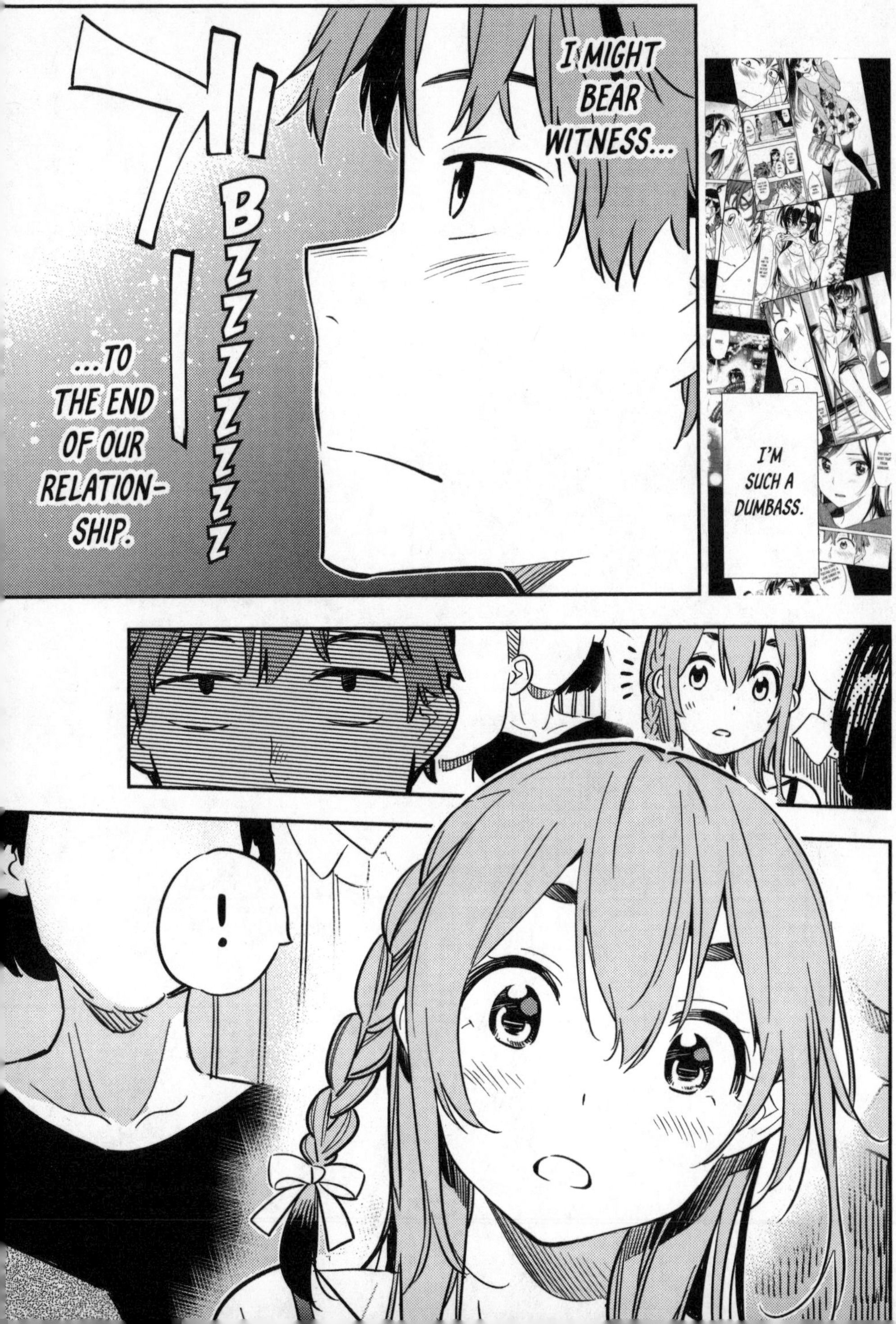
I'M SUCH A DUMBASS.
I MIGHT BEAR WITNESS...
BZZZZZZZZZ
...TO THE END OF OUR RELATION-SHIP.
!

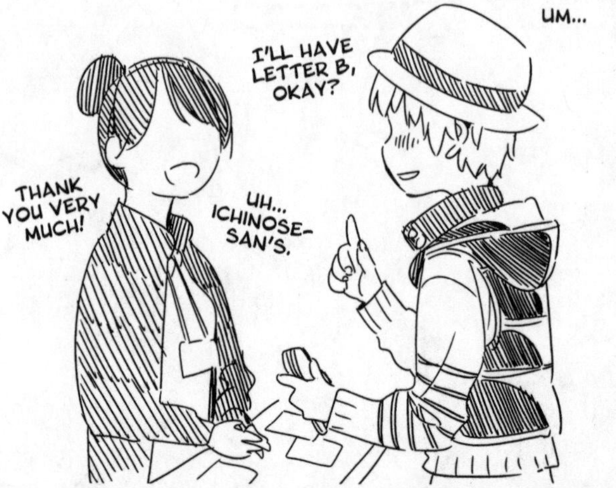
UM...
I'LL HAVE LETTER B, OKAY?
UH... ICHINOSE-SAN'S.
THANK YOU VERY MUCH!

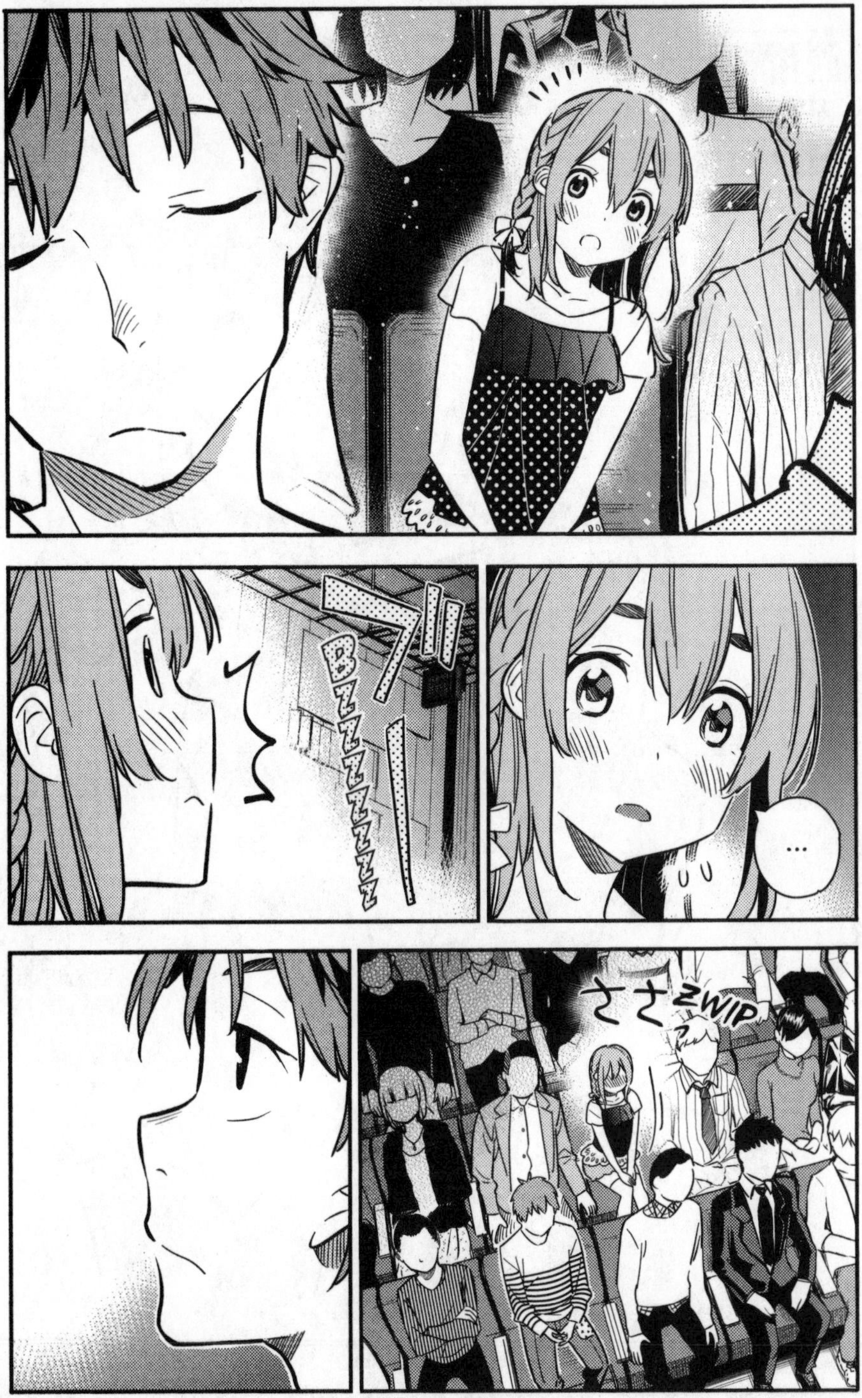
...
ブー
BZZZZZZZZZ
ささっ
ZWIP

RATING 51

MY DREAMS AND MY GIRLFRIEND 2

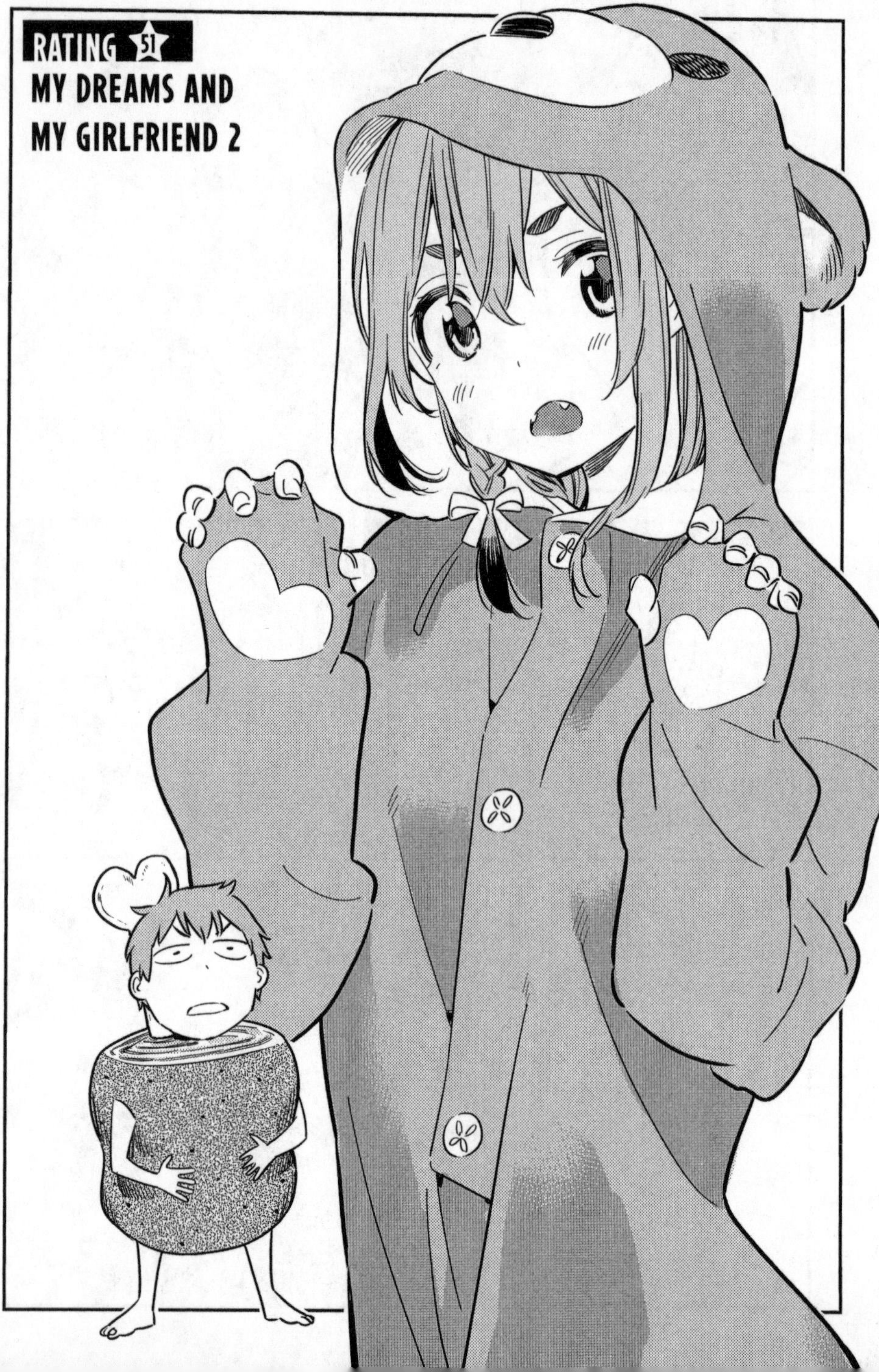

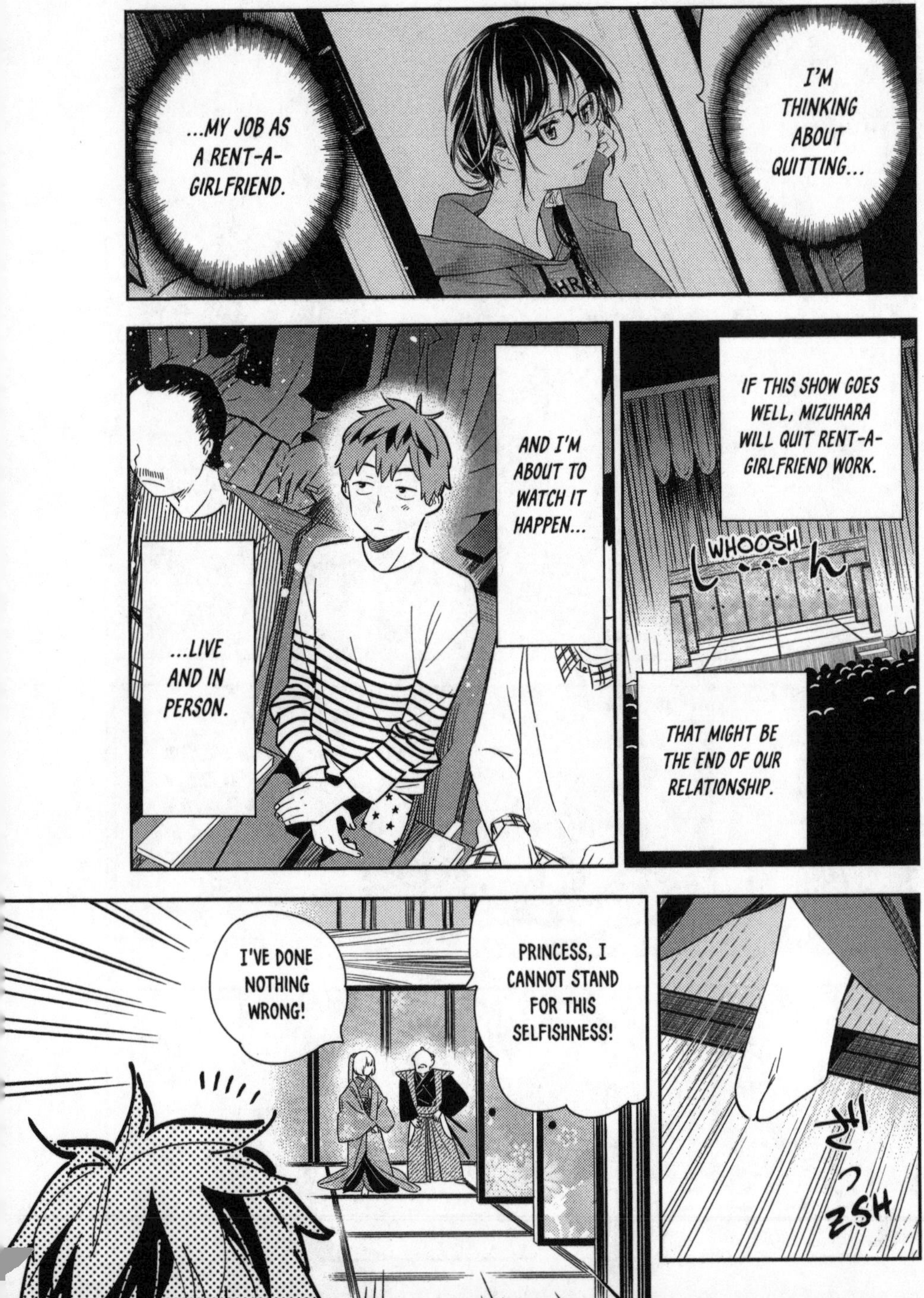
I'M THINKING ABOUT QUITTING...
...MY JOB AS A RENT-A-GIRLFRIEND.
IF THIS SHOW GOES WELL, MIZUHARA WILL QUIT RENT-A-GIRLFRIEND WORK.
WHOOSH
THAT MIGHT BE THE END OF OUR RELATIONSHIP.
AND I'M ABOUT TO WATCH IT HAPPEN...
...LIVE AND IN PERSON.
ZSH
PRINCESS, I CANNOT STAND FOR THIS SELFISHNESS!
I'VE DONE NOTHING WRONG!

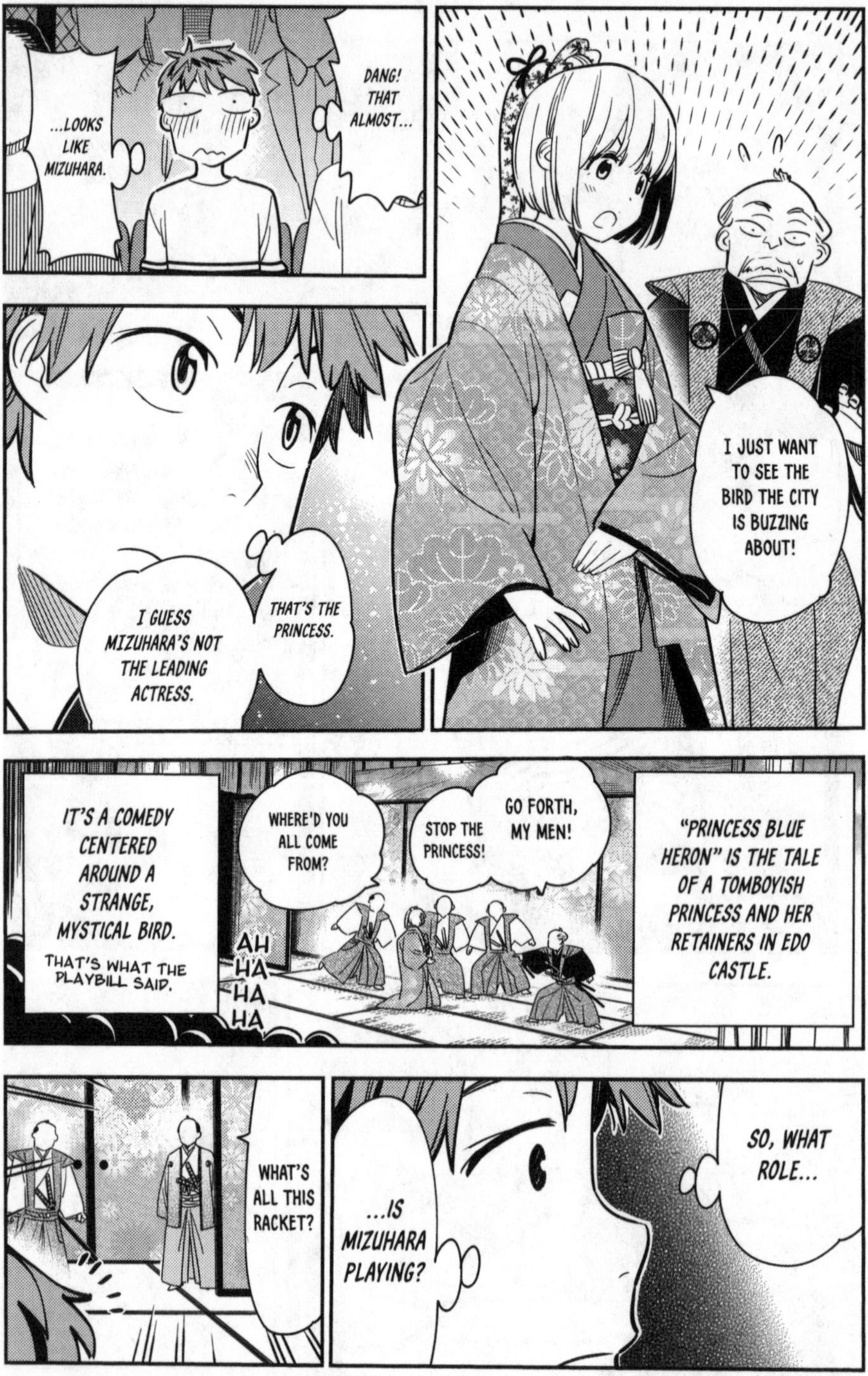
I JUST WANT TO SEE THE BIRD THE CITY IS BUZZING ABOUT!
DANG! THAT ALMOST...
...LOOKS LIKE MIZUHARA.
THAT'S THE PRINCESS.
I GUESS MIZUHARA'S NOT THE LEADING ACTRESS.
"PRINCESS BLUE HERON" IS THE TALE OF A TOMBOYISH PRINCESS AND HER RETAINERS IN EDO CASTLE.
GO FORTH, MY MEN!
STOP THE PRINCESS!
WHERE'D YOU ALL COME FROM?
AH HA HA HA
IT'S A COMEDY CENTERED AROUND A STRANGE, MYSTICAL BIRD.
THAT'S WHAT THE PLAYBILL SAID.
SO, WHAT ROLE...
...IS MIZUHARA PLAYING?
WHAT'S ALL THIS RACKET?

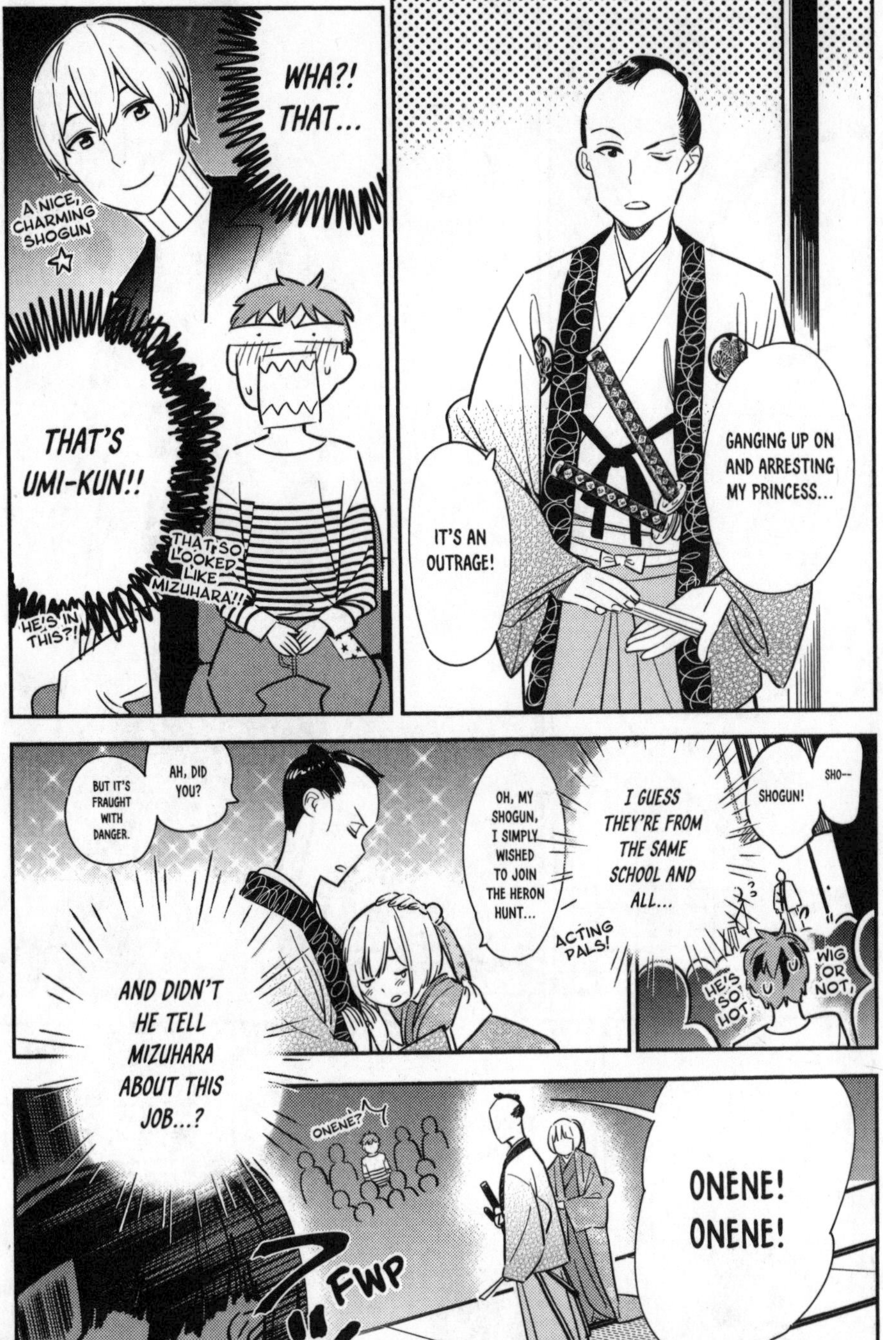
GANGING UP ON AND ARRESTING MY PRINCESS...
IT'S AN OUTRAGE!
WHA?! THAT...
A NICE, CHARMING SHOGUN ☆
THAT'S UMI-KUN!!
THAT SO LOOKED LIKE MIZUHARA!!
HE'S IN THIS?!
SHO--
SHOGUN!
WIG OR NOT,
HE'S SO HOT.
I GUESS THEY'RE FROM THE SAME SCHOOL AND ALL...
ACTING PALS!
OH, MY SHOGUN, I SIMPLY WISHED TO JOIN THE HERON HUNT...
AH, DID YOU?
BUT IT'S FRAUGHT WITH DANGER.
AND DIDN'T HE TELL MIZUHARA ABOUT THIS JOB...?
ONENE! ONENE!
ONENE?
FWP

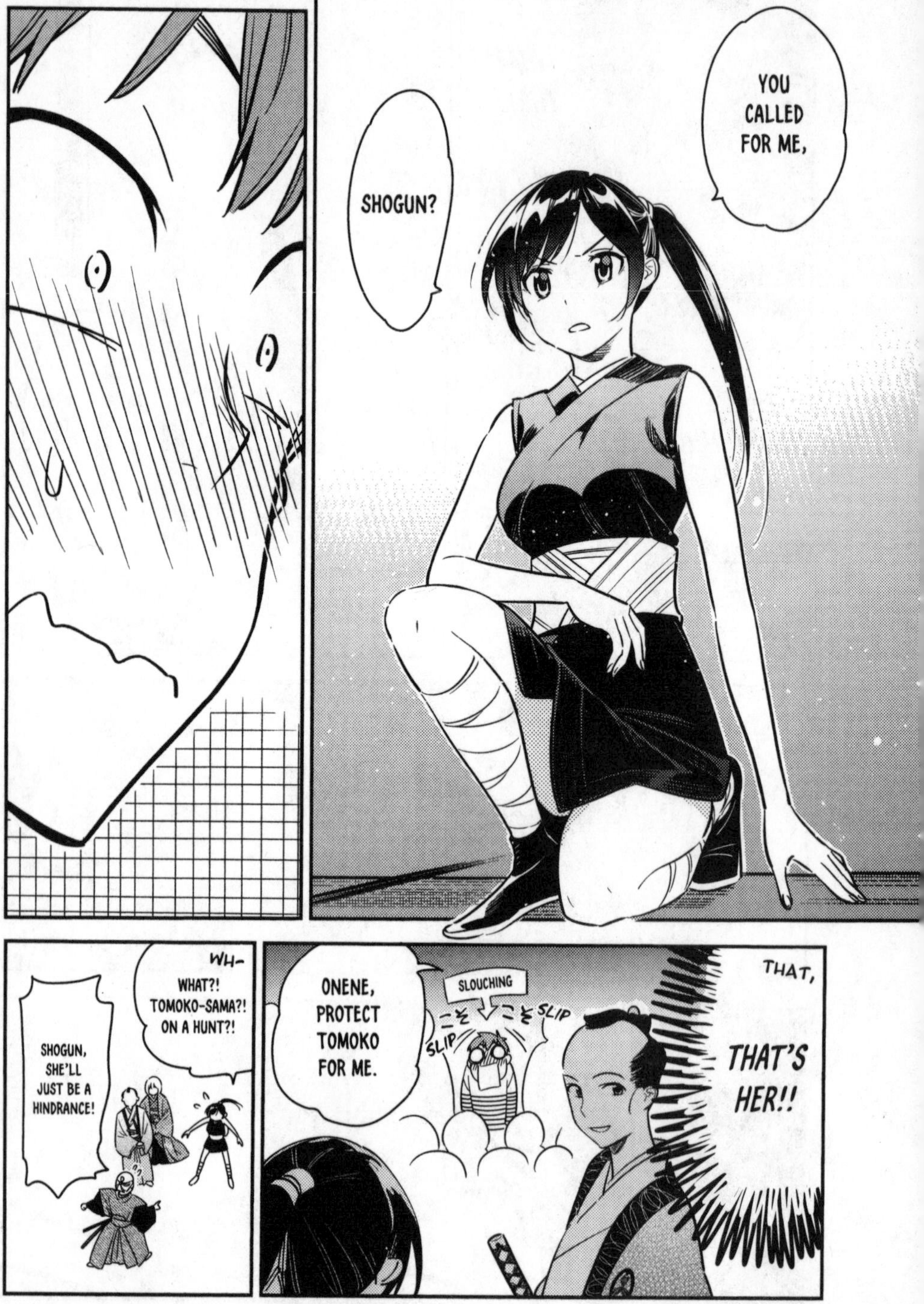
YOU CALLED FOR ME,
SHOGUN?
THAT,
THAT'S HER!!
ONENE, PROTECT TOMOKO FOR ME.
SLOUCHING
こそ こそ
SLIP SLIP
WH- WHAT?! TOMOKO-SAMA?! ON A HUNT?!
SHOGUN, SHE'LL JUST BE A HINDRANCE!

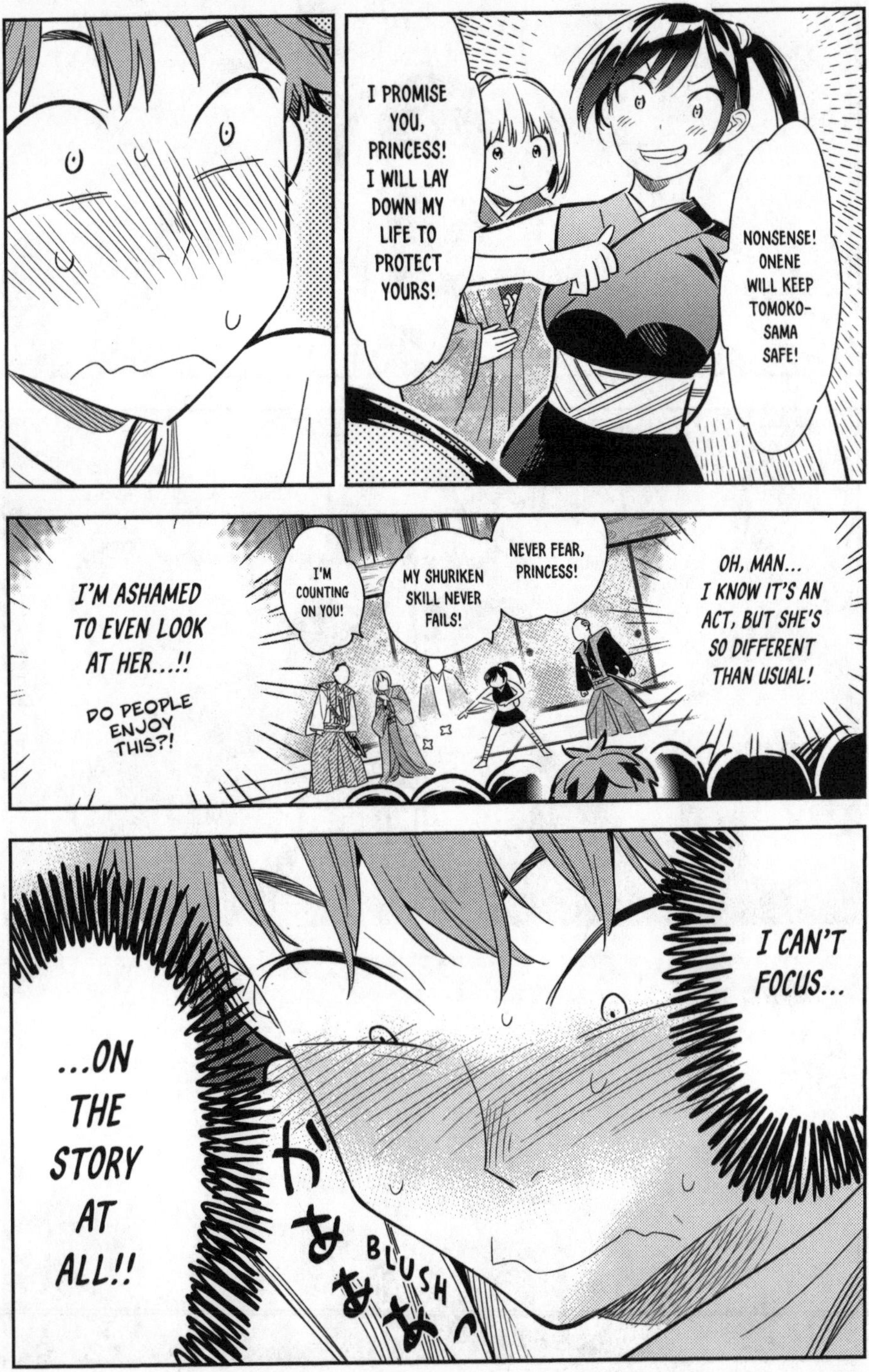
I PROMISE YOU, PRINCESS! I WILL LAY DOWN MY LIFE TO PROTECT YOURS!
NONSENSE! ONENE WILL KEEP TOMOKO-SAMA SAFE!
OH, MAN... I KNOW IT'S AN ACT, BUT SHE'S SO DIFFERENT THAN USUAL!
NEVER FEAR, PRINCESS!
MY SHURIKEN SKILL NEVER FAILS!
I'M COUNTING ON YOU!
I'M ASHAMED TO EVEN LOOK AT HER...!!
DO PEOPLE ENJOY THIS?!
I CAN'T FOCUS...
...ON THE STORY AT ALL!!
かあああ
BLUSH

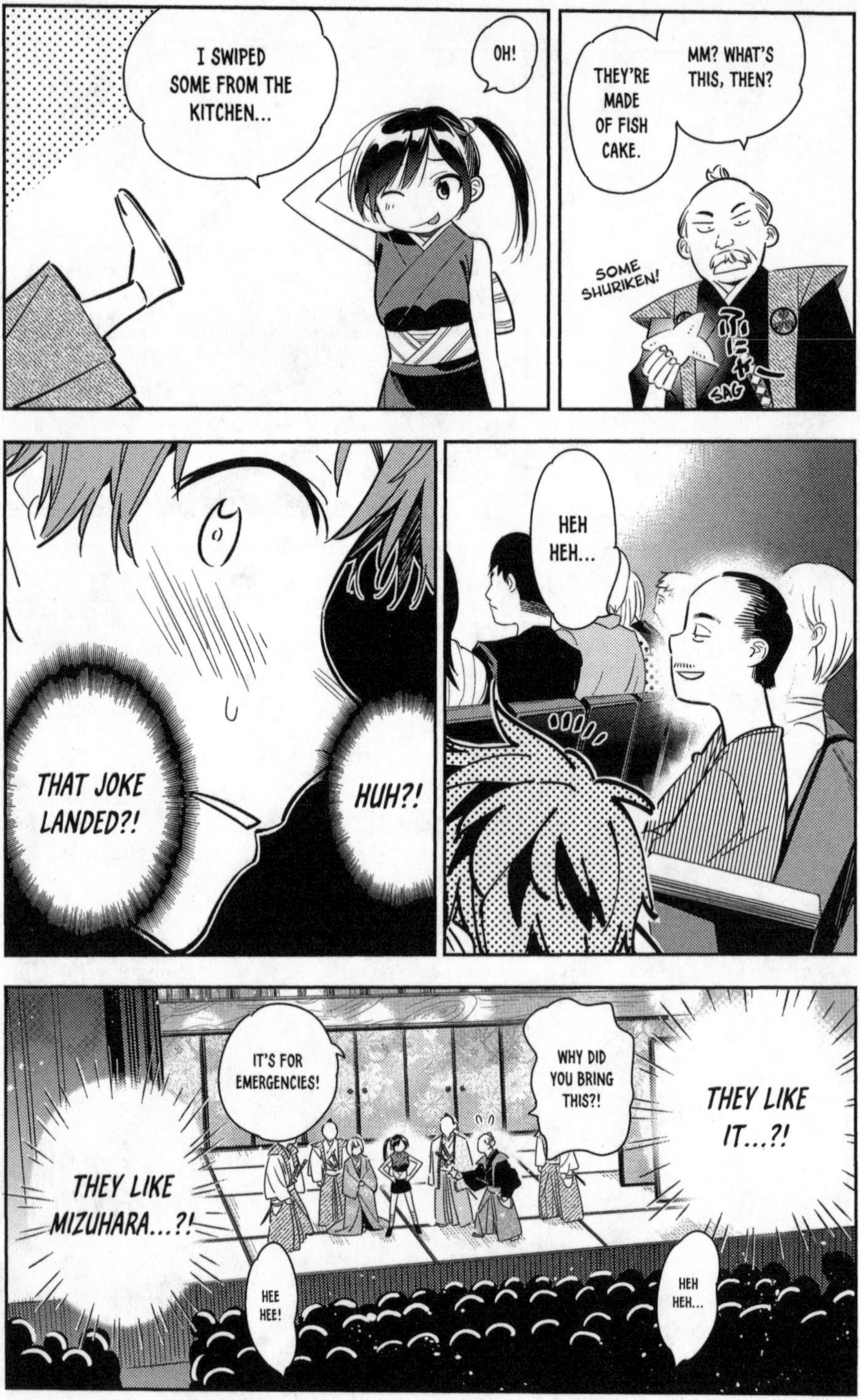
MM? WHAT'S THIS, THEN?
THEY'RE MADE OF FISH CAKE.
SOME SHURIKEN!
SAG
OH!
I SWIPED SOME FROM THE KITCHEN...
HEH HEH...
HUH?!
THAT JOKE LANDED?!
THEY LIKE IT...?!
WHY DID YOU BRING THIS?!
IT'S FOR EMERGENCIES!
HEH HEH...
THEY LIKE MIZUHARA...?!
HEE HEE!

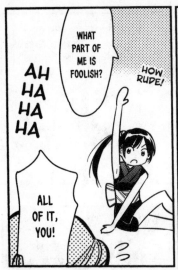

THERE'S NO WAY OUR FOES CAN STARVE US OUT NOW!
THIS IS A HUNT, NOT A SIEGE!
WHAT A FOOLISH GIRL YOU ARE!
WHAT PART OF ME IS FOOLISH?
HOW RUDE!
AH HA HA HA
ALL OF IT, YOU!
AH HA HA!
SHE'S FUNNY!
IT'S CRAZY HOW SHE CAN BE THIS WHOLE OTHER PERSON...
...IN FRONT OF THIS CROWD!
I MEAN, YEAH, SHE'S AN ACTRESS, BUT...
MNCH MNCH
DON'T EAT IT!!
AH HA HA HA
HA HA HA HA HA

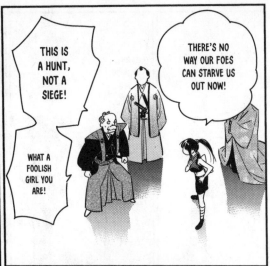

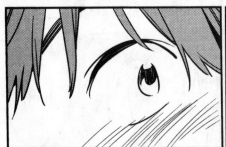

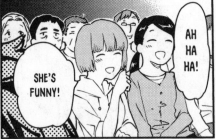

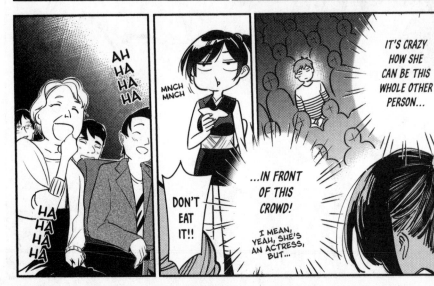

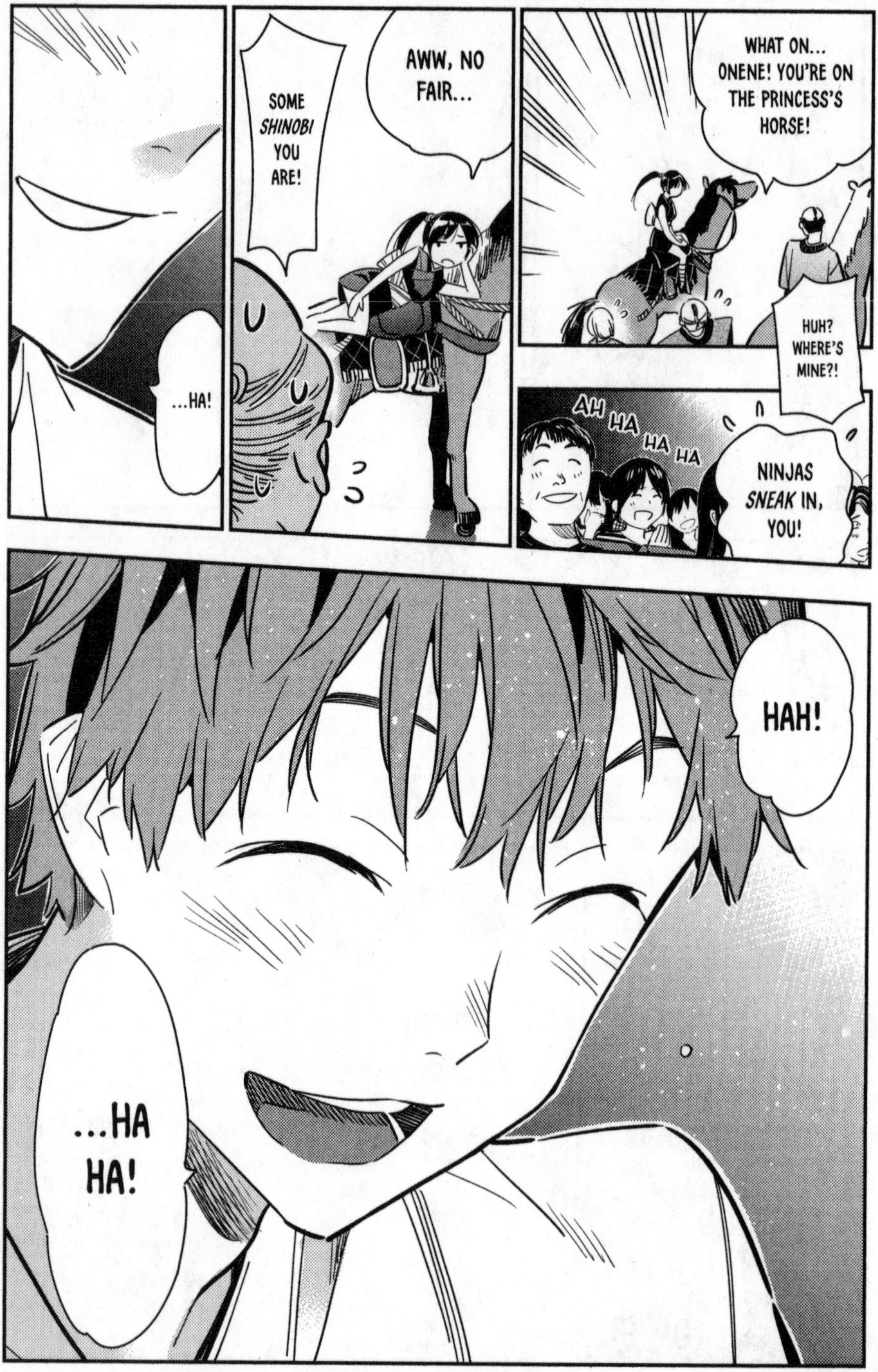
WHAT ON... ONENE! YOU'RE ON THE PRINCESS'S HORSE!
HUH? WHERE'S MINE?!
AH HA HA HA
NINJAS *SNEAK* IN, YOU!
AWW, NO FAIR...
SOME *SHINOBI* YOU ARE!
...HA!
HAH!
...HA HA!

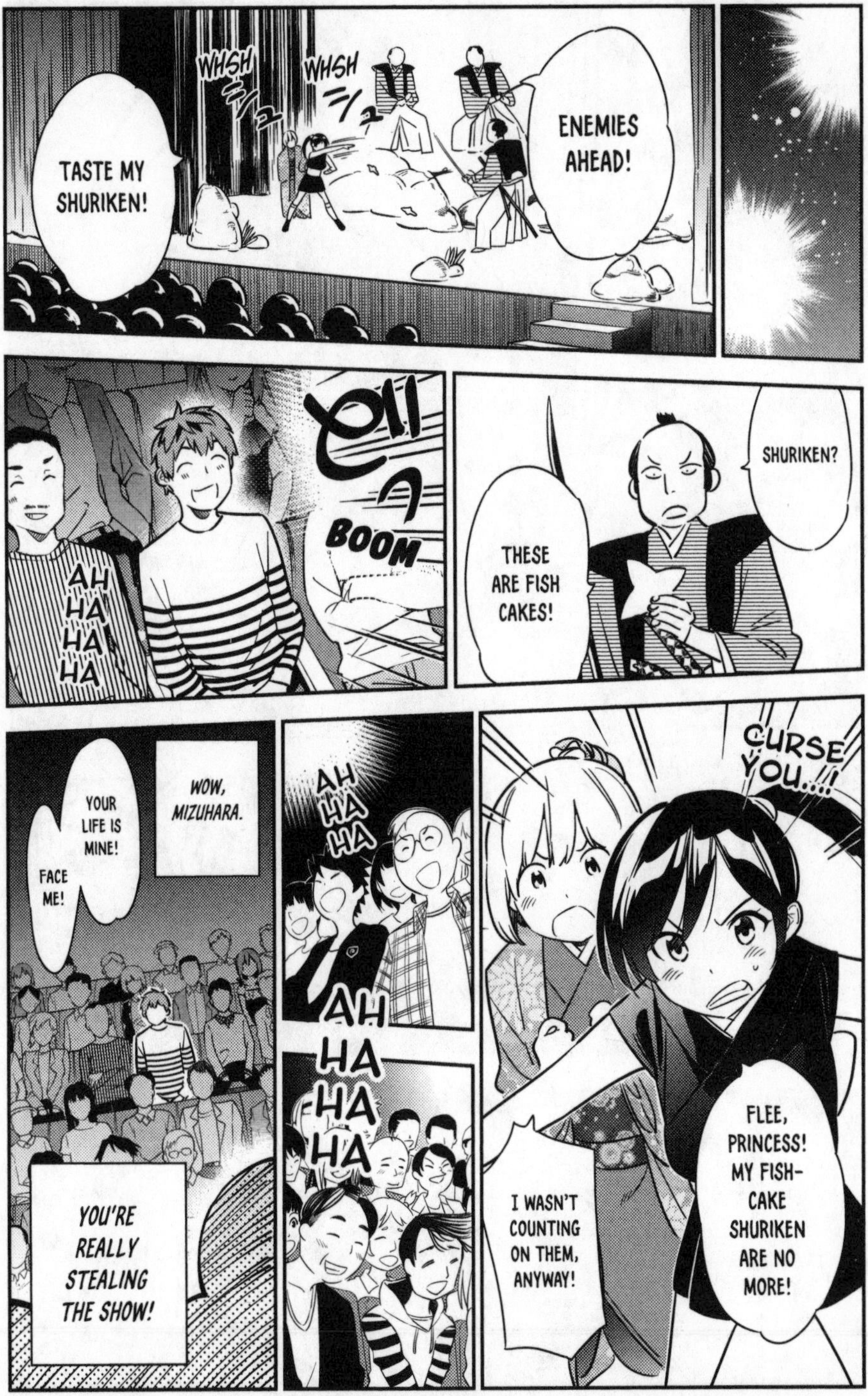
ENEMIES AHEAD!
WHSH
WHSH
TASTE MY SHURIKEN!
SHURIKEN?
THESE ARE FISH CAKES!
BOOM
AH HA HA HA
CURSE YOU...!
FLEE, PRINCESS! MY FISH-CAKE SHURIKEN ARE NO MORE!
I WASN'T COUNTING ON THEM, ANYWAY!
AH HA HA
AH HA HA HA HA
WOW, MIZUHARA.
YOUR LIFE IS MINE!
FACE ME!
YOU'RE REALLY STEALING THE SHOW!

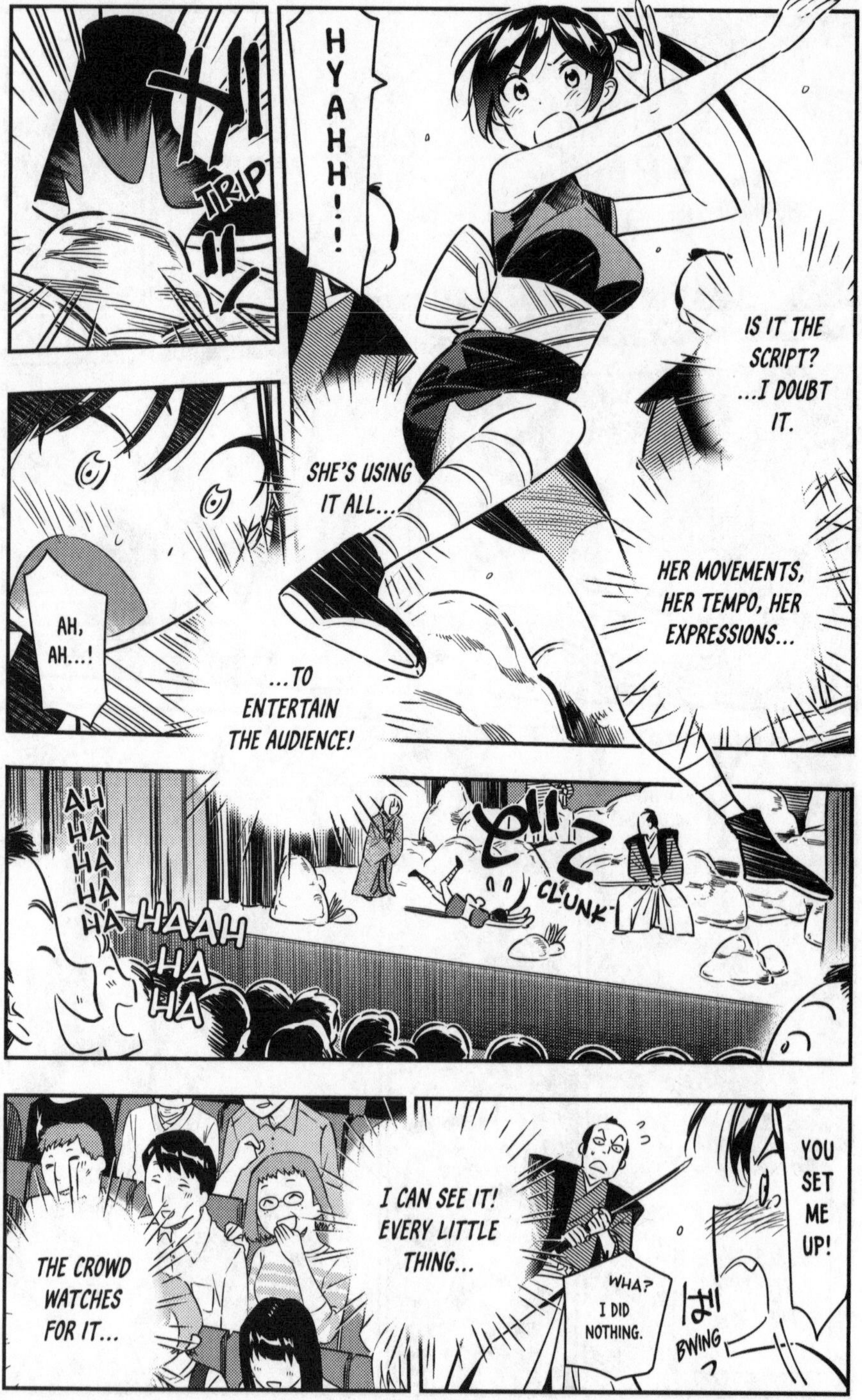
HYAHH!!
IS IT THE SCRIPT? ...I DOUBT IT.
HER MOVEMENTS, HER TEMPO, HER EXPRESSIONS...
SHE'S USING IT ALL...
...TO ENTERTAIN THE AUDIENCE!
TRIP!!
AH, AH...!
CLUNK
AH HA HA HA HA HA
HAAAH HA HA
YOU SET ME UP!
BWING
WHA? I DID NOTHING.
I CAN SEE IT! EVERY LITTLE THING...
THE CROWD WATCHES FOR IT...

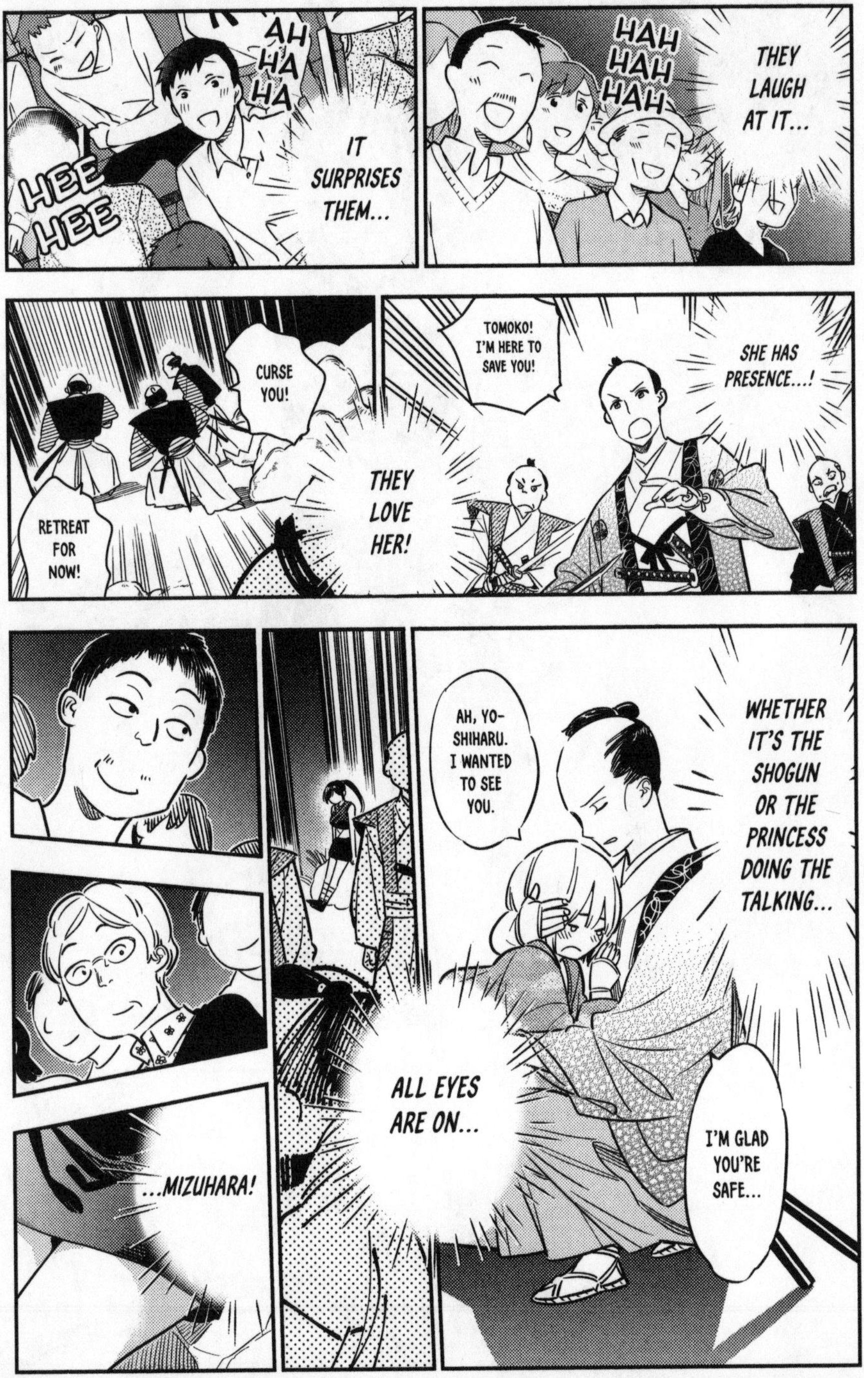
HAH HAH HAH
THEY LAUGH AT IT...
AH HA HA
IT SURPRISES THEM...
HEE HEE
TOMOKO! I'M HERE TO SAVE YOU!
SHE HAS PRESENCE...!
THEY LOVE HER!
CURSE YOU!
RETREAT FOR NOW!
WHETHER IT'S THE SHOGUN OR THE PRINCESS DOING THE TALKING...
AH, YO-SHIHARU. I WANTED TO SEE YOU.
I'M GLAD YOU'RE SAFE...
ALL EYES ARE ON...
...MIZUHARA!

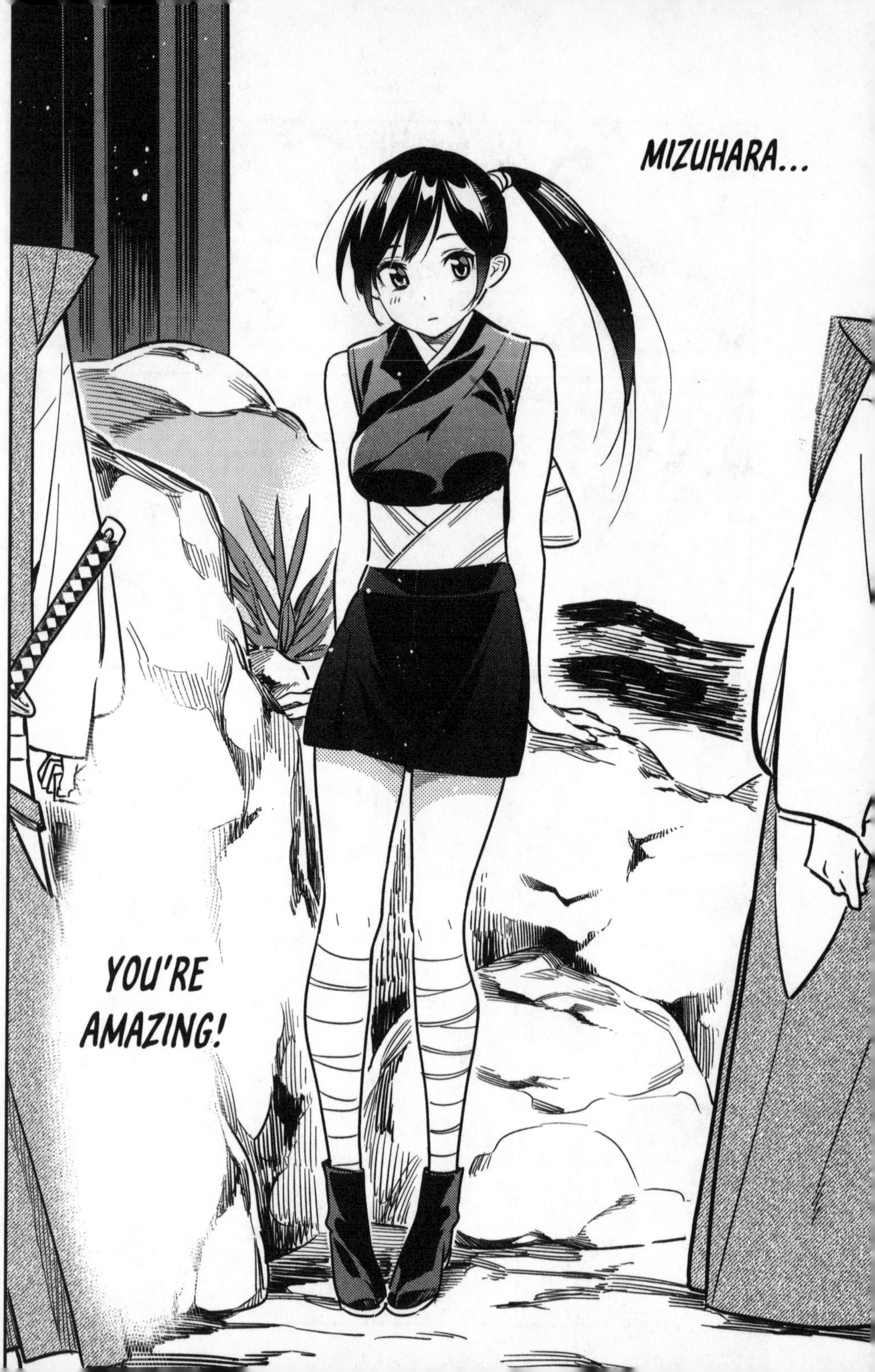
MIZUHARA...
YOU'RE AMAZING!

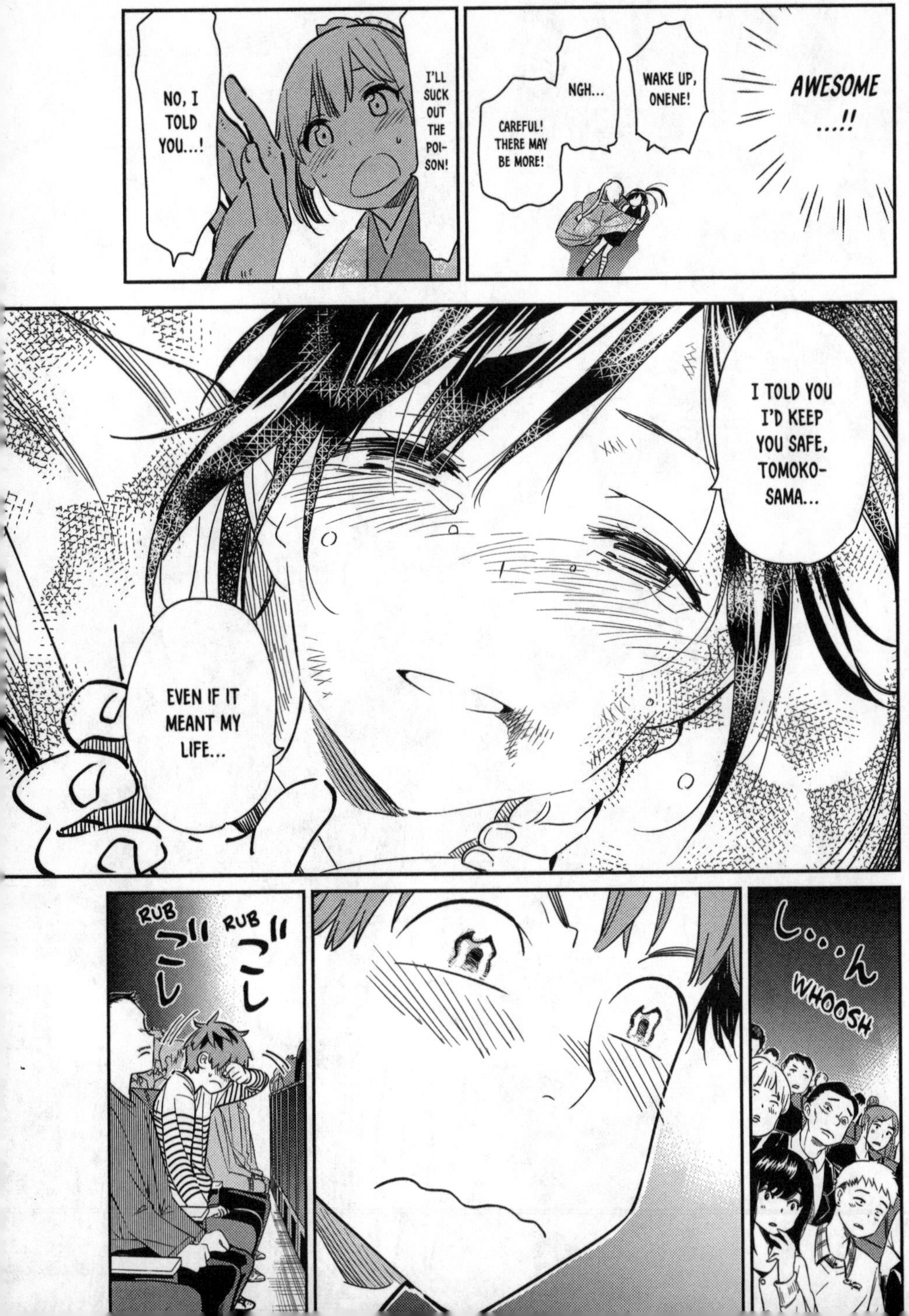
AWESOME ...!!
WAKE UP, ONENE!
NGH...
CAREFUL! THERE MAY BE MORE!
I'LL SUCK OUT THE POI- SON!
NO, I TOLD YOU...!
I TOLD YOU I'D KEEP YOU SAFE, TOMOKO- SAMA...
EVEN IF IT MEANT MY LIFE...
し…ん
WHOOSH
RUB
ごし
RUB
ごし

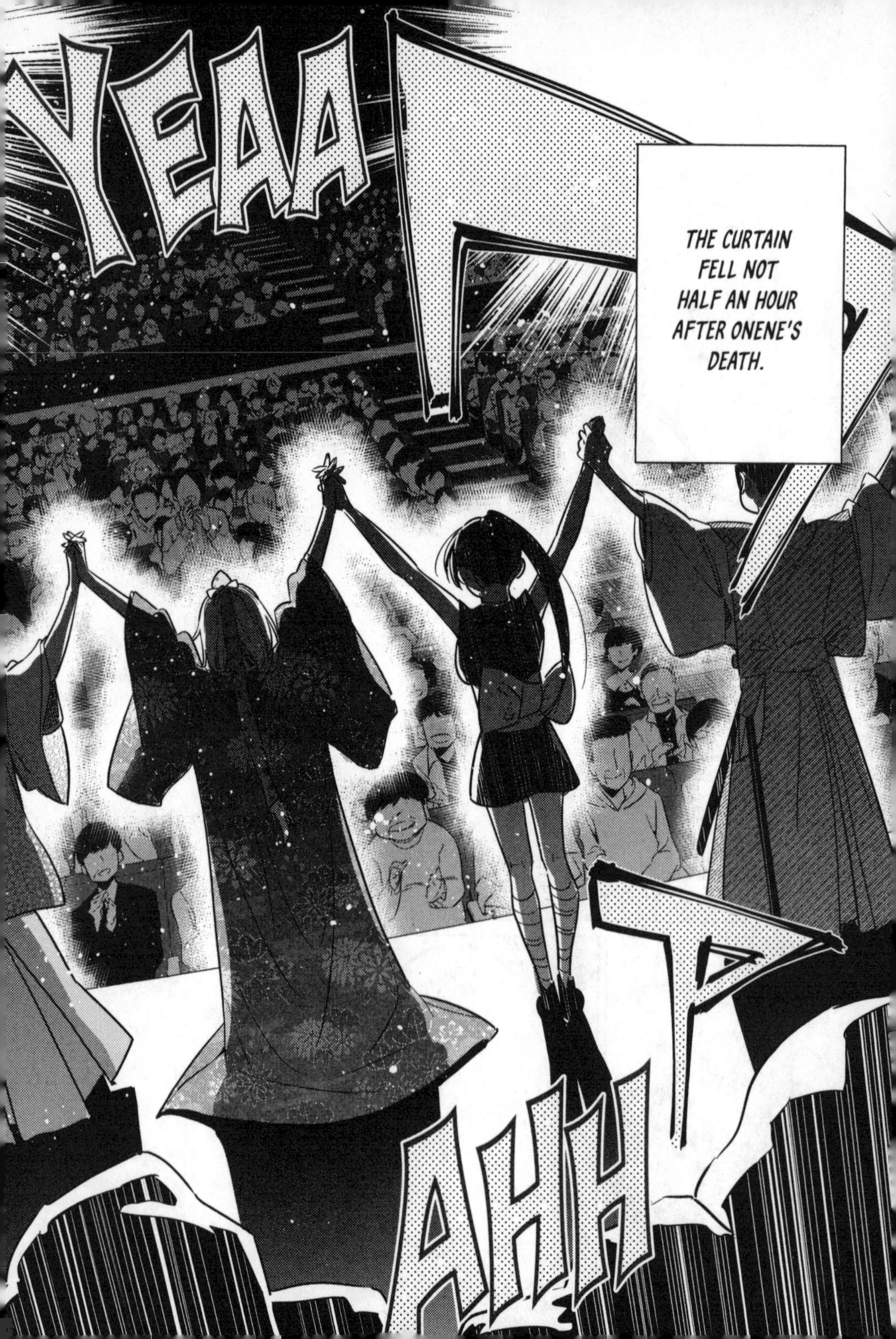
THE CURTAIN FELL NOT HALF AN HOUR AFTER ONENE'S DEATH.
YEAAAAAHHH

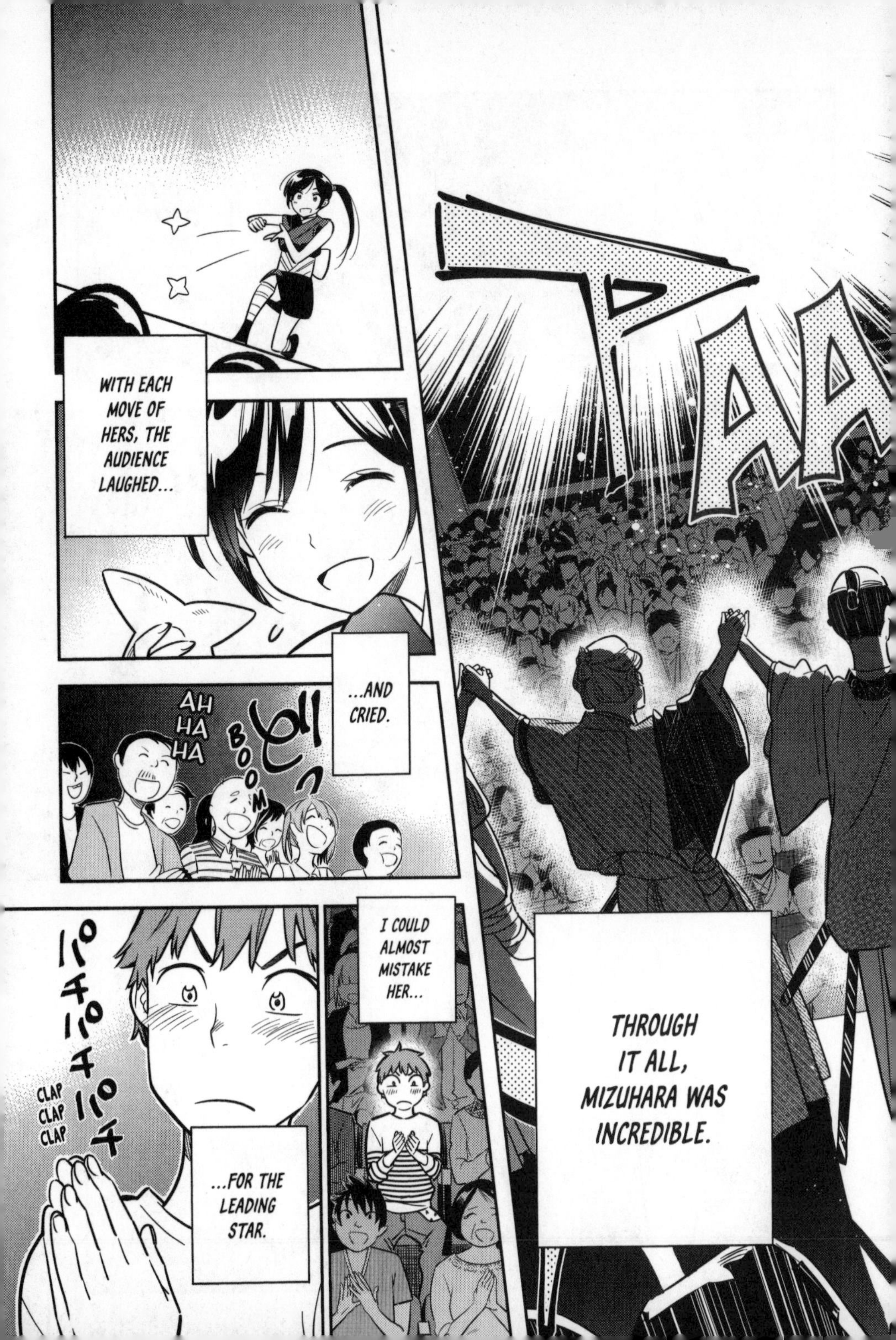
PAA
THROUGH IT ALL, MIZUHARA WAS INCREDIBLE.
WITH EACH MOVE OF HERS, THE AUDIENCE LAUGHED...
...AND CRIED.
AH HA HA
BOOM
I COULD ALMOST MISTAKE HER...
パチパチパチ
CLAP CLAP CLAP
...FOR THE LEADING STAR.

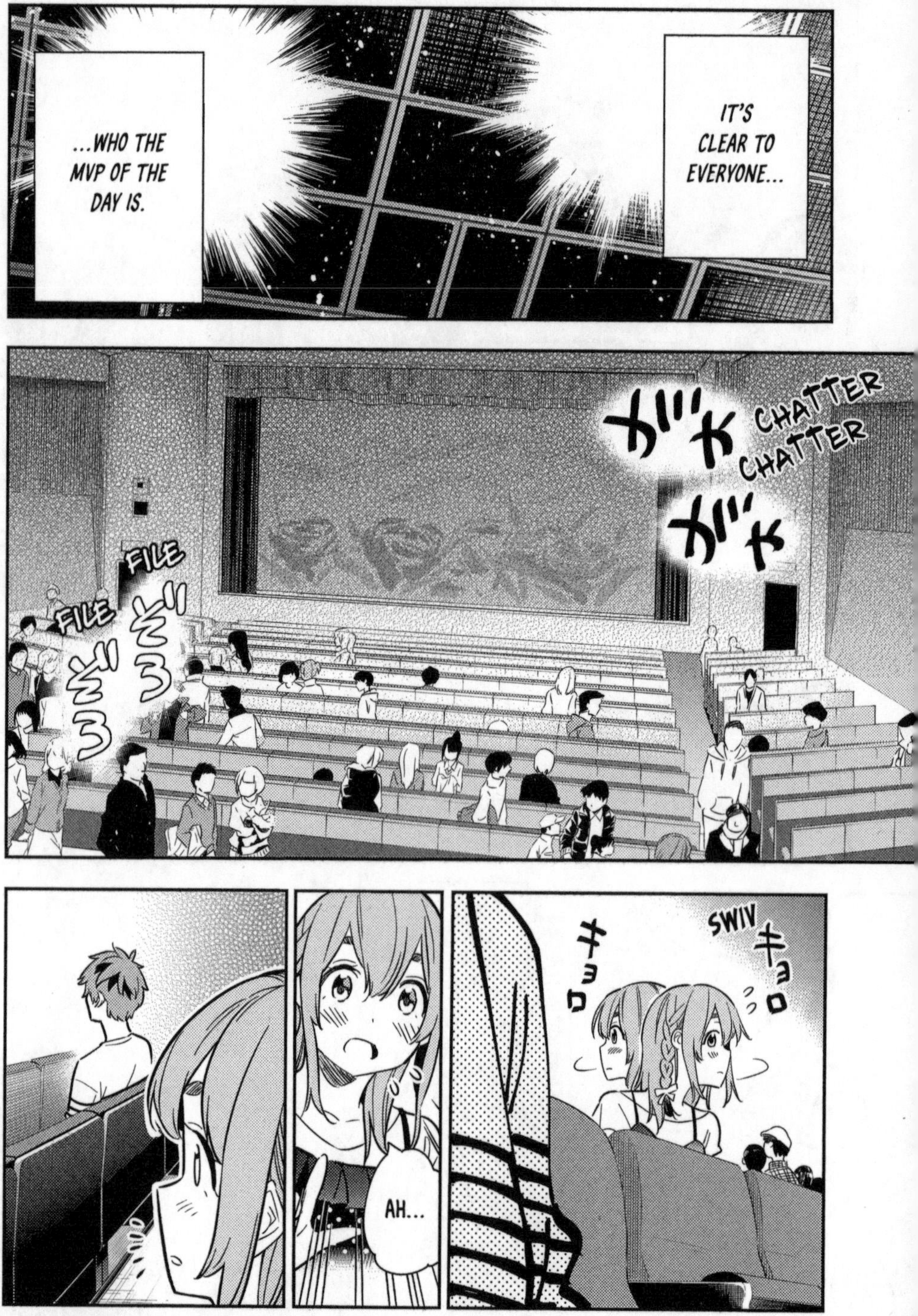
IT'S CLEAR TO EVERYONE...
...WHO THE MVP OF THE DAY IS.
ガヤガヤ
CHATTER CHATTER
ぞろぞろ
FILE FILE
キョロキョロ
SWIV
AH...

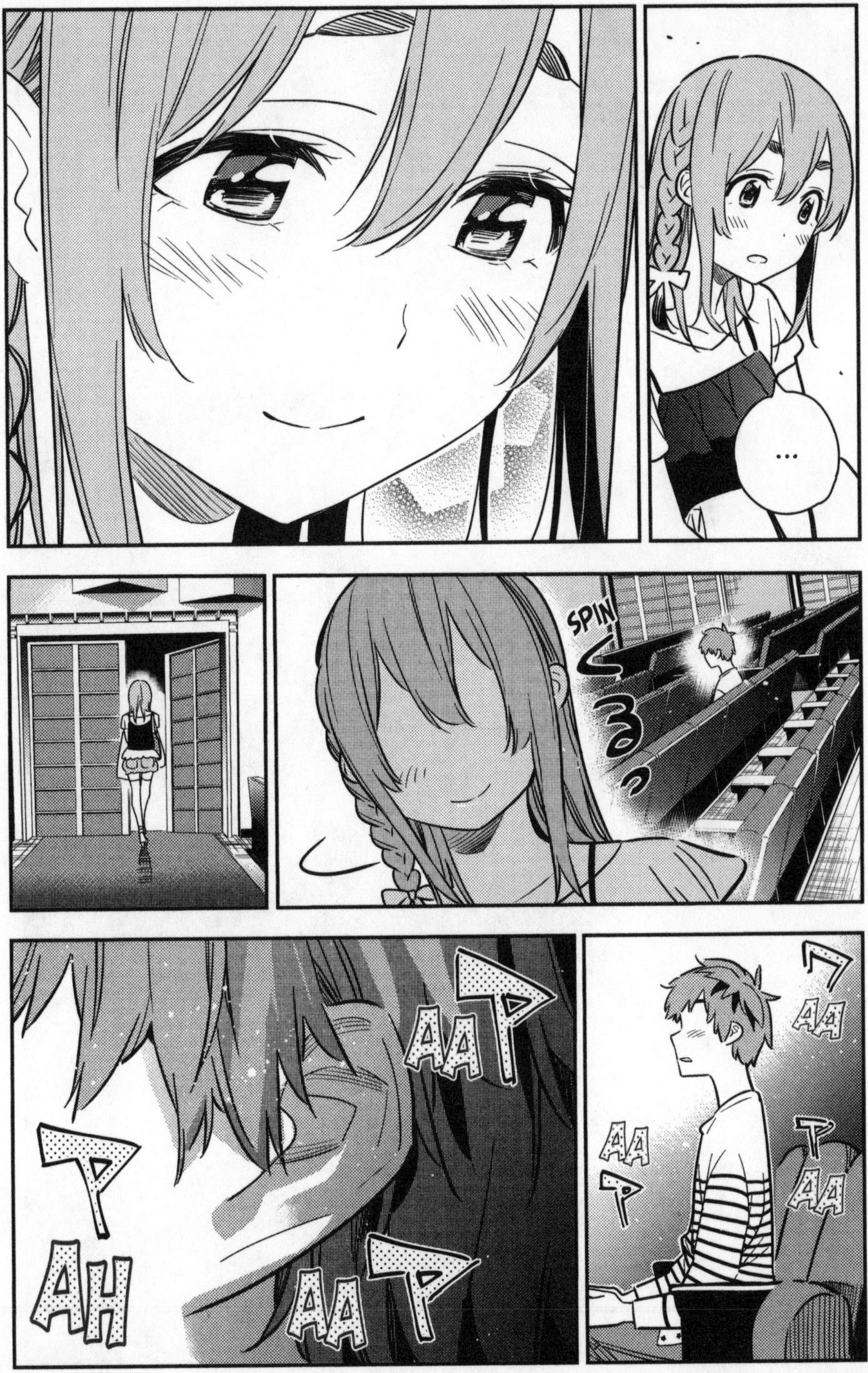
...
SPIN
AA
AA
AA
AA
AA
AH

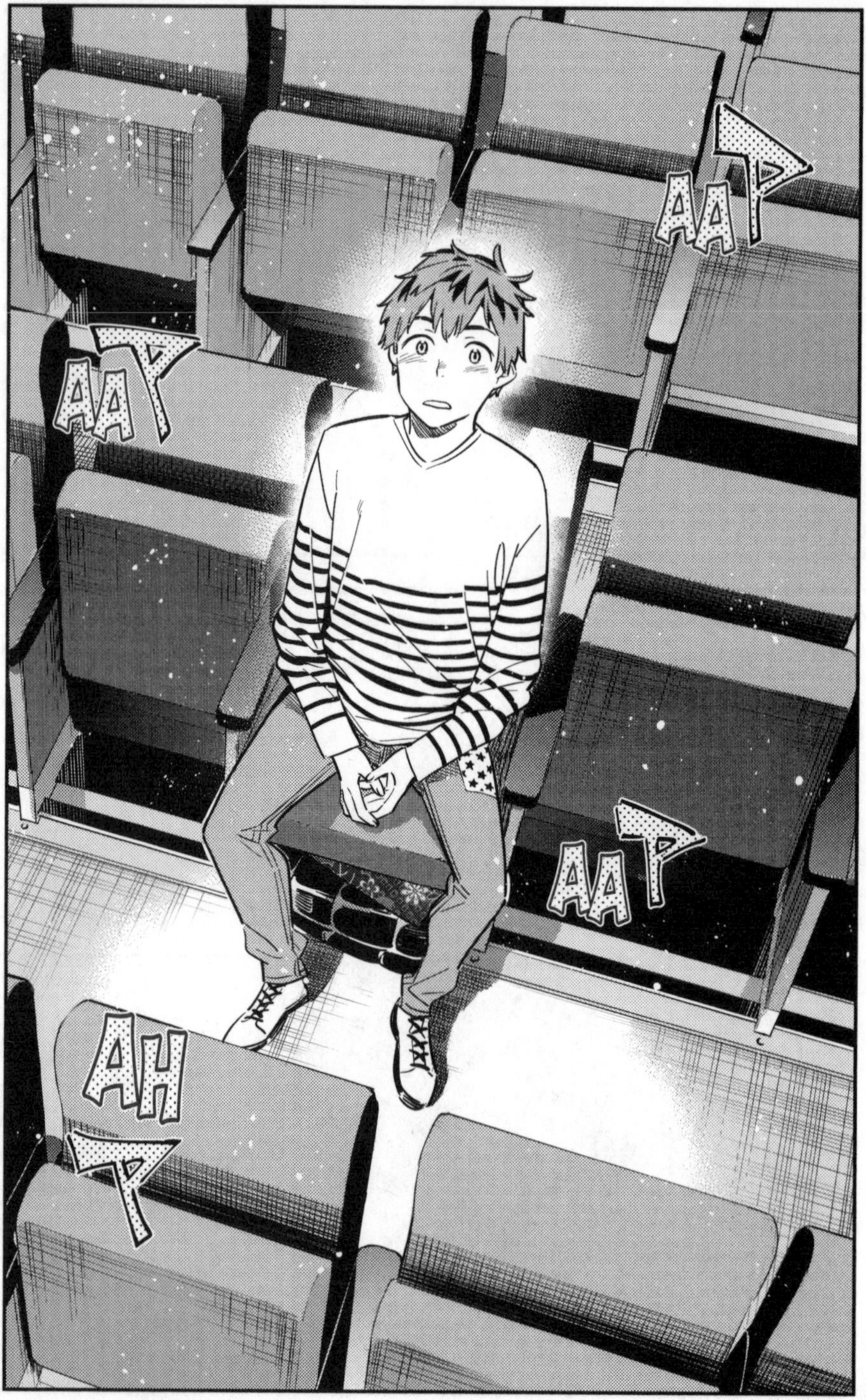
AAP
AAP
AAP
AHP

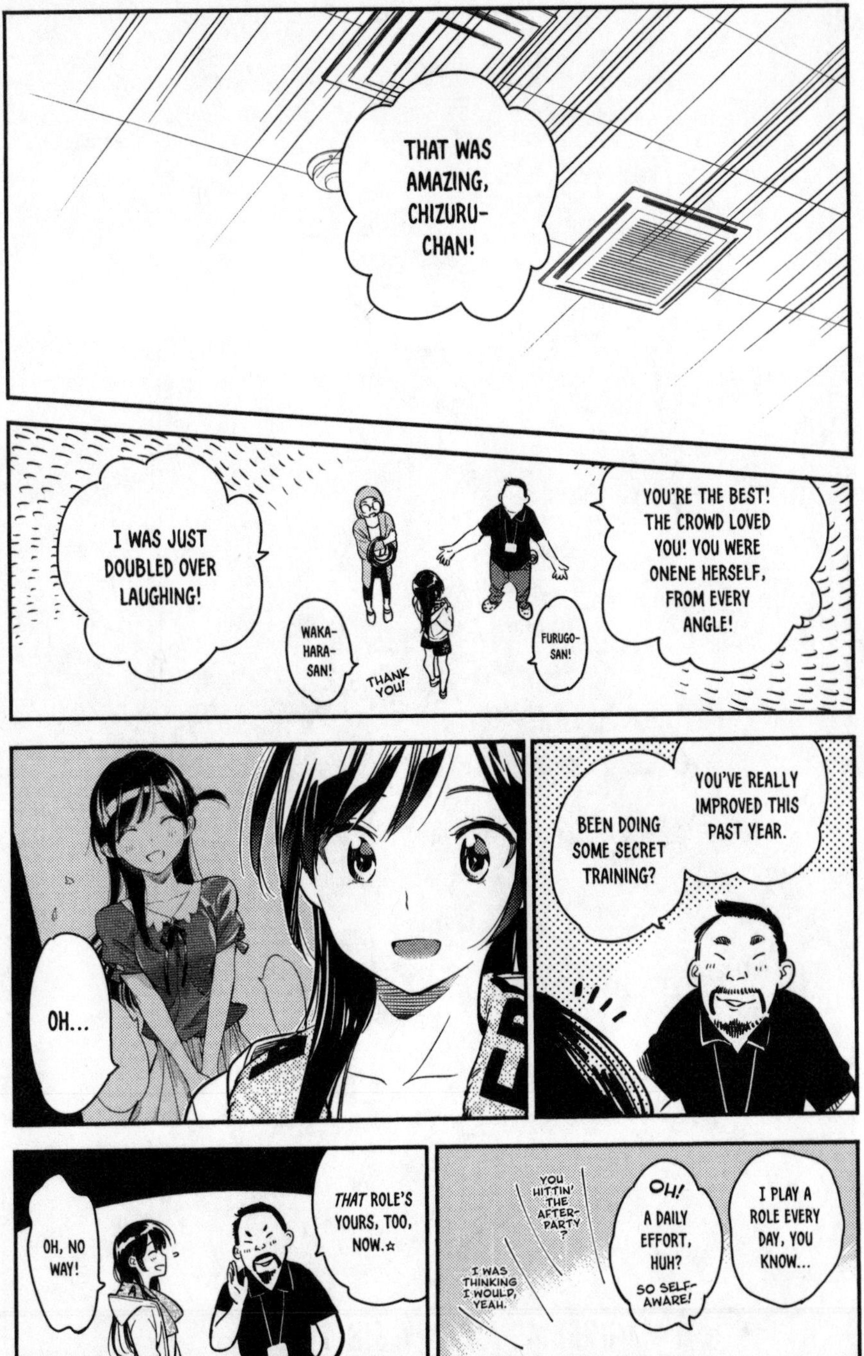

THAT WAS AMAZING, CHIZURU-CHAN!
YOU'RE THE BEST! THE CROWD LOVED YOU! YOU WERE ONENE HERSELF, FROM EVERY ANGLE!
FURUGO-SAN!
THANK YOU!
WAKA-HARA-SAN!
I WAS JUST DOUBLED OVER LAUGHING!
YOU'VE REALLY IMPROVED THIS PAST YEAR.
BEEN DOING SOME SECRET TRAINING?
OH...
I PLAY A ROLE EVERY DAY, YOU KNOW...
OH! A DAILY EFFORT, HUH?
SO SELF-AWARE!
YOU HITTIN' THE AFTER-PARTY?
I WAS THINKING I WOULD, YEAH.
THAT ROLE'S YOURS, TOO, NOW.☆
OH, NO WAY!

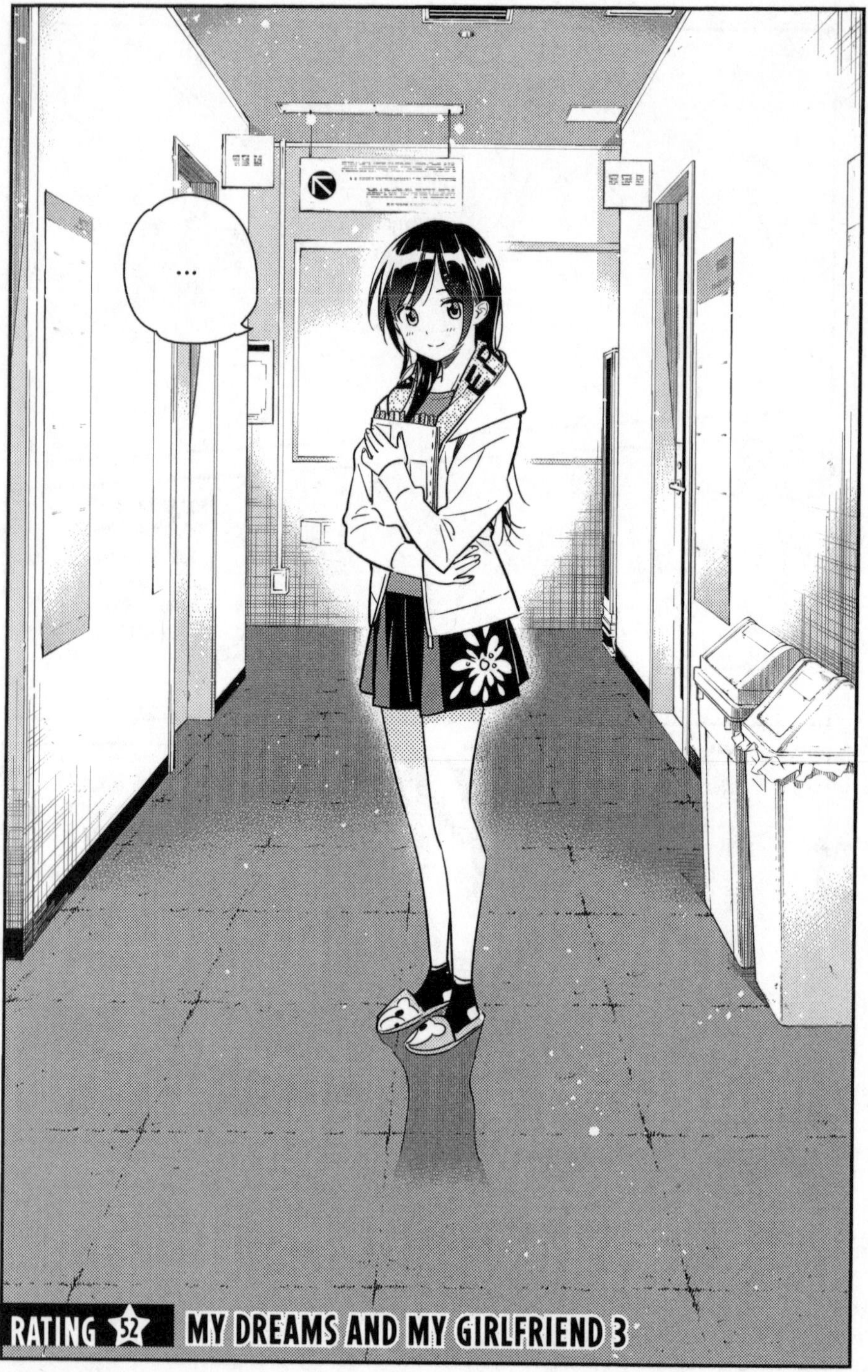
...

RATING 52 MY DREAMS AND MY GIRLFRIEND 3

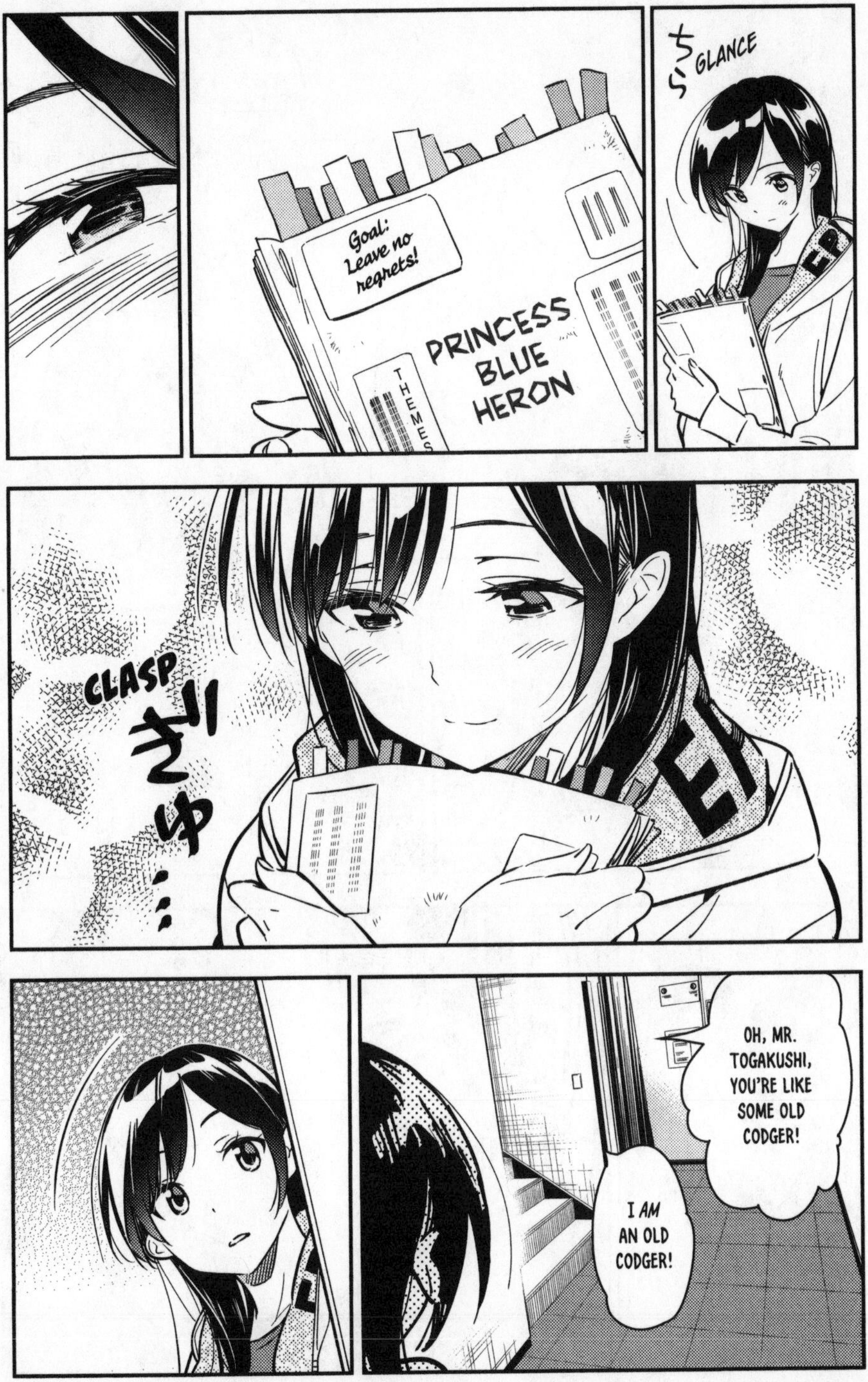
ちら
GLANCE
Goal: Leave no regrets!
PRINCESS BLUE HERON
THEMES
CLASP
ぎゅ…
OH, MR. TOGAKUSHI, YOU'RE LIKE SOME OLD CODGER!
I AM AN OLD CODGER!

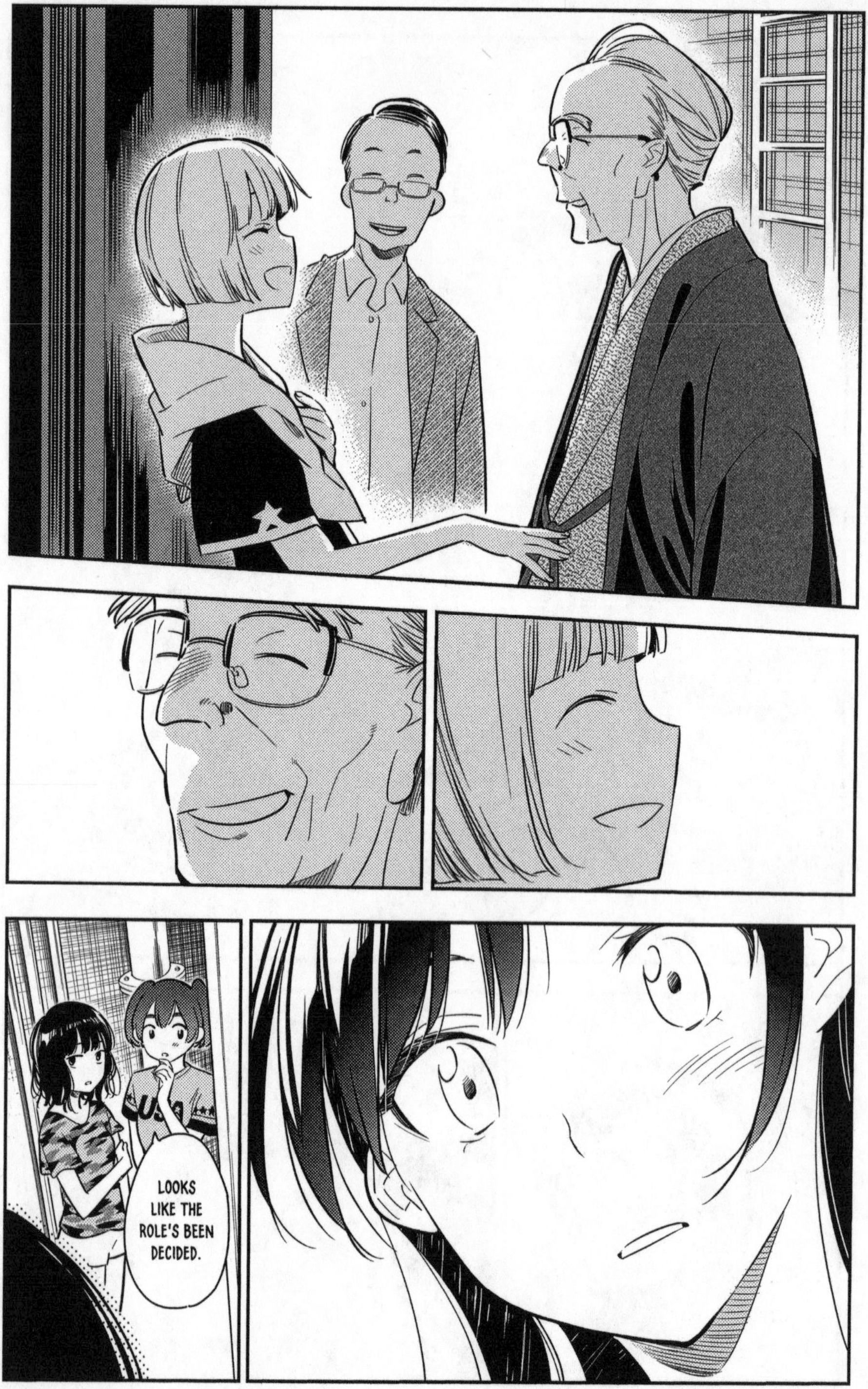
LOOKS LIKE THE ROLE'S BEEN DECIDED.

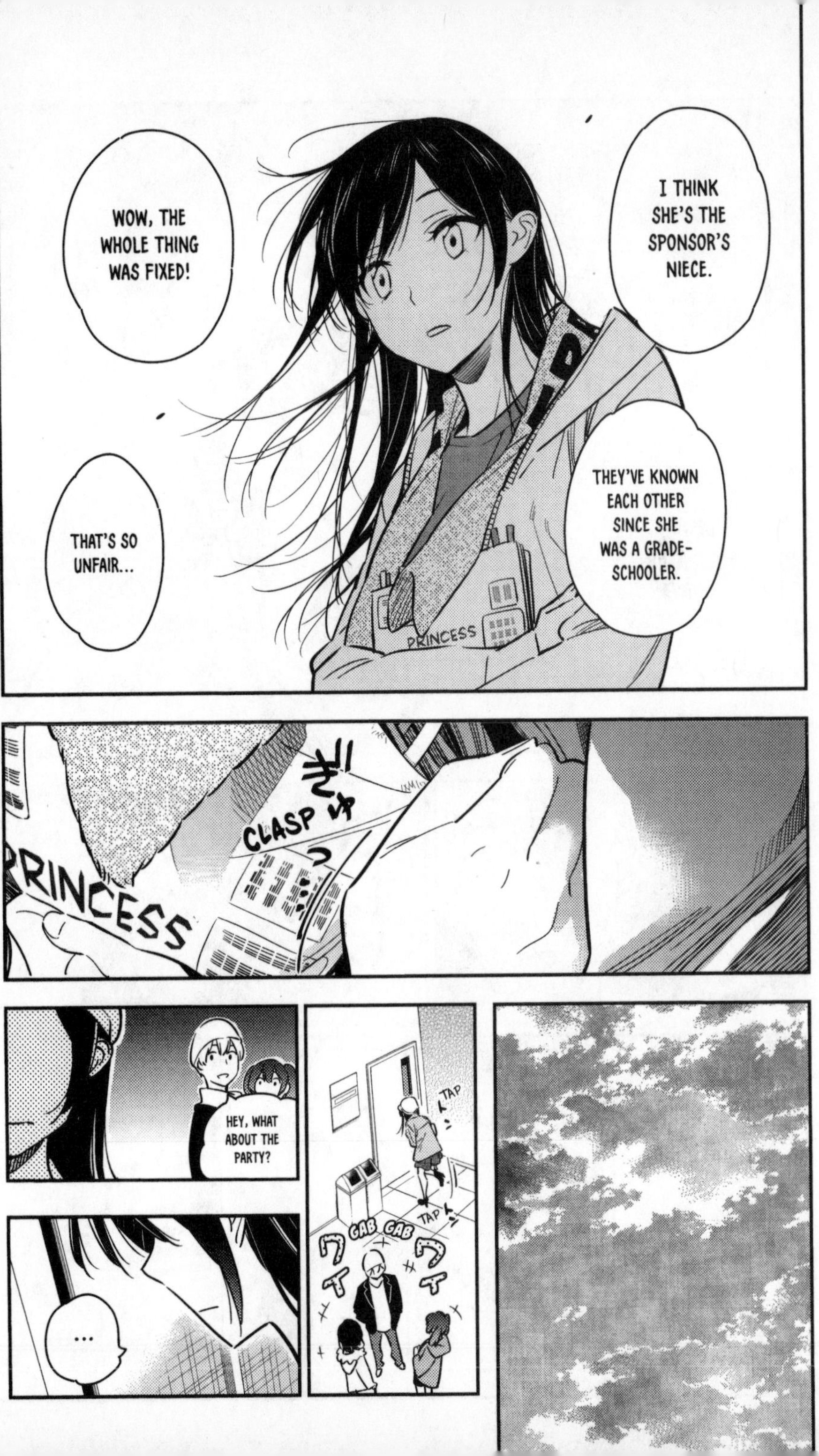
I THINK SHE'S THE SPONSOR'S NIECE.
THEY'VE KNOWN EACH OTHER SINCE SHE WAS A GRADE-SCHOOLER.
WOW, THE WHOLE THING WAS FIXED!
THAT'S SO UNFAIR...
PRINCESS
CLASP
PRINCESS
TAP
TAP
GAB GAB
HEY, WHAT ABOUT THE PARTY?
...

I'M SORRY!

I'LL CALL YOU LATER, OKAY?

...

BA-TAM

OH...

NGH

IF I CAN STAY...

...AFLOAT AS AN ACTRESS...

IF I DO WELL, THE AGENCY SAID...

...IT'D LEAD TO MORE WORK.

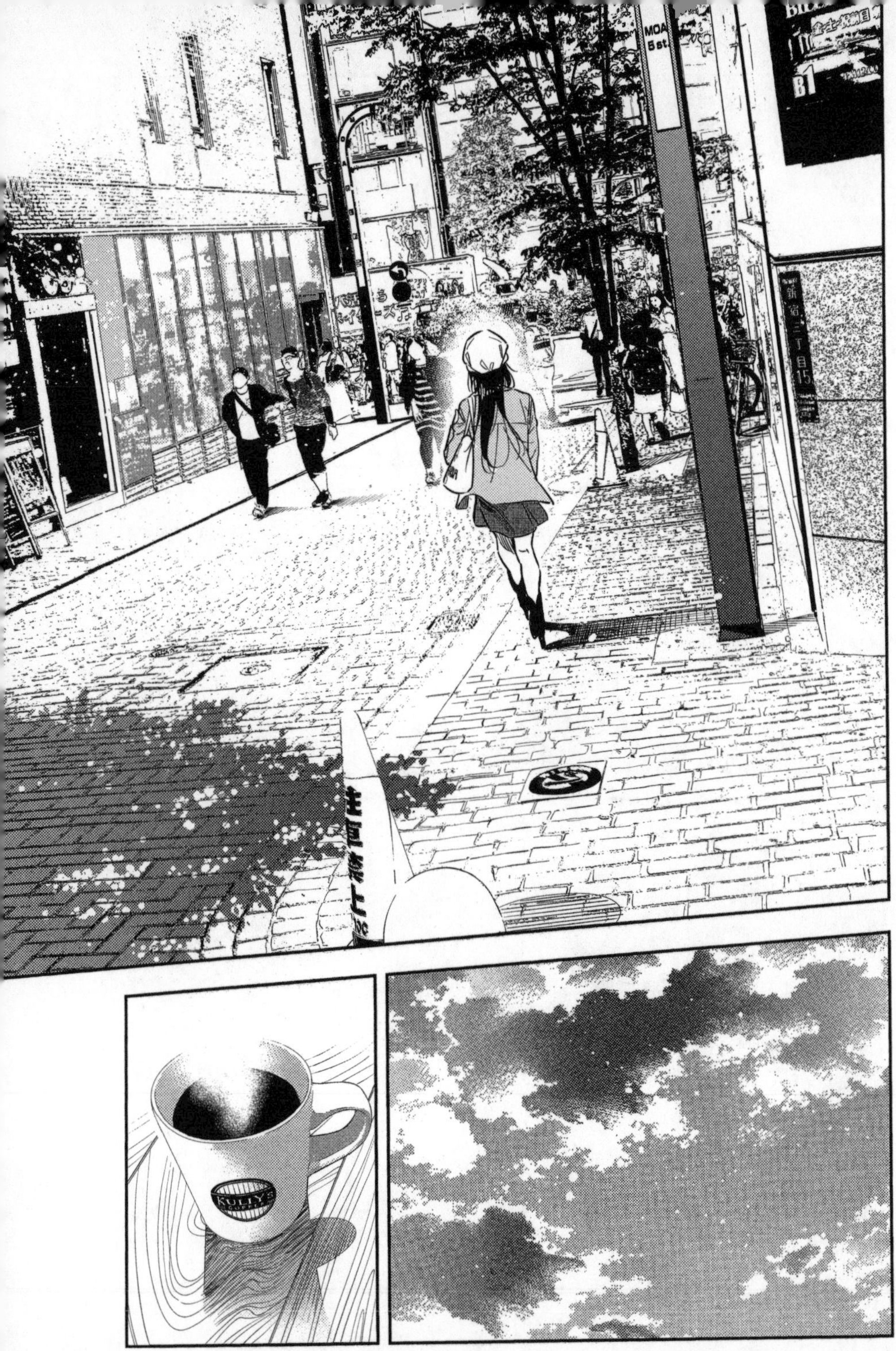
MOA
5 st.
B1
新宿三丁目15

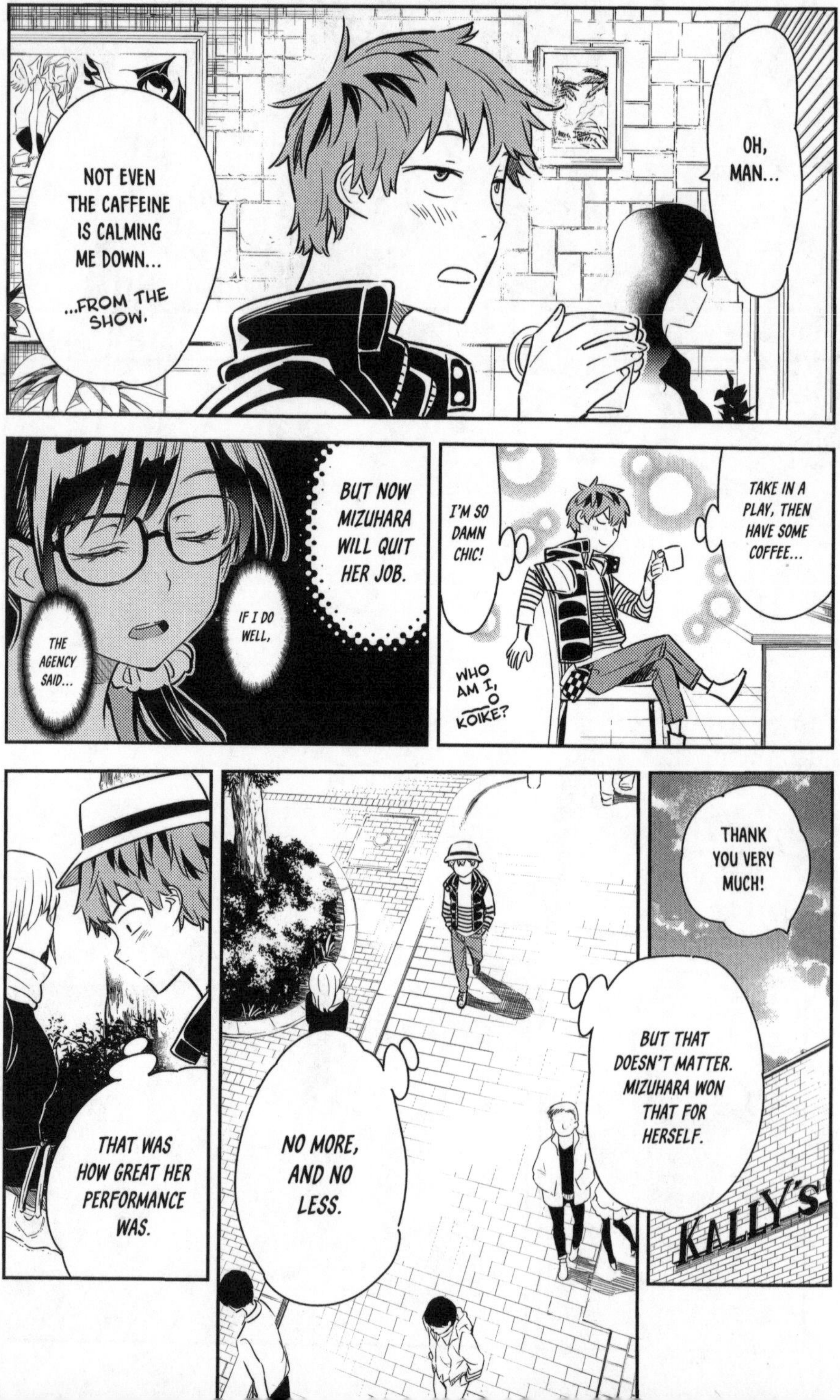
OH, MAN...
NOT EVEN THE CAFFEINE IS CALMING ME DOWN...
...FROM THE SHOW.
TAKE IN A PLAY, THEN HAVE SOME COFFEE...
I'M SO DAMN CHIC!
WHO AM I, KOIKE?
BUT NOW MIZUHARA WILL QUIT HER JOB.
IF I DO WELL,
THE AGENCY SAID...
THANK YOU VERY MUCH!
KALLY'S
BUT THAT DOESN'T MATTER. MIZUHARA WON THAT FOR HERSELF.
NO MORE, AND NO LESS.
THAT WAS HOW GREAT HER PERFORMANCE WAS.

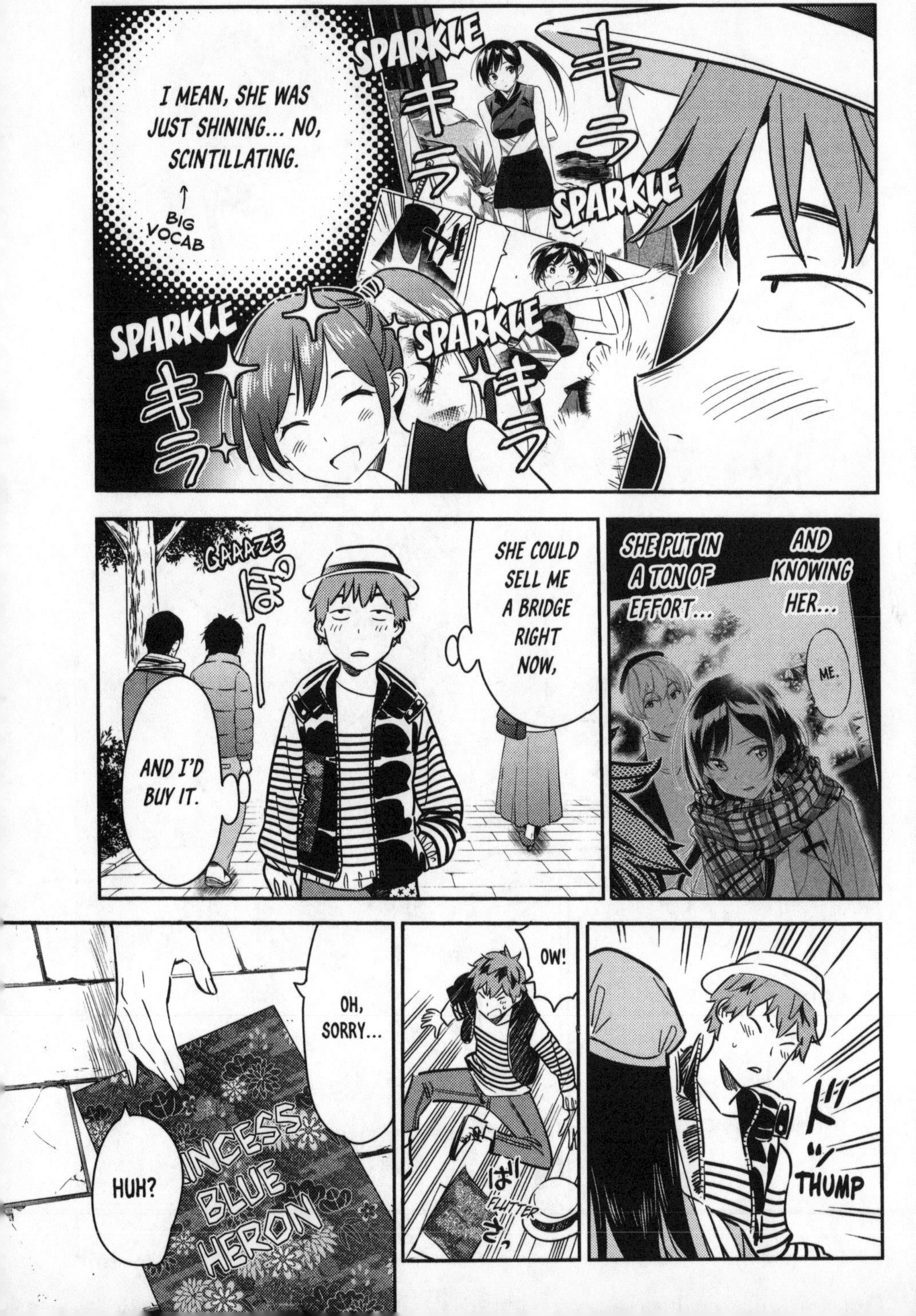
キラ
SPARKLE
SPARKLE
キラ
SPARKLE
I MEAN, SHE WAS JUST SHINING... NO, SCINTILLATING.
↑ BIG VOCAB
SPARKLE
キラ
キラ
SHE PUT IN A TON OF EFFORT...
AND KNOWING HER...
ME.
SHE COULD SELL ME A BRIDGE RIGHT NOW,
GAAAZE
ぽー
AND I'D BUY IT.
ドッ
THUMP
OW!
ばっ
FLUTTER
さっ
OH, SORRY...
INCESS BLUE HERON
HUH?

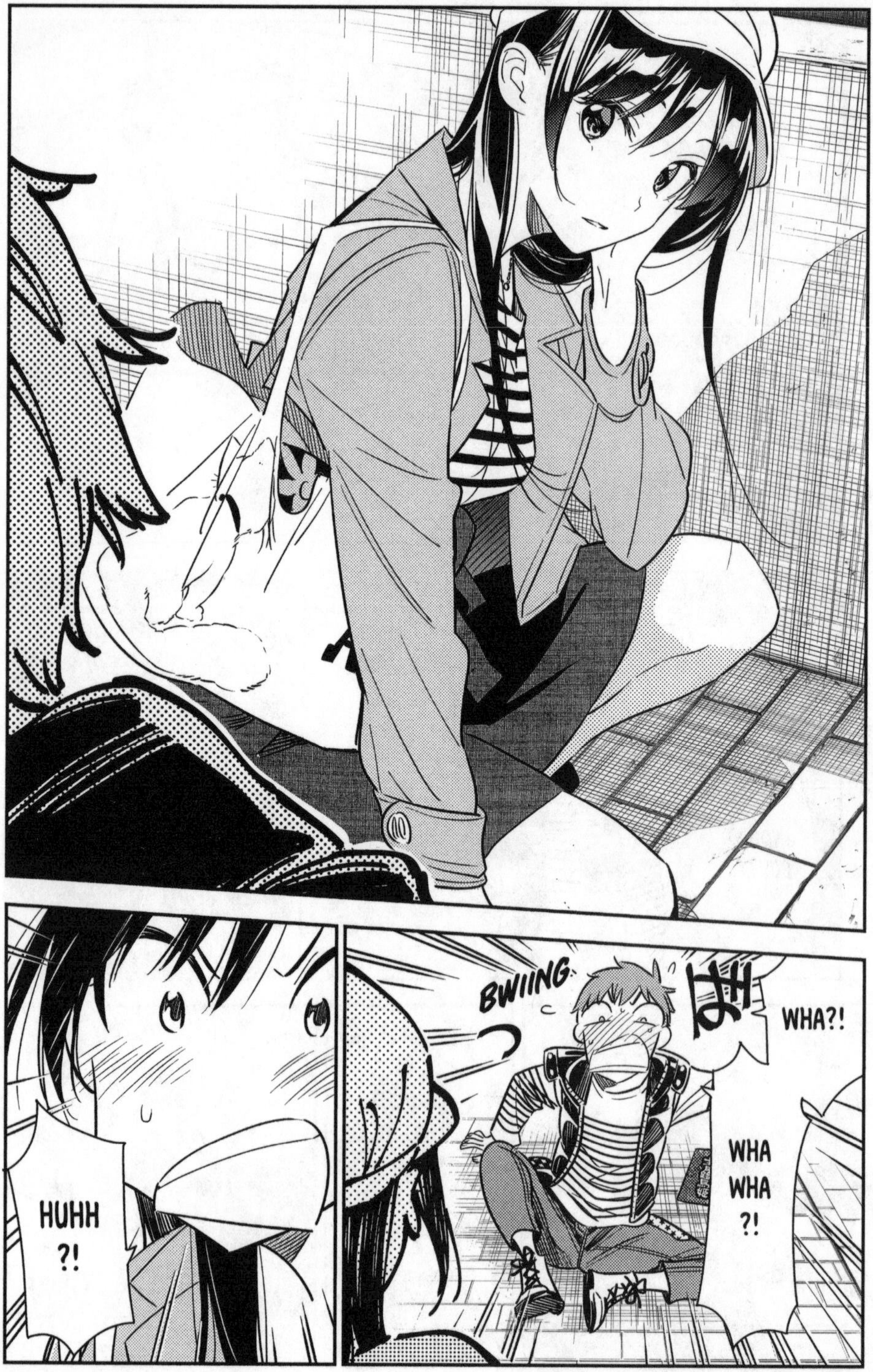
WHA?!
BWIING
WHA WHA ?!
HUHH ?!

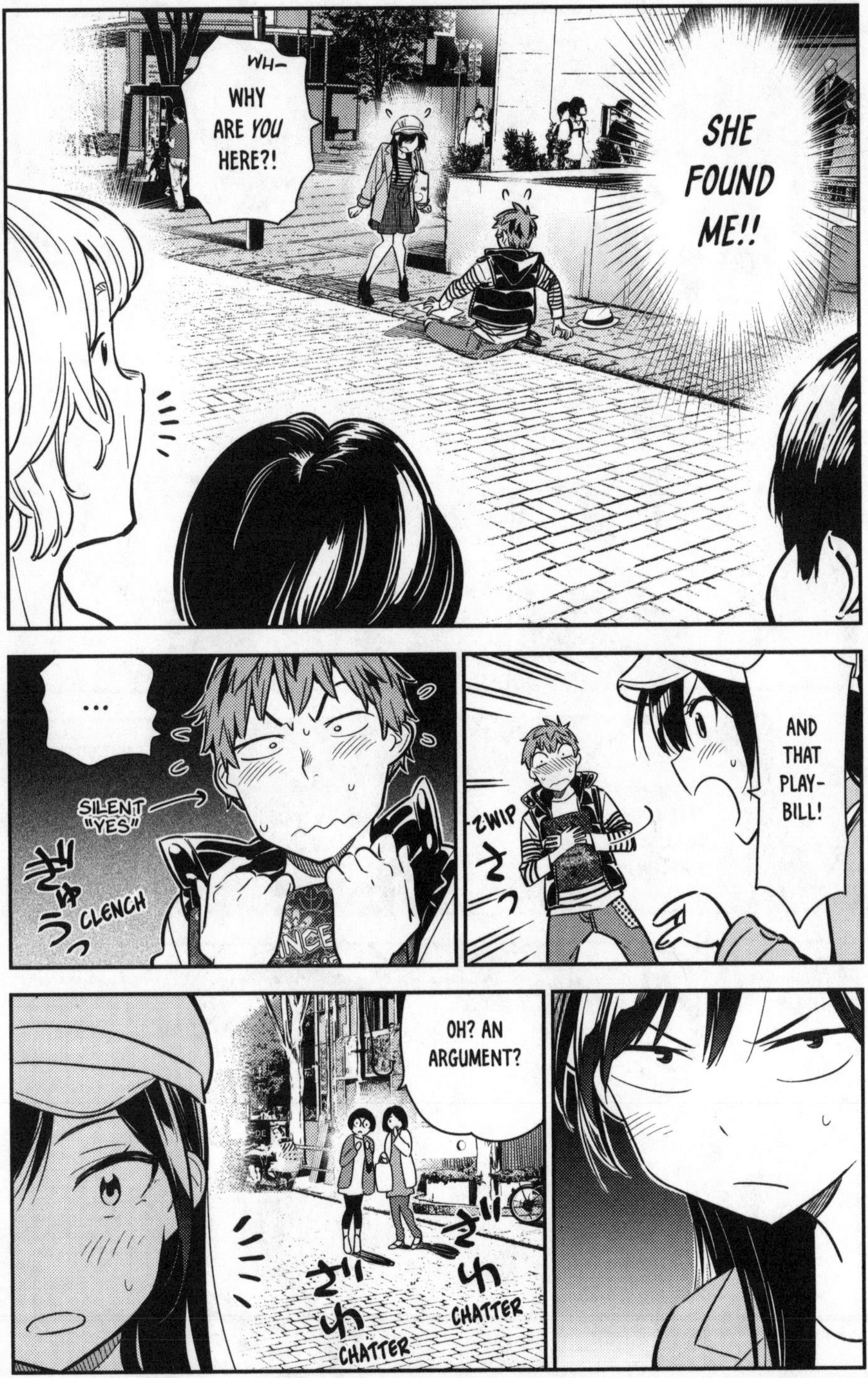
SHE FOUND ME!!
WH- WHY ARE YOU HERE?!
AND THAT PLAY-BILL!
さっ
ZWIP
...
SILENT "YES"
ぎゅうっ
CLENCH
OH? AN ARGUMENT?
ざわ
CHATTER
ざわ
CHATTER

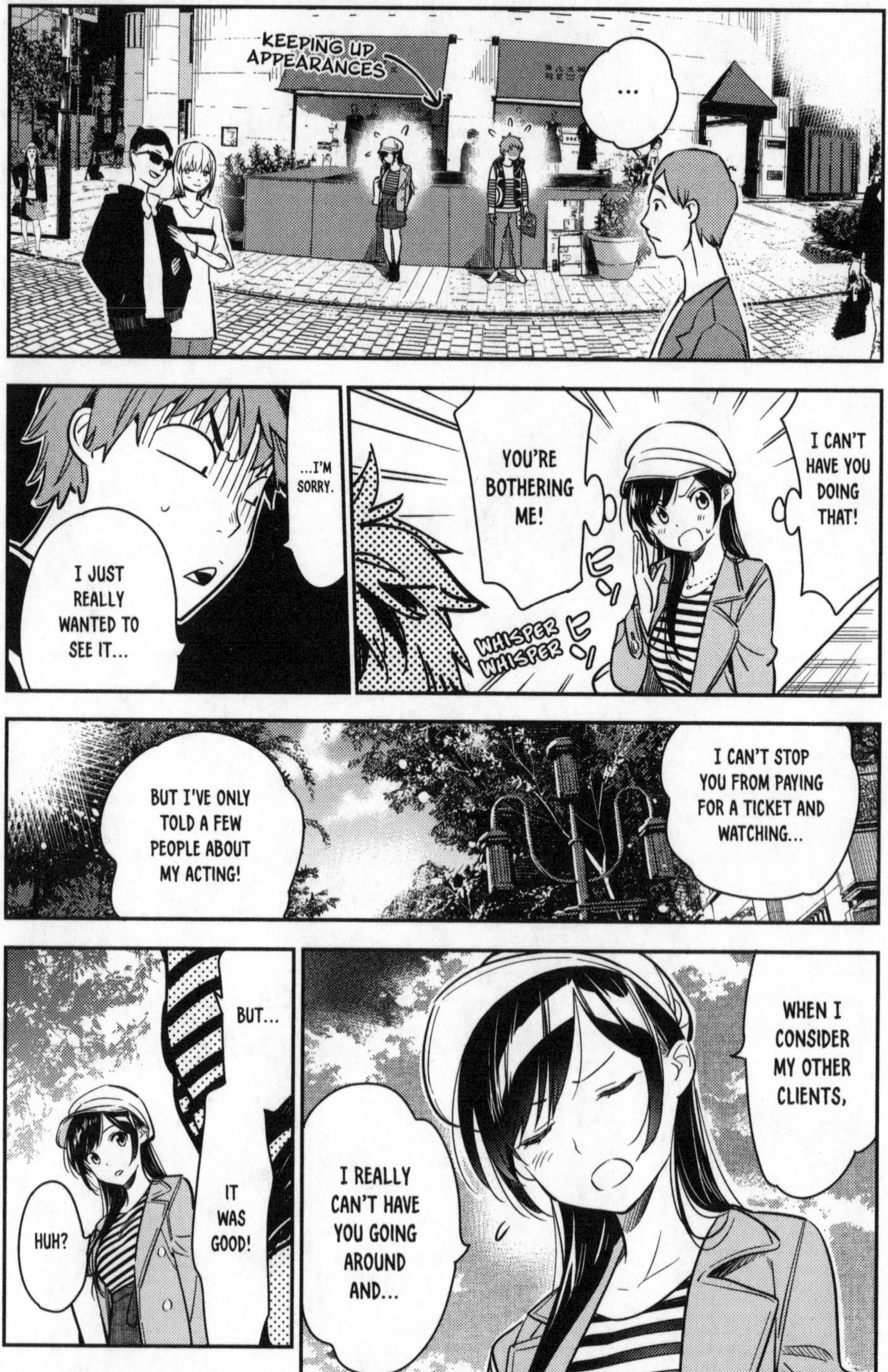
...
KEEPING UP APPEARANCES
I CAN'T HAVE YOU DOING THAT!
YOU'RE BOTHERING ME!
WHISPER WHISPER
...I'M SORRY.
I JUST REALLY WANTED TO SEE IT...
I CAN'T STOP YOU FROM PAYING FOR A TICKET AND WATCHING...
BUT I'VE ONLY TOLD A FEW PEOPLE ABOUT MY ACTING!
WHEN I CONSIDER MY OTHER CLIENTS,
I REALLY CAN'T HAVE YOU GOING AROUND AND...
BUT...
IT WAS GOOD!
HUH?

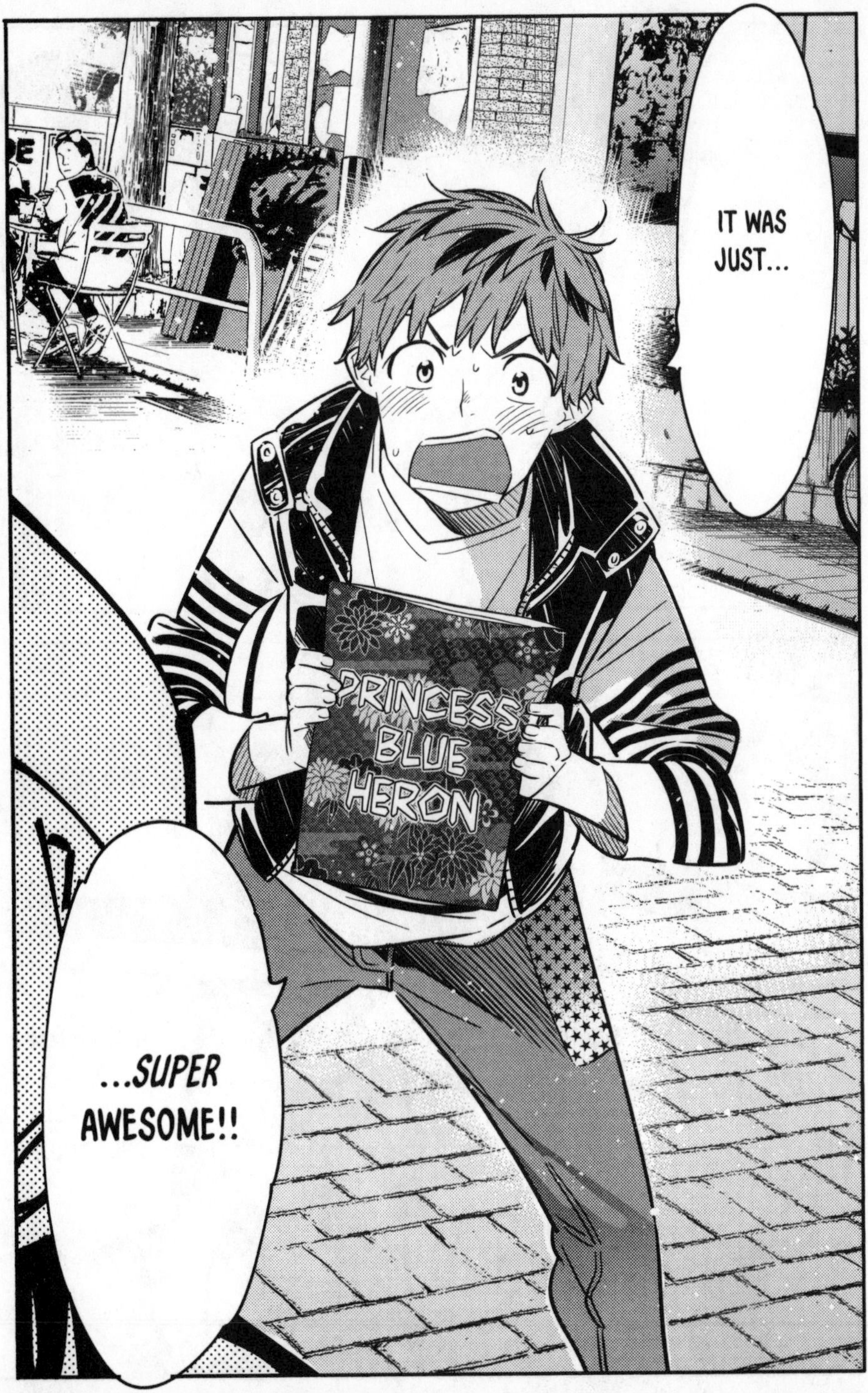
IT WAS JUST...
PRINCESS BLUE HERON
...SUPER AWESOME!!

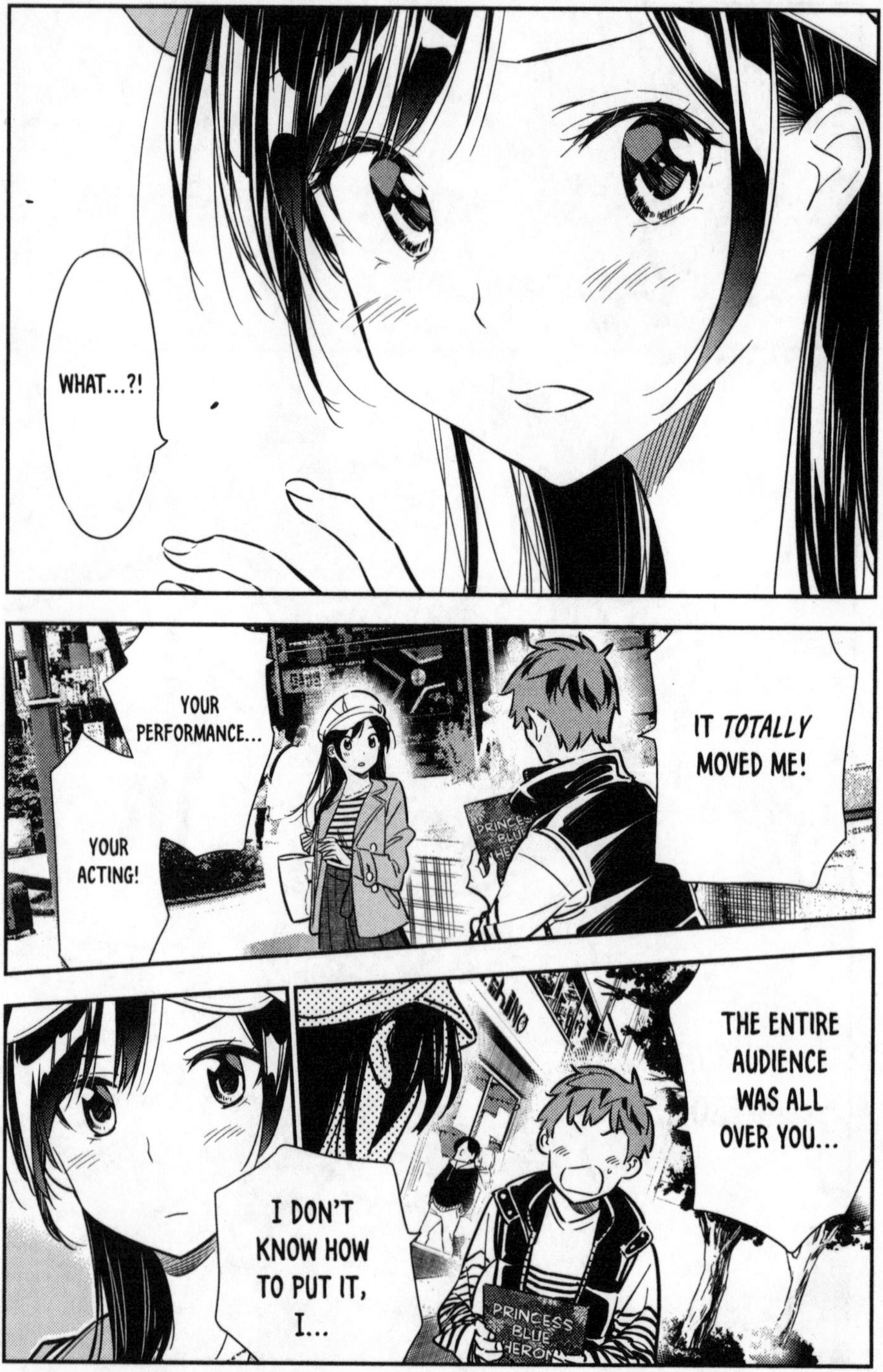
WHAT...?!
IT *TOTALLY* MOVED ME!
YOUR PERFORMANCE...
YOUR ACTING!
THE ENTIRE AUDIENCE WAS ALL OVER YOU...
I DON'T KNOW HOW TO PUT IT, I...
PRINCESS BLUE HERON

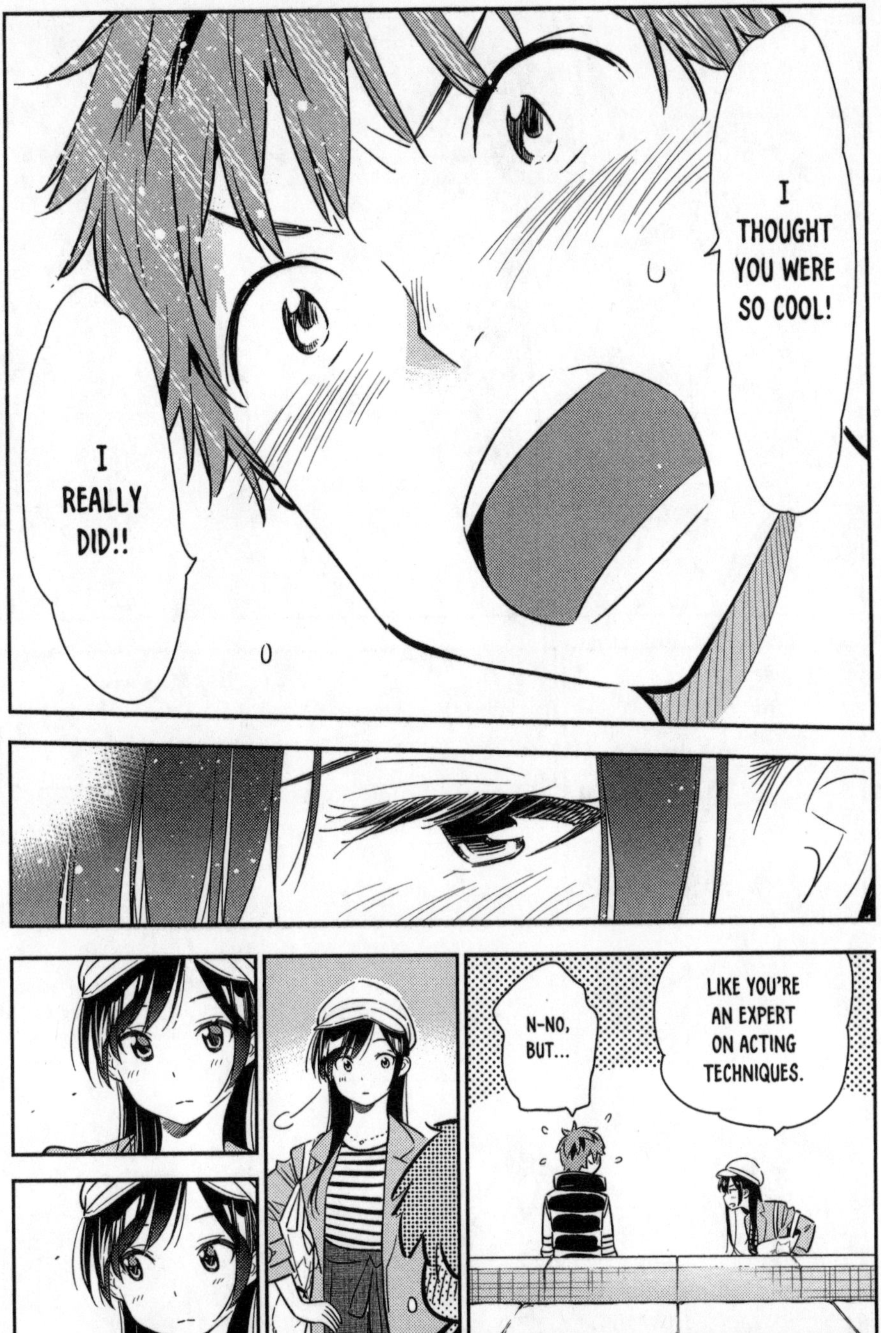
I THOUGHT YOU WERE SO COOL!
I REALLY DID!!
LIKE YOU'RE AN EXPERT ON ACTING TECHNIQUES.
N-NO, BUT...

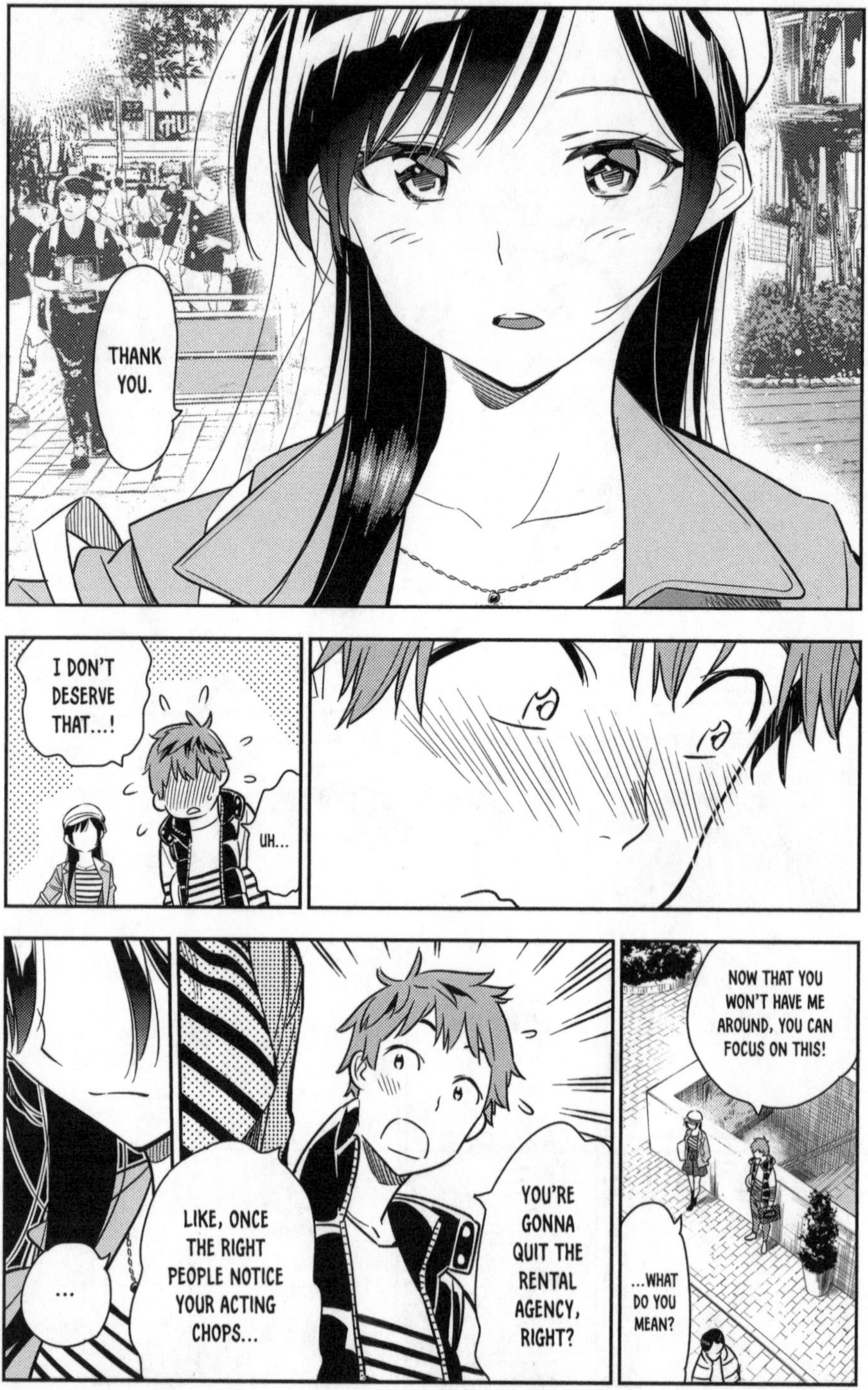
THANK YOU.
I DON'T DESERVE THAT...!
UH...
NOW THAT YOU WON'T HAVE ME AROUND, YOU CAN FOCUS ON THIS!
...WHAT DO YOU MEAN?
YOU'RE GONNA QUIT THE RENTAL AGENCY, RIGHT?
LIKE, ONCE THE RIGHT PEOPLE NOTICE YOUR ACTING CHOPS...
...

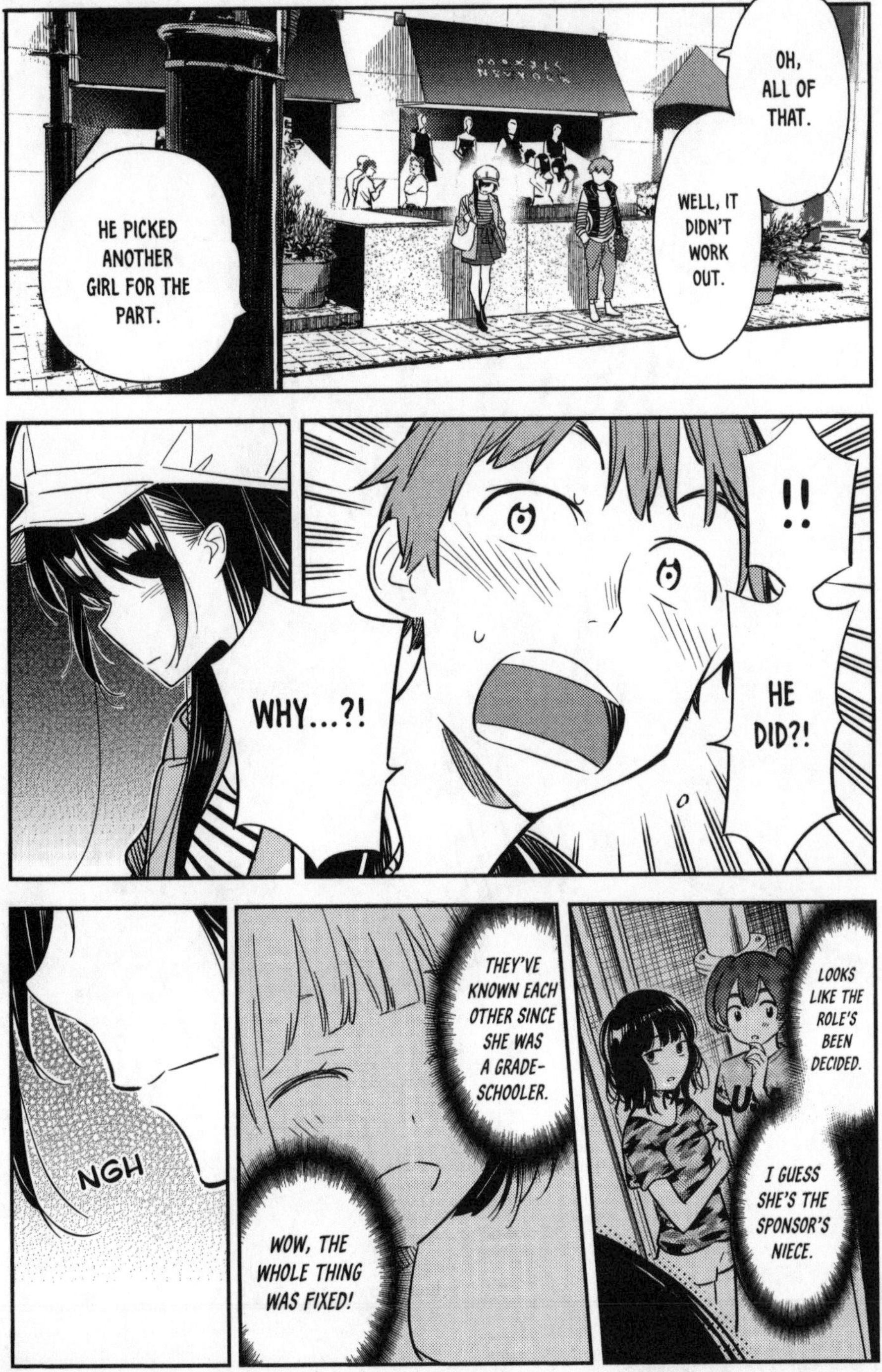
OH, ALL OF THAT.
WELL, IT DIDN'T WORK OUT.
HE PICKED ANOTHER GIRL FOR THE PART.
!!
HE DID?!
WHY...?!
LOOKS LIKE THE ROLE'S BEEN DECIDED.
I GUESS SHE'S THE SPONSOR'S NIECE.
THEY'VE KNOWN EACH OTHER SINCE SHE WAS A GRADE-SCHOOLER.
WOW, THE WHOLE THING WAS FIXED!
NGH

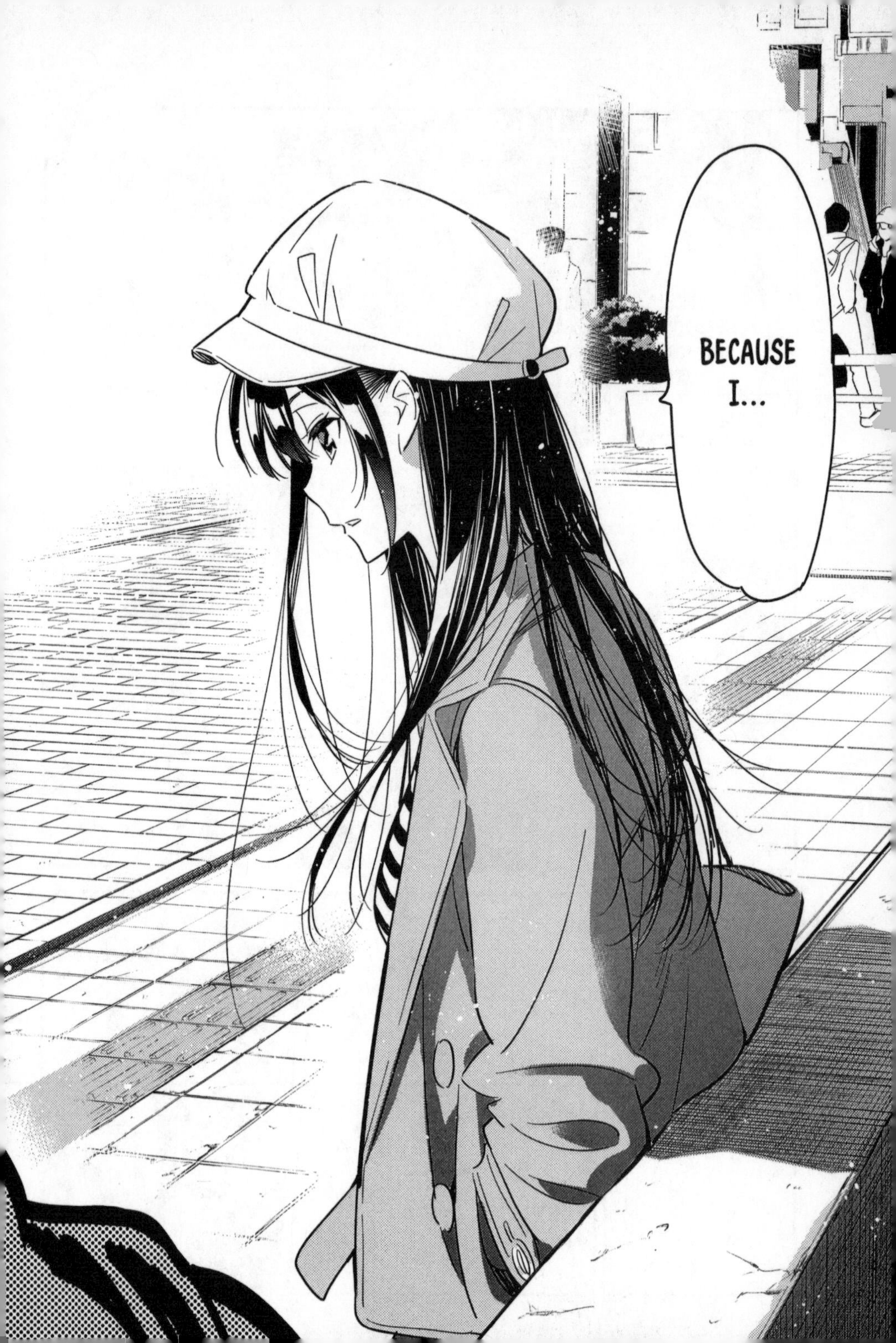
BECAUSE I...

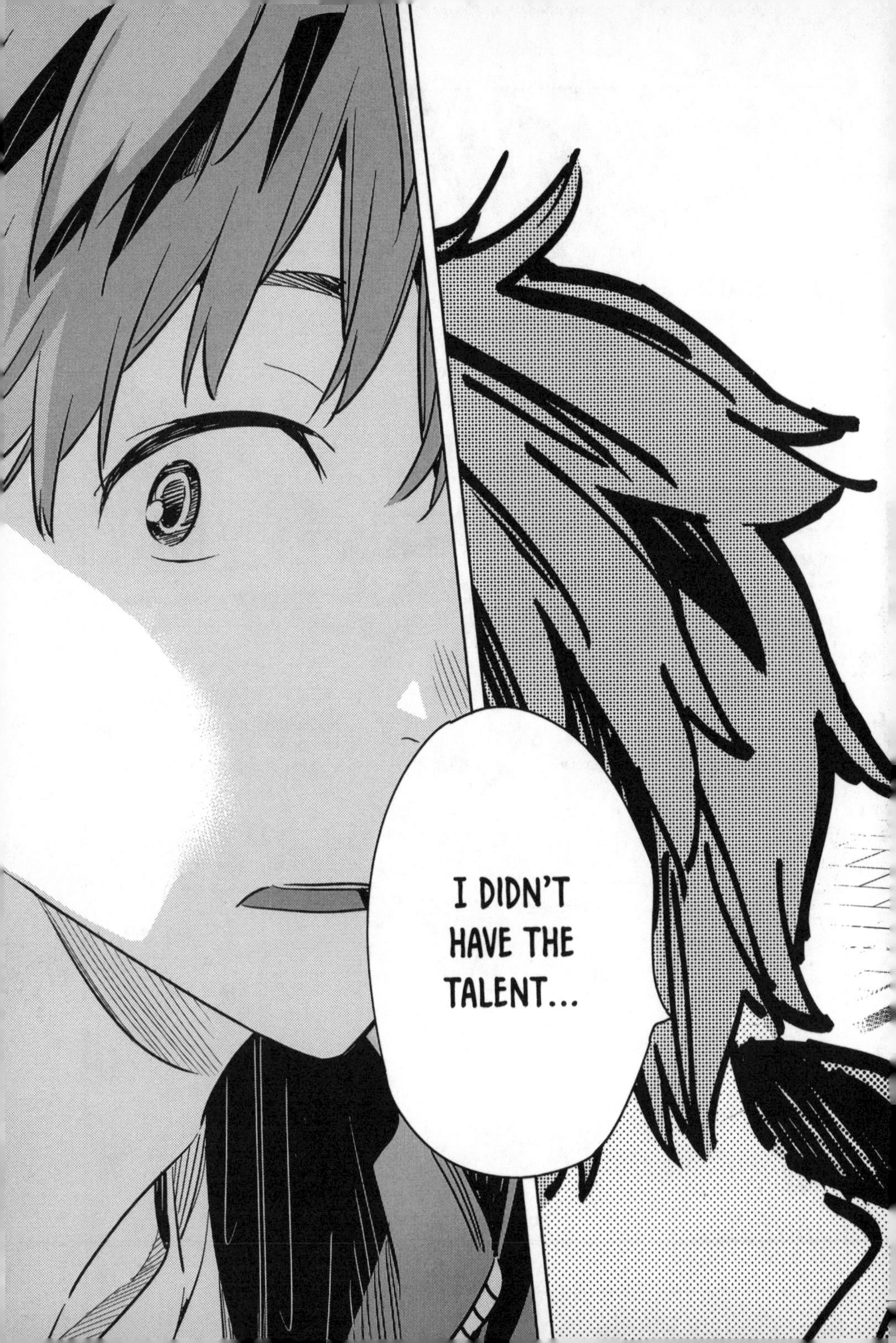
I DIDN'T HAVE THE TALENT...

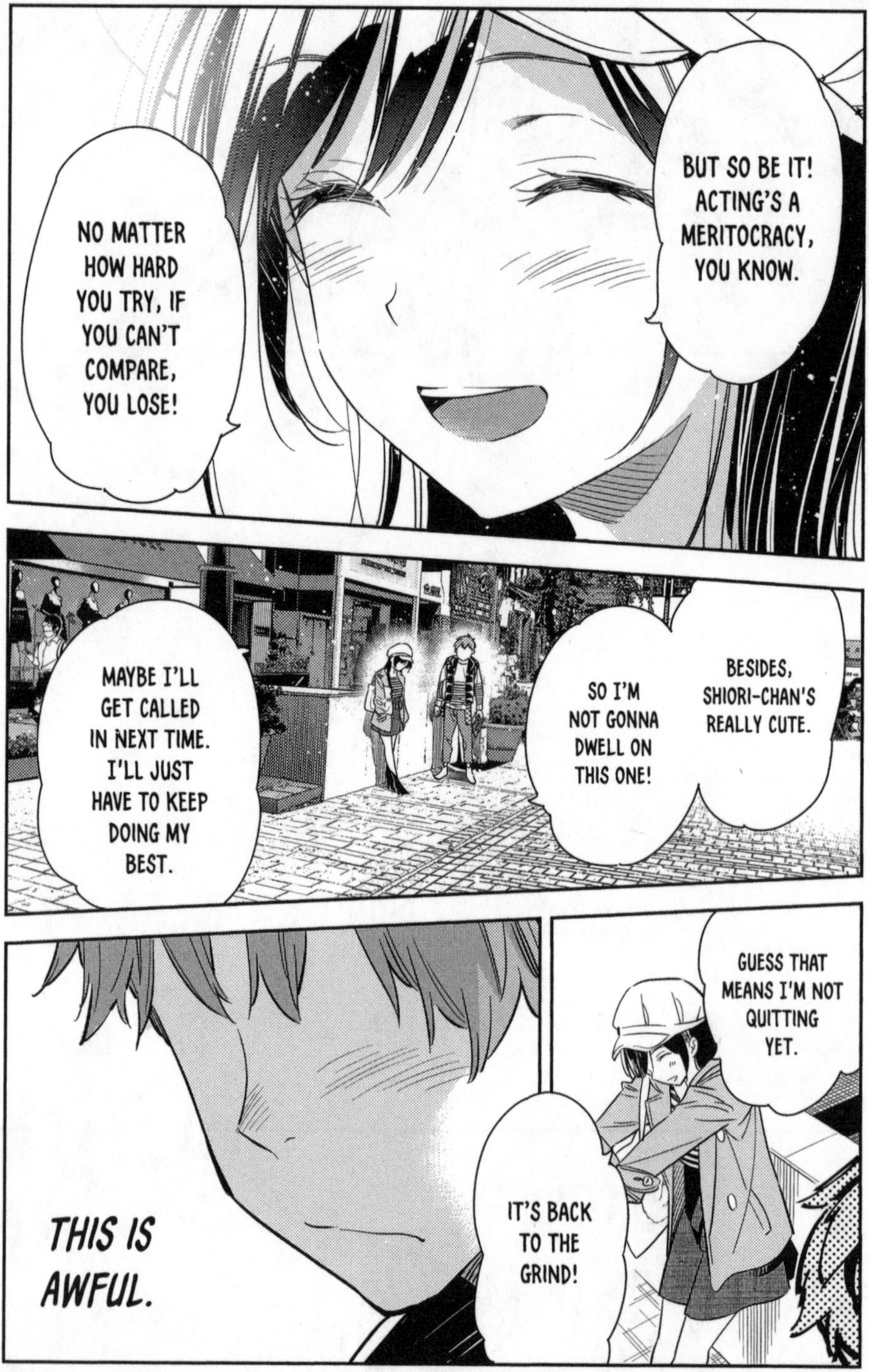
BUT SO BE IT! ACTING'S A MERITOCRACY, YOU KNOW.
NO MATTER HOW HARD YOU TRY, IF YOU CAN'T COMPARE, YOU LOSE!
BESIDES, SHIORI-CHAN'S REALLY CUTE.
SO I'M NOT GONNA DWELL ON THIS ONE!
MAYBE I'LL GET CALLED IN NEXT TIME. I'LL JUST HAVE TO KEEP DOING MY BEST.
GUESS THAT MEANS I'M NOT QUITTING YET.
IT'S BACK TO THE GRIND!
THIS IS AWFUL.

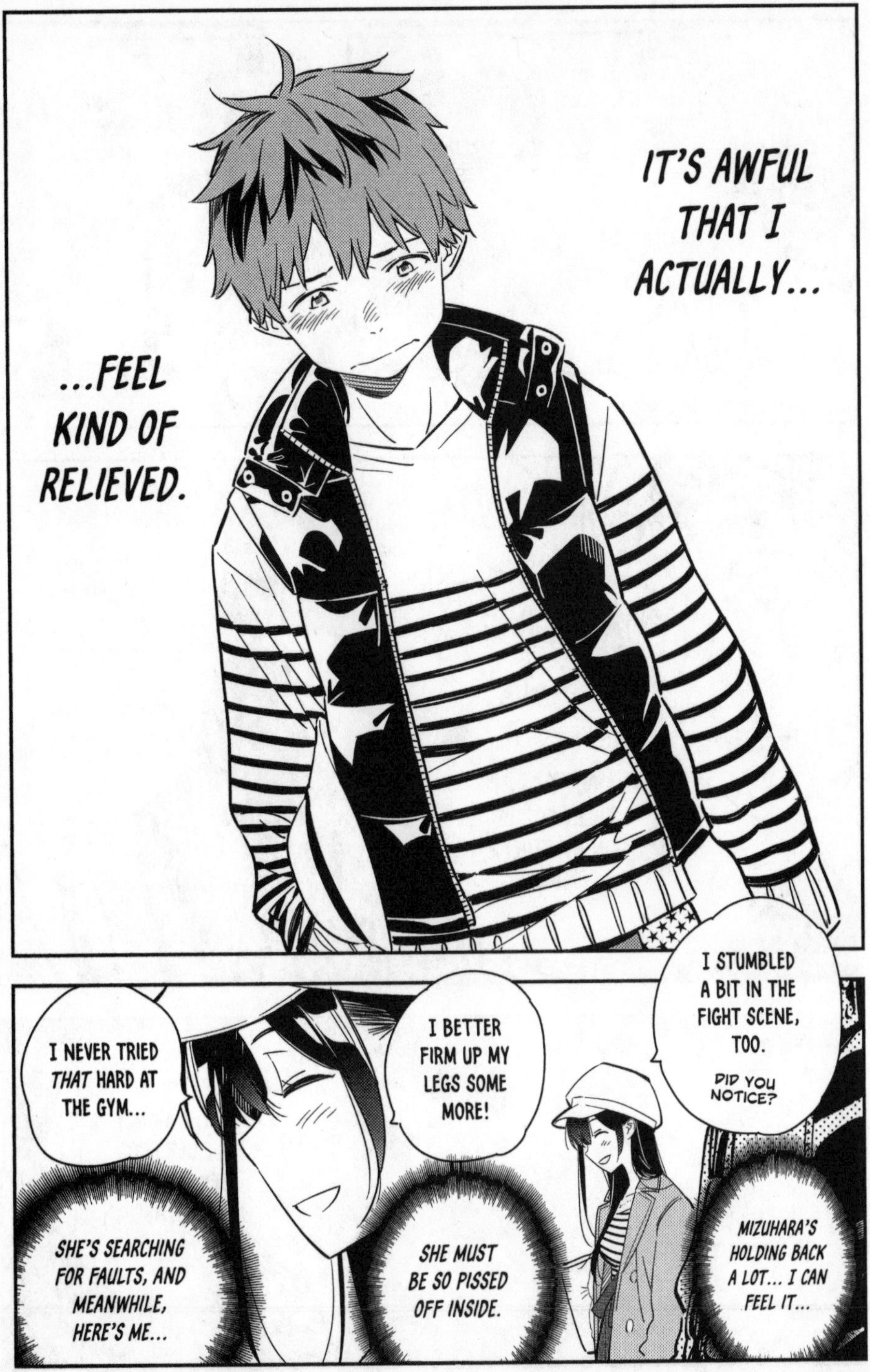
IT'S AWFUL THAT I ACTUALLY...
...FEEL KIND OF RELIEVED.
I STUMBLED A BIT IN THE FIGHT SCENE, TOO.
DID YOU NOTICE?
I BETTER FIRM UP MY LEGS SOME MORE!
I NEVER TRIED *THAT* HARD AT THE GYM...
MIZUHARA'S HOLDING BACK A LOT... I CAN FEEL IT...
SHE MUST BE SO PISSED OFF INSIDE.
SHE'S SEARCHING FOR FAULTS, AND MEANWHILE, HERE'S ME...

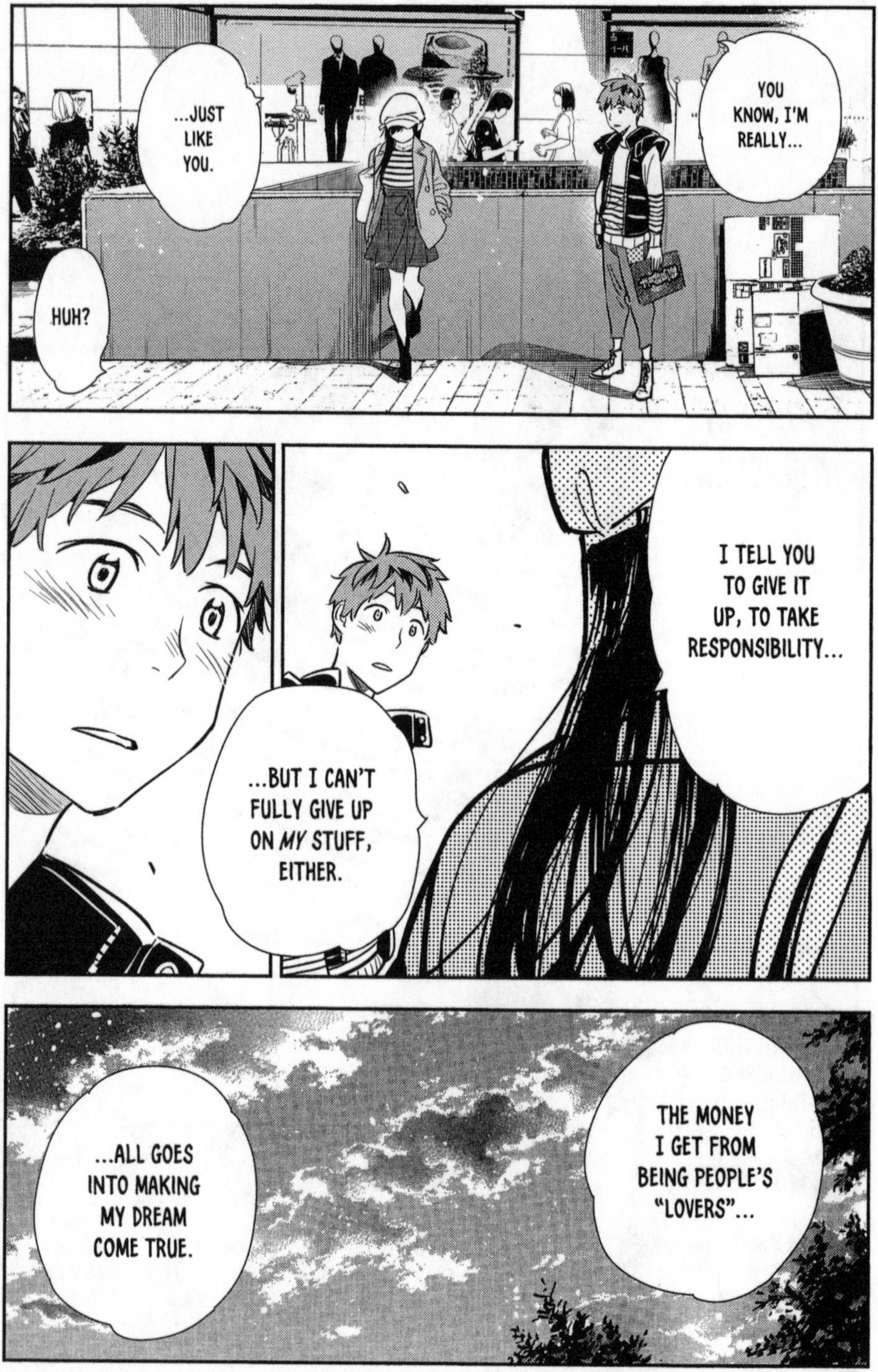
YOU KNOW, I'M REALLY...
...JUST LIKE YOU.
HUH?
I TELL YOU TO GIVE IT UP, TO TAKE RESPONSIBILITY...
...BUT I CAN'T FULLY GIVE UP ON *MY* STUFF, EITHER.
THE MONEY I GET FROM BEING PEOPLE'S "LOVERS"...
...ALL GOES INTO MAKING MY DREAM COME TRUE.

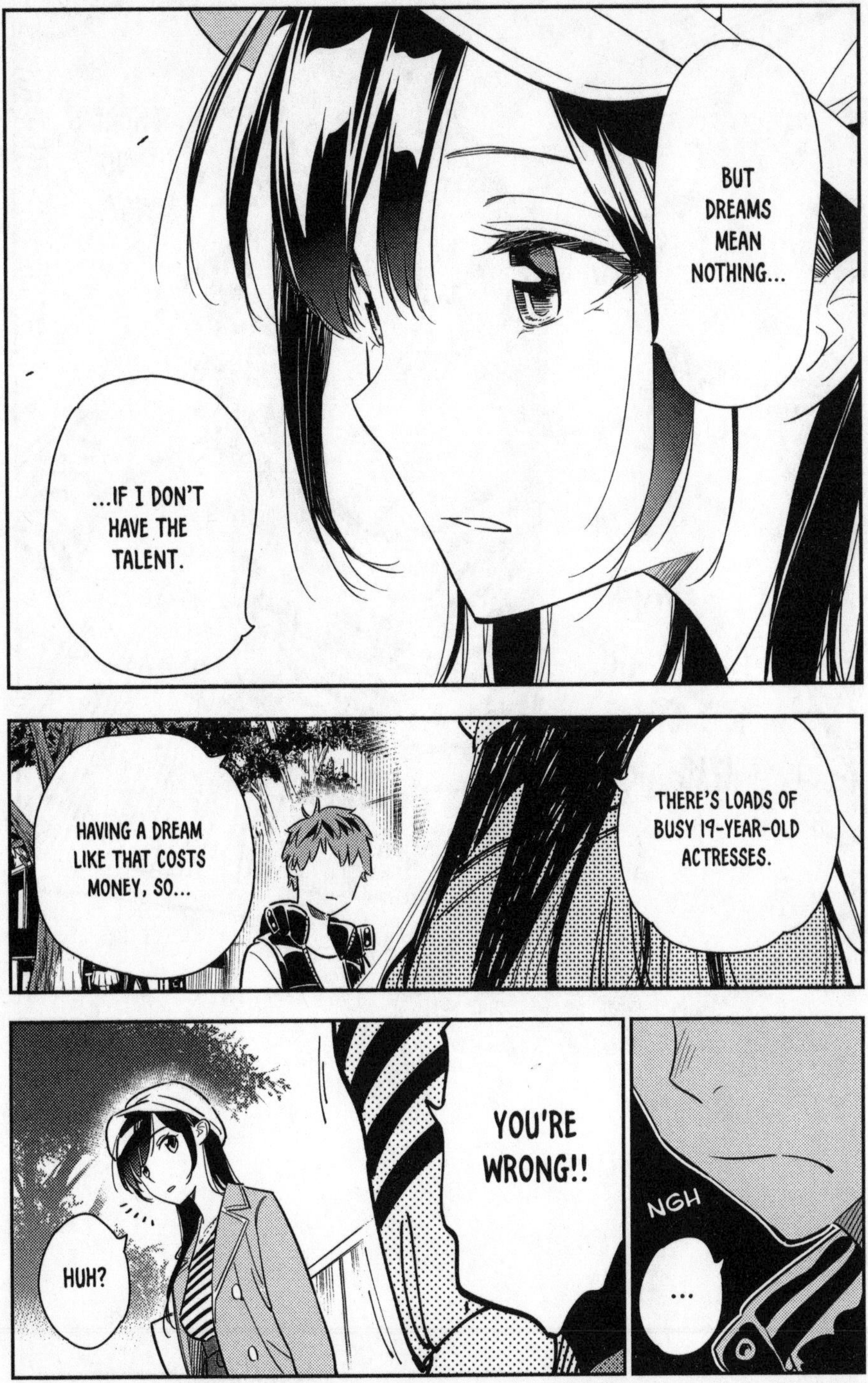
BUT DREAMS MEAN NOTHING...
...IF I DON'T HAVE THE TALENT.
THERE'S LOADS OF BUSY 19-YEAR-OLD ACTRESSES.
HAVING A DREAM LIKE THAT COSTS MONEY, SO...
NGH
...
YOU'RE WRONG!!
HUH?

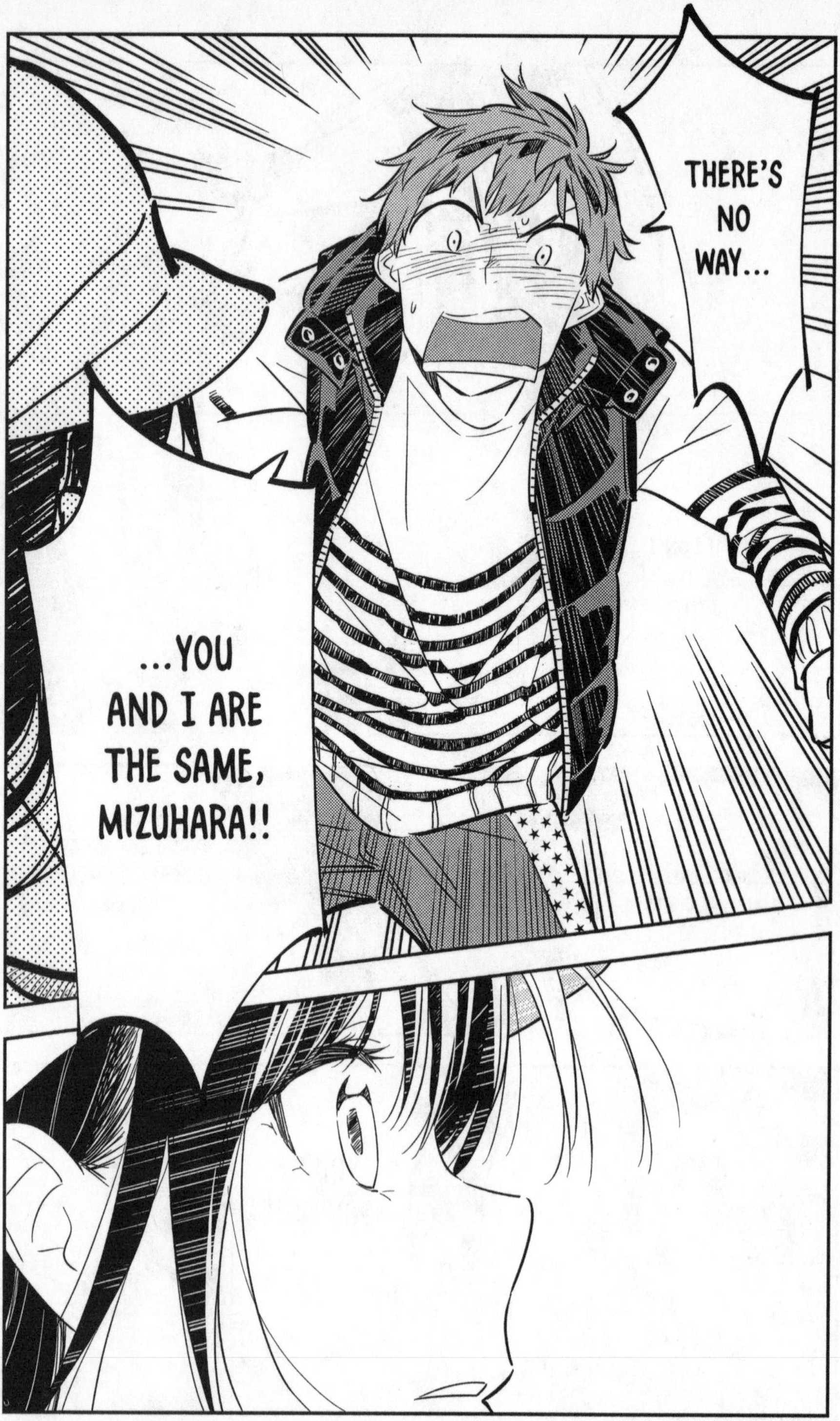
THERE'S NO WAY...
...YOU AND I ARE THE SAME, MIZUHARA!!

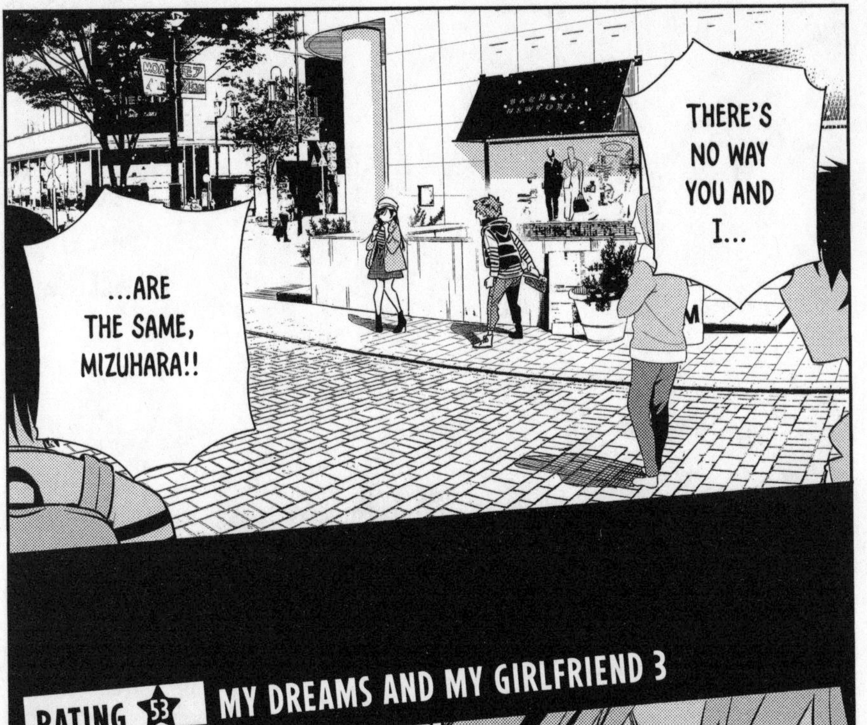
THERE'S NO WAY YOU AND I...
...ARE THE SAME, MIZUHARA!!

RATING 53 MY DREAMS AND MY GIRLFRIEND 3

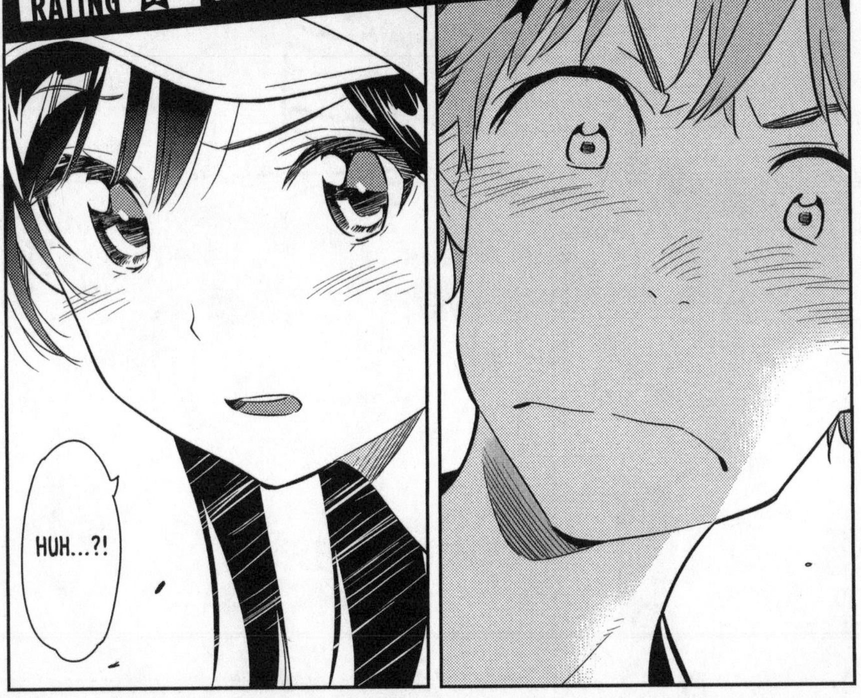
HUH...?!

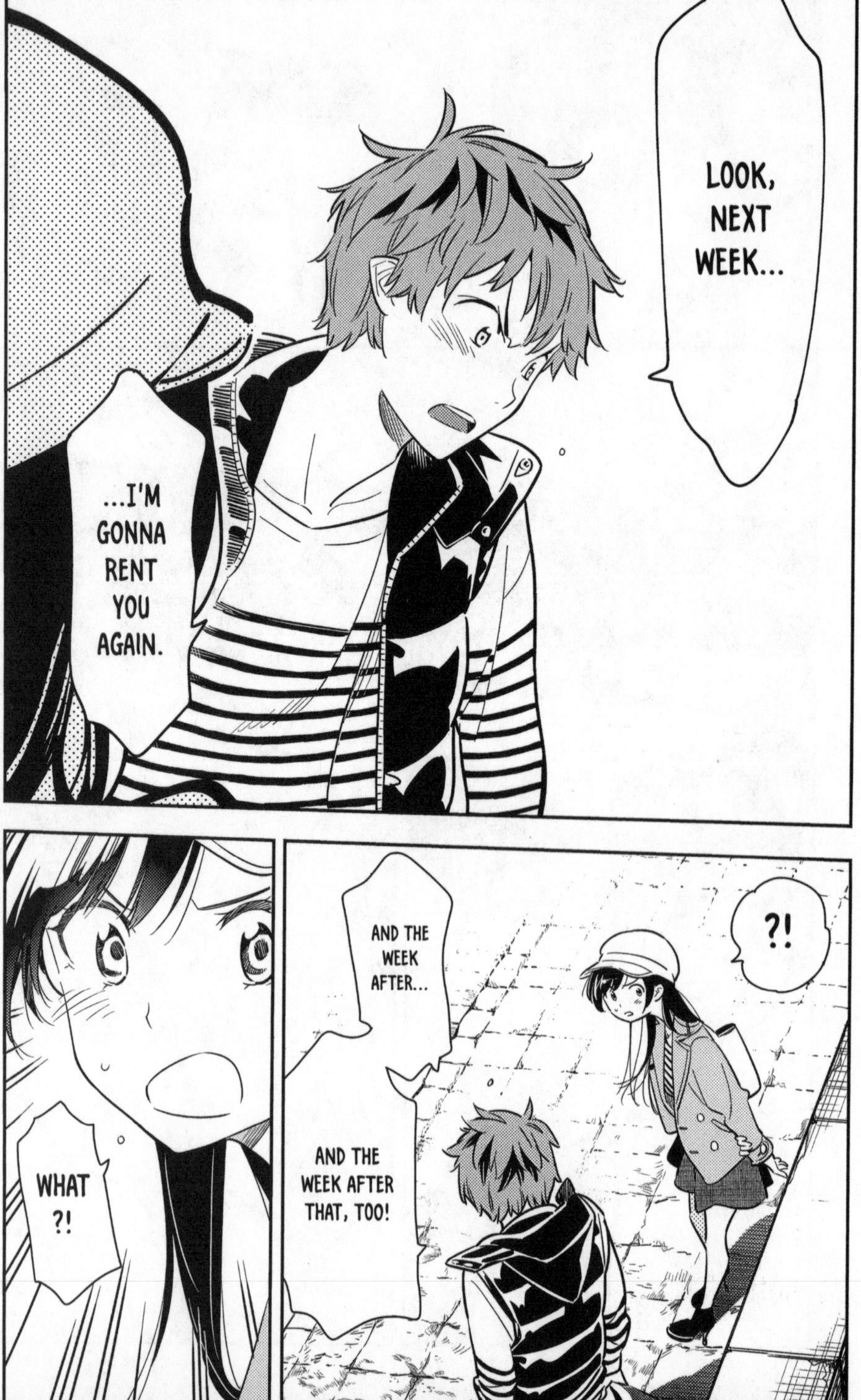
LOOK, NEXT WEEK...
...I'M GONNA RENT YOU AGAIN.
?!
AND THE WEEK AFTER...
AND THE WEEK AFTER THAT, TOO!
WHAT ?!

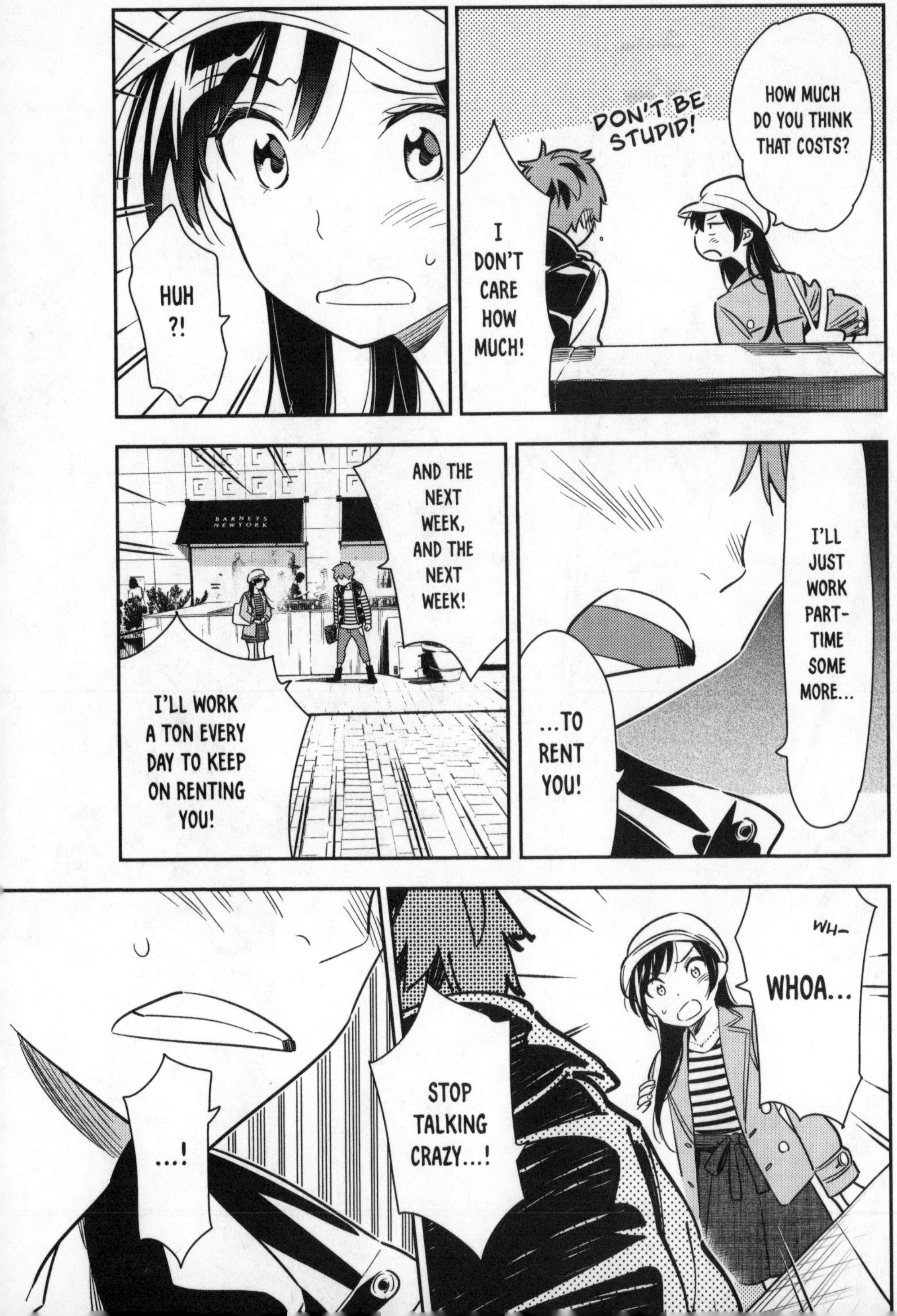
HOW MUCH DO YOU THINK THAT COSTS?
DON'T BE STUPID!
I DON'T CARE HOW MUCH!
HUH ?!
I'LL JUST WORK PART-TIME SOME MORE...
...TO RENT YOU!
AND THE NEXT WEEK, AND THE NEXT WEEK!
BARNEYS NEWYORK
I'LL WORK A TON EVERY DAY TO KEEP ON RENTING YOU!
WH-
WHOA...
STOP TALKING CRAZY...!
...!

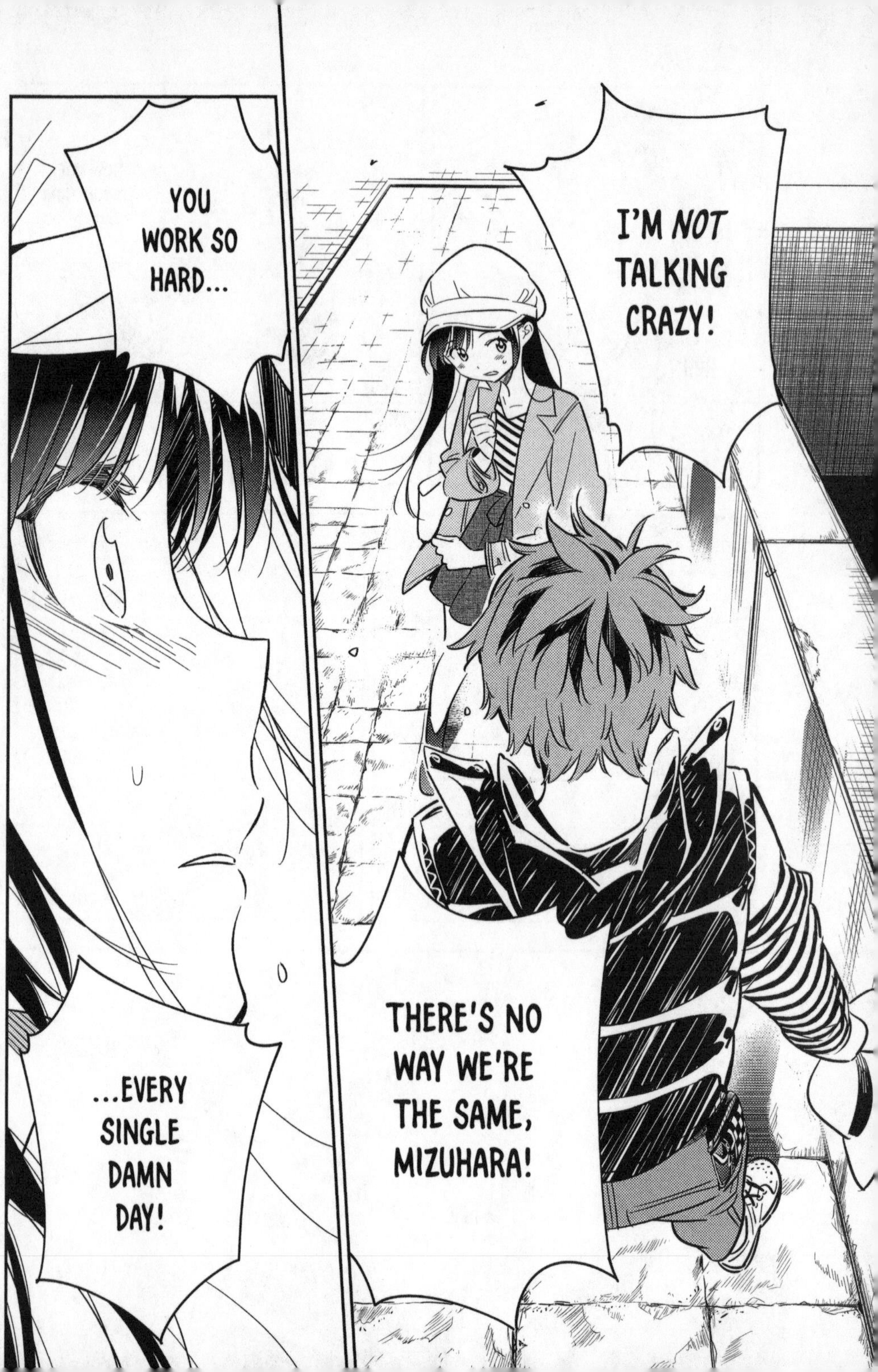
I'M NOT TALKING CRAZY!
THERE'S NO WAY WE'RE THE SAME, MIZUHARA!
YOU WORK SO HARD...
...EVERY SINGLE DAMN DAY!

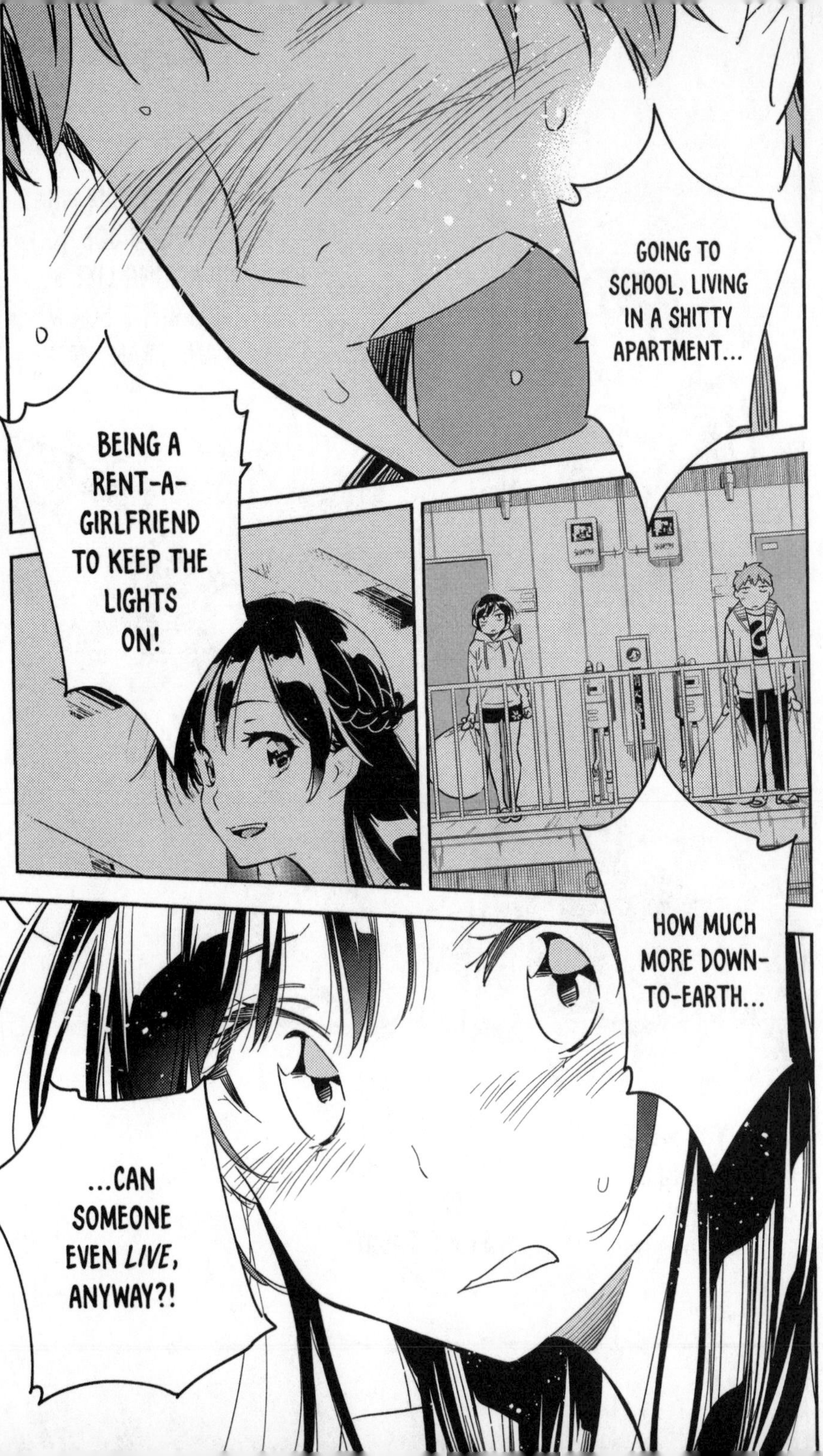
GOING TO SCHOOL, LIVING IN A SHITTY APARTMENT...
BEING A RENT-A-GIRLFRIEND TO KEEP THE LIGHTS ON!
HOW MUCH MORE DOWN-TO-EARTH...
...CAN SOMEONE EVEN *LIVE*, ANYWAY?!

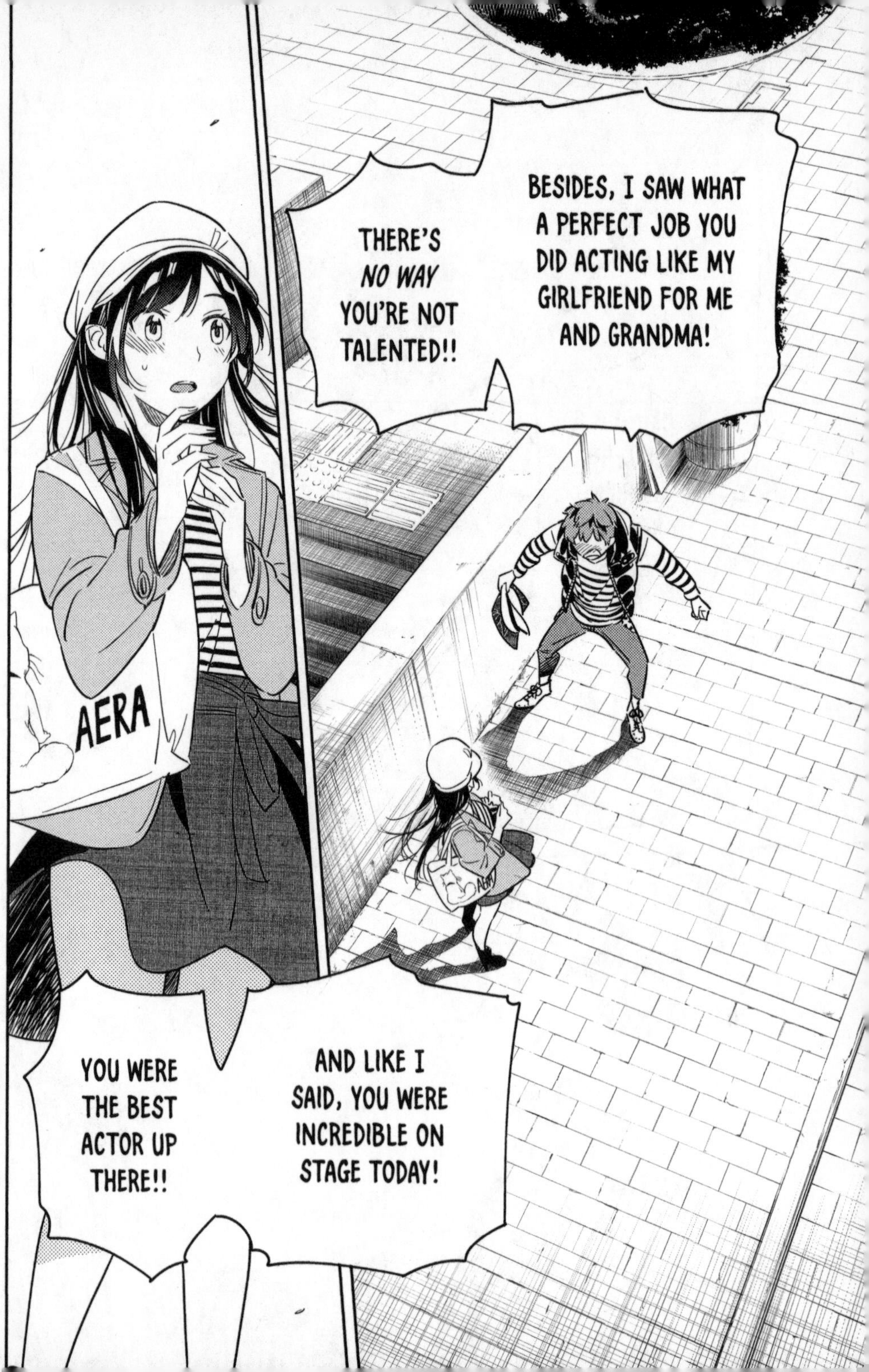

BESIDES, I SAW WHAT A PERFECT JOB YOU DID ACTING LIKE MY GIRLFRIEND FOR ME AND GRANDMA!
THERE'S *NO WAY* YOU'RE NOT TALENTED!!
AERA
AND LIKE I SAID, YOU WERE INCREDIBLE ON STAGE TODAY!
YOU WERE THE BEST ACTOR UP THERE!!

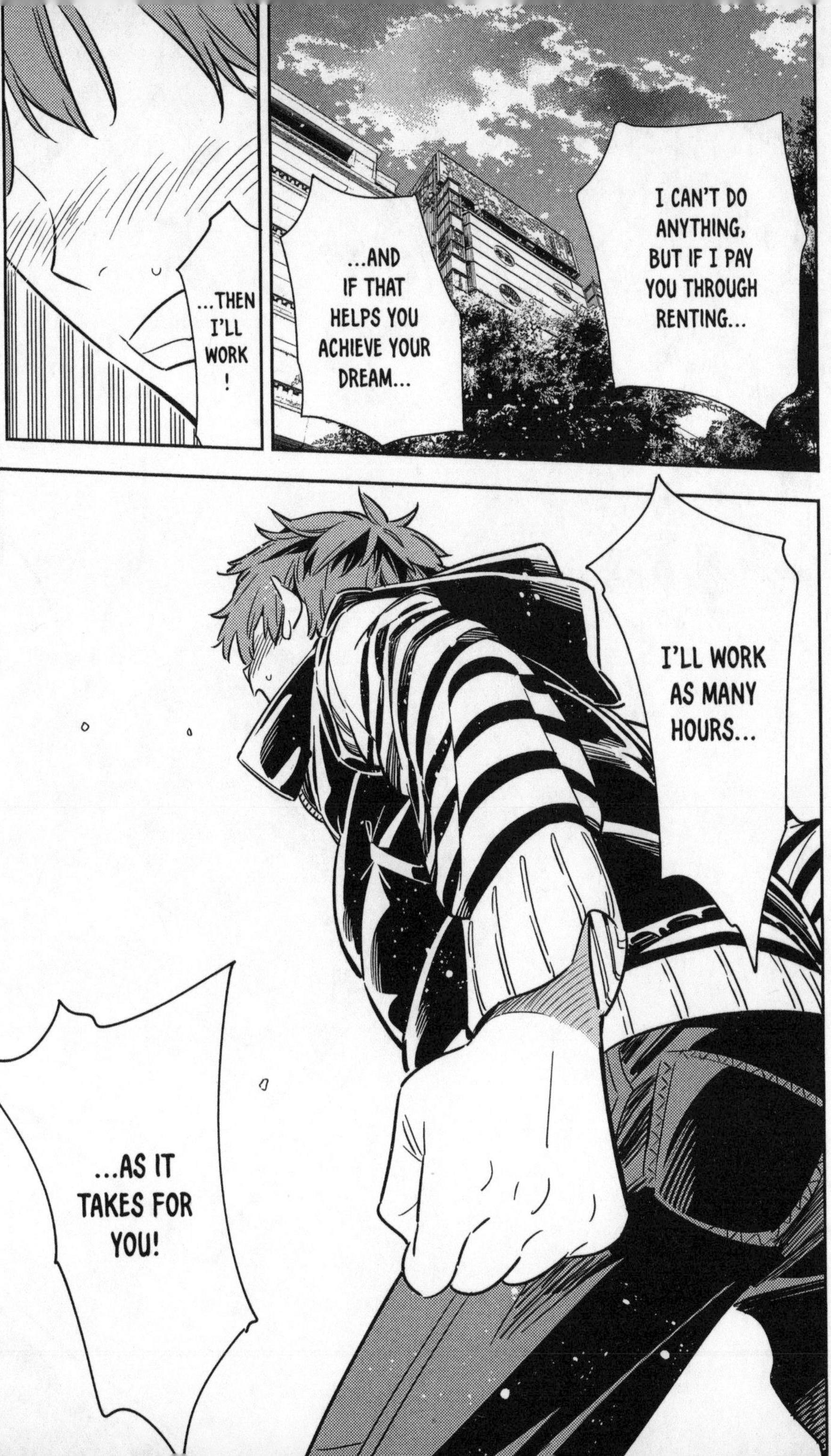
I CAN'T DO ANYTHING, BUT IF I PAY YOU THROUGH RENTING...
...AND IF THAT HELPS YOU ACHIEVE YOUR DREAM...
...THEN I'LL WORK!
I'LL WORK AS MANY HOURS...
...AS IT TAKES FOR YOU!

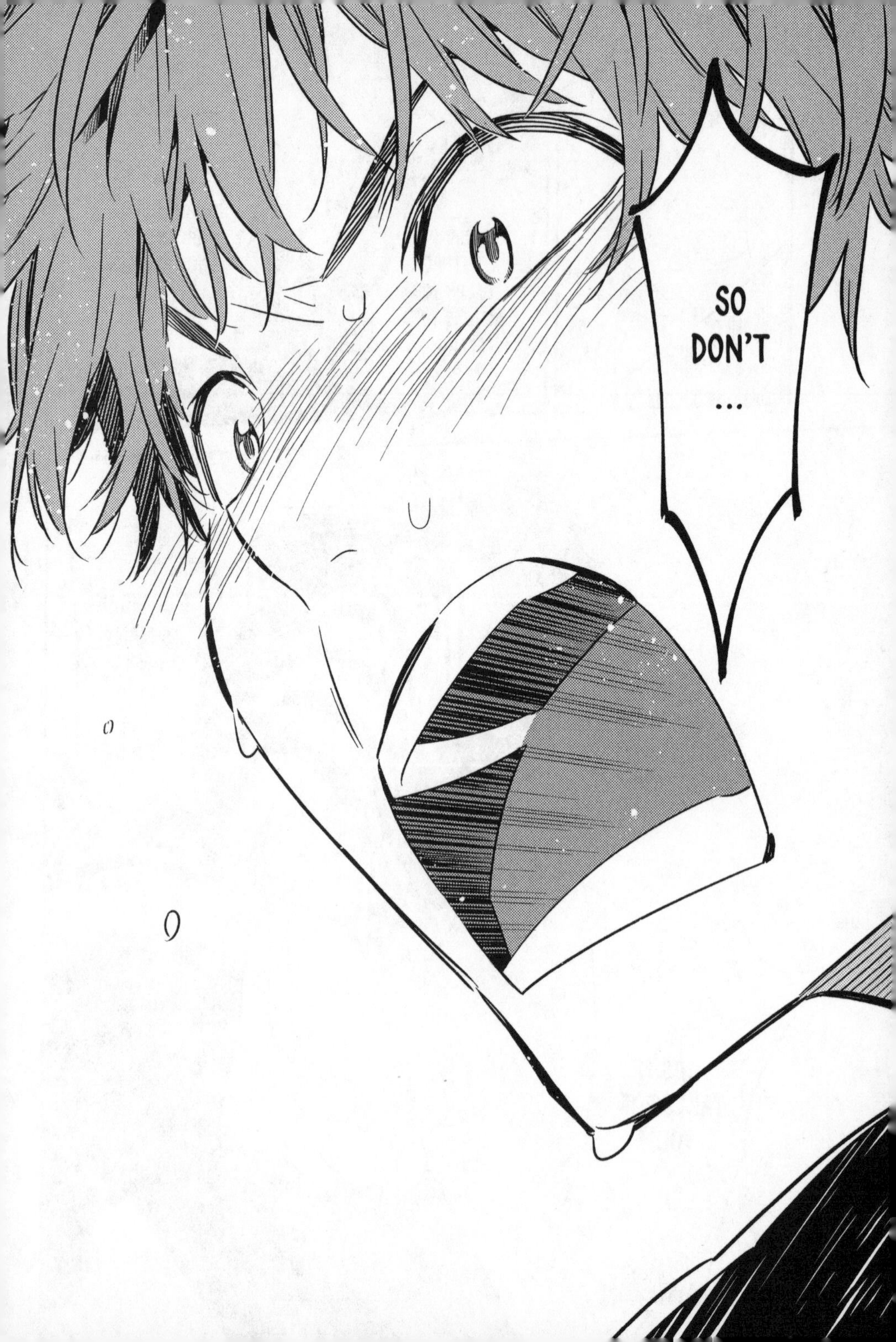
SO DON'T ...

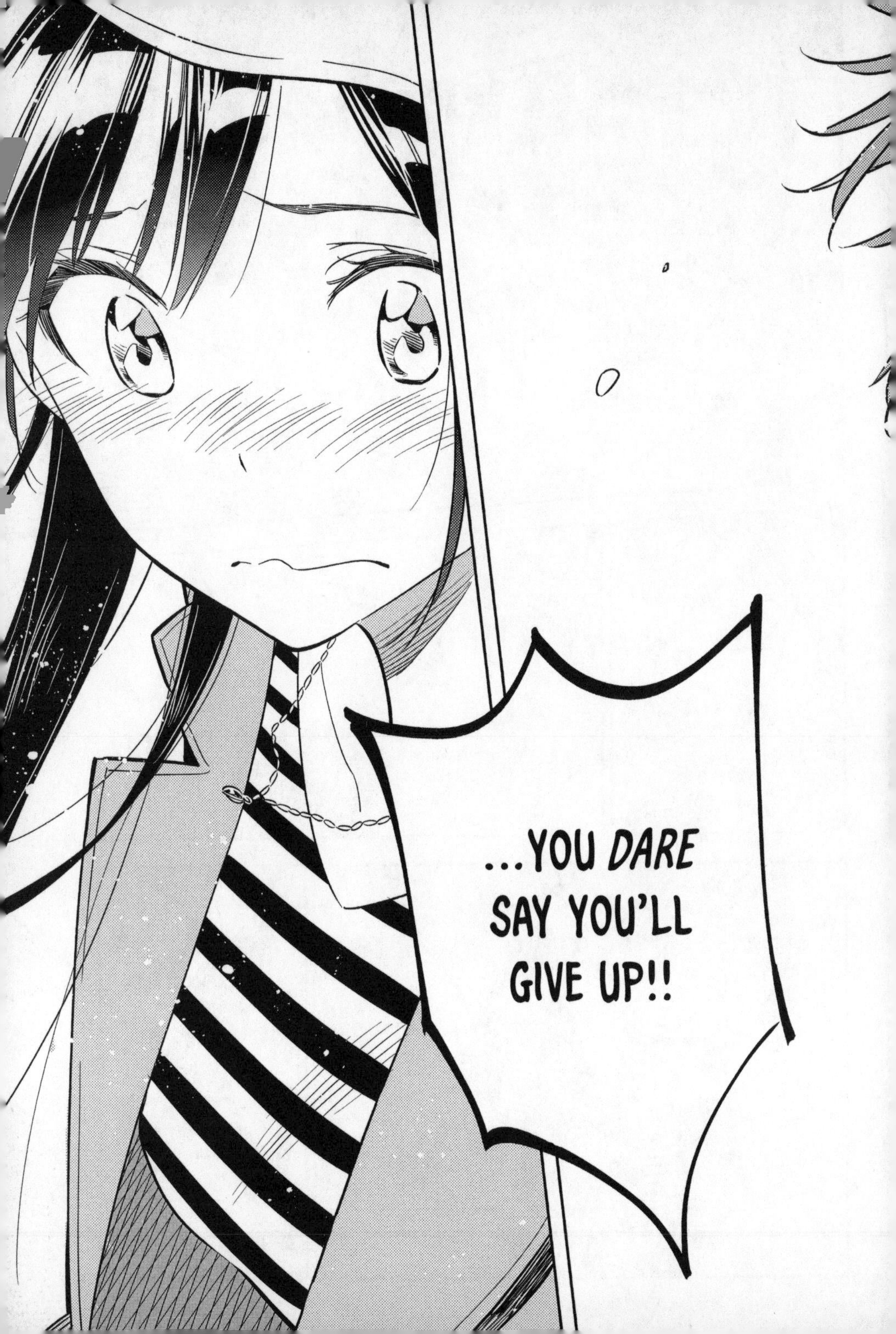
...YOU *DARE* SAY YOU'LL GIVE UP!!

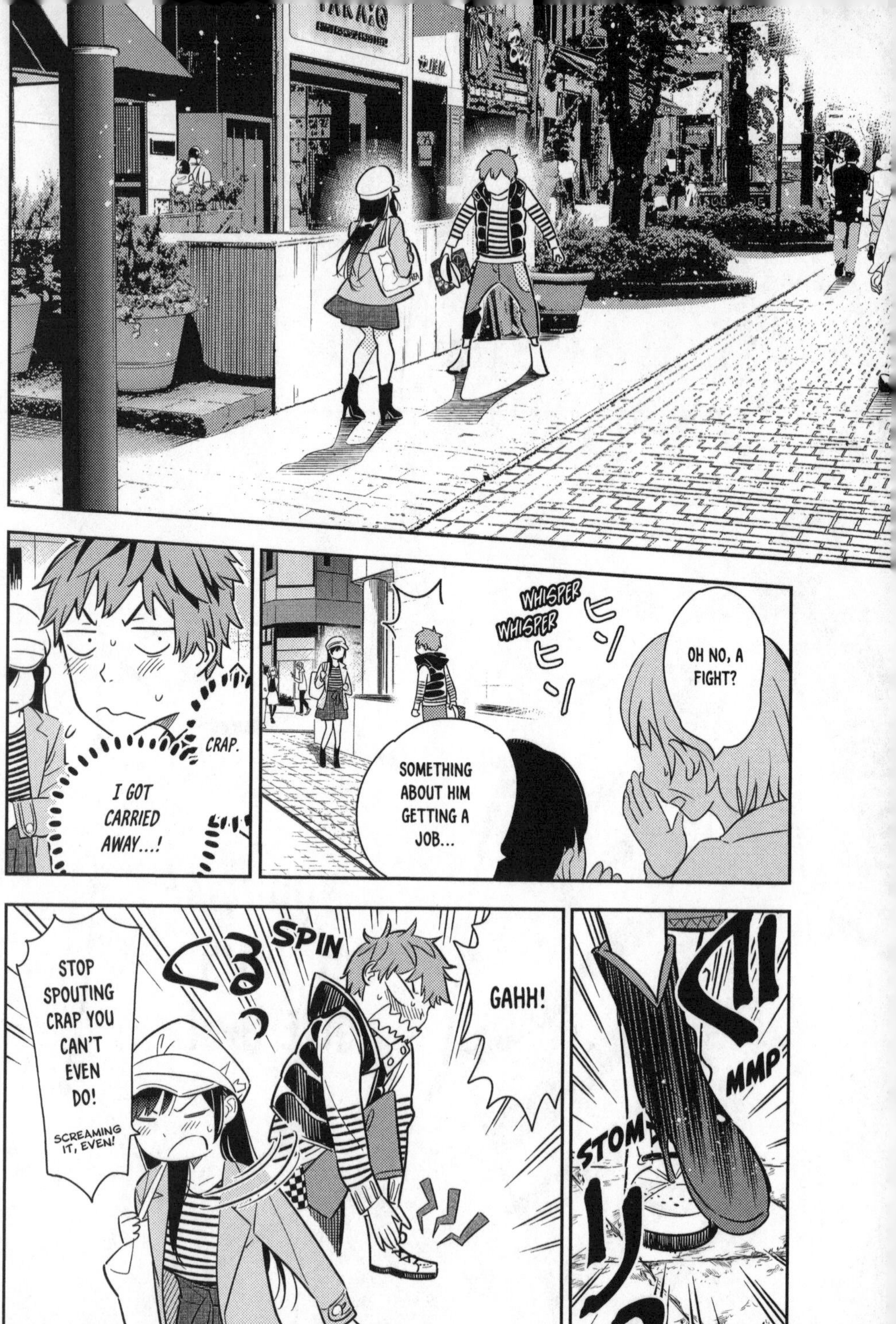
WHISPER
ヒソ
WHISPER
ヒソ
OH NO, A FIGHT?
SOMETHING ABOUT HIM GETTING A JOB...
CRAP.
I GOT CARRIED AWAY...!
MMP
STOM
SPIN
くるっ
GAHH!
STOP SPOUTING CRAP YOU CAN'T EVEN DO!
SCREAMING IT, EVEN!

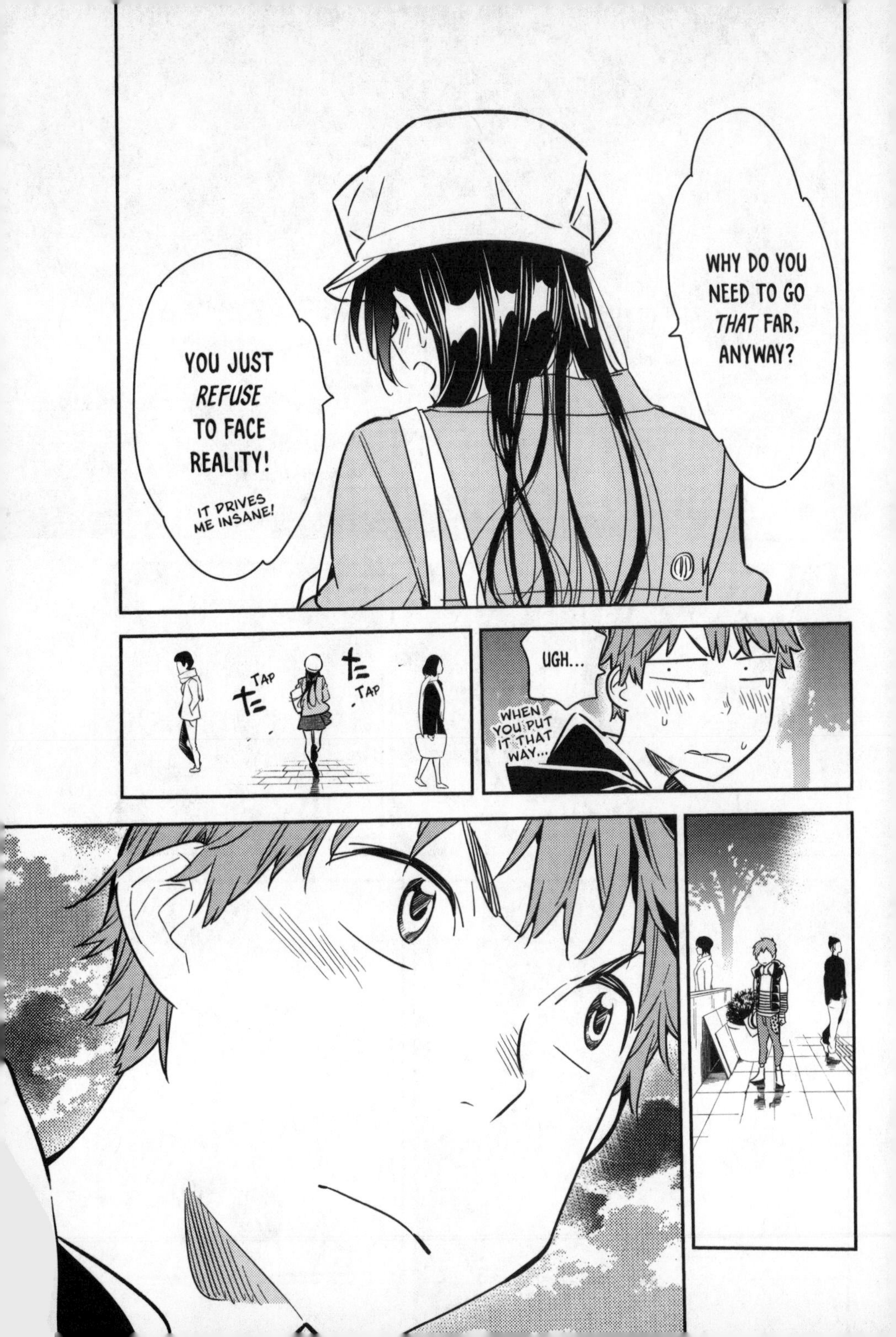
WHY DO YOU NEED TO GO THAT FAR, ANYWAY?
YOU JUST REFUSE TO FACE REALITY!
IT DRIVES ME INSANE!
UGH...
WHEN YOU PUT IT THAT WAY...
TAP
TAP

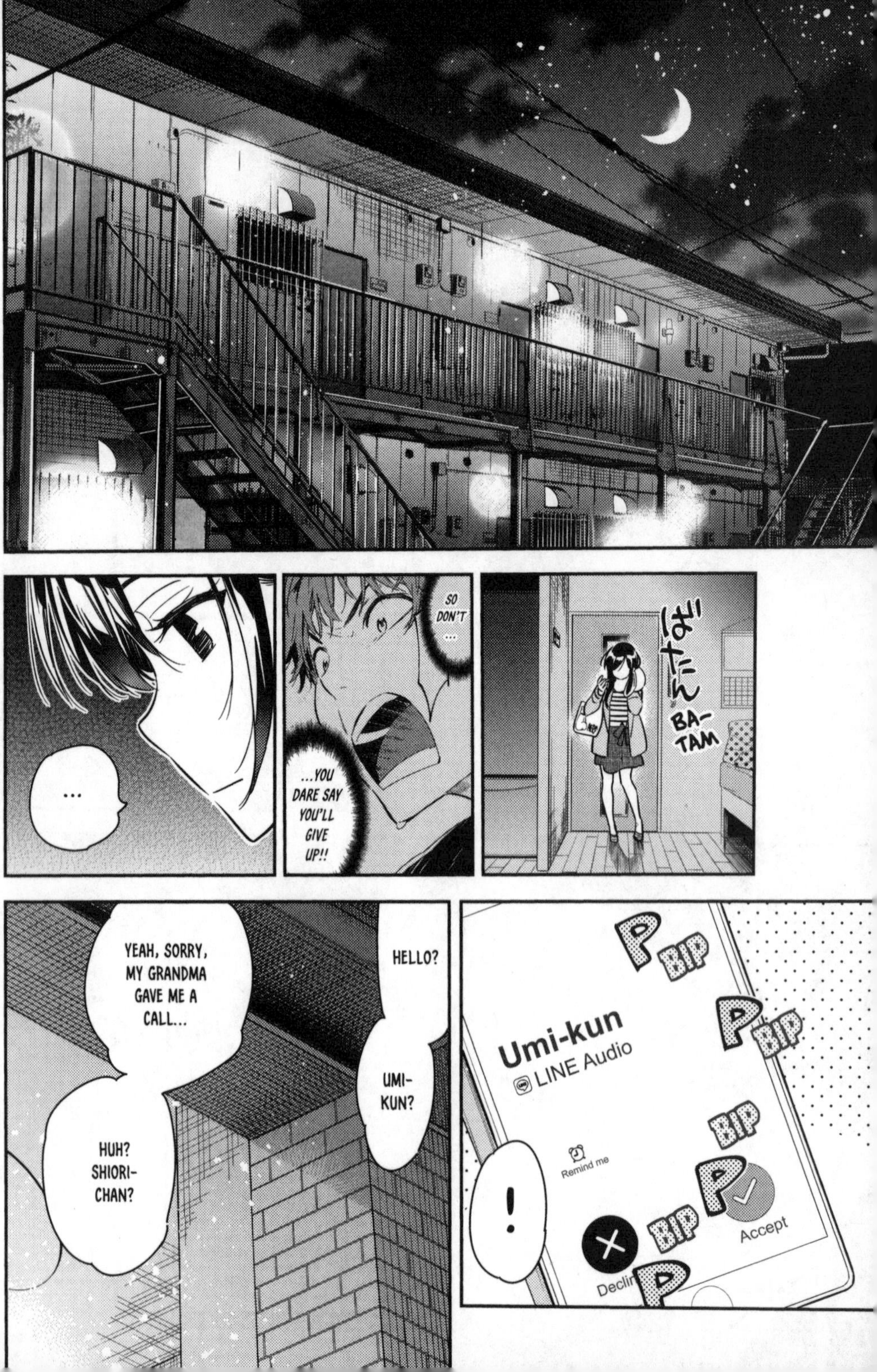
ばたん
BA-TAM
SO DON'T ...
...YOU DARE SAY YOU'LL GIVE UP!!
...
P BIP
P BIP
BIP P
BIP P
Umi-kun
LINE Audio
Remind me
Accept
Declin
!
HELLO?
YEAH, SORRY, MY GRANDMA GAVE ME A CALL...
UMI-KUN?
HUH? SHIORI-CHAN?

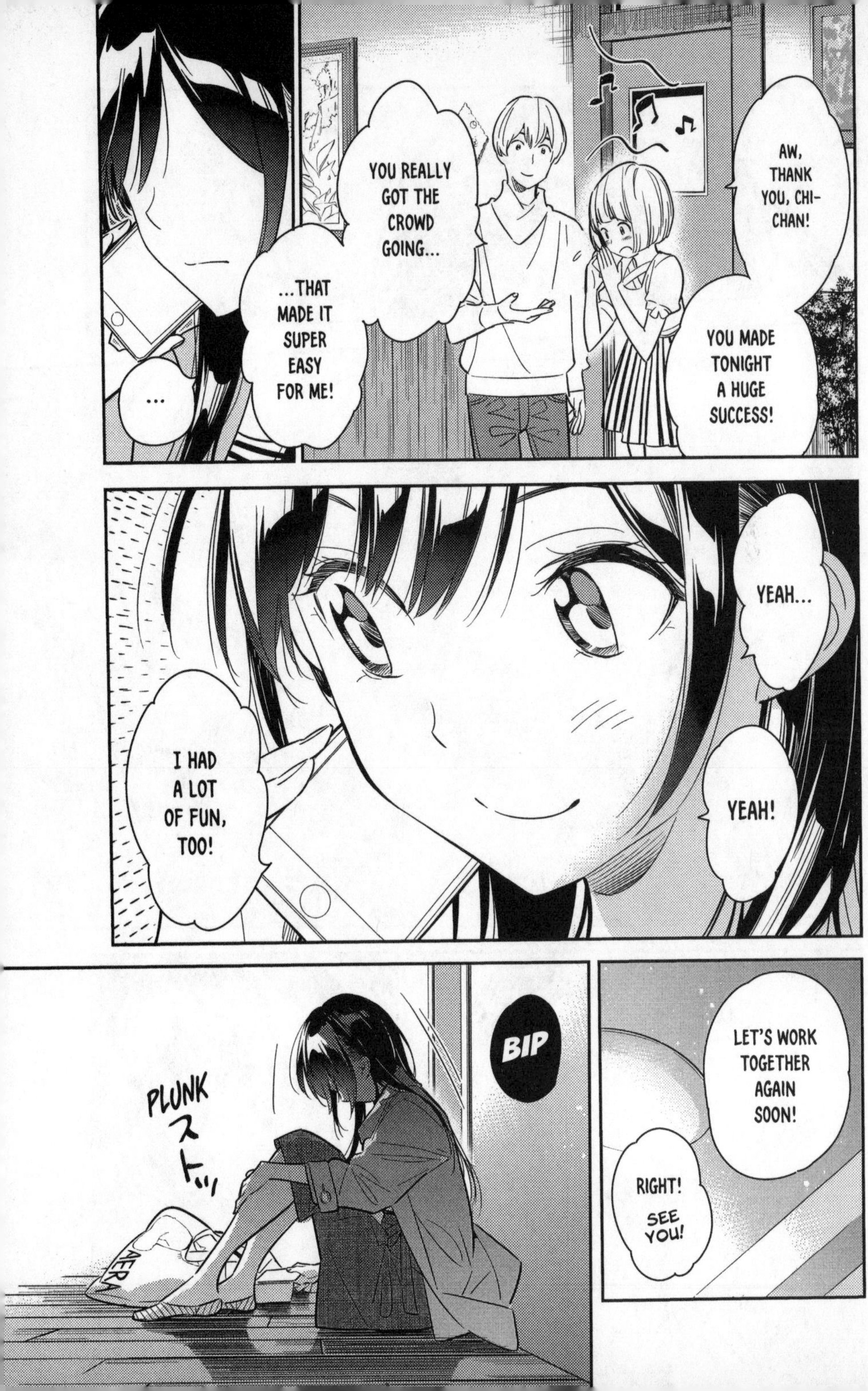
AW, THANK YOU, CHI-CHAN!
YOU MADE TONIGHT A HUGE SUCCESS!
YOU REALLY GOT THE CROWD GOING...
...THAT MADE IT SUPER EASY FOR ME!
...
YEAH...
YEAH!
I HAD A LOT OF FUN, TOO!
LET'S WORK TOGETHER AGAIN SOON!
RIGHT! SEE YOU!
BIP
PLUNK ストッ
AERA

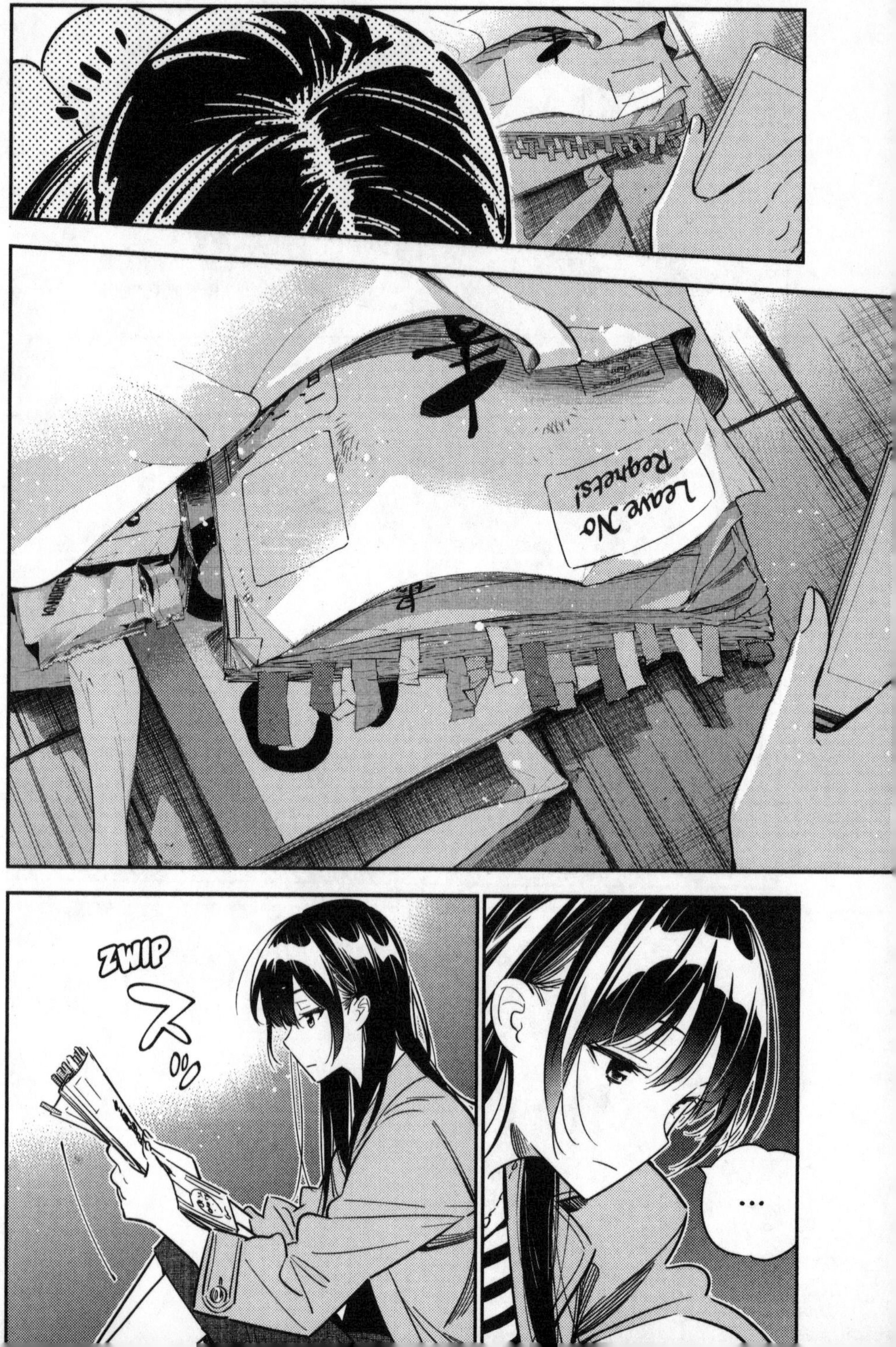

Leave No Regrets!
...
ZWIP
ス

Leave No Regrets!
FLIP
A ninja, moving to support Tomoko
Yoshiharu
Onene! Onene!
Onene enters and kneels
Onene
You called for me, shogun?
Keep it looking cool
Yoshiharu
Onene, protect Tomoko for me.
Onene
What?! Tomoko-sama, on a hunt?!
Look at Shiori-chan
Retainer
Shogun, she'll just be a hindrance!
(Nod)
Onene
Nonsense! Let Onene keep Tomoko-sama safe!
Leaves main impression of Onene character
I promise you, Princess! I will stake my life to protect yours!
Sensing Yoshiharu's suspicious eyes, Onene reveals her weapon.
Onene
A beat
No, never fear! With my shuriken skills…
What a foolish girl you are!
Onene takes a bite out of a fish-cake shuriken.
Give to Tajiri-san in wings at end of Act 2
Yoshiharu
Don't eat it!!
Keep eating it afterward
Do not get in Shiori-Chan's way
What on… Nene! You're on the Princess's horse! Stage
Onene
Huh? Where's mine?!
Really loud!!
Samurai
Ninjas sneak in, you!
Onene
Aww, no fair…
Pissed-off pose
Samurai
Fast-tempo and smooth
Onene
Hostile foes ahead! Taste my shuriken!
Oda
Shuriken? These are fish cakes!
Onene
Shoot! Flee, Princess!
Onene steps up to the front line, only to trip over a stone in the way and pratfall to the ground.
Onene
Dahhh!!
Don't get distracted by movements in front
Onene
Ah, ah…!
Trip!
Onene
You set me up!

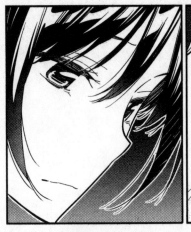

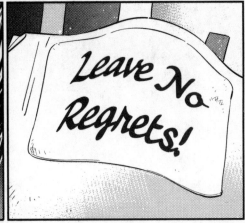

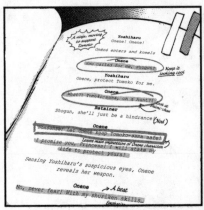

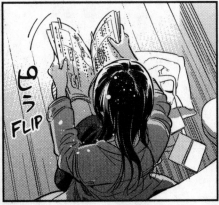

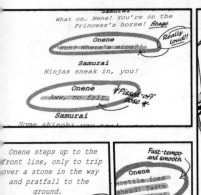

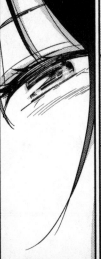

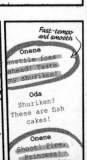

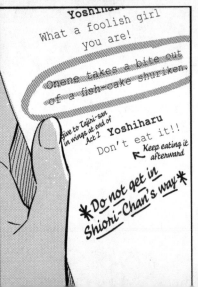

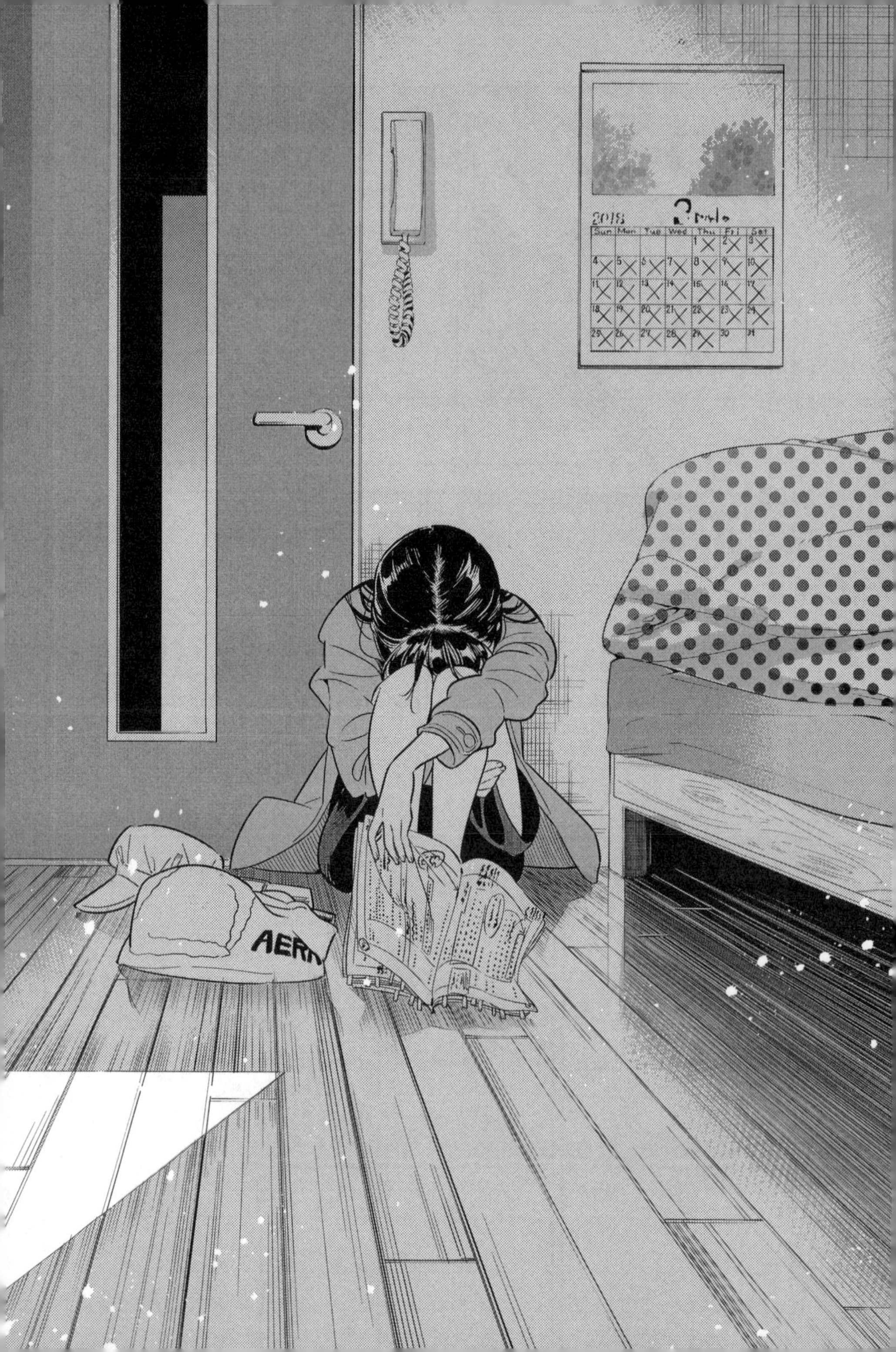
2018
Sun Mon Tue Wed Thu Fri Sat
AER

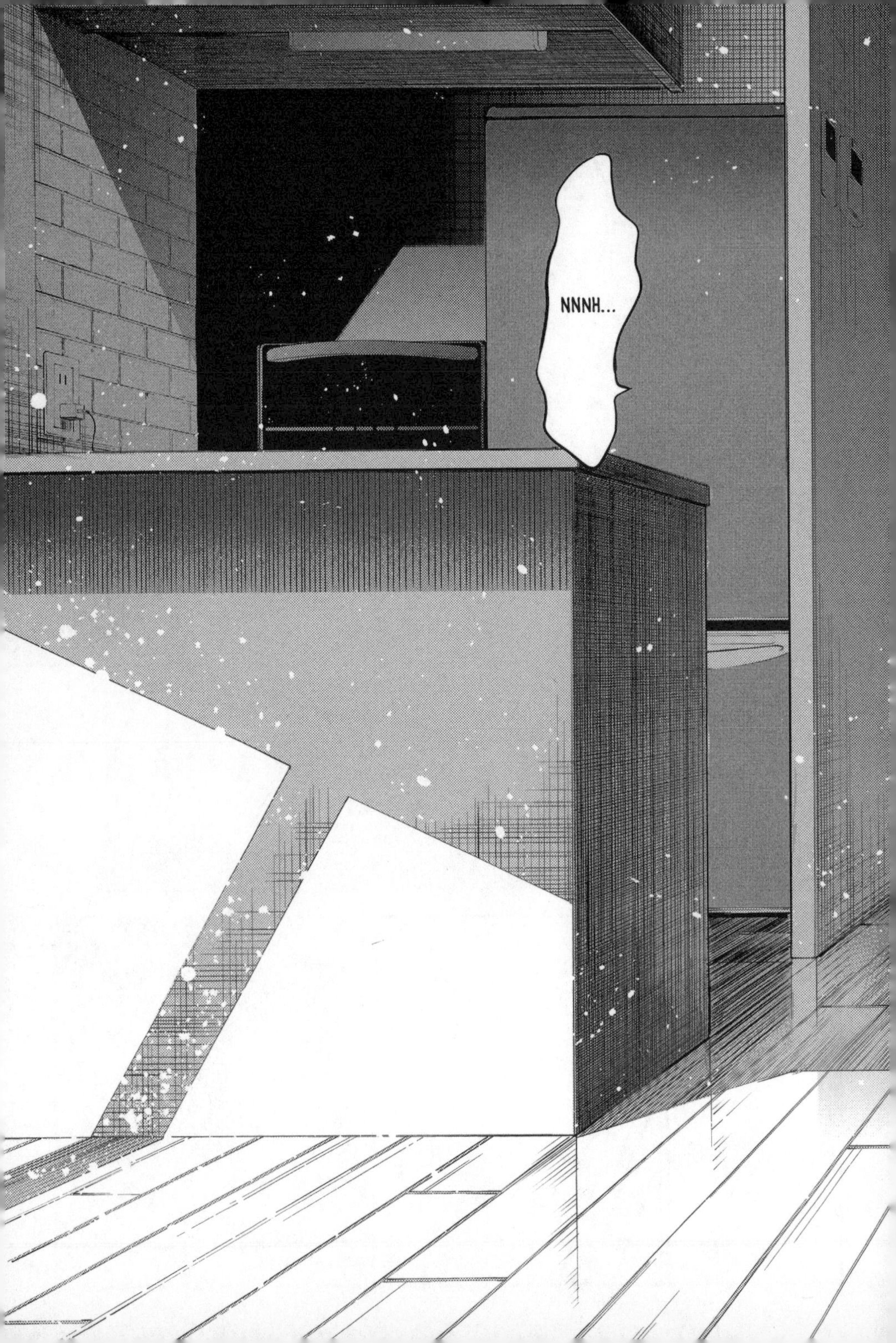
NNNH...

...NH...

TWING!

SWP

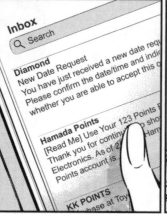

Inbox
🔍 Search

Diamond
New Date Request
You have just received a new date requ
Please confirm the date/time and indic
whether you are able to accept this o

Hamada Points
[Read Me] Use Your 123 Points
Thank you for contin o sho
Electronics. As of 2   Ham
Points account is

KK POINTS
   base at Toy

SWP

REA

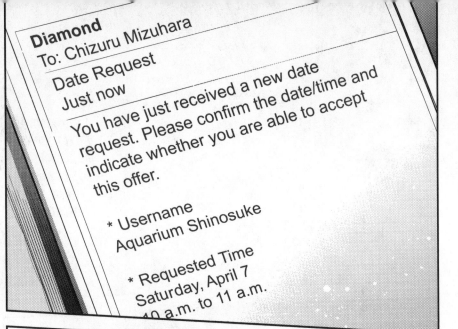

Diamond

To: Chizuru Mizuhara

Date Request
Just now

You have just received a new date request. Please confirm the date/time and indicate whether you are able to accept this offer.

* Username
Aquarium Shinosuke

* Requested Time
Saturday, April 7
10 a.m. to 11 a.m.

* Username
Aquarium Shinosuke

TWING!

LOOK, NEXT WEEK...

...I'M GONNA RENT YOU AGAIN.

AERA

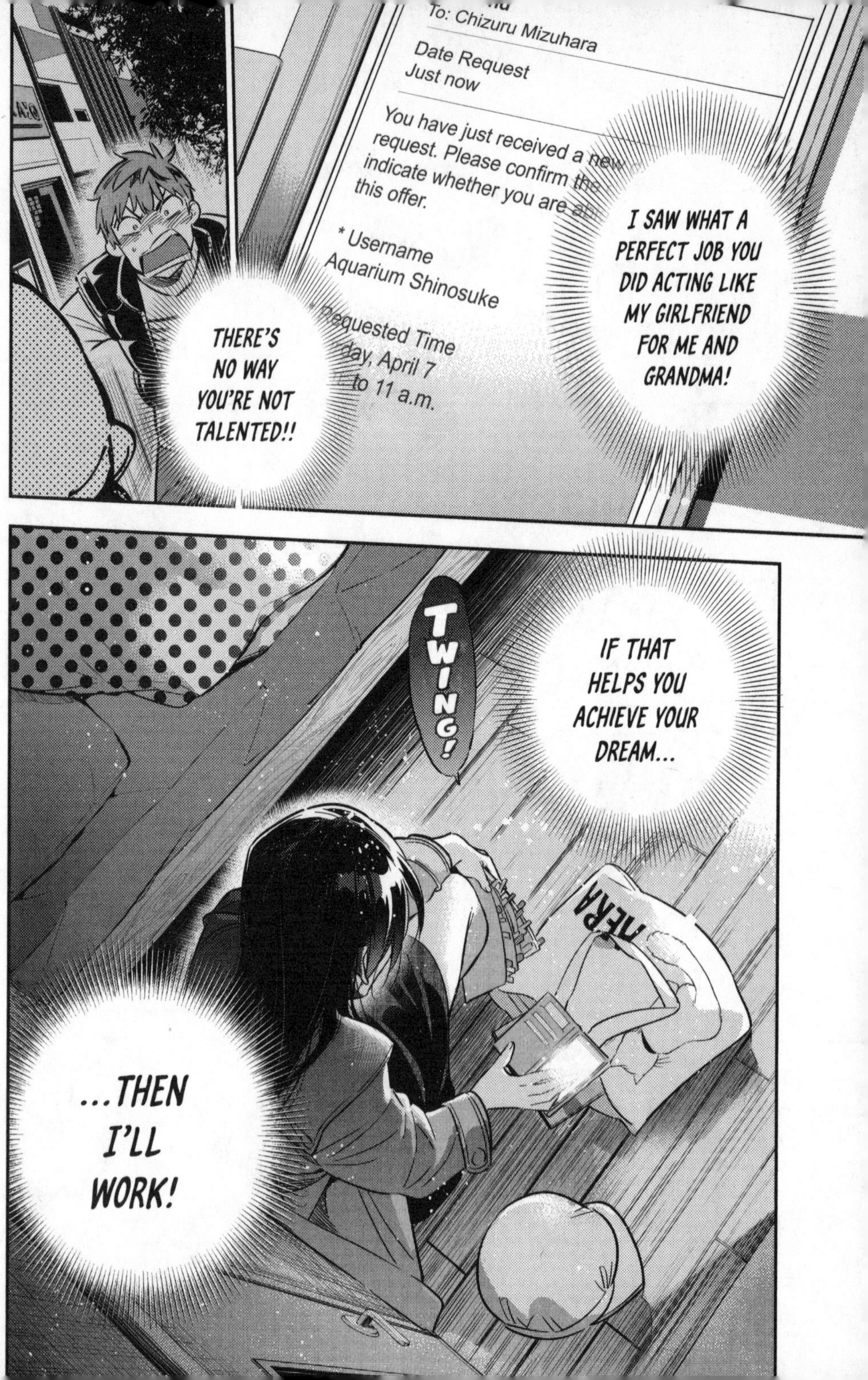
To: Chizuru Mizuhara
Date Request
Just now
You have just received a new request. Please confirm the indicate whether you are ab this offer.
* Username
Aquarium Shinosuke
equested Time
day, April 7
to 11 a.m.
I SAW WHAT A PERFECT JOB YOU DID ACTING LIKE MY GIRLFRIEND FOR ME AND GRANDMA!
THERE'S NO WAY YOU'RE NOT TALENTED!!
IF THAT HELPS YOU ACHIEVE YOUR DREAM...
TWING!
...THEN I'LL WORK!

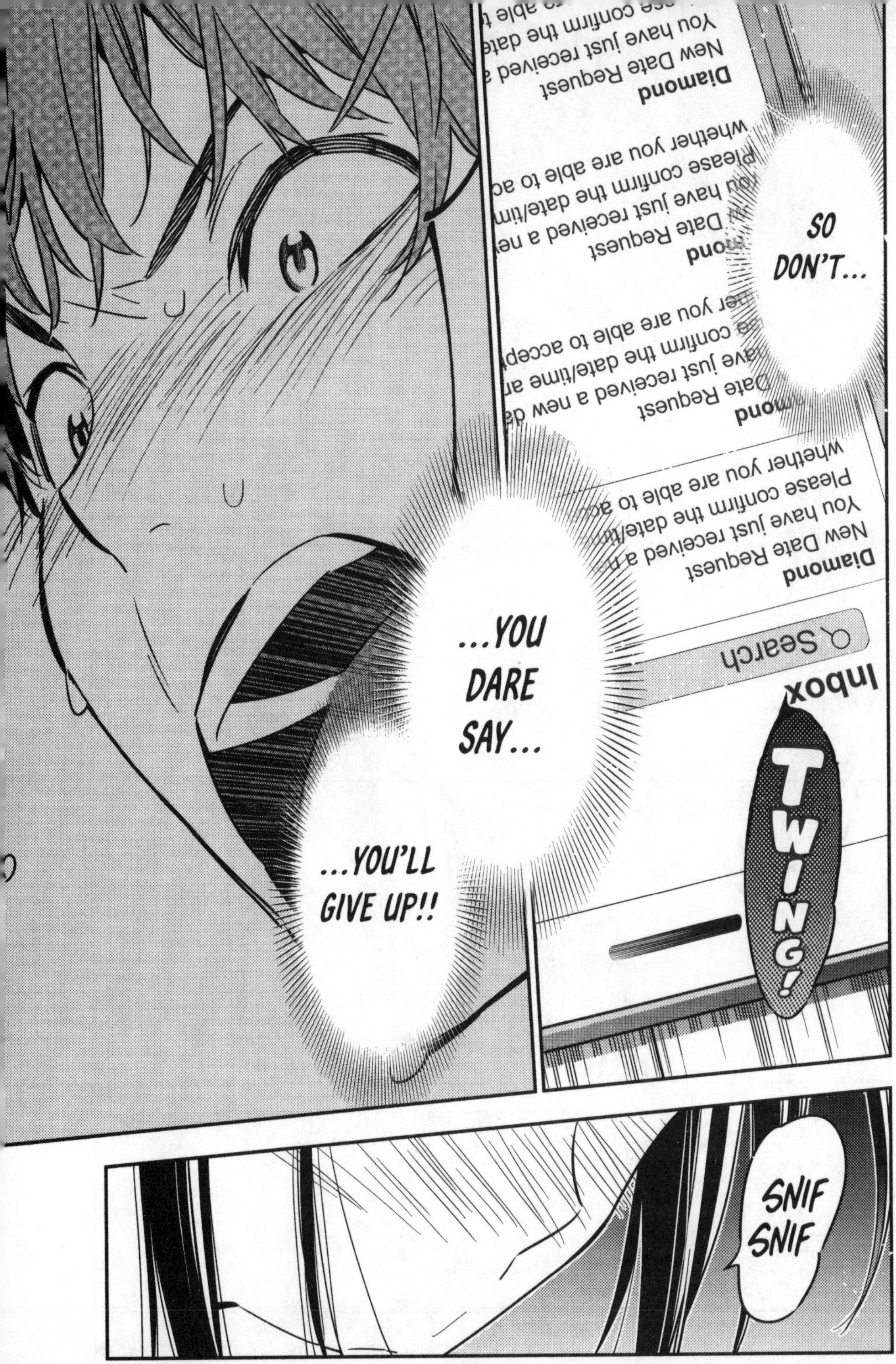
SO DON'T...
Inbox
Search
Diamond
New Date Request
...YOU DARE SAY...
...YOU'LL GIVE UP!!
TWING!
SNIF SNIF

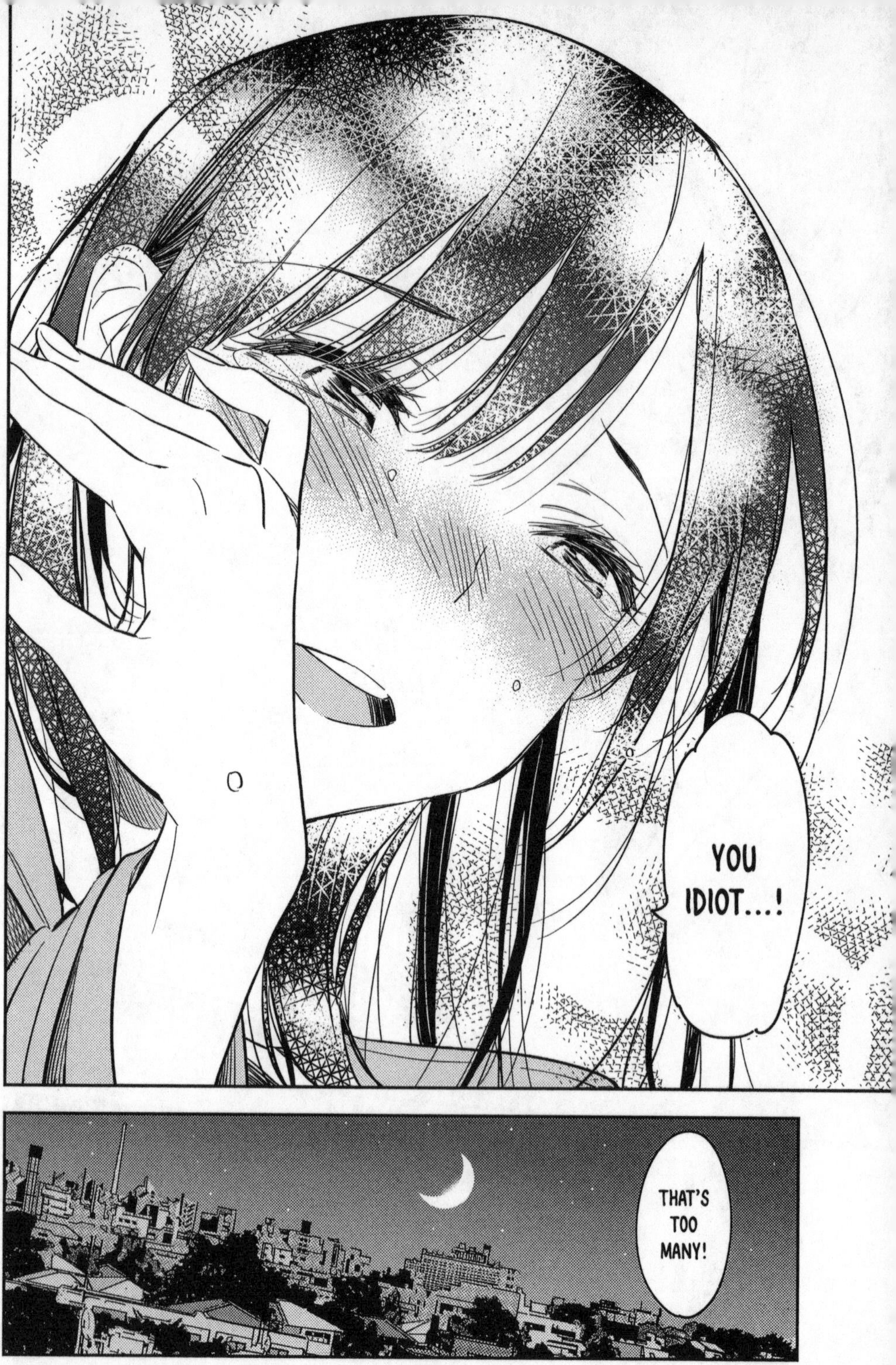
YOU IDIOT...!
THAT'S TOO MANY!

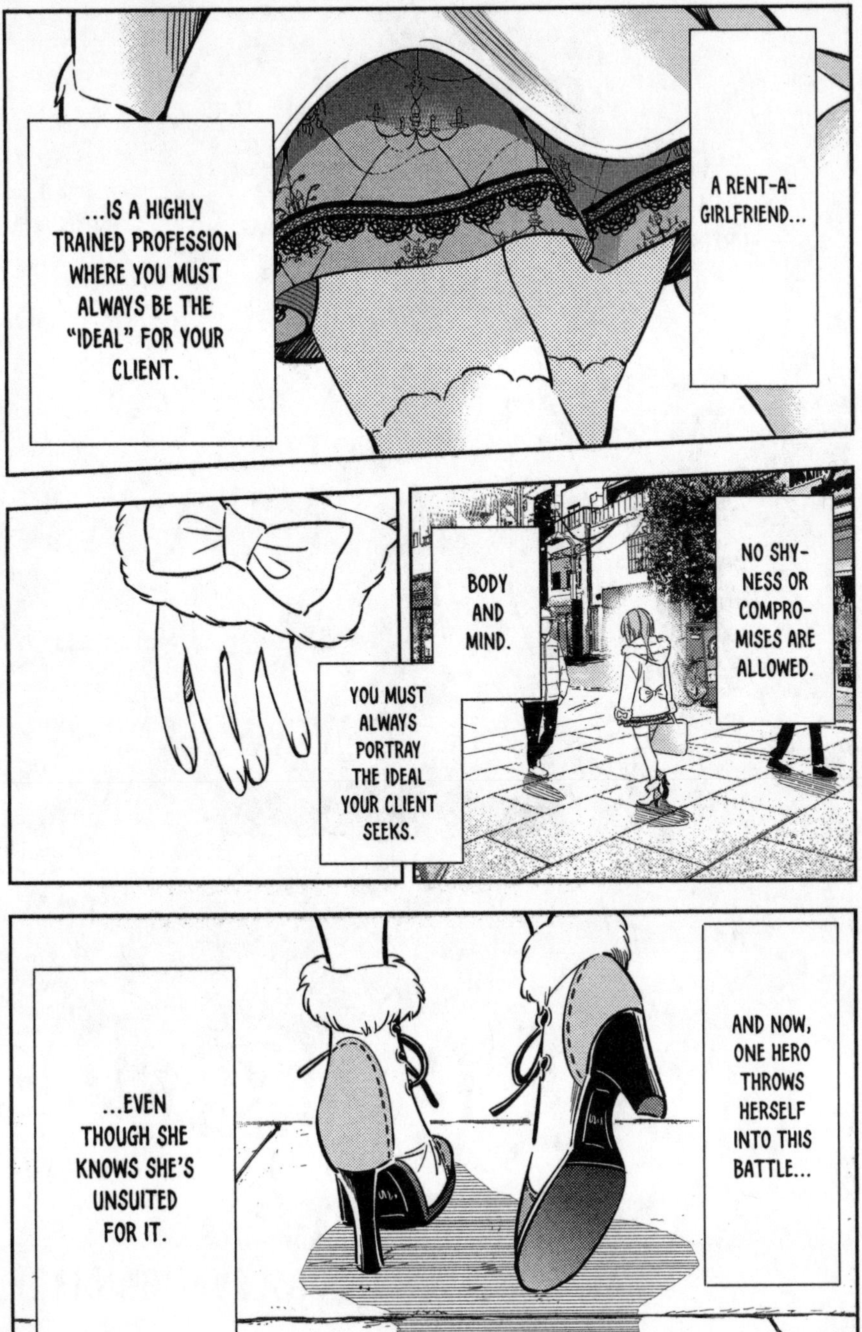
A RENT-A-GIRLFRIEND...
...IS A HIGHLY TRAINED PROFESSION WHERE YOU MUST ALWAYS BE THE "IDEAL" FOR YOUR CLIENT.
NO SHYNESS OR COMPROMISES ARE ALLOWED.
BODY AND MIND.
YOU MUST ALWAYS PORTRAY THE IDEAL YOUR CLIENT SEEKS.
AND NOW, ONE HERO THROWS HERSELF INTO THIS BATTLE...
...EVEN THOUGH SHE KNOWS SHE'S UNSUITED FOR IT.

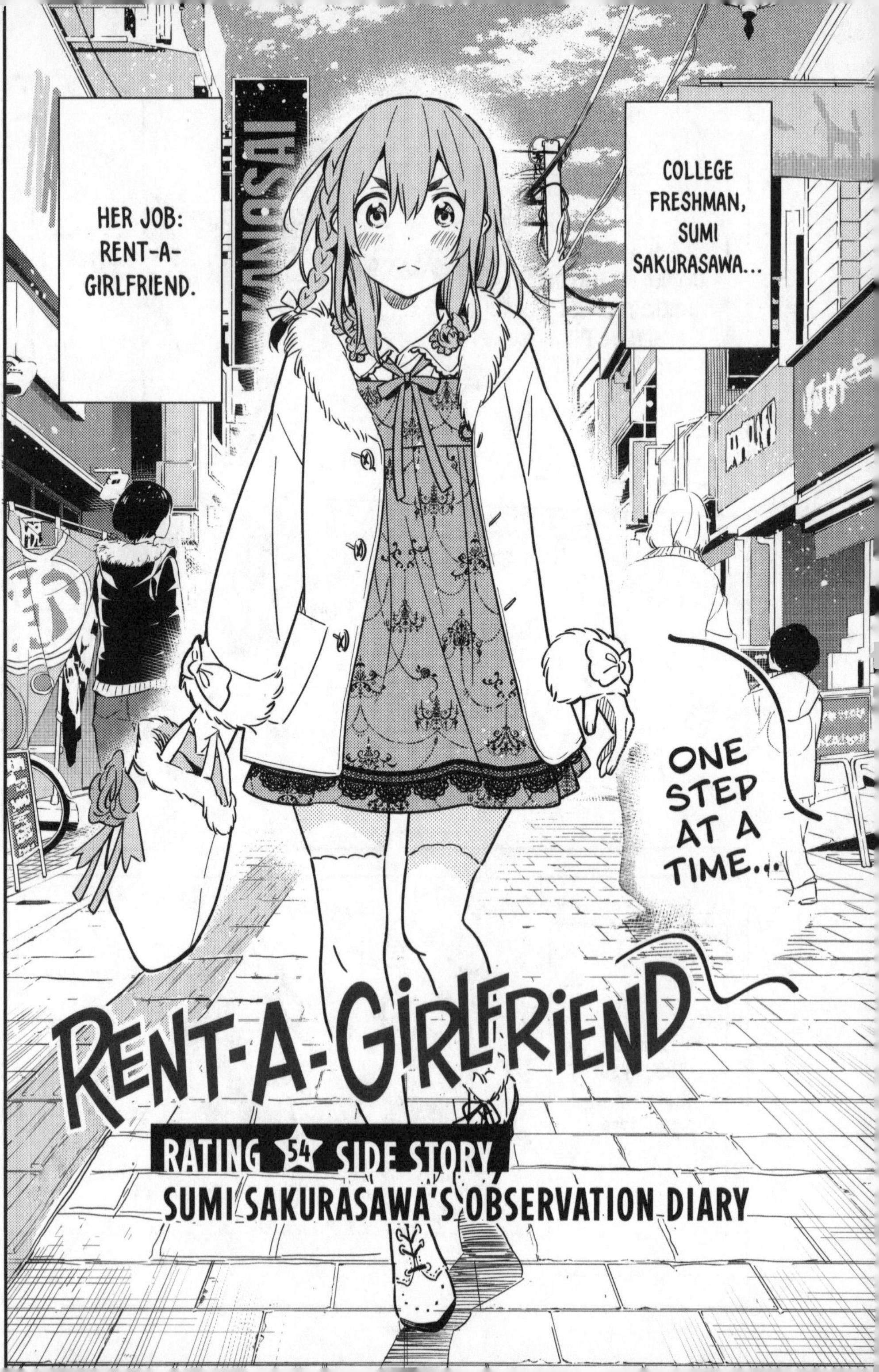
COLLEGE FRESHMAN, SUMI SAKURASAWA...
HER JOB: RENT-A-GIRLFRIEND.
ONE STEP AT A TIME...
RENT-A-GIRLFRIEND
RATING 54 SIDE STORY
SUMI SAKURASAWA'S OBSERVATION DIARY

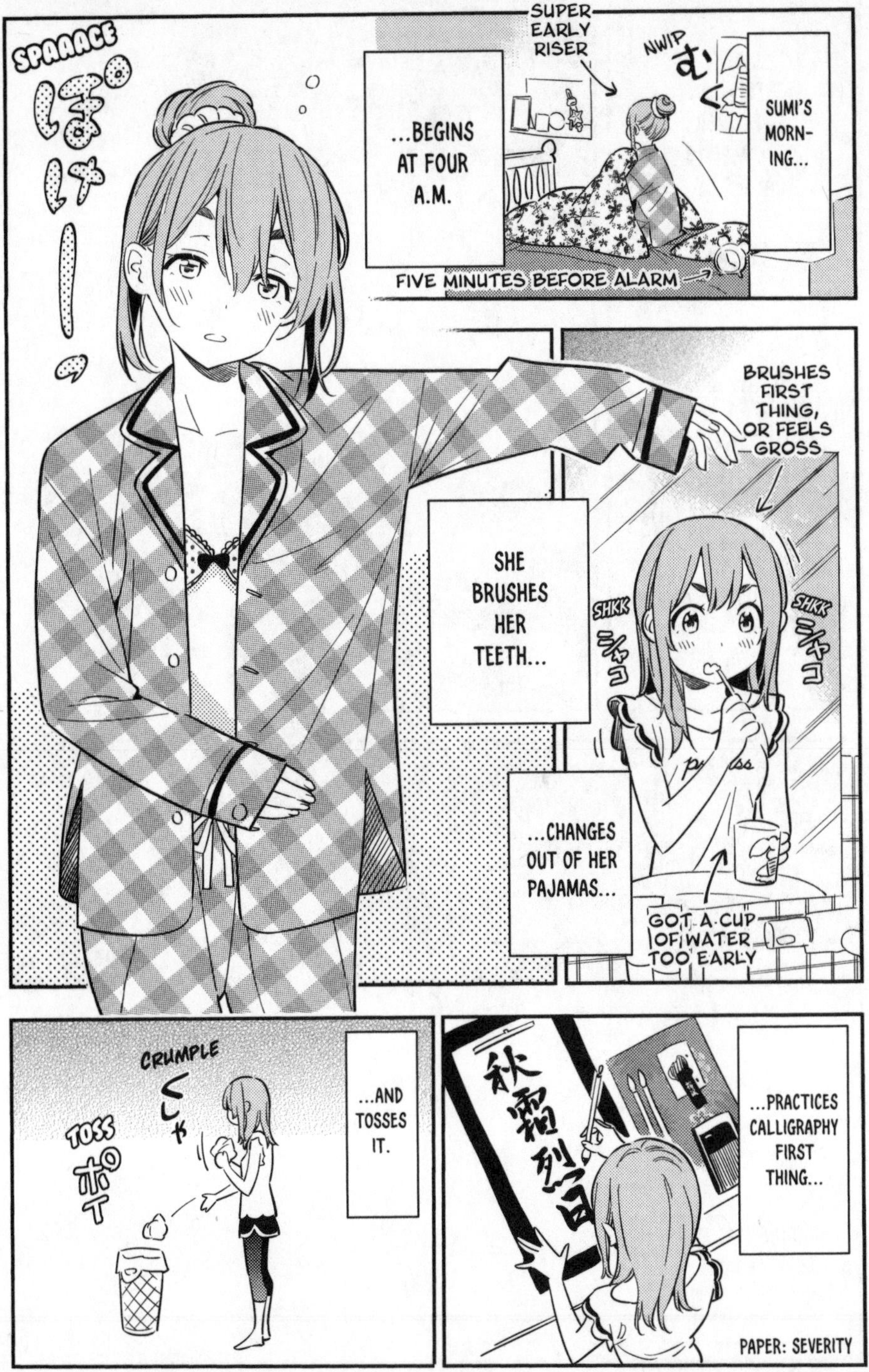
SUMI'S MORN-ING...
NWIP
むく
SUPER EARLY RISER
...BEGINS AT FOUR A.M.
FIVE MINUTES BEFORE ALARM
BRUSHES FIRST THING, OR FEELS GROSS
SHE BRUSHES HER TEETH...
SHKK
シャコ
SHKK
シャコ
...CHANGES OUT OF HER PAJAMAS...
GOT A CUP OF WATER TOO EARLY
SPAAACE
ぽけーっ
...PRACTICES CALLIGRAPHY FIRST THING...
秋霜烈日
PAPER: SEVERITY
...AND TOSSES IT.
CRUMPLE
くしゃ
TOSS
ポイ

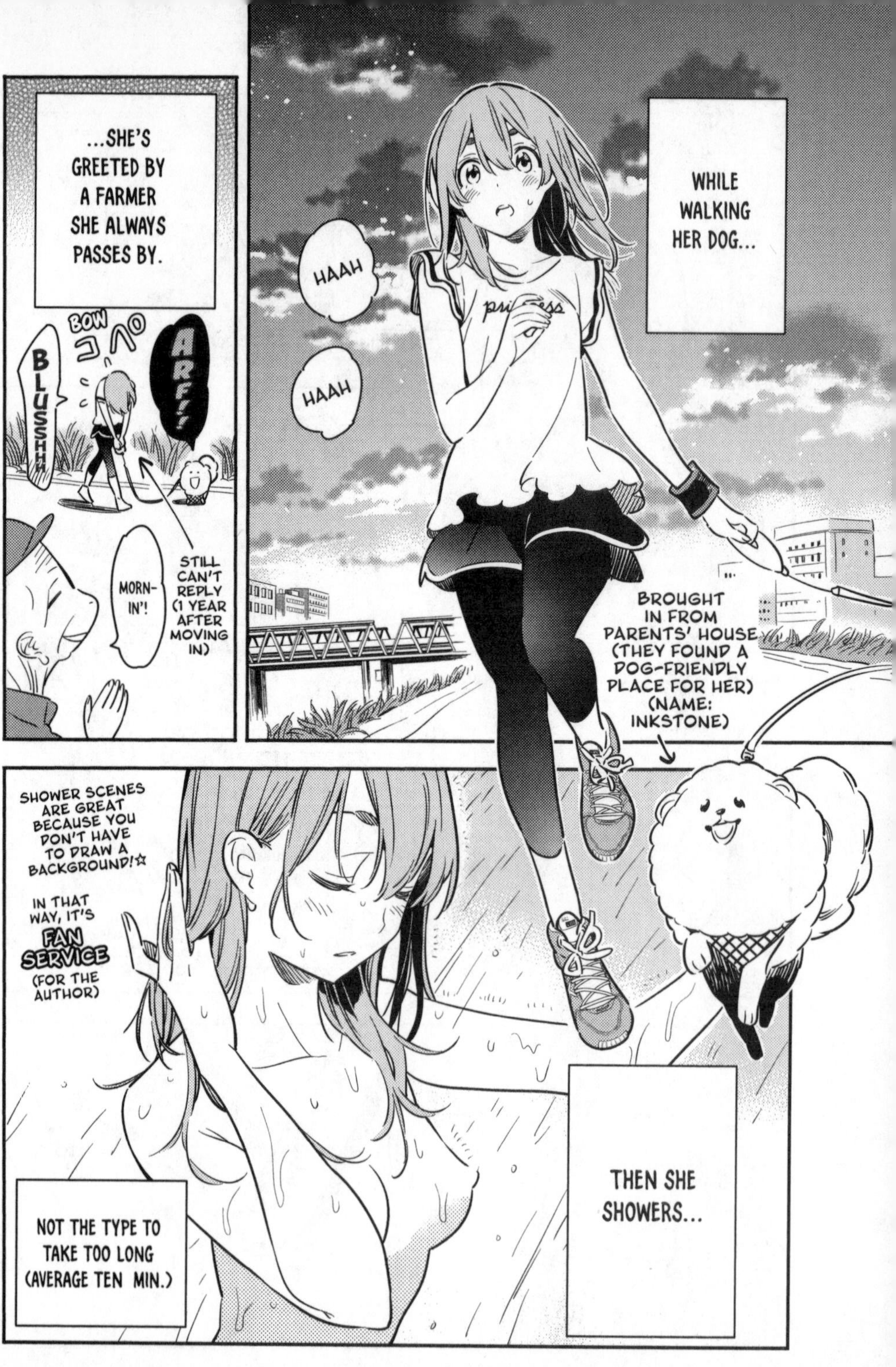
WHILE WALKING HER DOG...
HAAH
HAAH
BROUGHT IN FROM PARENTS' HOUSE (THEY FOUND A DOG-FRIENDLY PLACE FOR HER) (NAME: INKSTONE)
...SHE'S GREETED BY A FARMER SHE ALWAYS PASSES BY.
ARF!?
BOW
コヘ
BLUSHH
MORN-IN'!
STILL CAN'T REPLY (1 YEAR AFTER MOVING IN)
THEN SHE SHOWERS...
SHOWER SCENES ARE GREAT BECAUSE YOU DON'T HAVE TO DRAW A BACKGROUND!☆
IN THAT WAY, IT'S FAN SERVICE (FOR THE AUTHOR)
NOT THE TYPE TO TAKE TOO LONG (AVERAGE TEN MIN.)

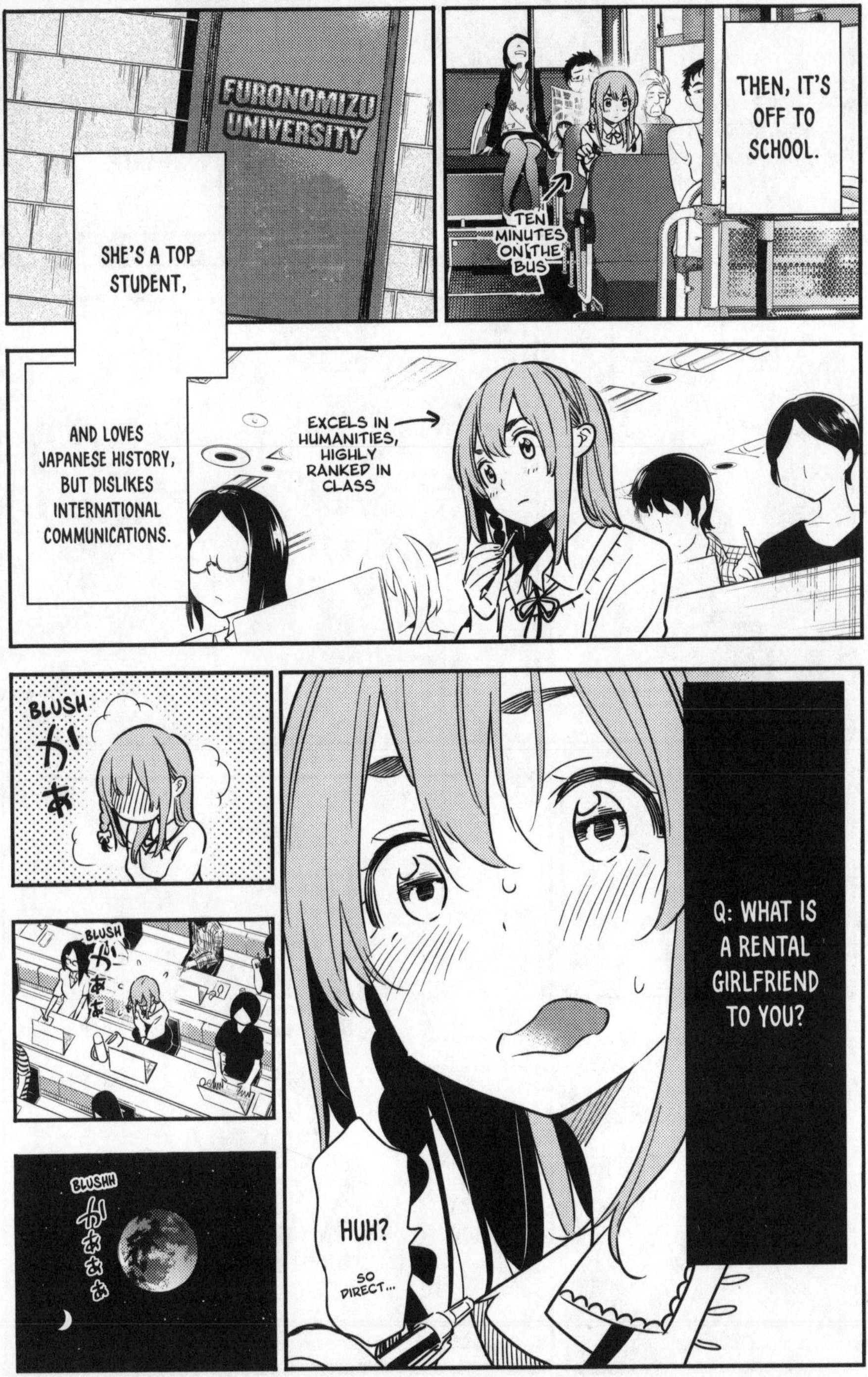
THEN, IT'S OFF TO SCHOOL.
TEN MINUTES ON THE BUS
FURONOMIZU UNIVERSITY
SHE'S A TOP STUDENT,
AND LOVES JAPANESE HISTORY, BUT DISLIKES INTERNATIONAL COMMUNICATIONS.
EXCELS IN HUMANITIES, HIGHLY RANKED IN CLASS
Q: WHAT IS A RENTAL GIRLFRIEND TO YOU?
HUH?
SO DIRECT...
BLUSH
かあ
BLUSH
かあぁ
BLUSHH
かあぁぁ

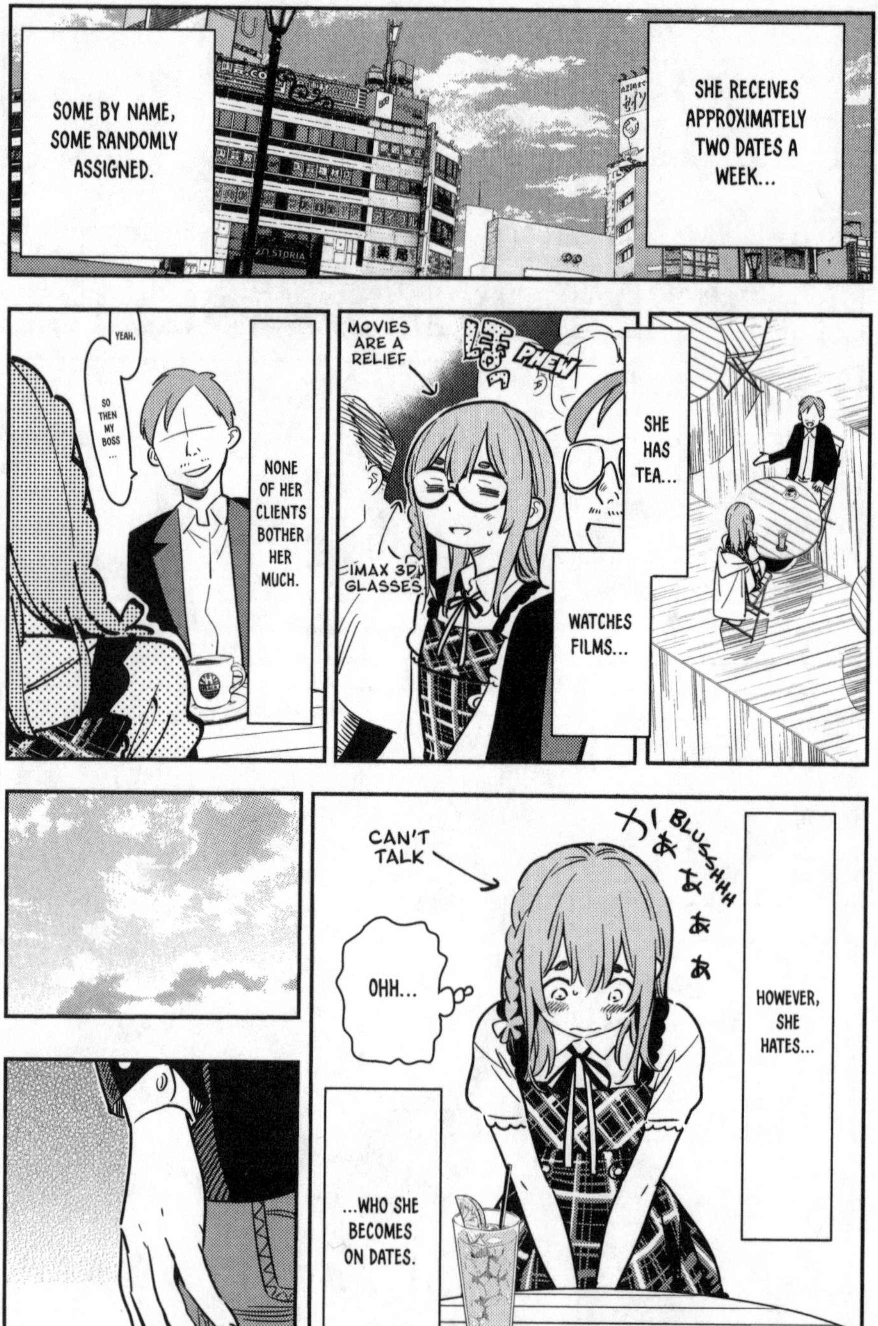
SHE RECEIVES APPROXIMATELY TWO DATES A WEEK...
SOME BY NAME, SOME RANDOMLY ASSIGNED.
SHE HAS TEA...
WATCHES FILMS...
PHEW
MOVIES ARE A RELIEF
IMAX 3D GLASSES
NONE OF HER CLIENTS BOTHER HER MUCH.
YEAH,
SO THEN MY BOSS ...
HOWEVER, SHE HATES...
BLUSHHH
CAN'T TALK
OHH...
...WHO SHE BECOMES ON DATES.

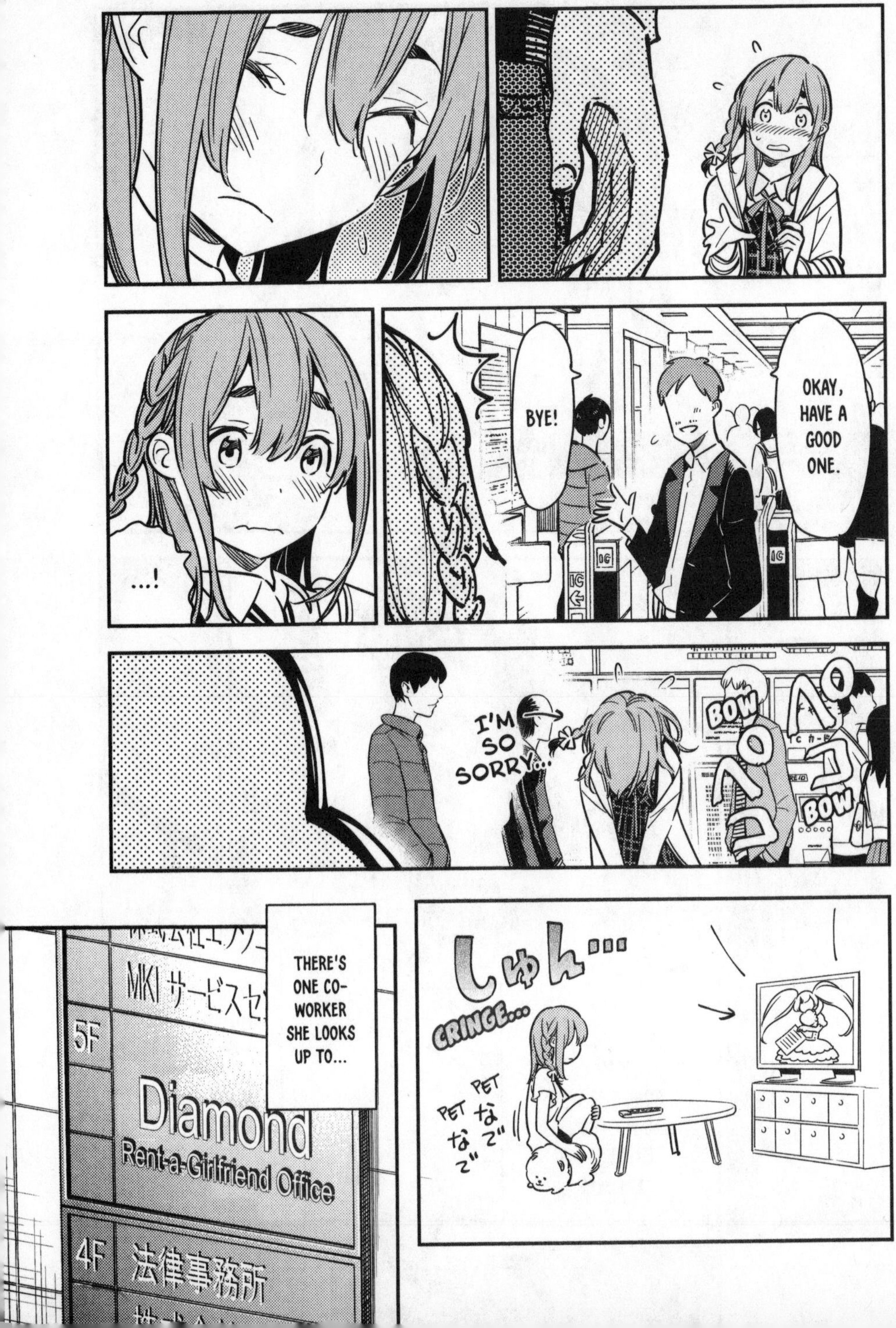
OKAY, HAVE A GOOD ONE.
BYE!
...!
BOW
BOW
I'M SO SORRY...
しゅん…
CRINGE...
PET なで
PET なで
THERE'S ONE CO-WORKER SHE LOOKS UP TO...
MKI サービスセ
5F
Diamond
Rent-a-Girlfriend Office
4F
法律事務所

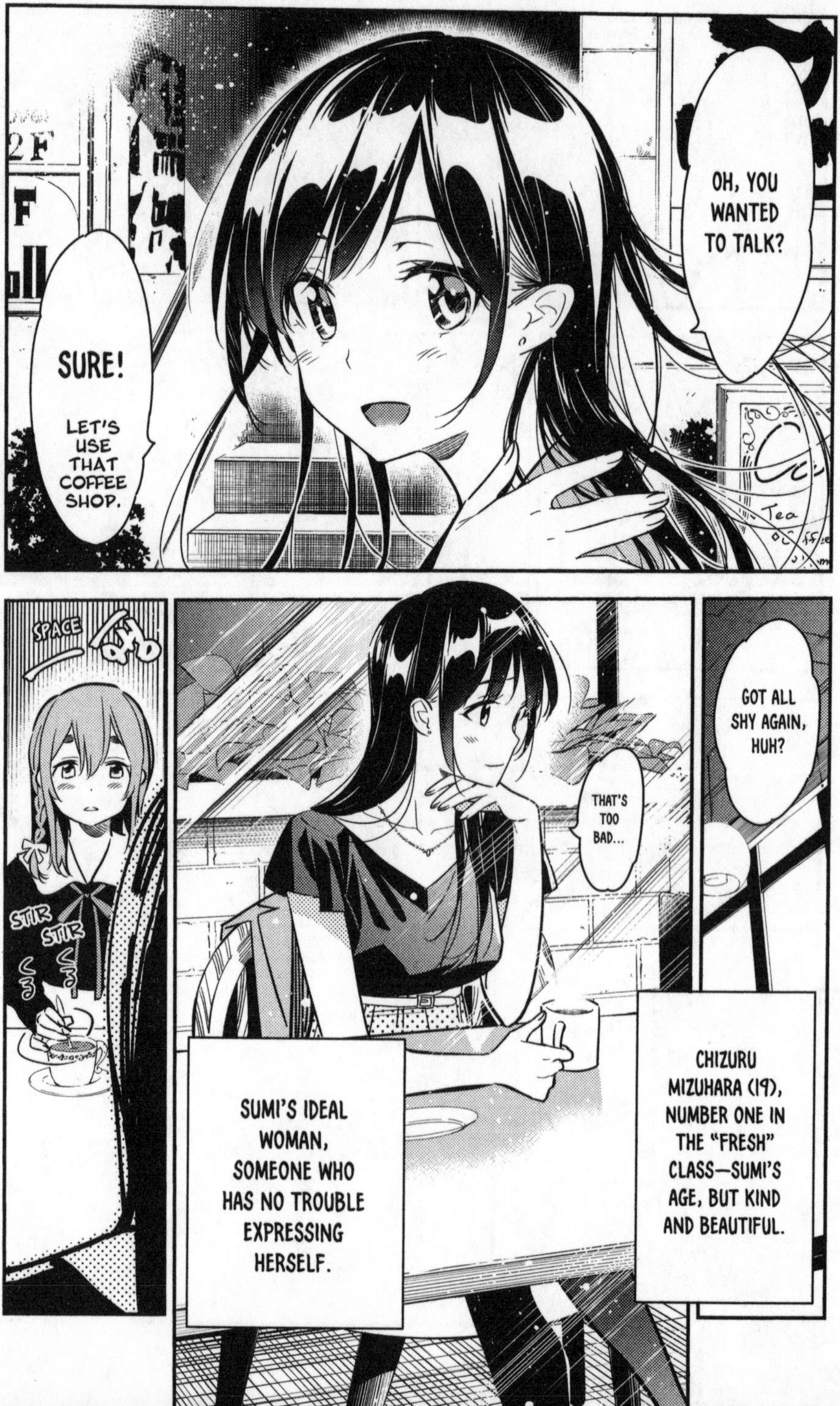
OH, YOU WANTED TO TALK?
SURE!
LET'S USE THAT COFFEE SHOP.
GOT ALL SHY AGAIN, HUH?
CHIZURU MIZUHARA (19), NUMBER ONE IN THE "FRESH" CLASS—SUMI'S AGE, BUT KIND AND BEAUTIFUL.
THAT'S TOO BAD...
SUMI'S IDEAL WOMAN, SOMEONE WHO HAS NO TROUBLE EXPRESSING HERSELF.
SPACE
STIR STIR

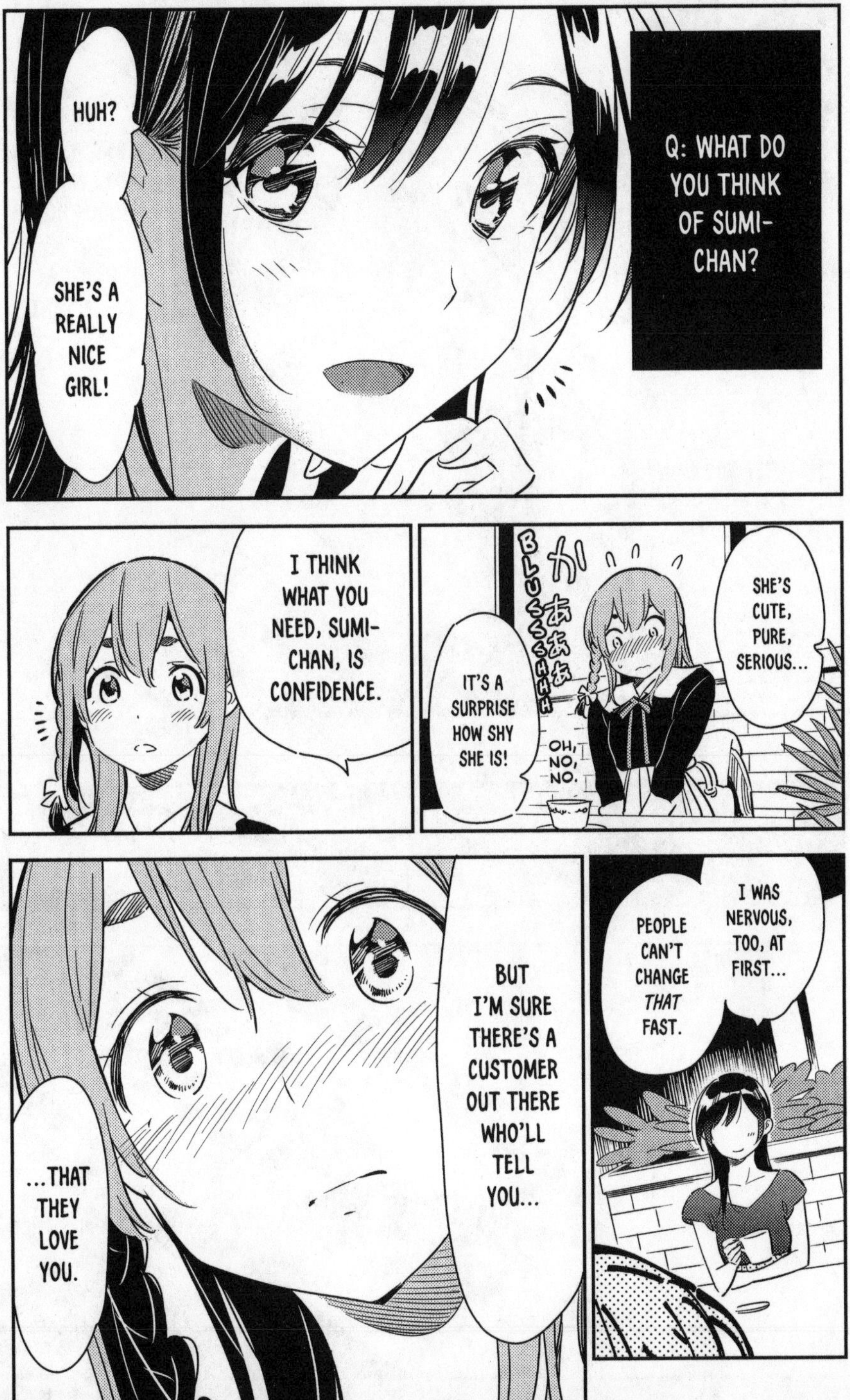
Q: WHAT DO YOU THINK OF SUMI-CHAN?
HUH?
SHE'S A REALLY NICE GIRL!
SHE'S CUTE, PURE, SERIOUS...
かあああ
BLUSSHHH
IT'S A SURPRISE HOW SHY SHE IS!
OH, NO, NO.
I THINK WHAT YOU NEED, SUMI-CHAN, IS CONFIDENCE.
I WAS NERVOUS, TOO, AT FIRST...
PEOPLE CAN'T CHANGE *THAT* FAST.
BUT I'M SURE THERE'S A CUSTOMER OUT THERE WHO'LL TELL YOU...
...THAT THEY LOVE YOU.

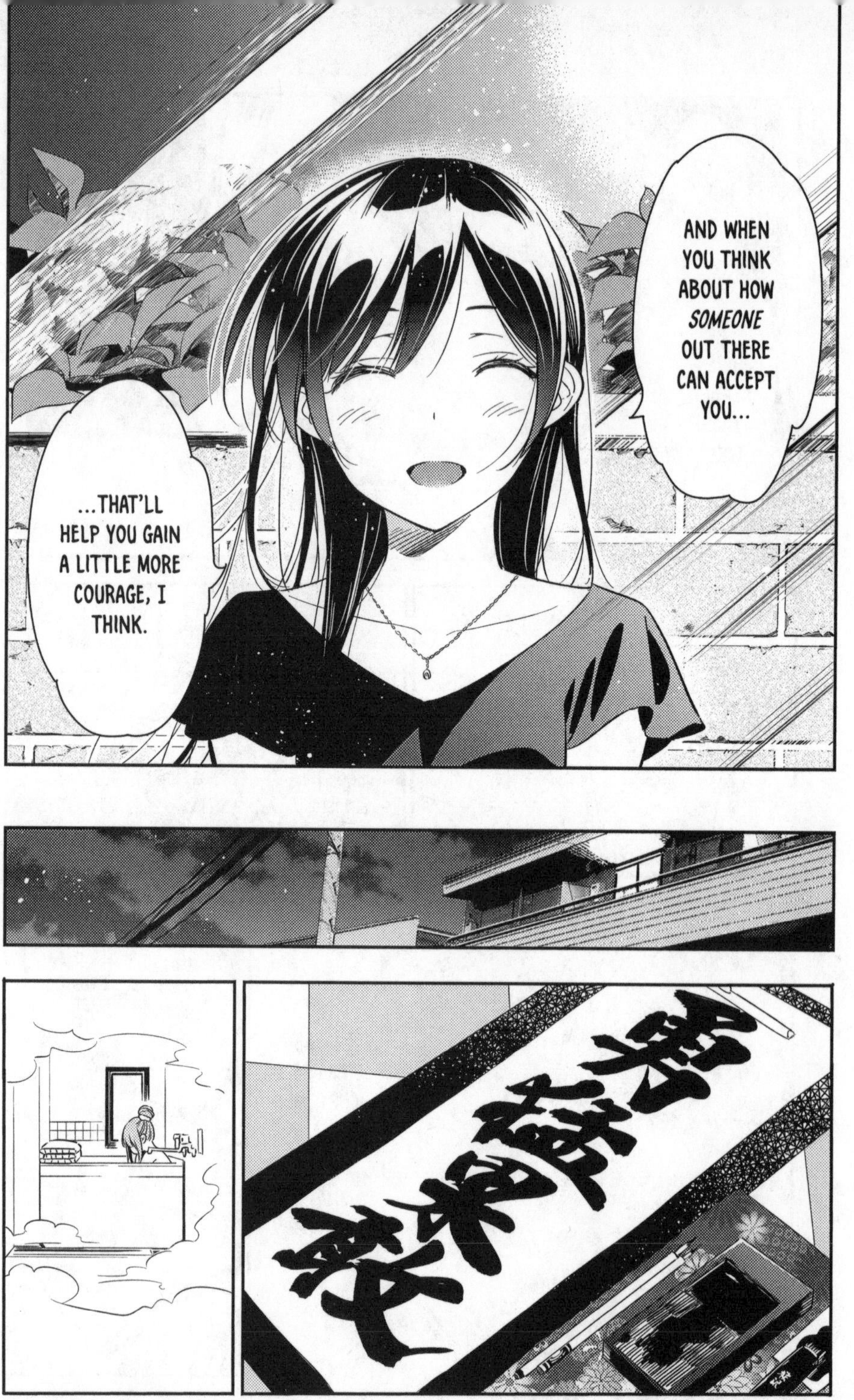
AND WHEN YOU THINK ABOUT HOW *SOMEONE* OUT THERE CAN ACCEPT YOU...
...THAT'LL HELP YOU GAIN A LITTLE MORE COURAGE, I THINK.

PAPER: DAUNTLESS COURAGE

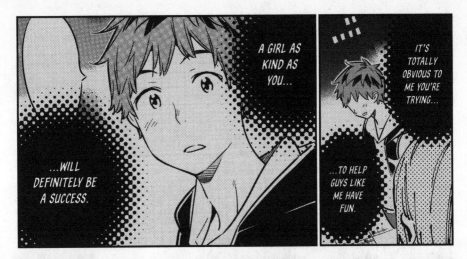

IT'S TOTALLY OBVIOUS TO ME YOU'RE TRYING...
...TO HELP GUYS LIKE ME HAVE FUN.
A GIRL AS KIND AS YOU...
...WILL DEFINITELY BE A SUCCESS.
NGH
HNGH

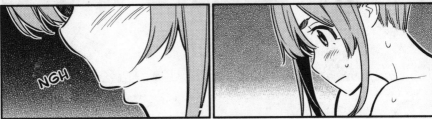

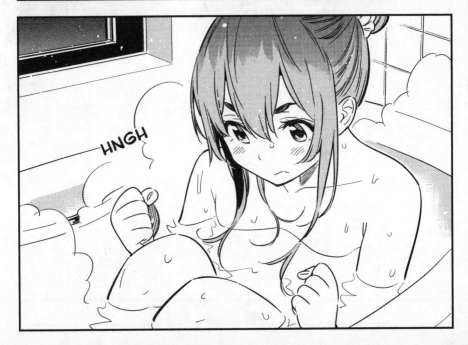

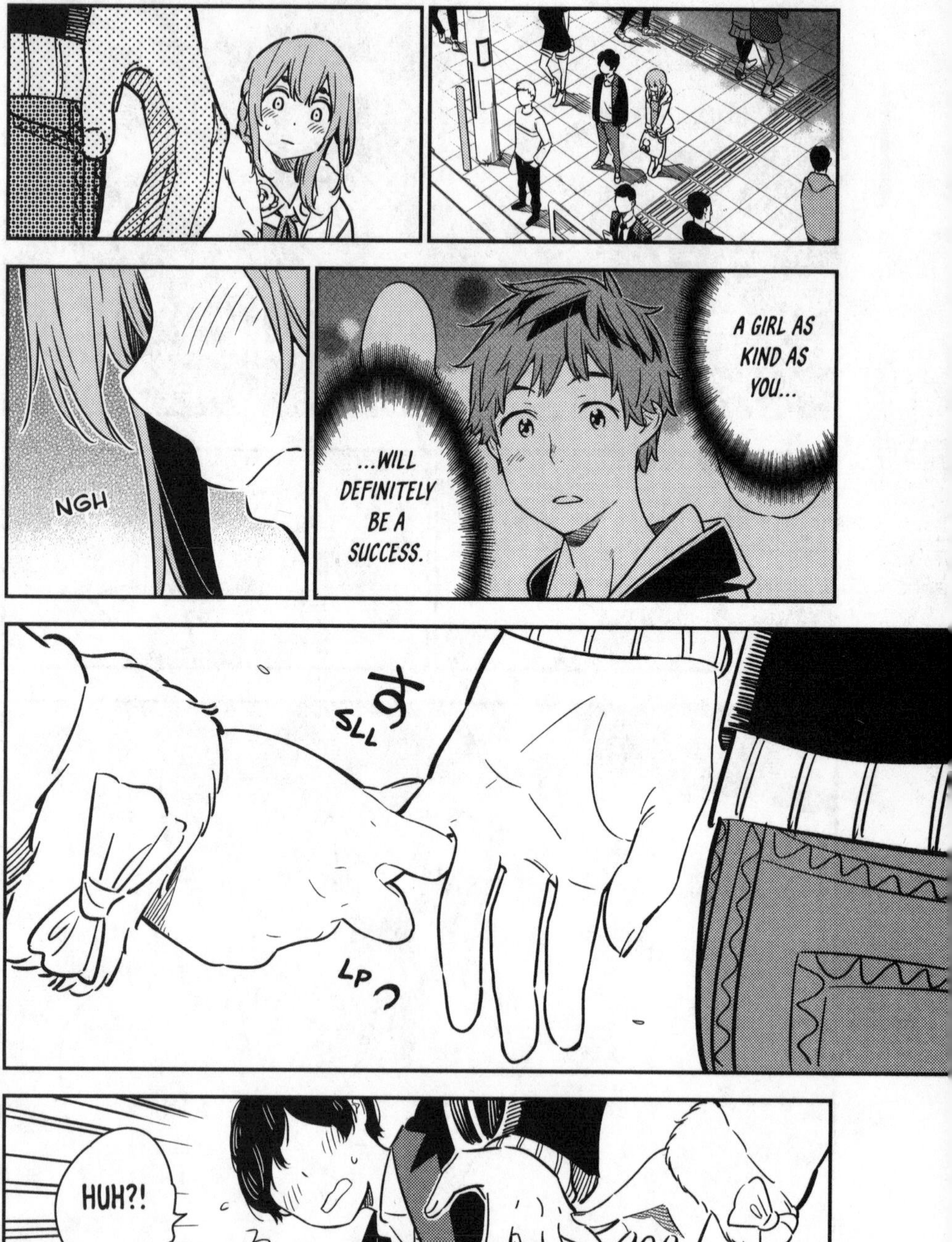
A GIRL AS KIND AS YOU...
...WILL DEFINITELY BE A SUCCESS.
NGH
す
SLL
LP
HUH?!

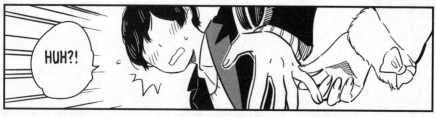

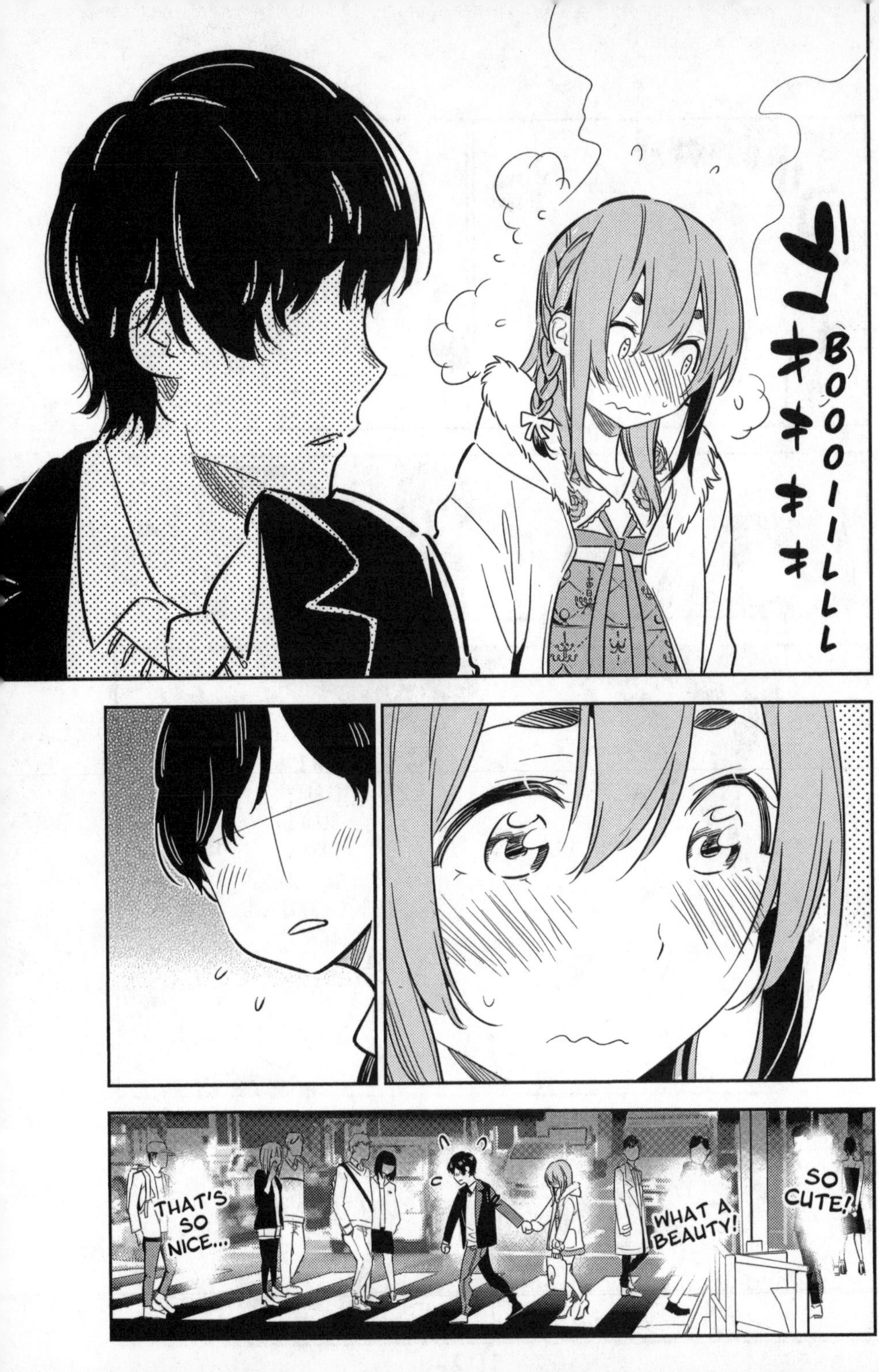
BOOOIILLL
SO CUTE!
WHAT A BEAUTY!
THAT'S SO NICE...

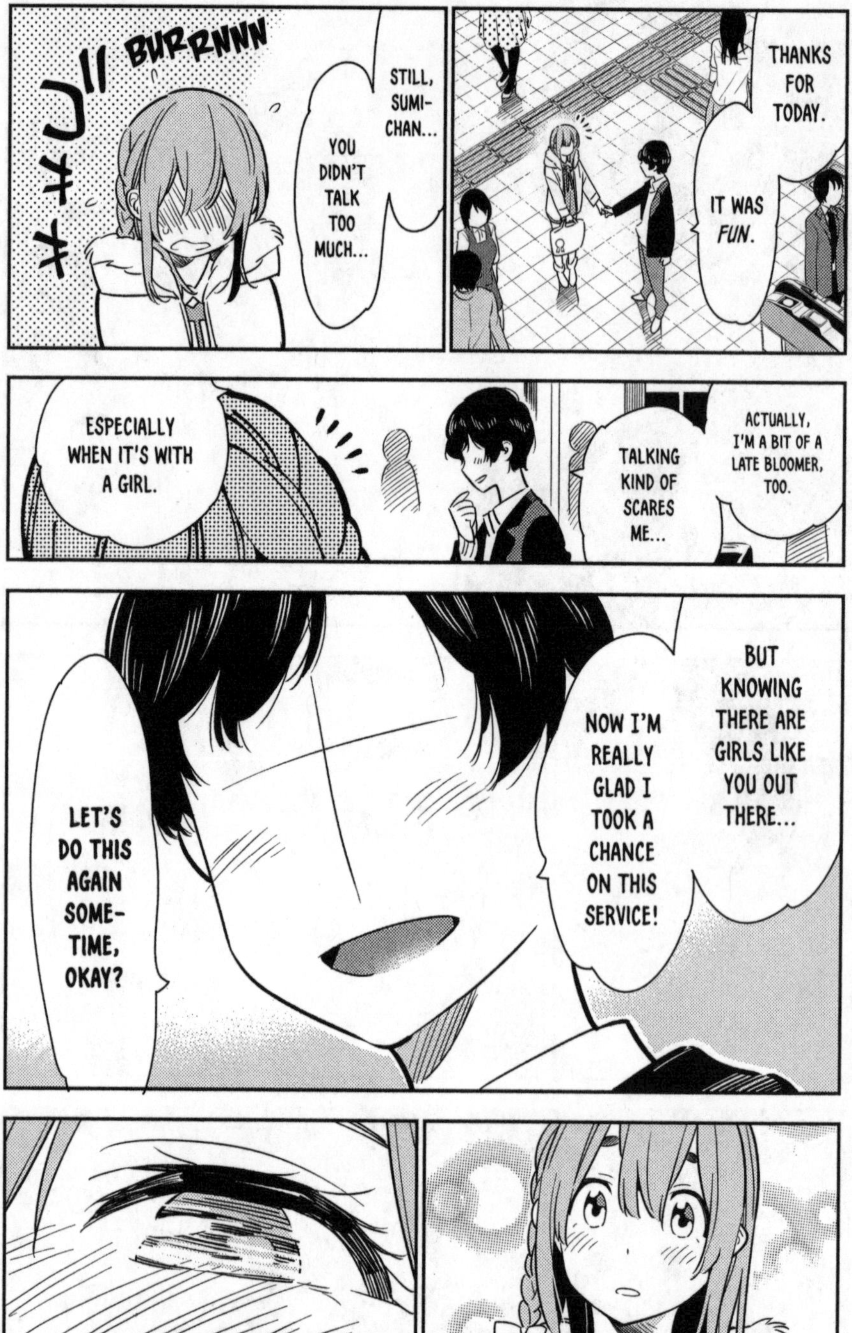
THANKS FOR TODAY.
IT WAS FUN.
STILL, SUMI-CHAN...
YOU DIDN'T TALK TOO MUCH...
BURRNNN
ACTUALLY, I'M A BIT OF A LATE BLOOMER, TOO.
TALKING KIND OF SCARES ME...
ESPECIALLY WHEN IT'S WITH A GIRL.
BUT KNOWING THERE ARE GIRLS LIKE YOU OUT THERE...
NOW I'M REALLY GLAD I TOOK A CHANCE ON THIS SERVICE!
LET'S DO THIS AGAIN SOMETIME, OKAY?

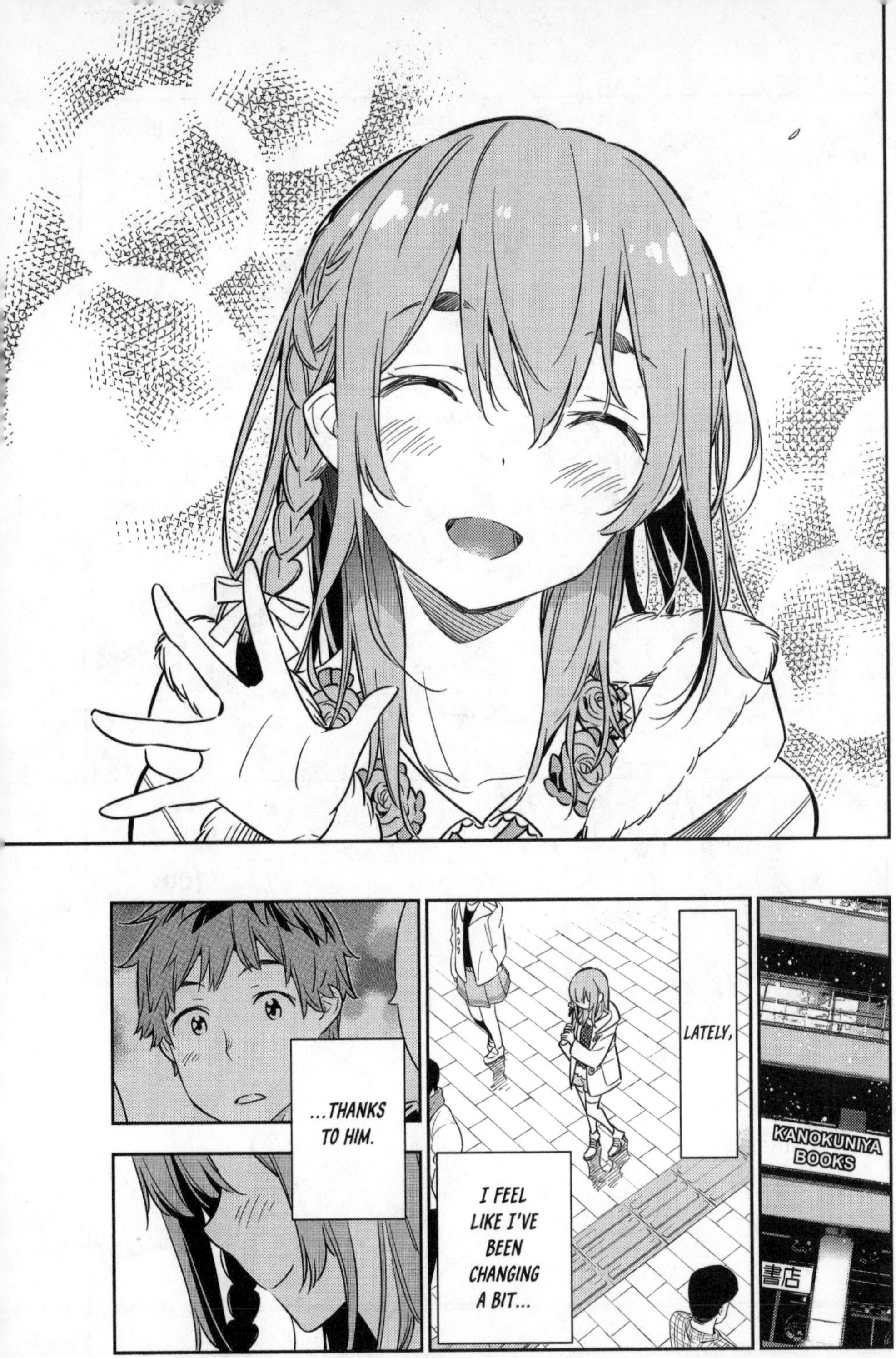
KANOKUNIYA BOOKS
書店
LATELY,
I FEEL LIKE I'VE BEEN CHANGING A BIT...
...THANKS TO HIM.

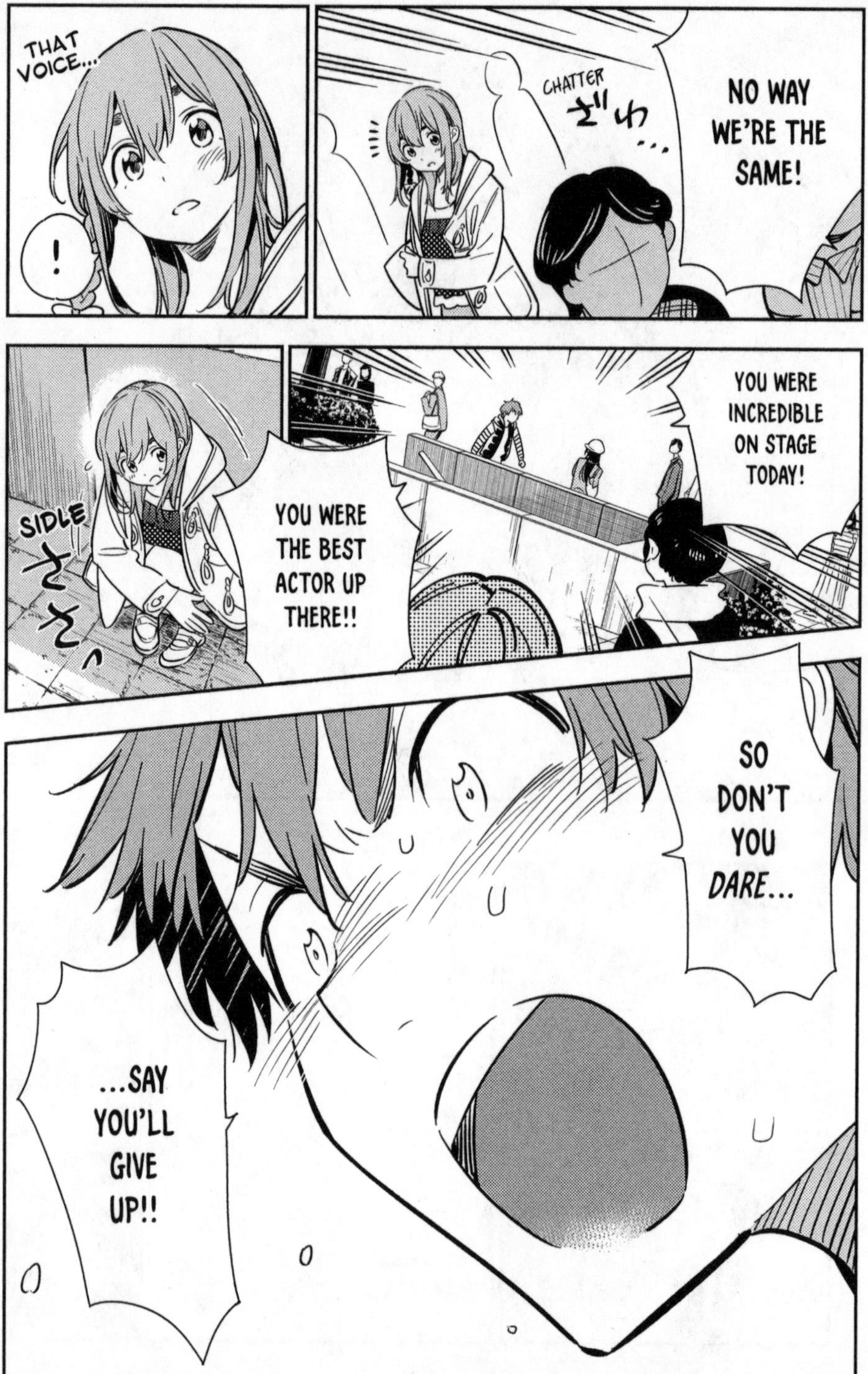
NO WAY WE'RE THE SAME!
CHATTER
ざわ...
THAT VOICE...
!
YOU WERE INCREDIBLE ON STAGE TODAY!
YOU WERE THE BEST ACTOR UP THERE!!
SIDLE
さそ
SO DON'T YOU *DARE*...
...SAY YOU'LL GIVE UP!!

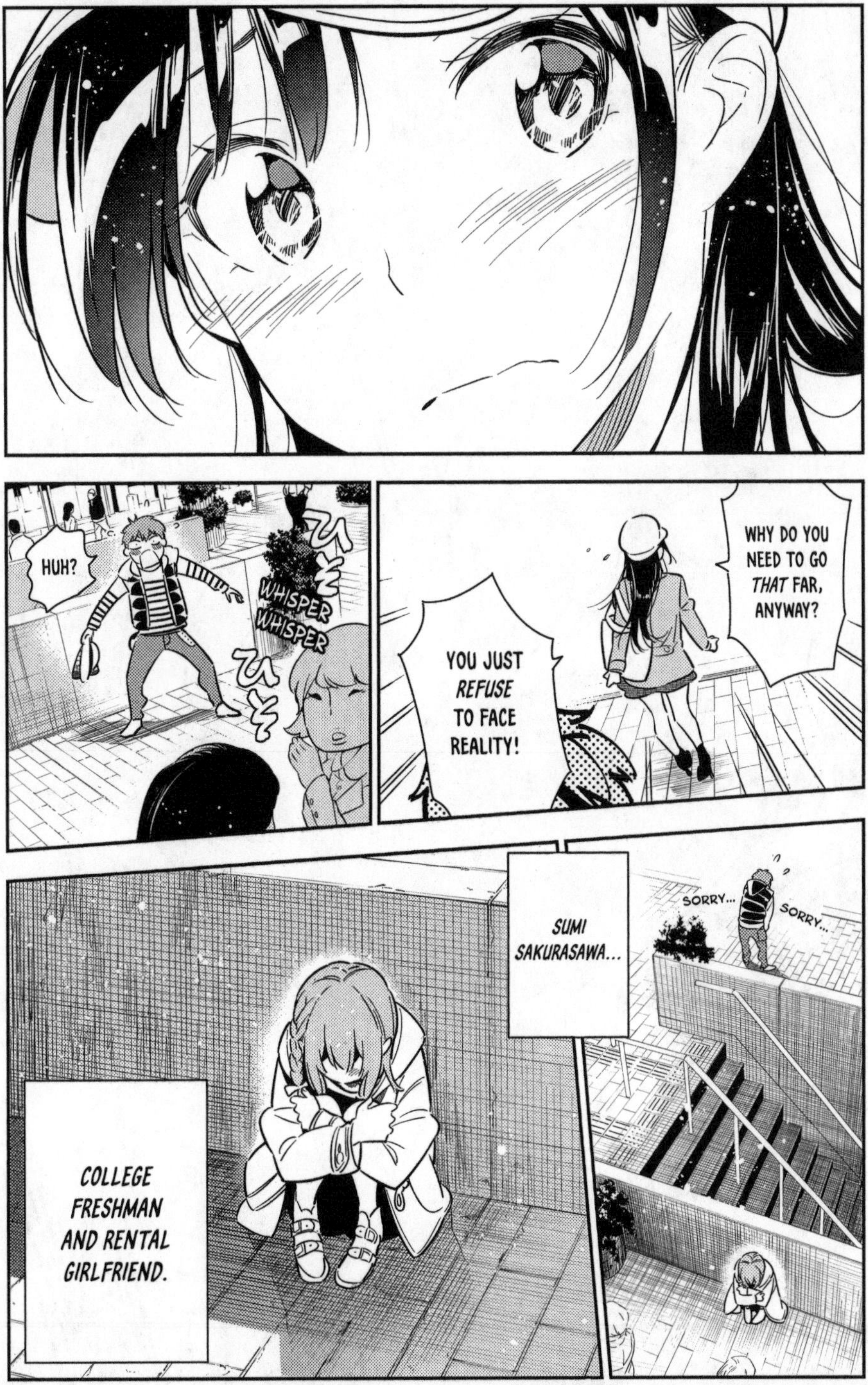
WHY DO YOU NEED TO GO *THAT* FAR, ANYWAY?
YOU JUST *REFUSE* TO FACE REALITY!
ひそ
WHISPER WHISPER
ひそ
HUH?
SORRY... SORRY...
SUMI SAKURASAWA...
COLLEGE FRESHMAN AND RENTAL GIRLFRIEND.

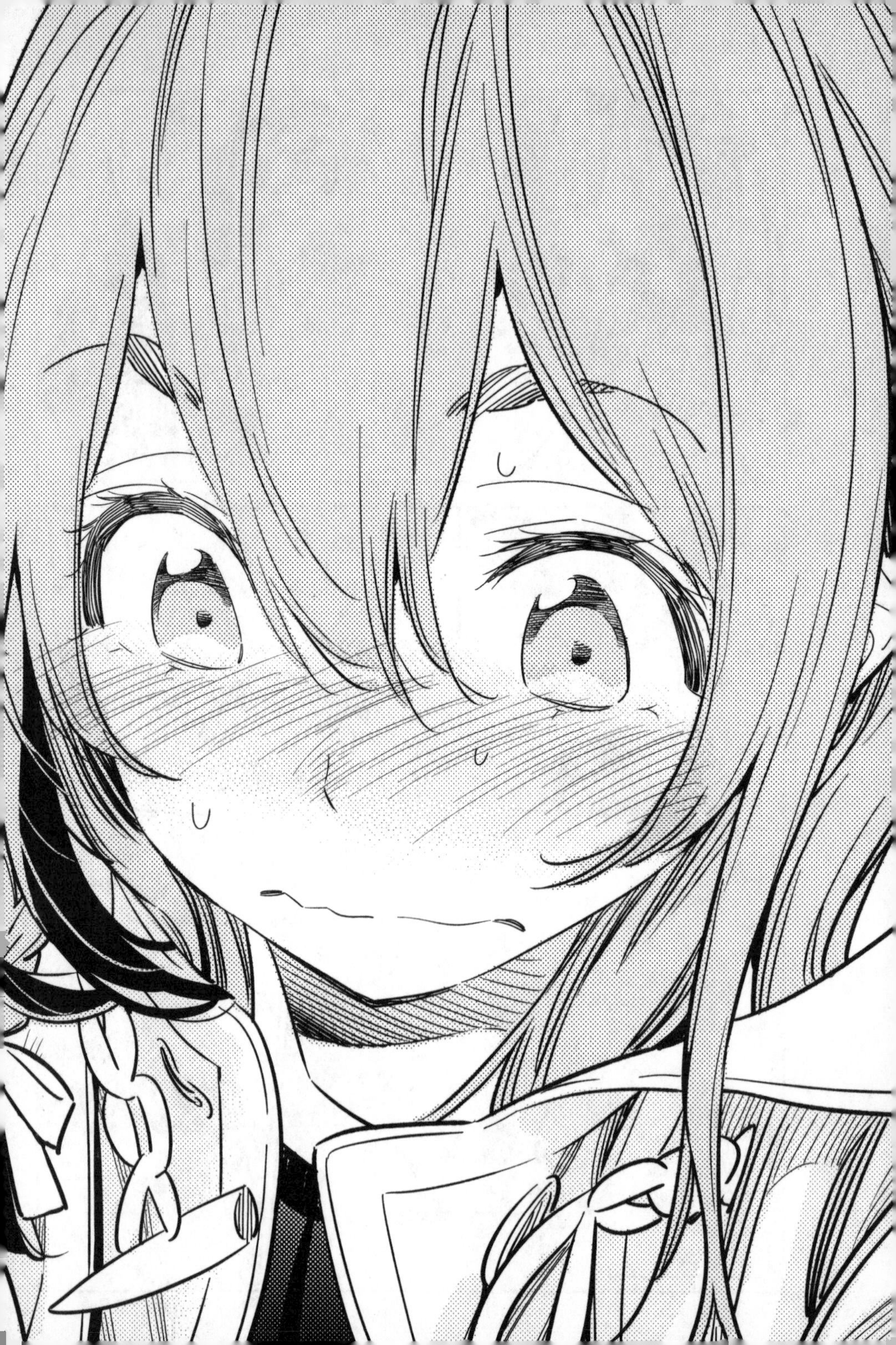

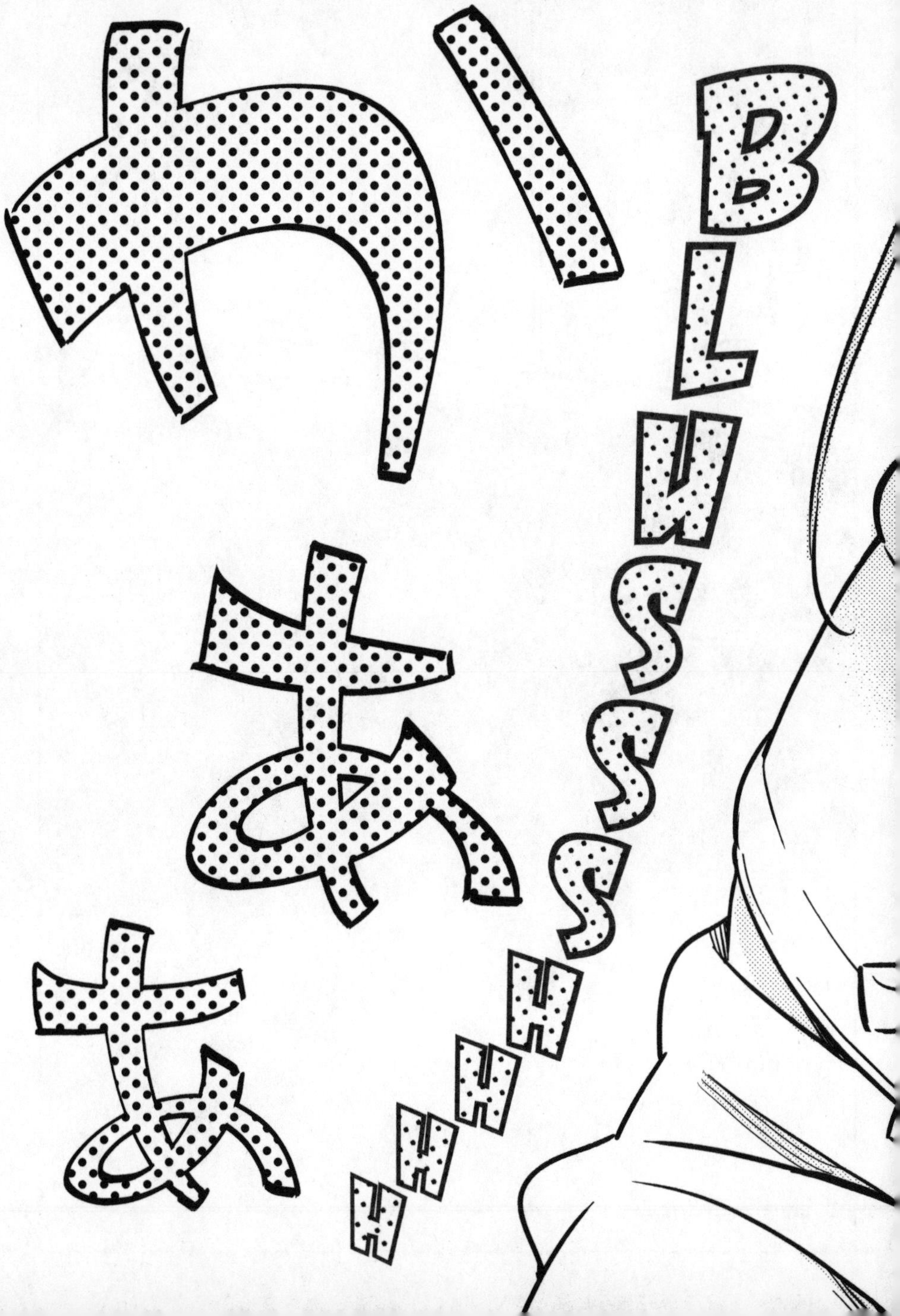
カーああ
BLUSSSHHHH

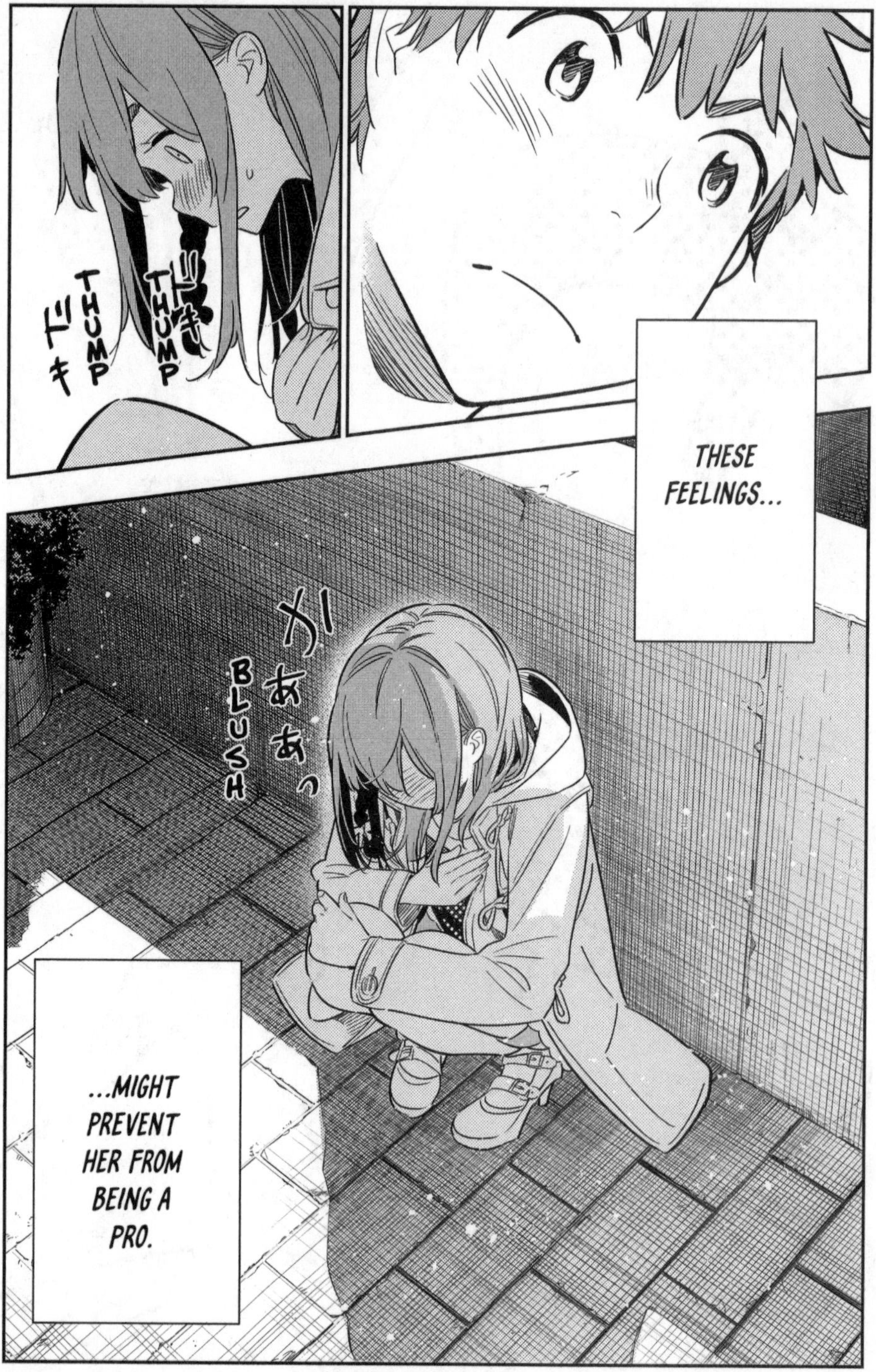
ドキ
THUMP
THUMP
ドキ
THESE FEELINGS...
かあぁっ
BLUSH
...MIGHT PREVENT HER FROM BEING A PRO.

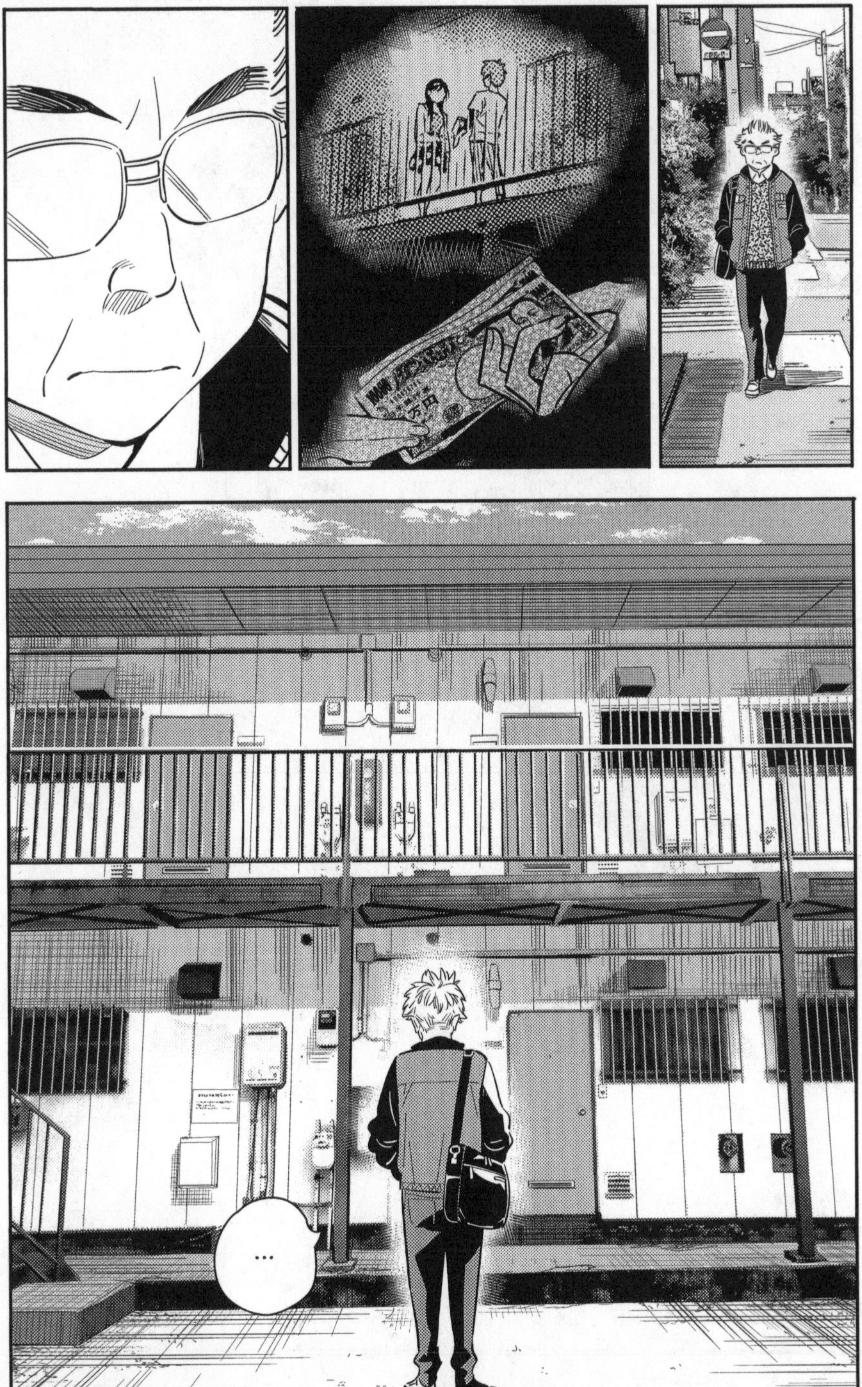
...

RATING 55 MY GIRLFRIEND AND MY FATHER

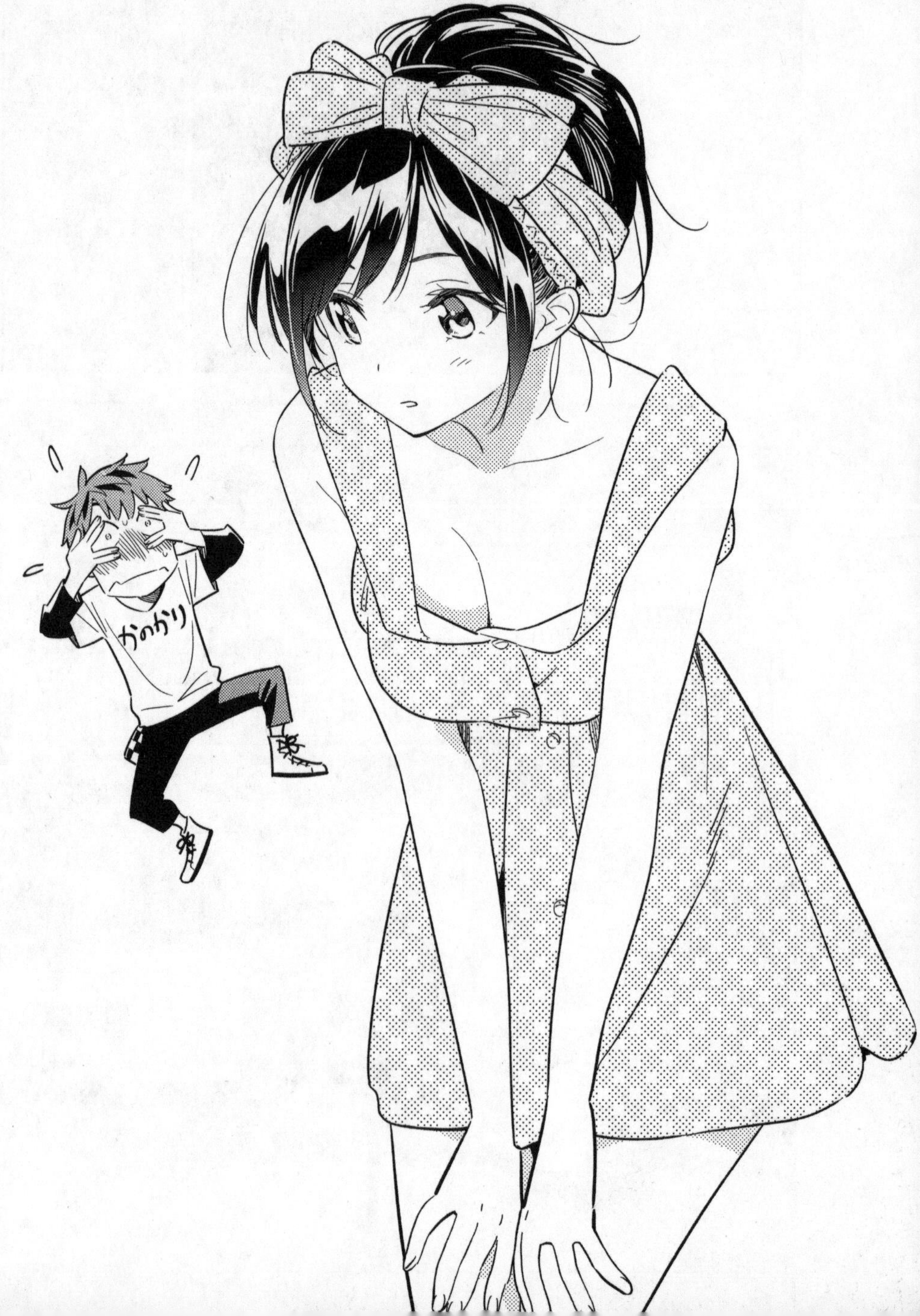
かのかり

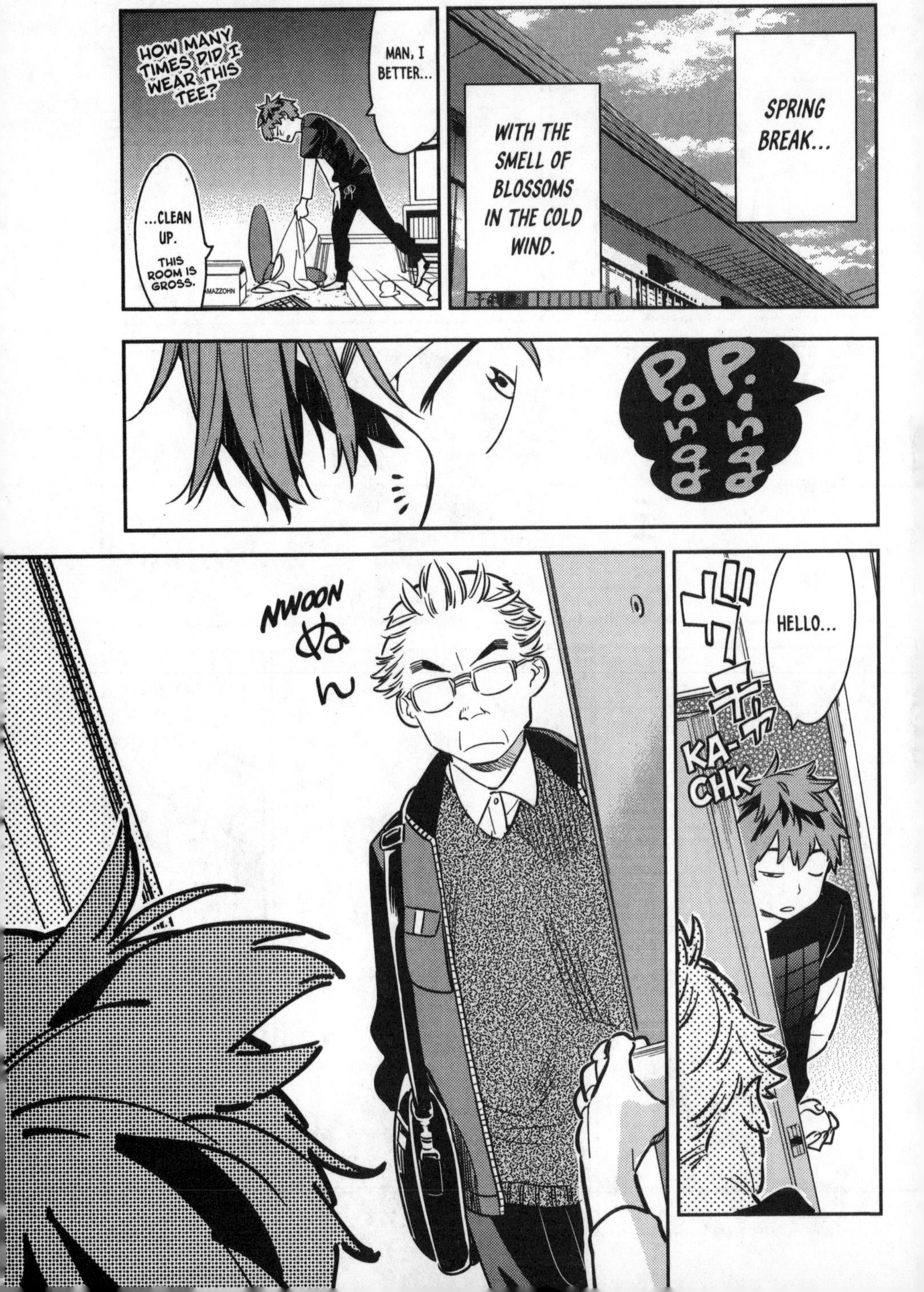
SPRING BREAK...
WITH THE SMELL OF BLOSSOMS IN THE COLD WIND.
MAN, I BETTER...
HOW MANY TIMES DID I WEAR THIS TEE?
...CLEAN UP.
THIS ROOM IS GROSS.
AMAZZOHN
Ping
Pong
HELLO...
ガチャ
KA-CHK
NWOON
ぬん

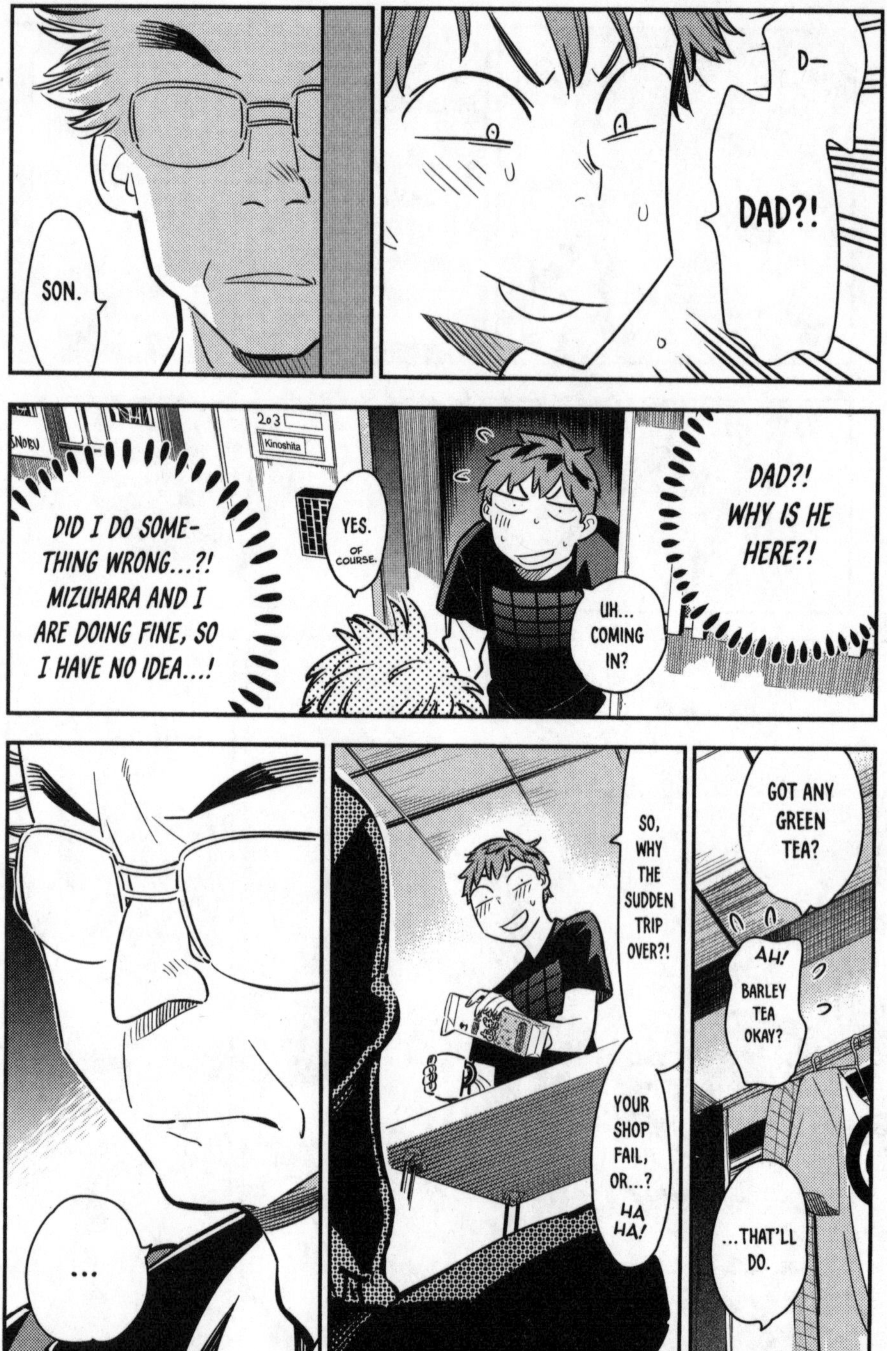
D—
DAD?!
SON.
DAD?! WHY IS HE HERE?!
UH... COMING IN?
YES. OF COURSE.
203
Kinoshita
DID I DO SOMETHING WRONG...?! MIZUHARA AND I ARE DOING FINE, SO I HAVE NO IDEA...!
GOT ANY GREEN TEA?
AH! BARLEY TEA OKAY?
...THAT'LL DO.
SO, WHY THE SUDDEN TRIP OVER?!
YOUR SHOP FAIL, OR...?
HA HA!
...

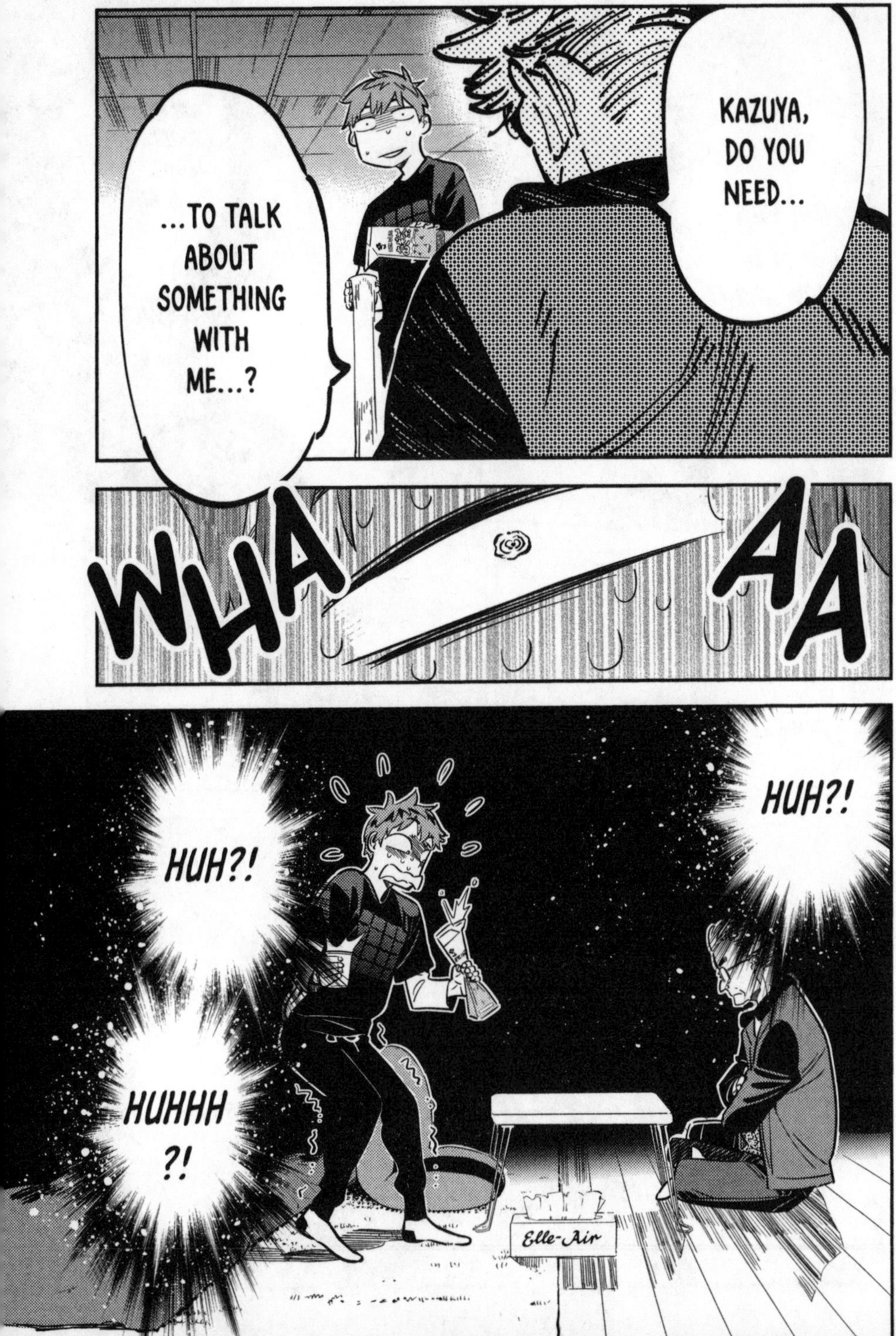
KAZUYA, DO YOU NEED...
...TO TALK ABOUT SOMETHING WITH ME...?
WHAAA
HUH?!
HUH?!
HUHHH ?!
Elle-Air

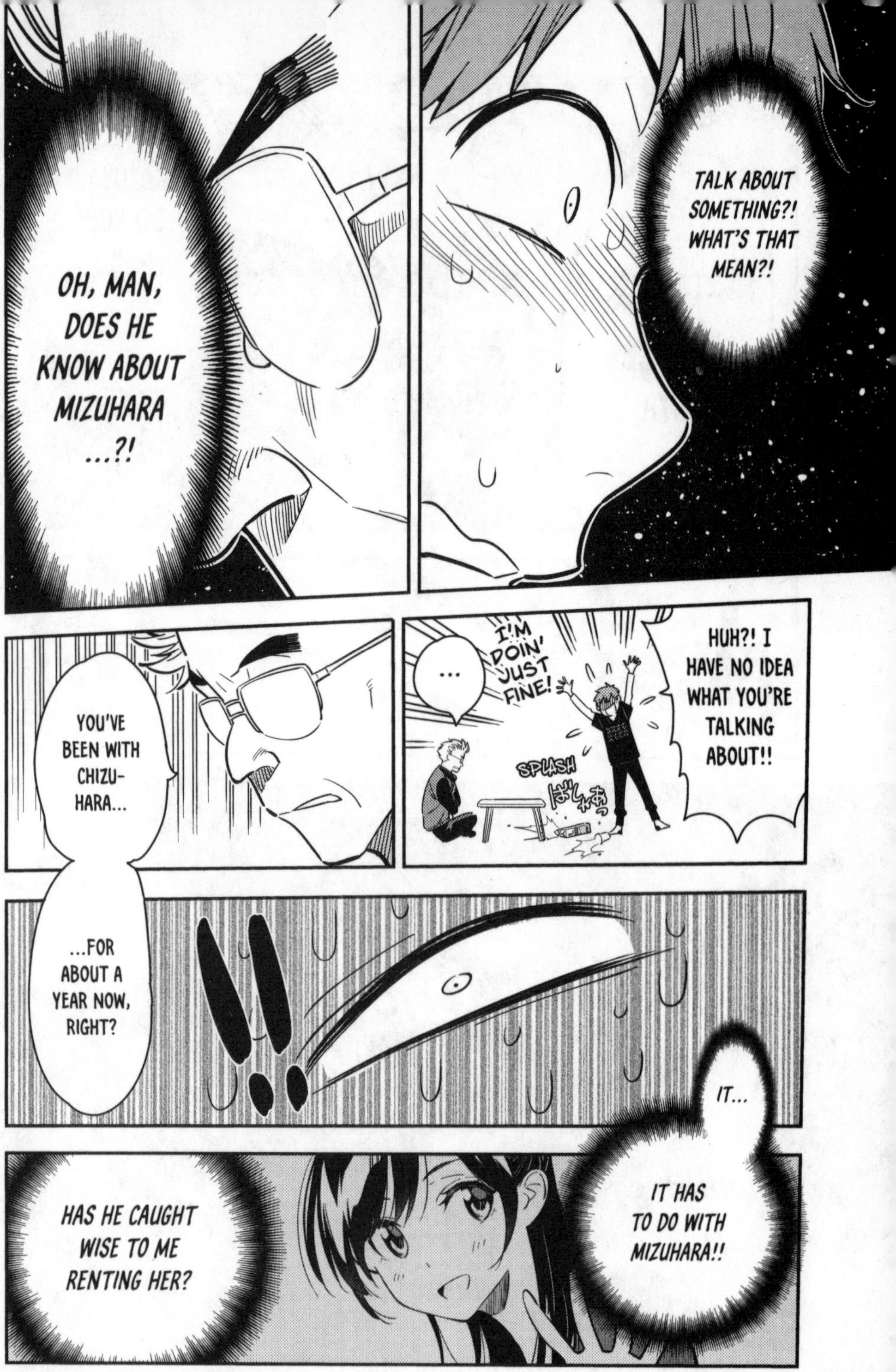

TALK ABOUT SOMETHING?! WHAT'S THAT MEAN?!
OH, MAN, DOES HE KNOW ABOUT MIZUHARA ...?!
HUH?! I HAVE NO IDEA WHAT YOU'RE TALKING ABOUT!!
I'M DOIN' JUST FINE!
...
SPLASH
YOU'VE BEEN WITH CHIZU-HARA...
...FOR ABOUT A YEAR NOW, RIGHT?
IT...
IT HAS TO DO WITH MIZUHARA!!
HAS HE CAUGHT WISE TO ME RENTING HER?

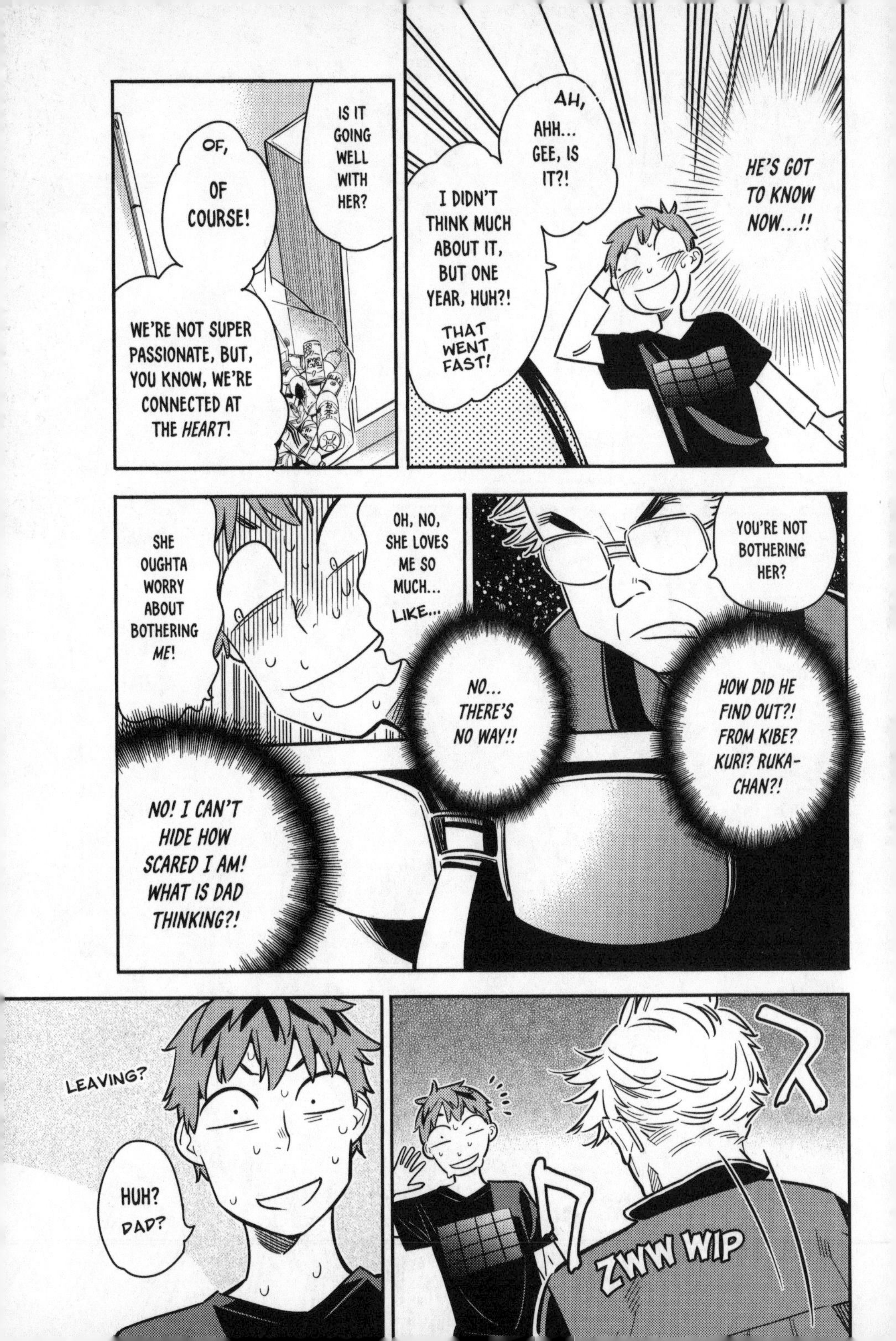
AH, AHH... GEE, IS IT?!
I DIDN'T THINK MUCH ABOUT IT, BUT ONE YEAR, HUH?!
THAT WENT FAST!
HE'S GOT TO KNOW NOW...!!
IS IT GOING WELL WITH HER?
OF, OF COURSE!
WE'RE NOT SUPER PASSIONATE, BUT, YOU KNOW, WE'RE CONNECTED AT THE *HEART*!
YOU'RE NOT BOTHERING HER?
HOW DID HE FIND OUT?! FROM KIBE? KURI? RUKA-CHAN?!
NO... THERE'S NO WAY!!
OH, NO, SHE LOVES ME SO MUCH... LIKE...
SHE OUGHTA WORRY ABOUT BOTHERING *ME*!
NO! I CAN'T HIDE HOW SCARED I AM! WHAT IS DAD THINKING?!
ZWW WIP
LEAVING?
HUH? DAD?

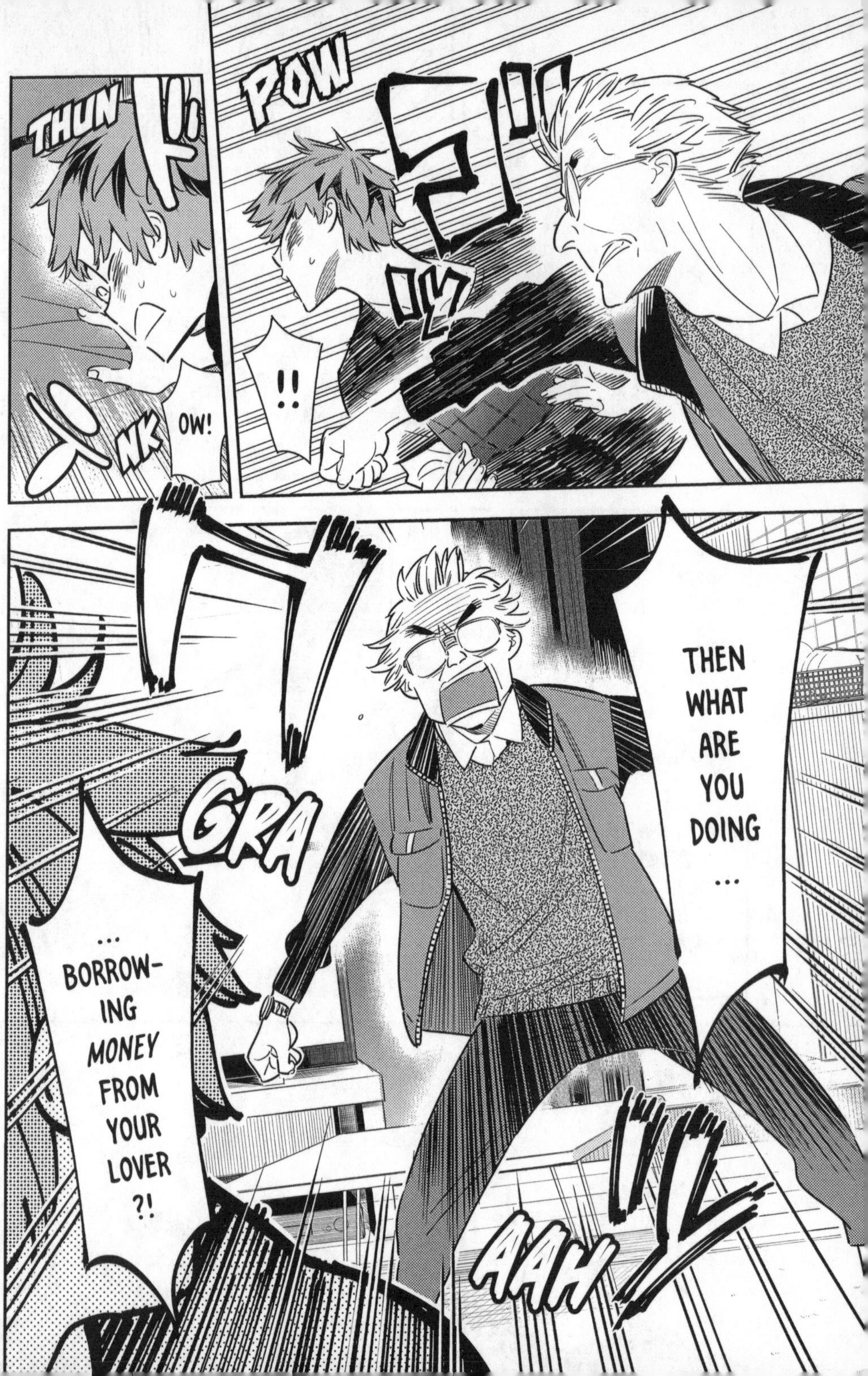
POW
!!
THUN
NK
OW!
THEN WHAT ARE YOU DOING...
GRA
AAH
...BORROWING MONEY FROM YOUR LOVER?!

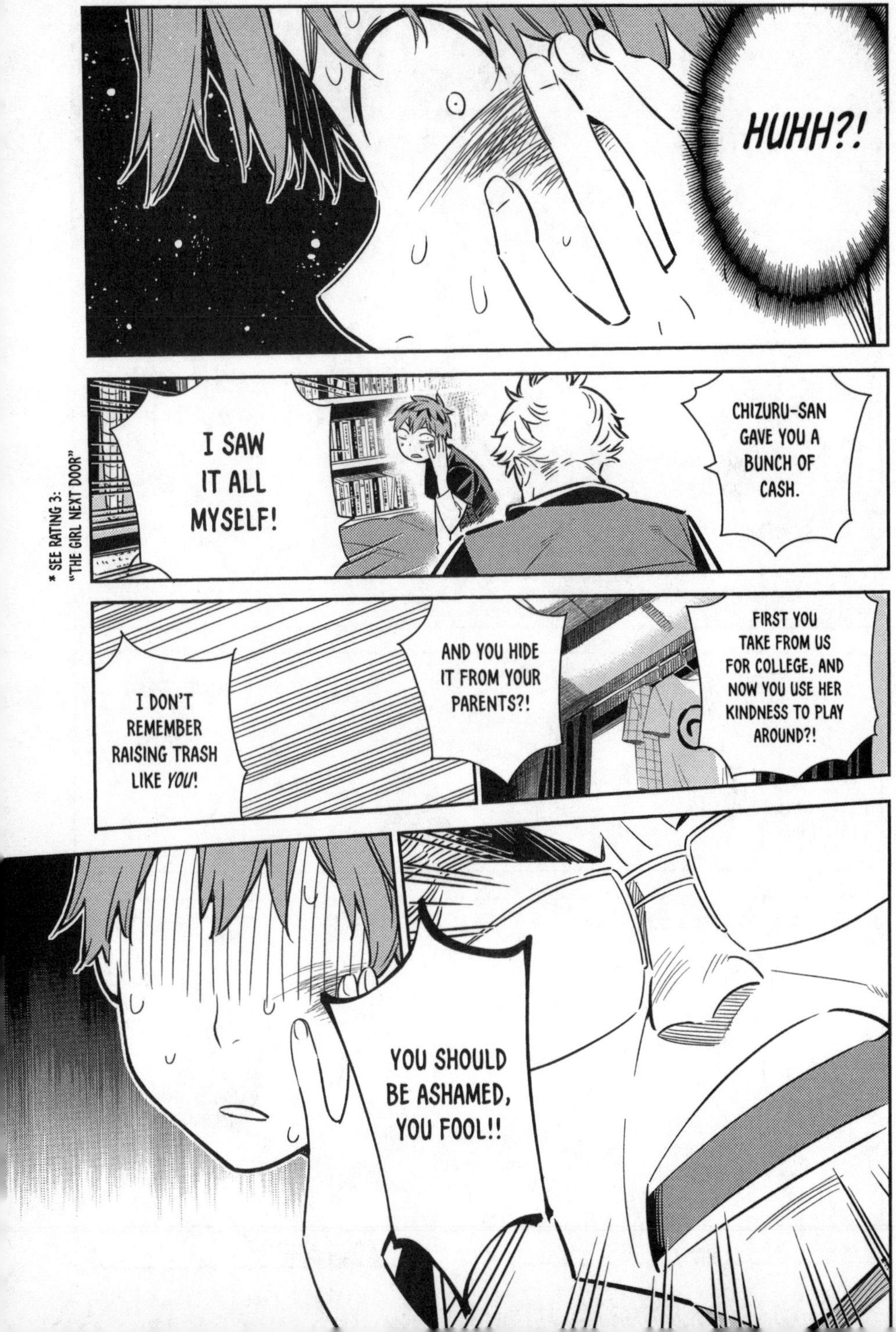
HUHH?!
CHIZURU-SAN GAVE YOU A BUNCH OF CASH.
I SAW IT ALL MYSELF!
FIRST YOU TAKE FROM US FOR COLLEGE, AND NOW YOU USE HER KINDNESS TO PLAY AROUND?!
AND YOU HIDE IT FROM YOUR PARENTS?!
I DON'T REMEMBER RAISING TRASH LIKE *YOU*!
YOU SHOULD BE ASHAMED, YOU FOOL!!

* SEE RATING 3: "THE GIRL NEXT DOOR"

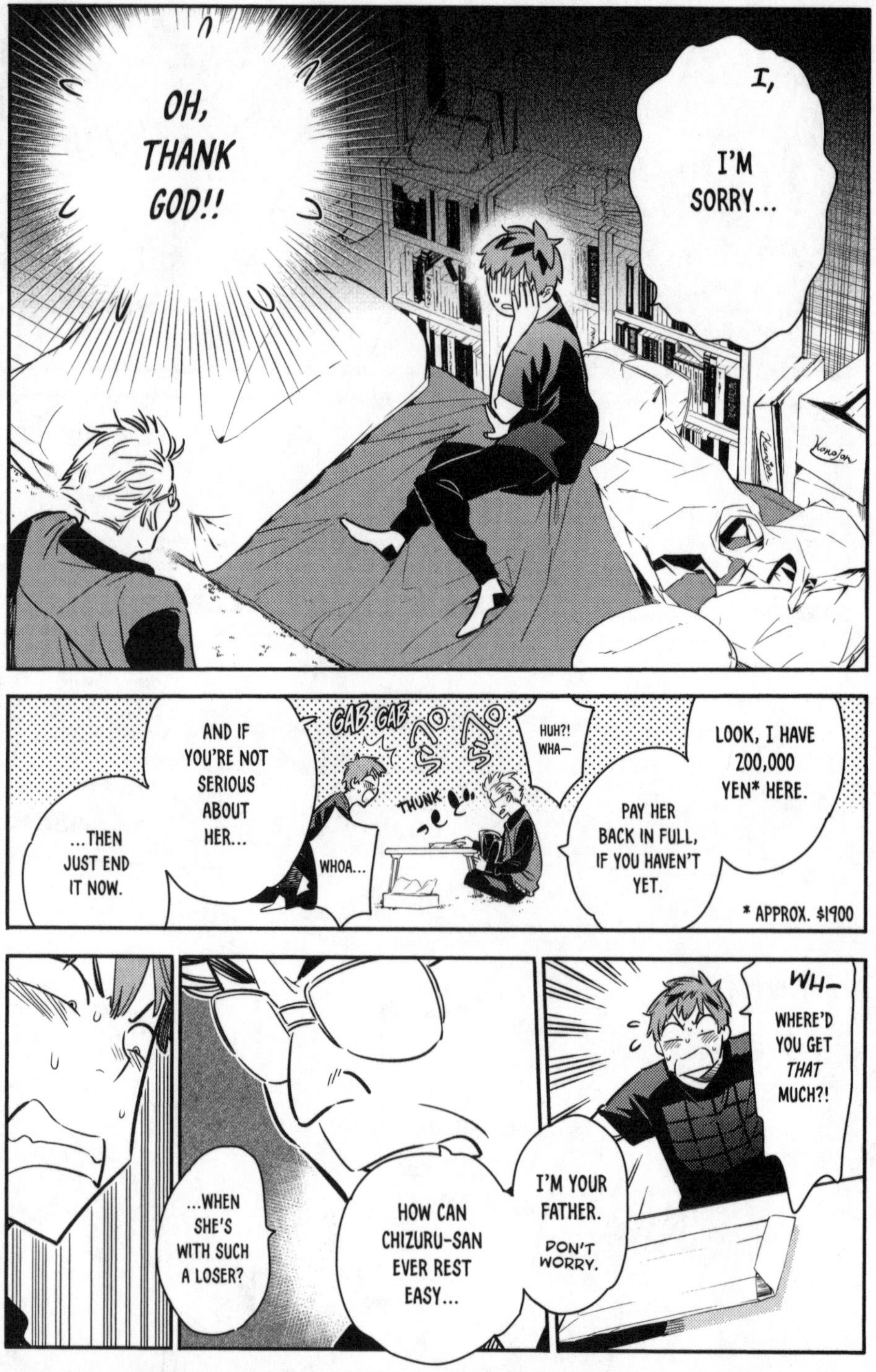
I,
I'M SORRY...
OH, THANK GOD!!
LOOK, I HAVE 200,000 YEN* HERE.
PAY HER BACK IN FULL, IF YOU HAVEN'T YET.
HUH?! WHA—
GAB GAB
THUNK
WHOA...
AND IF YOU'RE NOT SERIOUS ABOUT HER...
...THEN JUST END IT NOW.
* APPROX. $1900
WH—
WHERE'D YOU GET *THAT* MUCH?!
I'M YOUR FATHER.
DON'T WORRY.
HOW CAN CHIZURU-SAN EVER REST EASY...
...WHEN SHE'S WITH SUCH A LOSER?

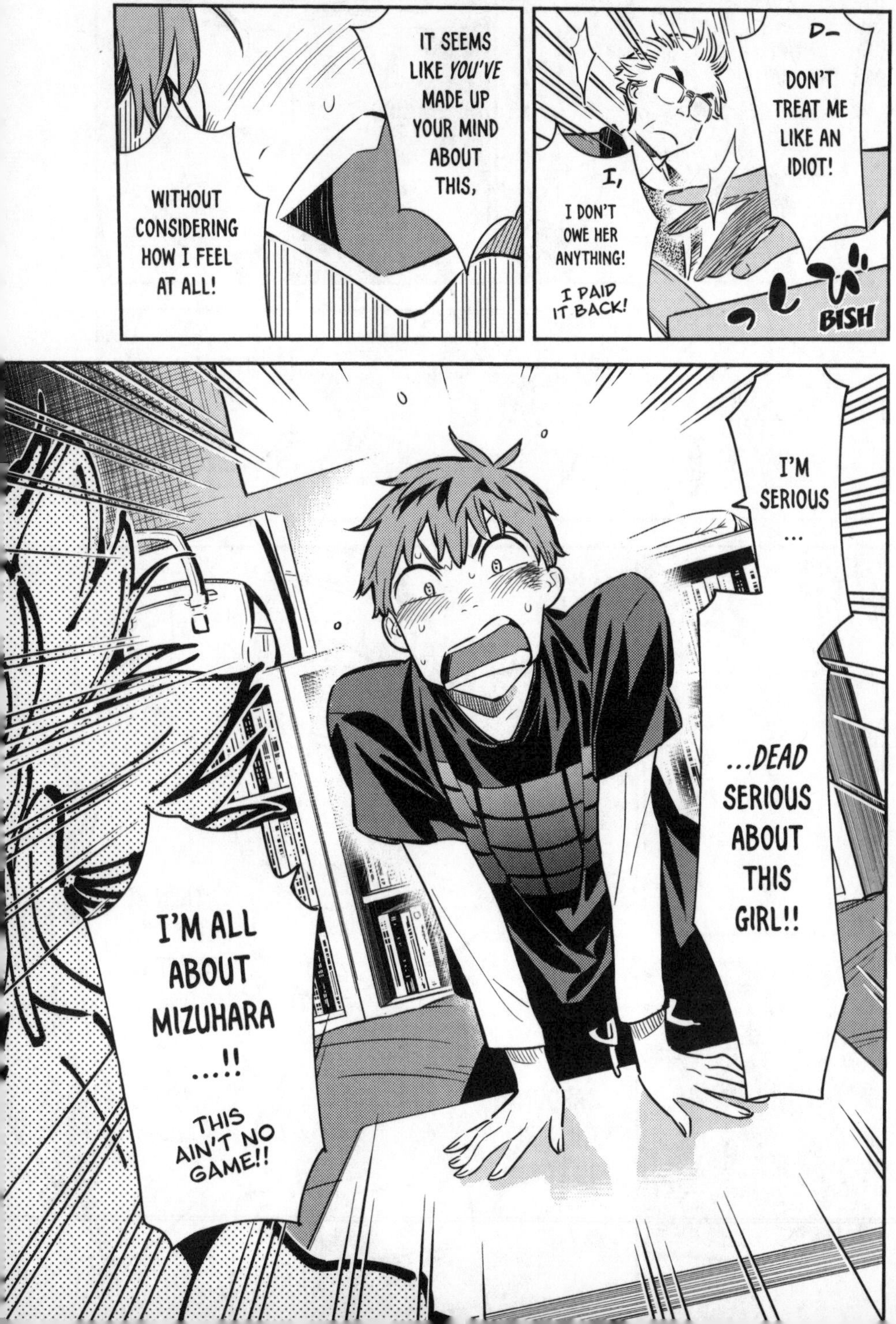
D–
DON'T TREAT ME LIKE AN IDIOT!
I,
I DON'T OWE HER ANYTHING!
I PAID IT BACK!
BISH
IT SEEMS LIKE *YOU'VE* MADE UP YOUR MIND ABOUT THIS,
WITHOUT CONSIDERING HOW I FEEL AT ALL!
I'M SERIOUS...
...*DEAD* SERIOUS ABOUT THIS GIRL!!
I'M ALL ABOUT MIZUHARA...!!
THIS AIN'T NO GAME!!

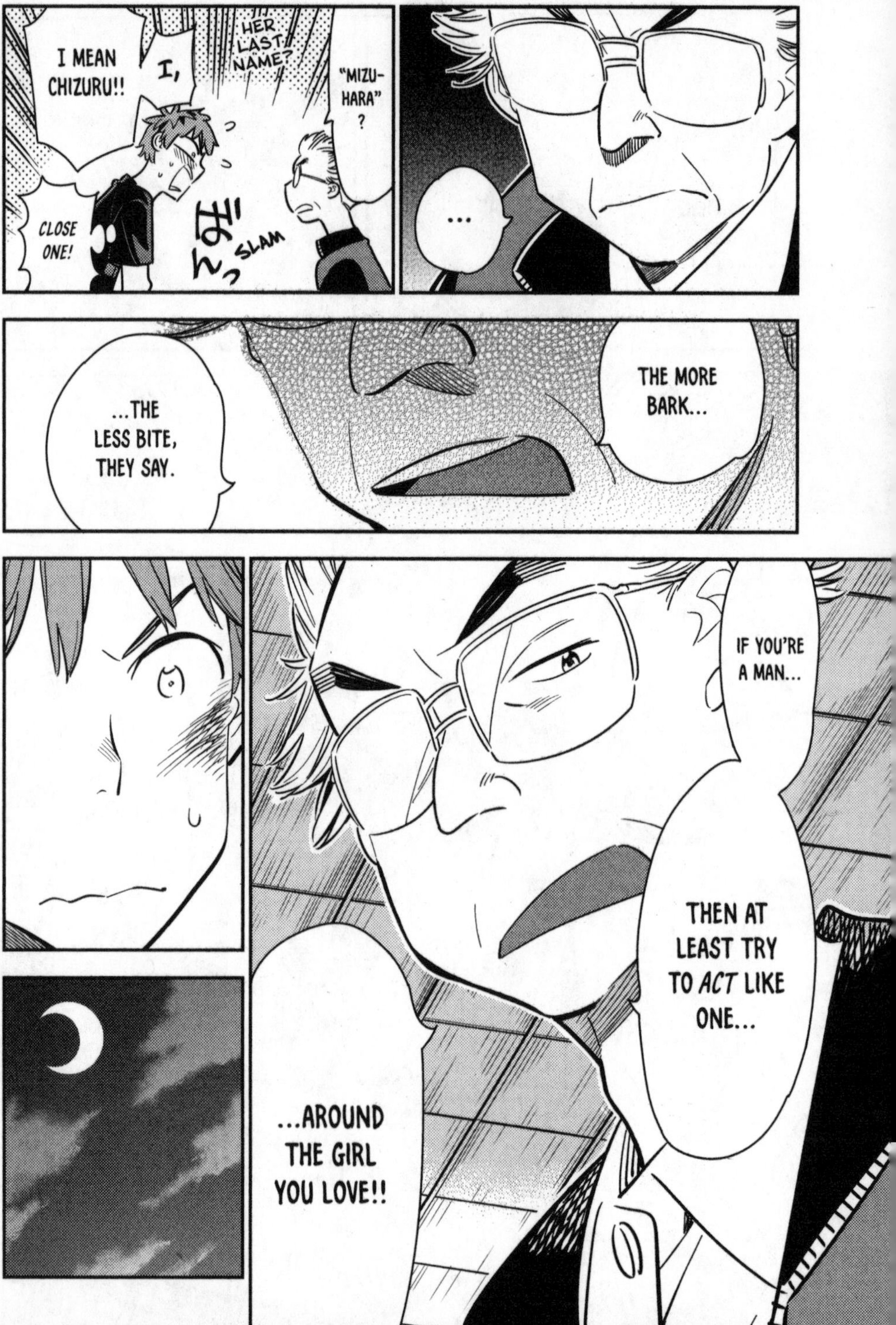
...
"MIZU-HARA"?
HER LAST NAME?
I,
I MEAN CHIZURU!!
ばんっ SLAM
CLOSE ONE!
THE MORE BARK...
...THE LESS BITE, THEY SAY.
IF YOU'RE A MAN...
THEN AT LEAST TRY TO *ACT* LIKE ONE...
...AROUND THE GIRL YOU LOVE!!

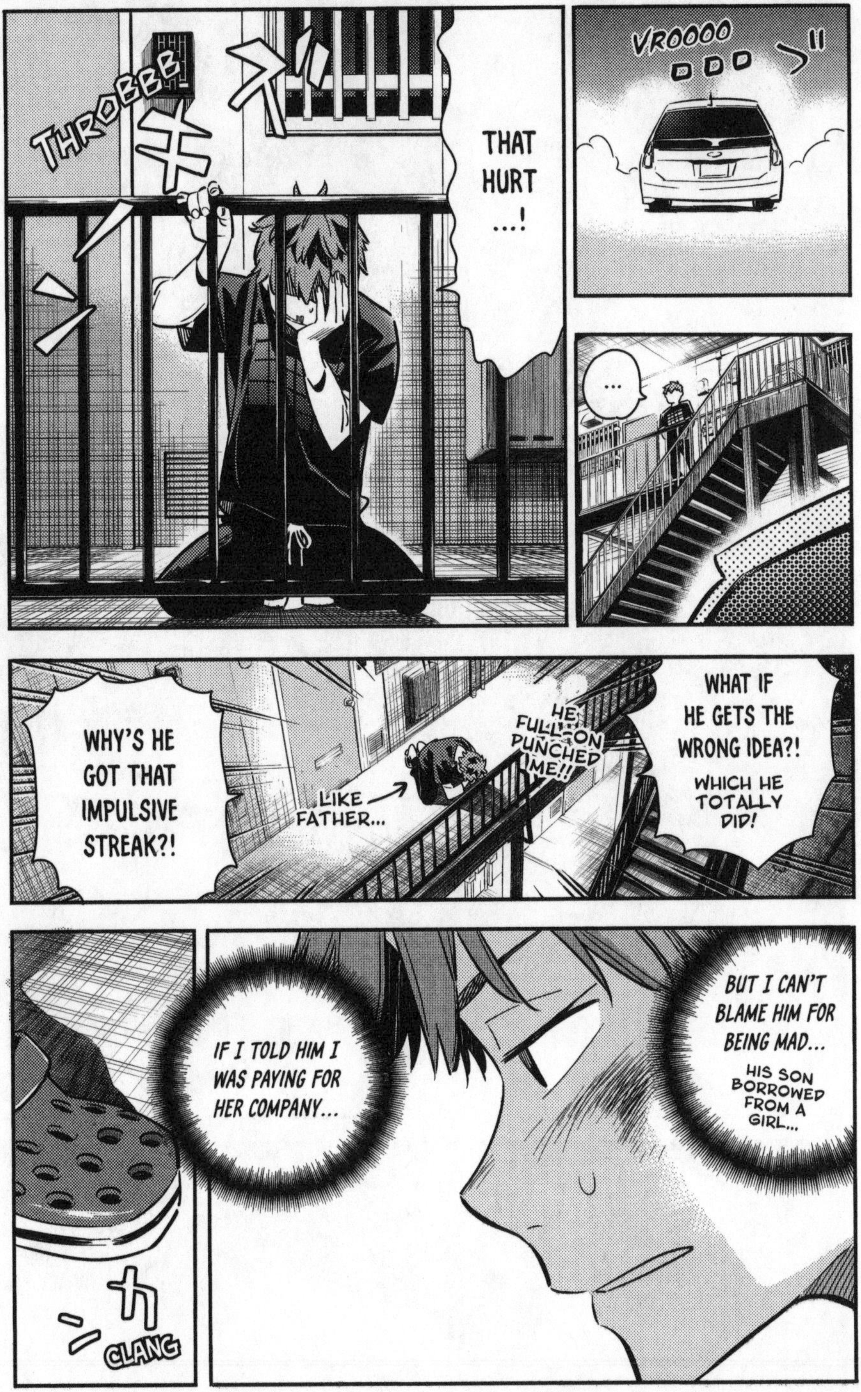

VROOOOOOO
...
THROBBB
THAT HURT ...!
WHAT IF HE GETS THE WRONG IDEA?!
WHICH HE TOTALLY DID!
HE FULL-ON PUNCHED ME!!
LIKE FATHER...
WHY'S HE GOT THAT IMPULSIVE STREAK?!
BUT I CAN'T BLAME HIM FOR BEING MAD...
HIS SON BORROWED FROM A GIRL...
IF I TOLD HIM I WAS PAYING FOR HER COMPANY...
CLANG

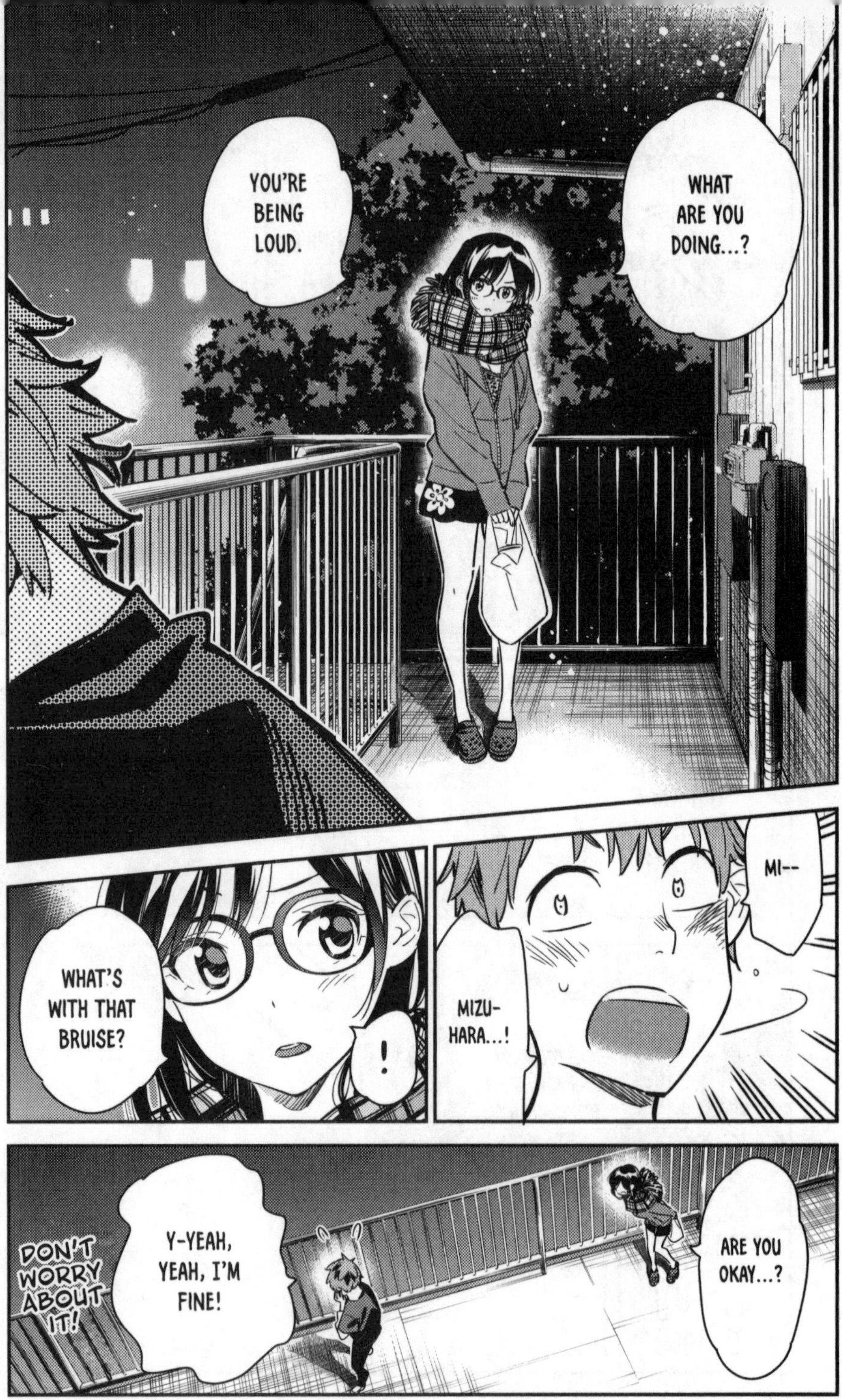
WHAT ARE YOU DOING...?
YOU'RE BEING LOUD.
MI--
MIZU-HARA...!
!
WHAT'S WITH THAT BRUISE?
ARE YOU OKAY...?
Y-YEAH, YEAH, I'M FINE!
DON'T WORRY ABOUT IT!

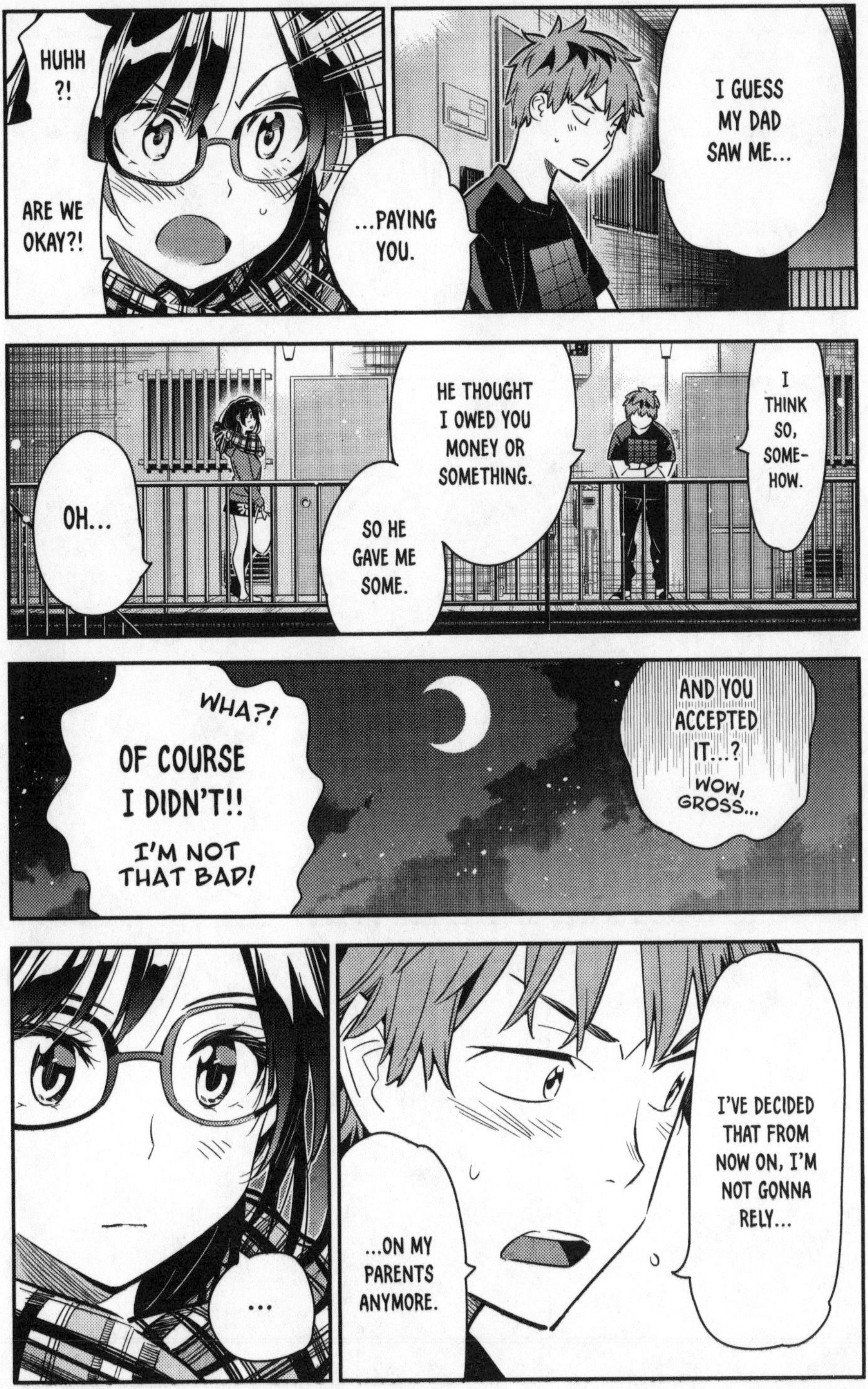
I GUESS MY DAD SAW ME...
...PAYING YOU.
HUHH ?!
ARE WE OKAY?!
I THINK SO, SOME-HOW.
HE THOUGHT I OWED YOU MONEY OR SOMETHING.
SO HE GAVE ME SOME.
OH...
AND YOU ACCEPTED IT...?
WOW, GROSS...
WHA?!
OF COURSE I DIDN'T!!
I'M NOT THAT BAD!
I'VE DECIDED THAT FROM NOW ON, I'M NOT GONNA RELY...
...ON MY PARENTS ANYMORE.
...

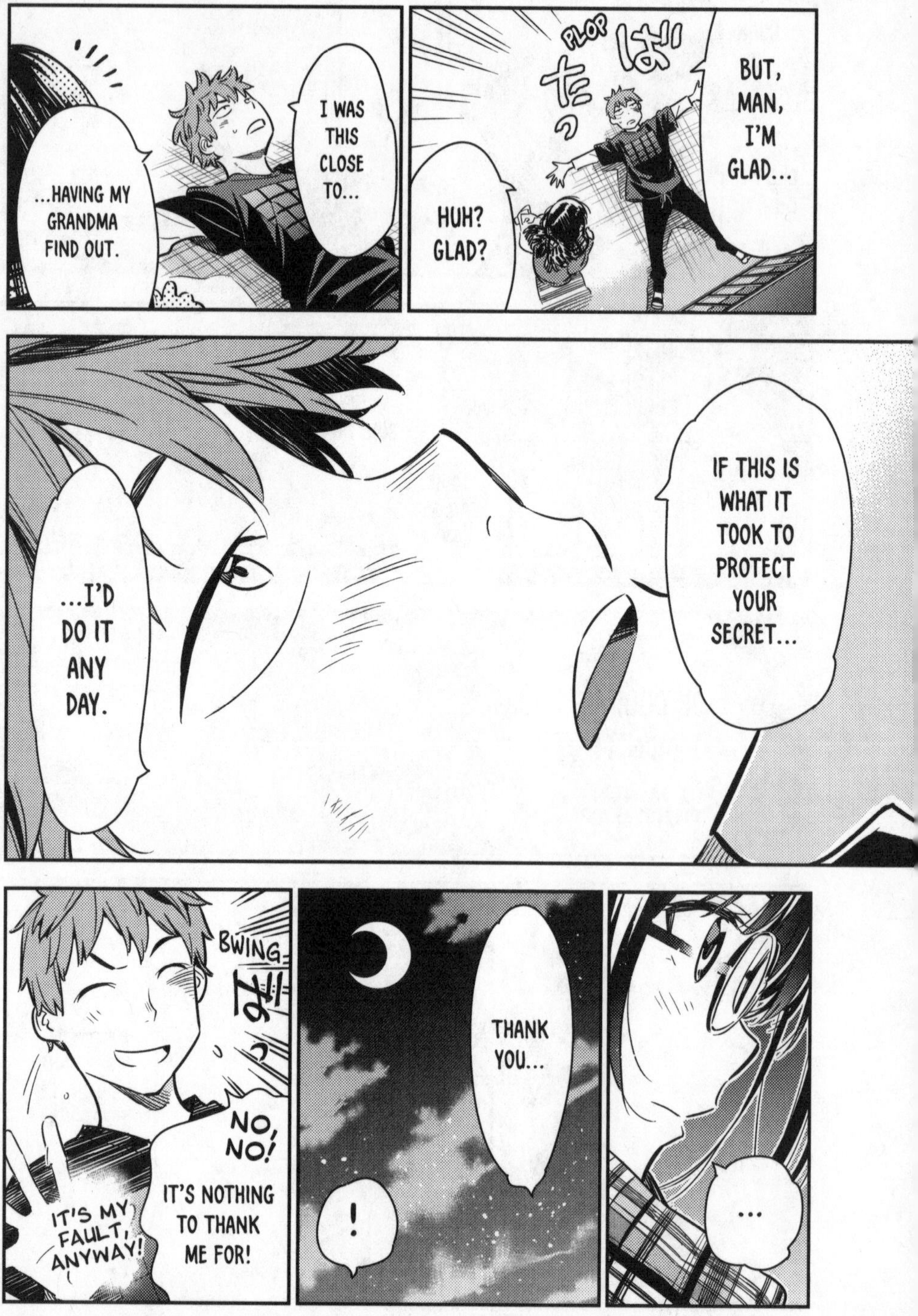
PLOP
BUT, MAN, I'M GLAD...
HUH? GLAD?
I WAS THIS CLOSE TO...
...HAVING MY GRANDMA FIND OUT.
IF THIS IS WHAT IT TOOK TO PROTECT YOUR SECRET...
...I'D DO IT ANY DAY.
...
THANK YOU...
!
BWING
NO, NO!
IT'S NOTHING TO THANK ME FOR!
IT'S MY FAULT, ANYWAY!

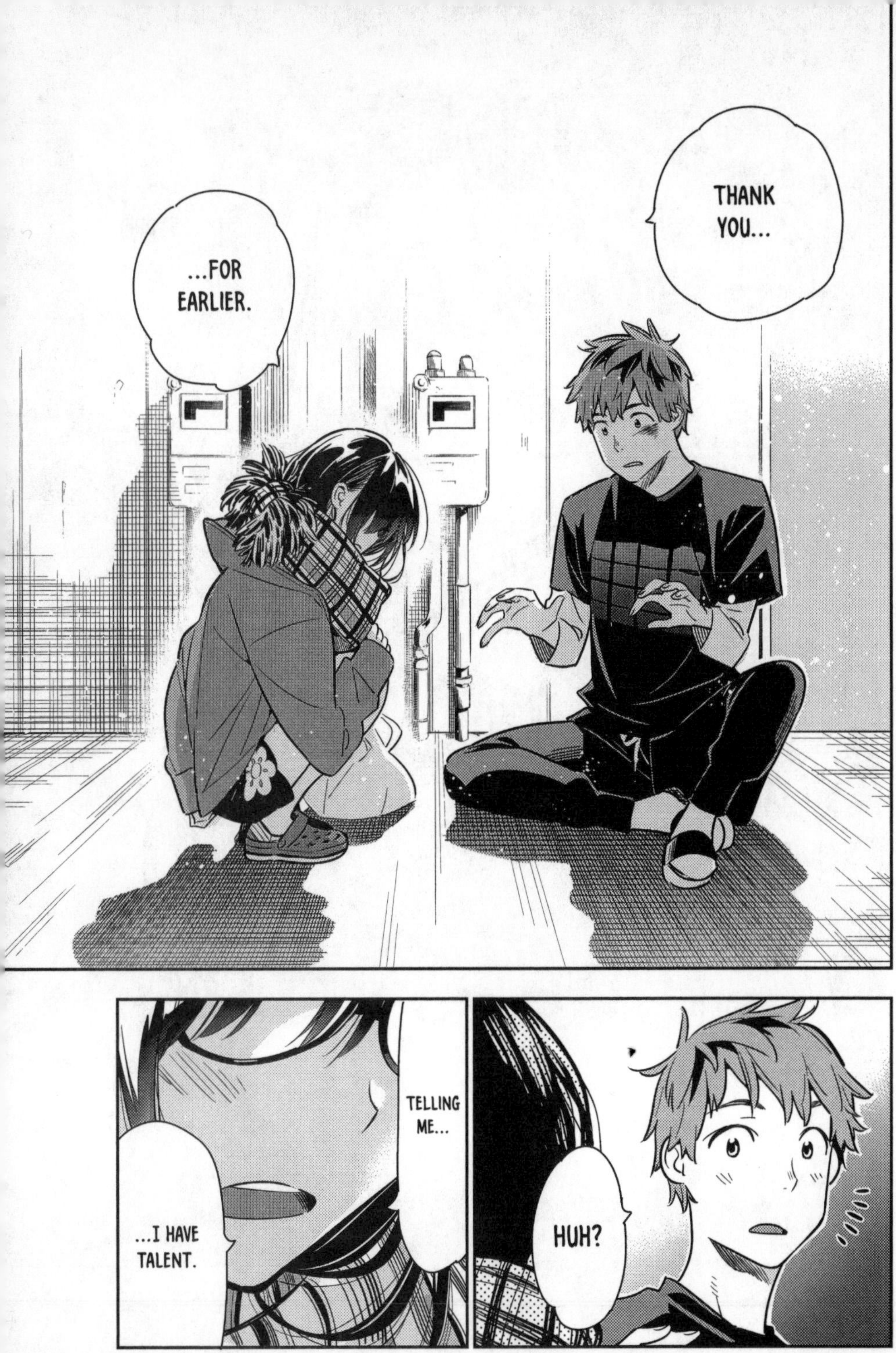
THANK YOU...
...FOR EARLIER.
HUH?
TELLING ME...
...I HAVE TALENT.

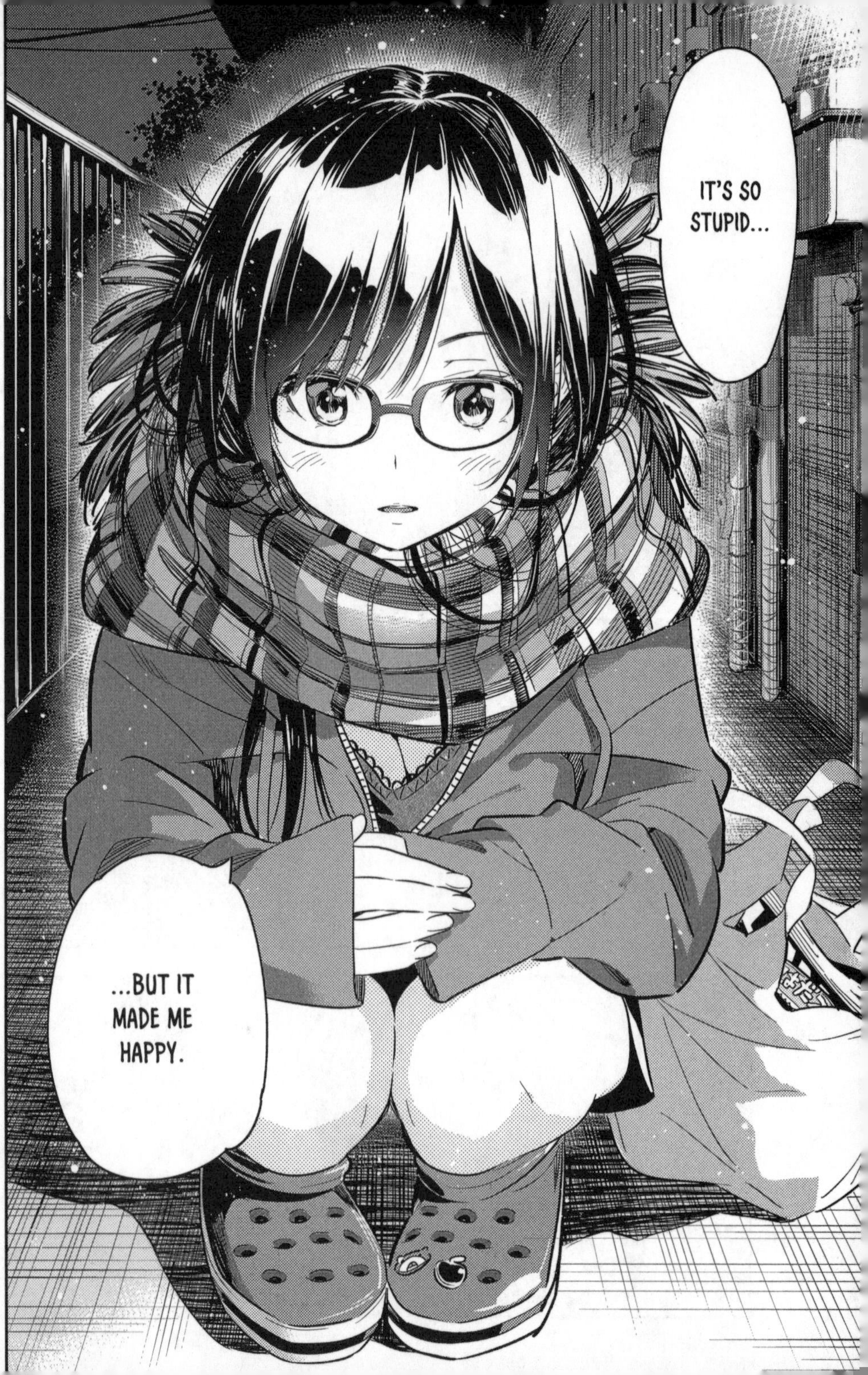
IT'S SO STUPID...
...BUT IT MADE ME HAPPY.

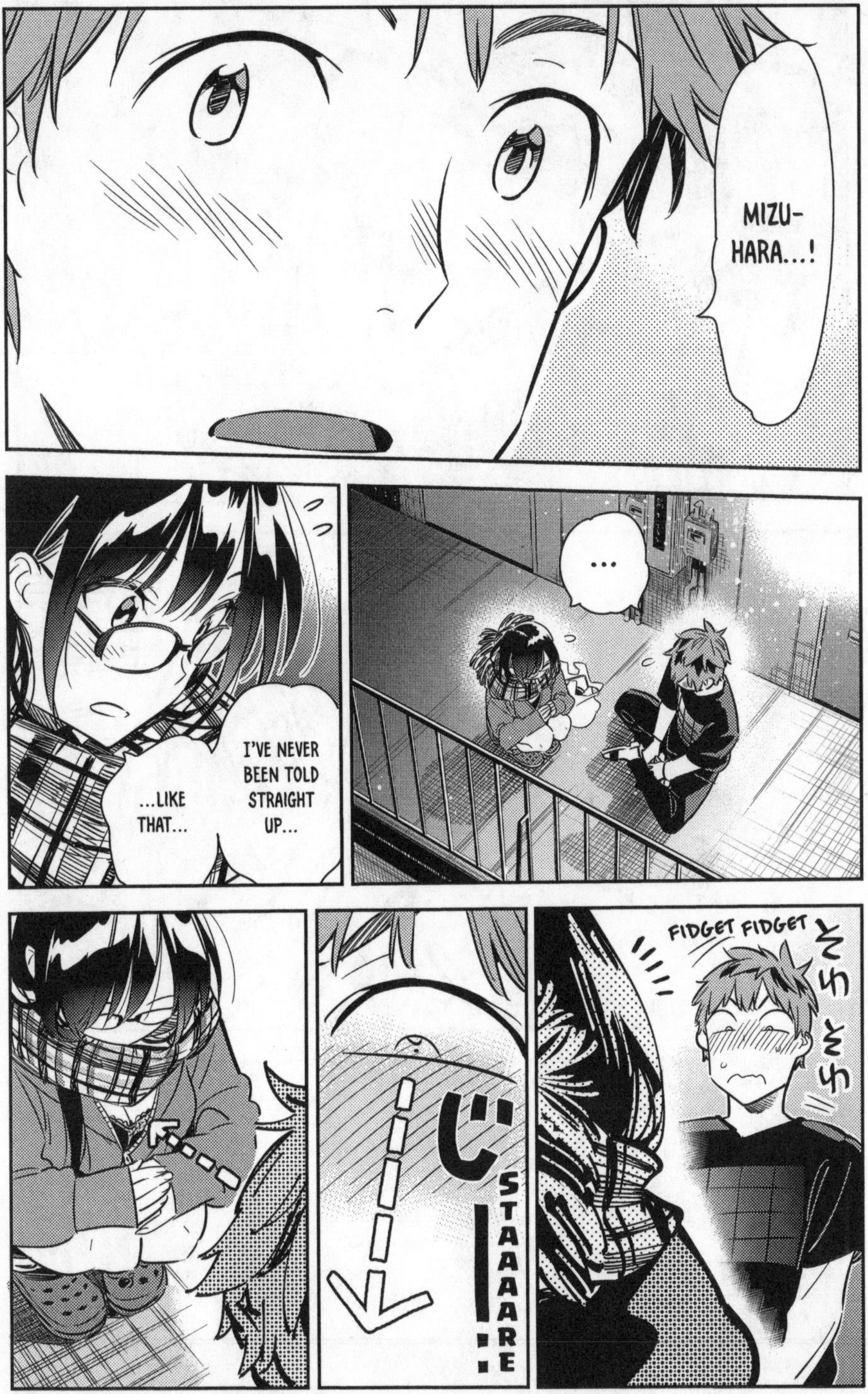
MIZU-HARA...!
...
I'VE NEVER BEEN TOLD STRAIGHT UP...
...LIKE THAT...
FIDGET FIDGET
STAAAARE

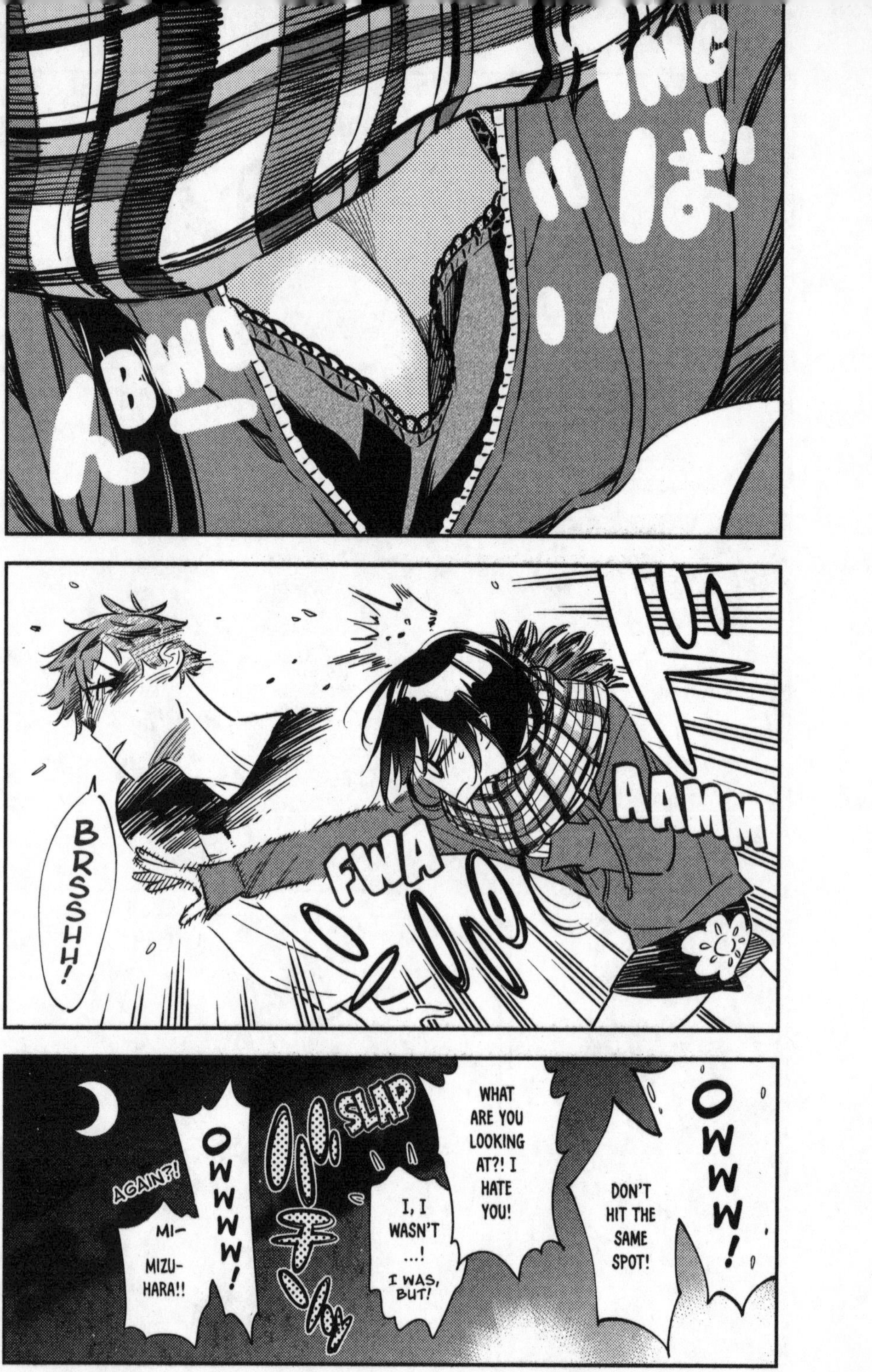
BWO
ING
AAMM
FWA
BRSSHH!
OWWW!
DON'T HIT THE SAME SPOT!
WHAT ARE YOU LOOKING AT?! I HATE YOU!
I, I WASN'T ...!
I WAS, BUT!
SLAP
OWWWWW!
MI-MIZUHARA!!
AGAIN?!

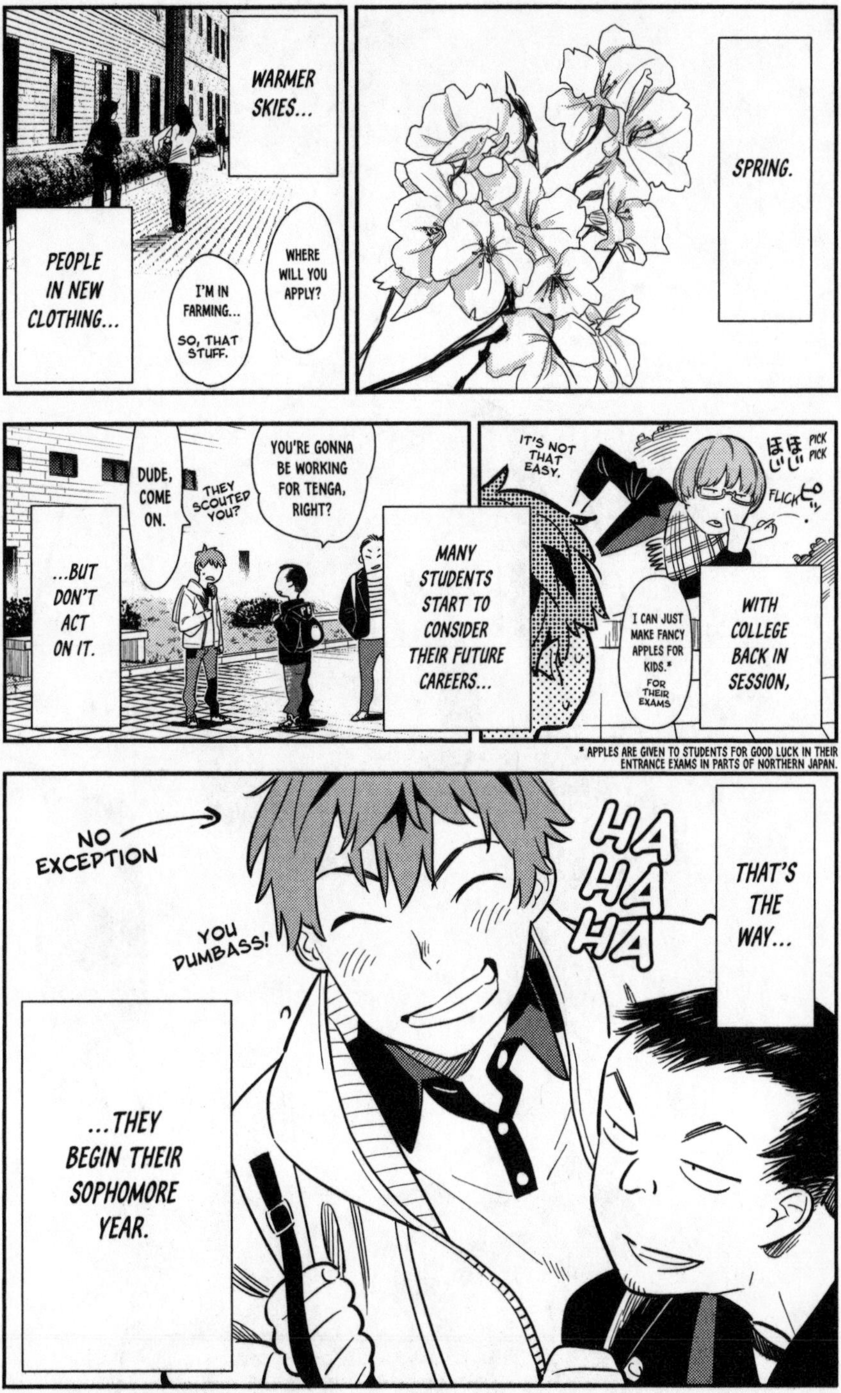
SPRING.
WARMER SKIES...
PEOPLE IN NEW CLOTHING...
WHERE WILL YOU APPLY?
I'M IN FARMING... SO, THAT STUFF.
WITH COLLEGE BACK IN SESSION,
IT'S NOT THAT EASY.
ほじほじ PICK PICK
ピッ FLICK
I CAN JUST MAKE FANCY APPLES FOR KIDS.* FOR THEIR EXAMS
MANY STUDENTS START TO CONSIDER THEIR FUTURE CAREERS...
YOU'RE GONNA BE WORKING FOR TENGA, RIGHT?
THEY SCOUTED YOU?
DUDE, COME ON.
...BUT DON'T ACT ON IT.
THAT'S THE WAY...
HA HA HA
NO EXCEPTION
YOU DUMBASS!
...THEY BEGIN THEIR SOPHOMORE YEAR.

* APPLES ARE GIVEN TO STUDENTS FOR GOOD LUCK IN THEIR ENTRANCE EXAMS IN PARTS OF NORTHERN JAPAN.

RATING 56 MY "GIRLFRIEND," CHIZURU ICHINOSE 1

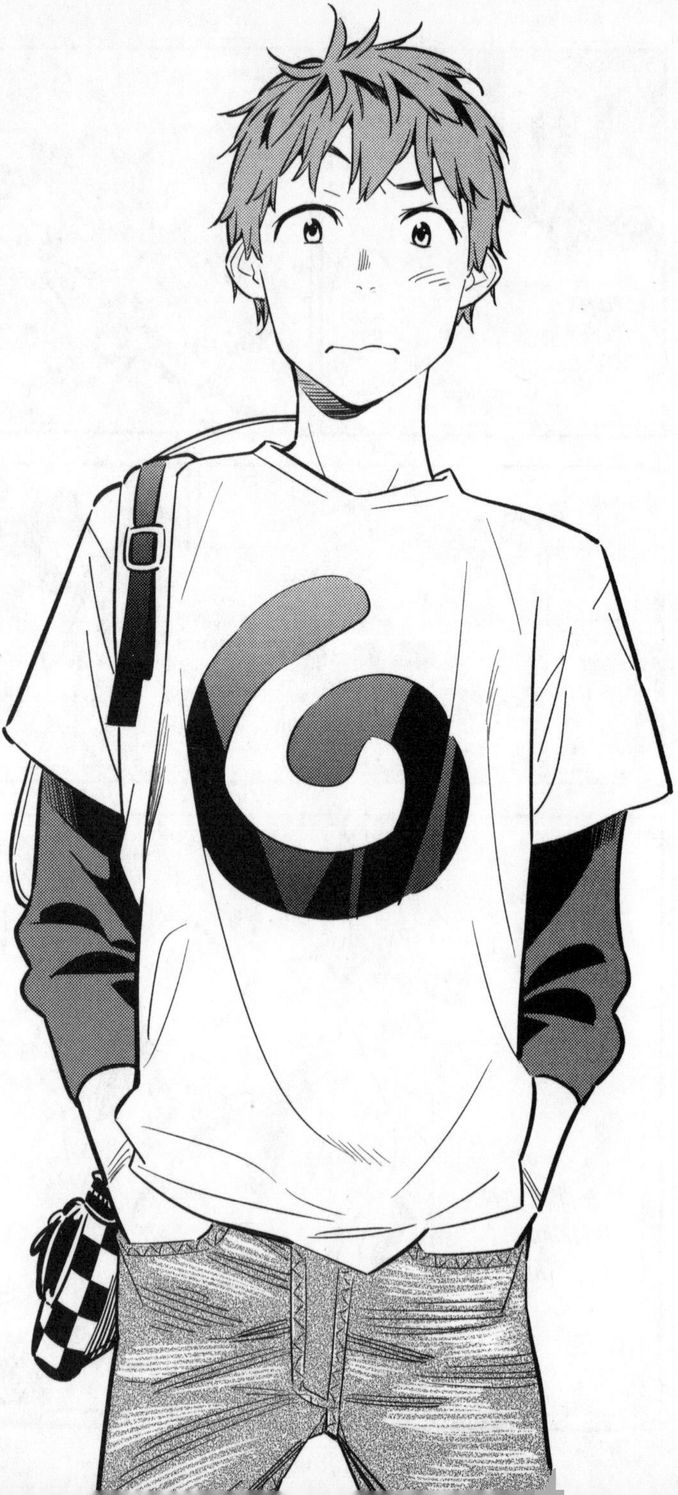

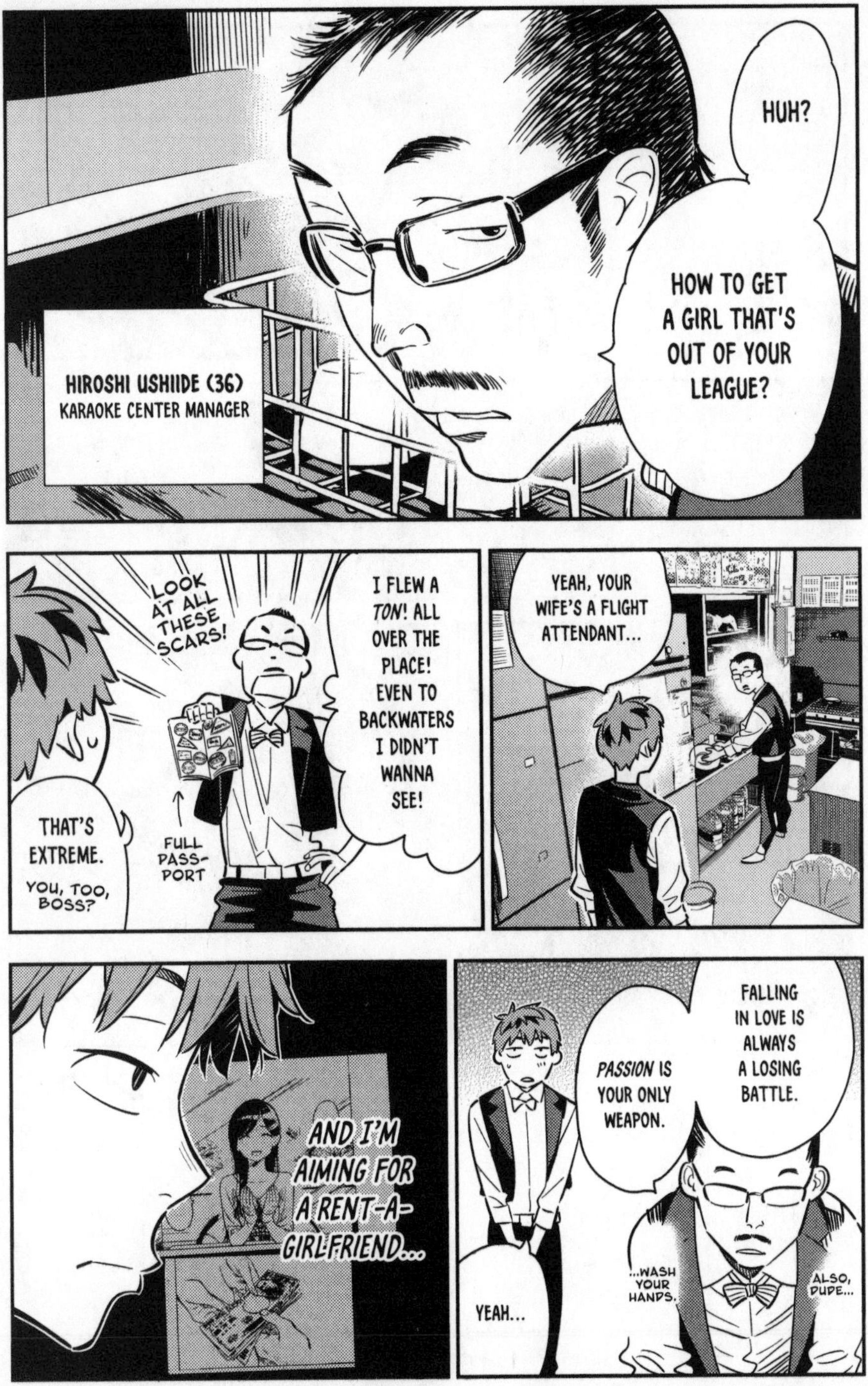
HUH?
HOW TO GET A GIRL THAT'S OUT OF YOUR LEAGUE?
HIROSHI USHIIDE (36)
KARAOKE CENTER MANAGER
YEAH, YOUR WIFE'S A FLIGHT ATTENDANT...
I FLEW A *TON*! ALL OVER THE PLACE! EVEN TO BACKWATERS I DIDN'T WANNA SEE!
LOOK AT ALL THESE SCARS!
FULL PASSPORT
THAT'S EXTREME.
YOU, TOO, BOSS?
FALLING IN LOVE IS ALWAYS A LOSING BATTLE.
PASSION IS YOUR ONLY WEAPON.
ALSO, DUDE...
...WASH YOUR HANDS.
YEAH...
AND I'M AIMING FOR A RENT-A-GIRLFRIEND...

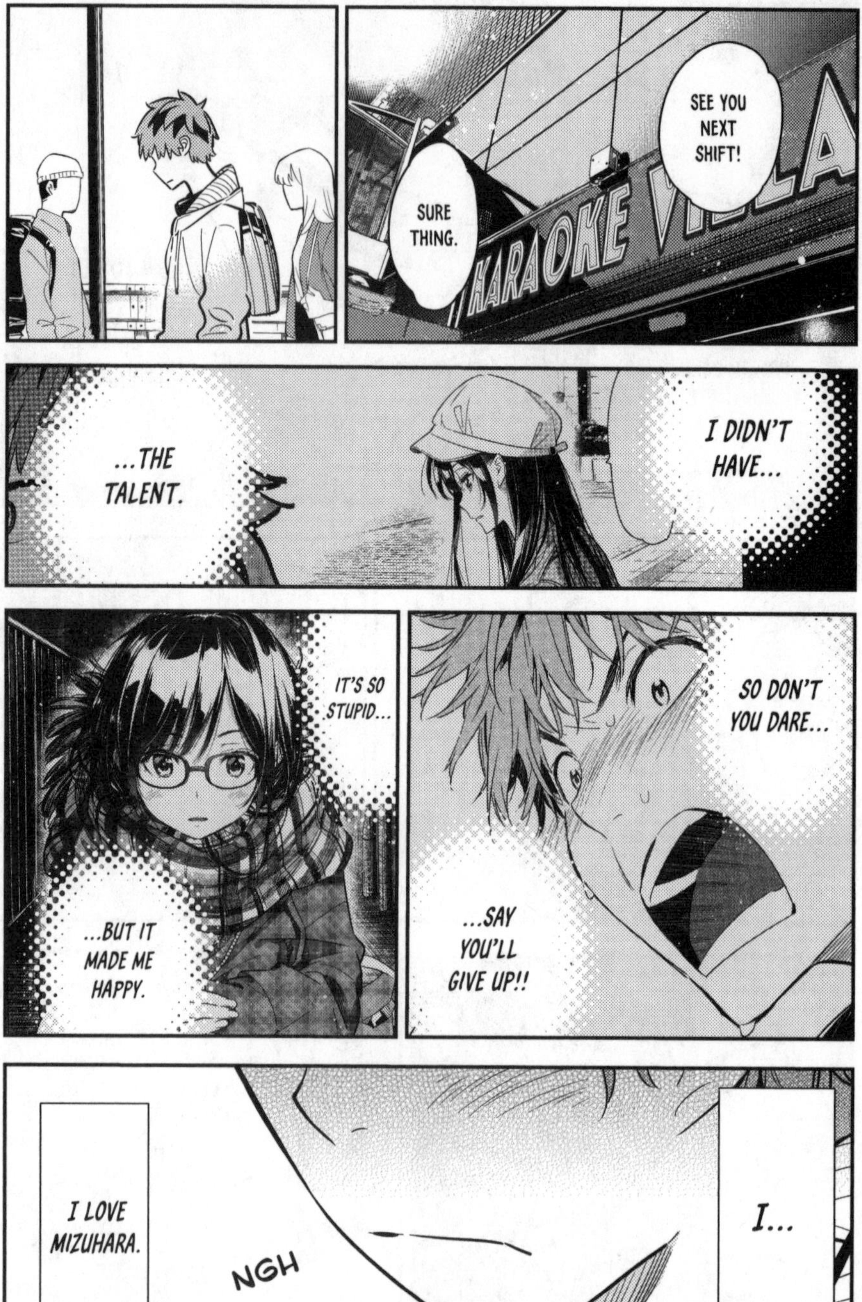
SEE YOU NEXT SHIFT!
SURE THING.
KARAOKE
I DIDN'T HAVE...
...THE TALENT.
SO DON'T YOU DARE...
...SAY YOU'LL GIVE UP!!
IT'S SO STUPID...
...BUT IT MADE ME HAPPY.
I...
NGH
I LOVE MIZUHARA.

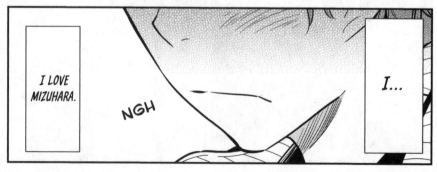

I LOVE...

MIZU-HARA!!

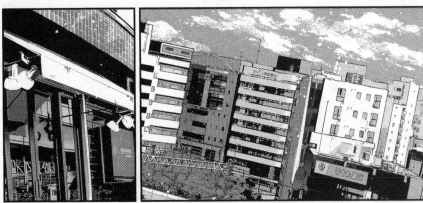

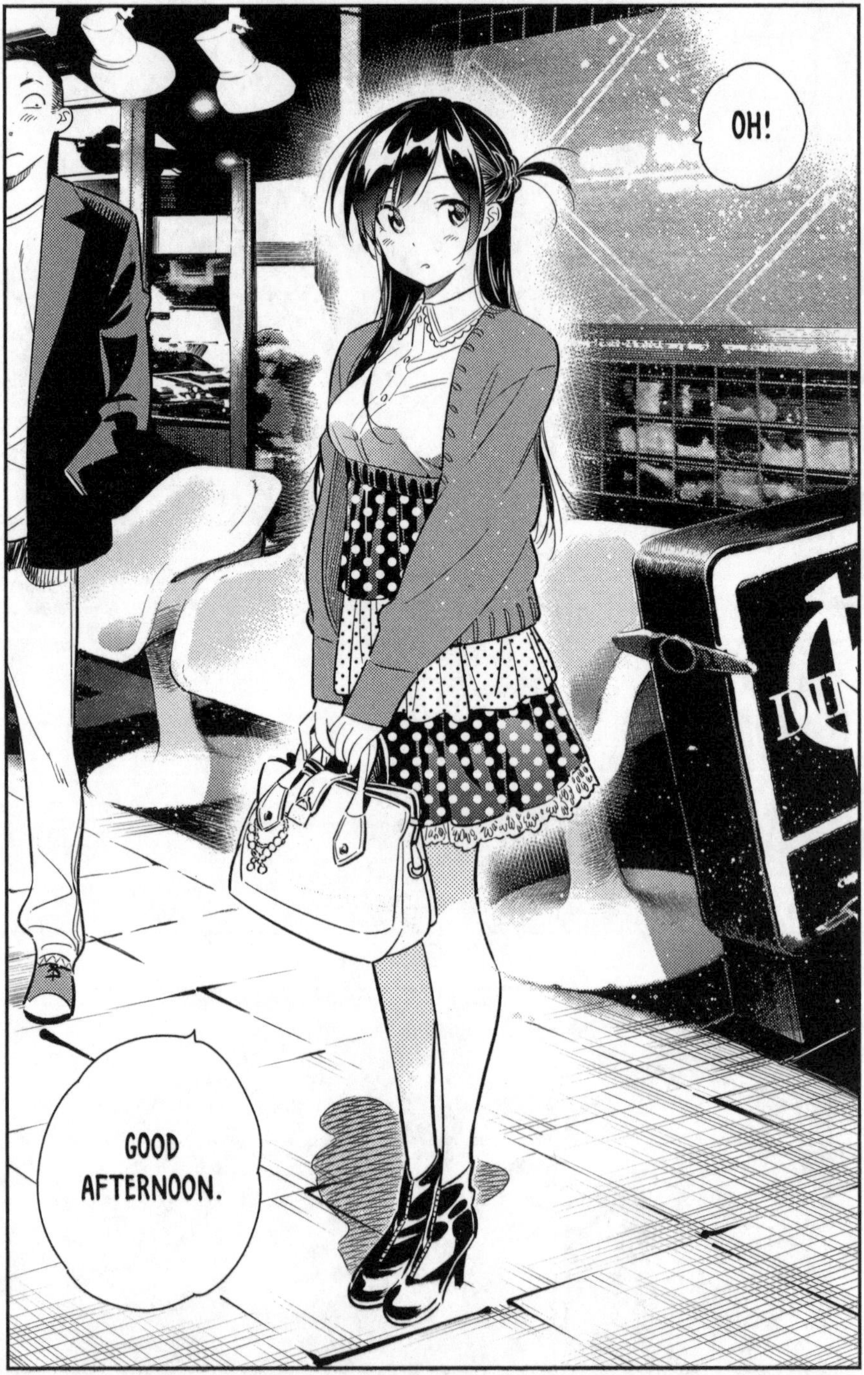
OH!
GOOD AFTERNOON.

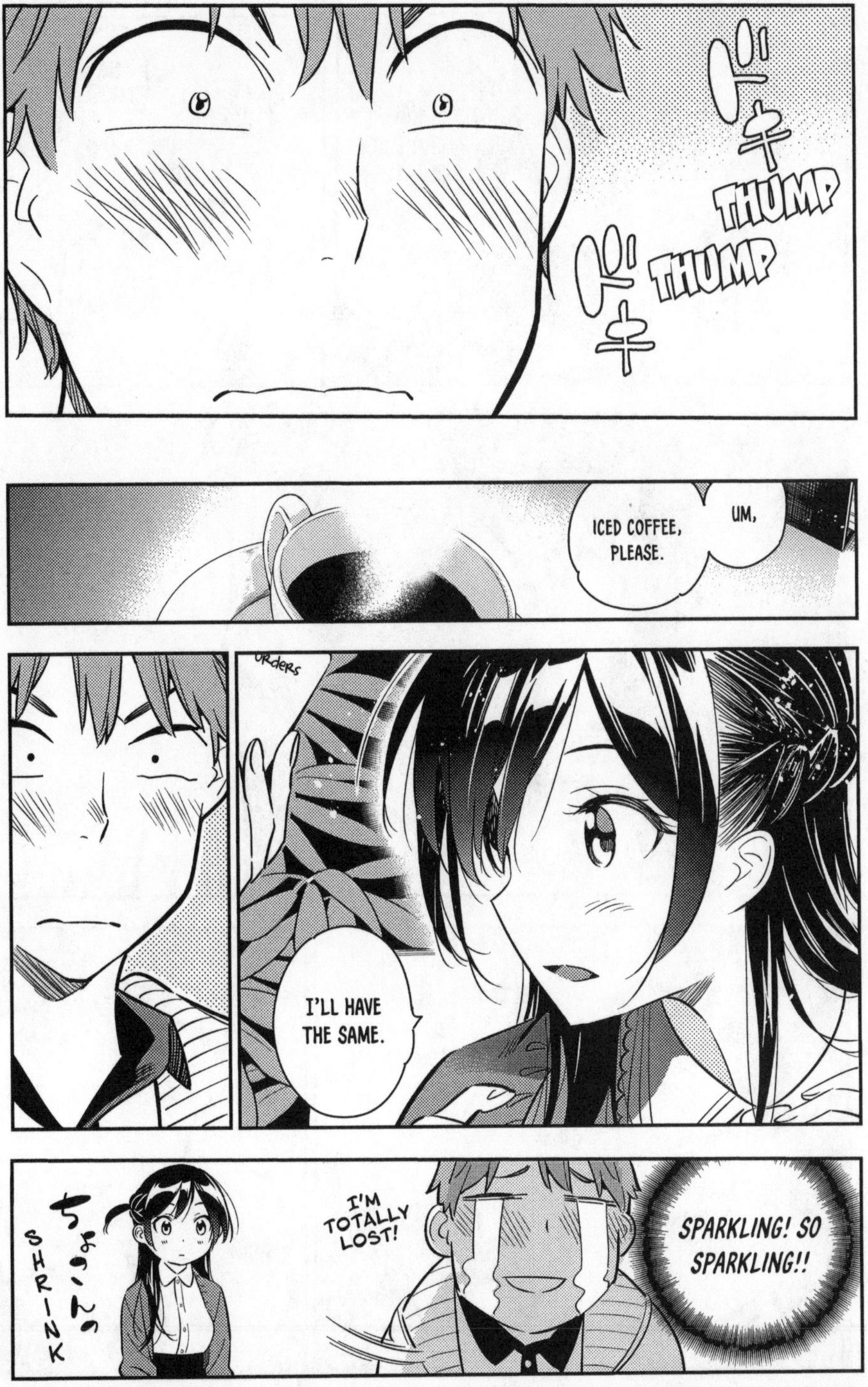

ドキ
THUMP
ドキ
THUMP
UM,
ICED COFFEE, PLEASE.
ORDERS
I'LL HAVE THE SAME.
SPARKLING! SO SPARKLING!!
I'M TOTALLY LOST!
SHRINK

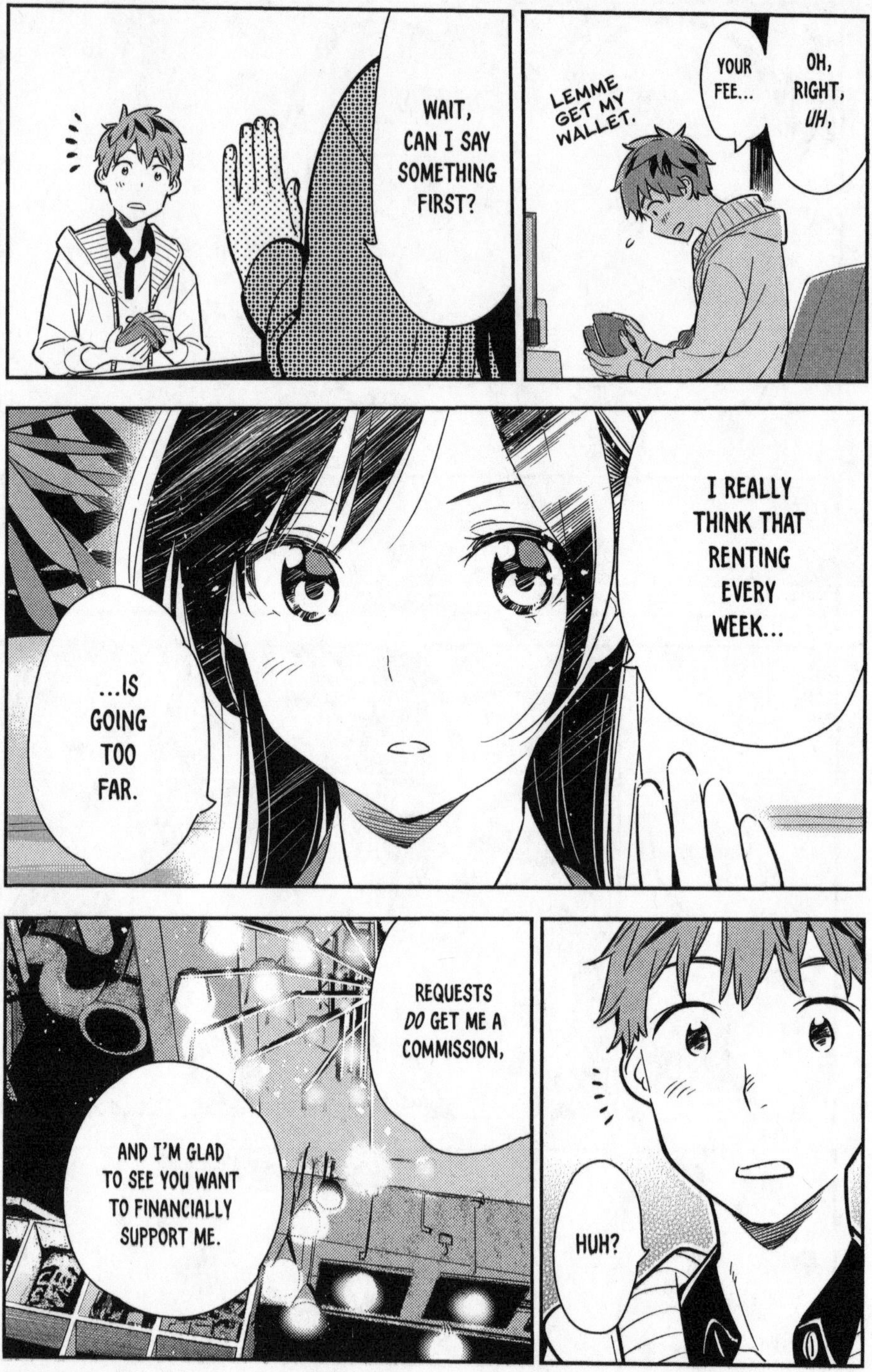

OH, RIGHT, *UH,*
YOUR FEE...
LEMME GET MY WALLET.
WAIT, CAN I SAY SOMETHING FIRST?
I REALLY THINK THAT RENTING EVERY WEEK...
...IS GOING TOO FAR.
HUH?
REQUESTS *DO* GET ME A COMMISSION,
AND I'M GLAD TO SEE YOU WANT TO FINANCIALLY SUPPORT ME.

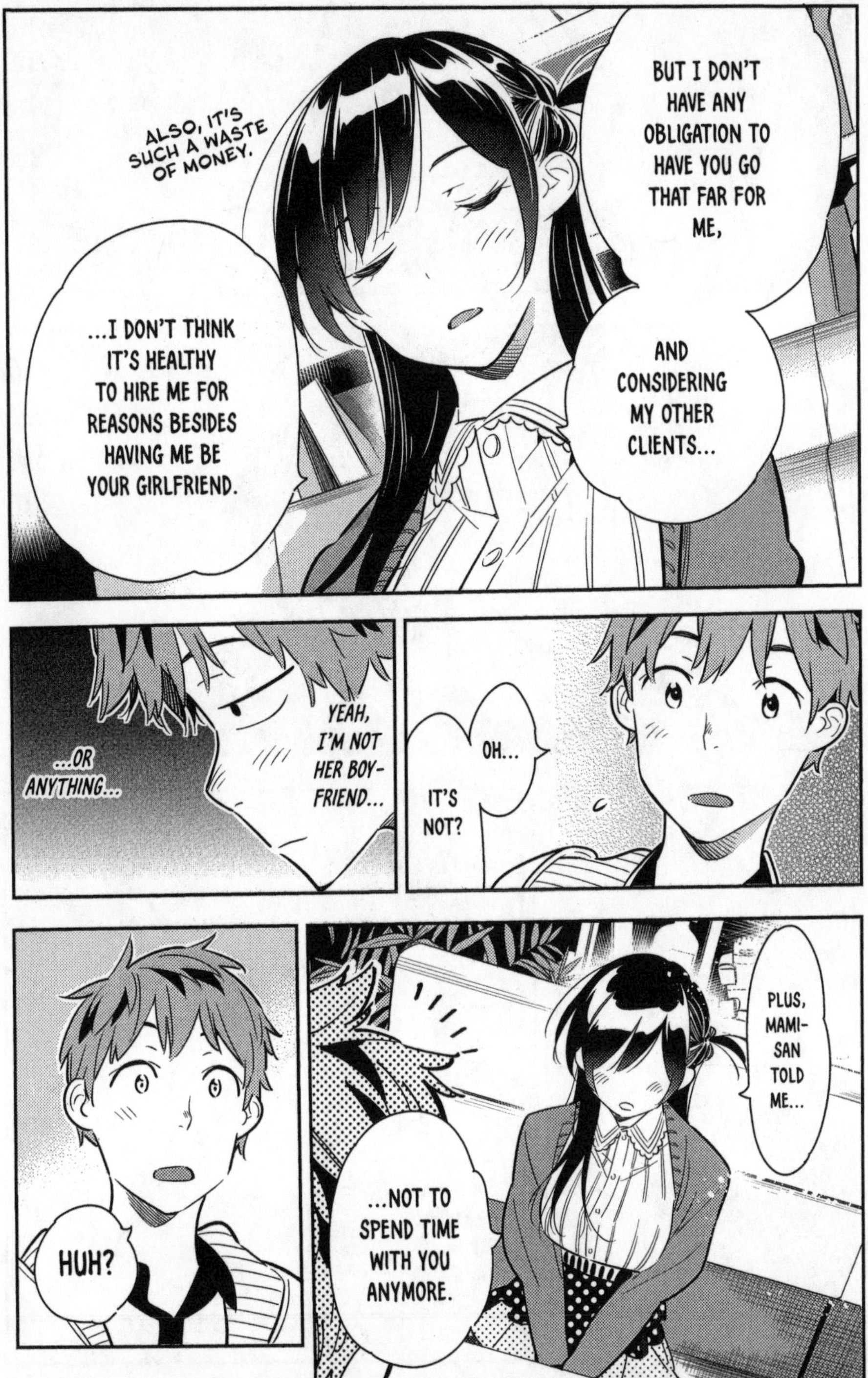
BUT I DON'T HAVE ANY OBLIGATION TO HAVE YOU GO THAT FAR FOR ME,
AND CONSIDERING MY OTHER CLIENTS...
...I DON'T THINK IT'S HEALTHY TO HIRE ME FOR REASONS BESIDES HAVING ME BE YOUR GIRLFRIEND.
ALSO, IT'S SUCH A WASTE OF MONEY.
OH...
IT'S NOT?
YEAH, I'M NOT HER BOY-FRIEND...
...OR ANYTHING...
PLUS, MAMI-SAN TOLD ME...
...NOT TO SPEND TIME WITH YOU ANYMORE.
HUH?

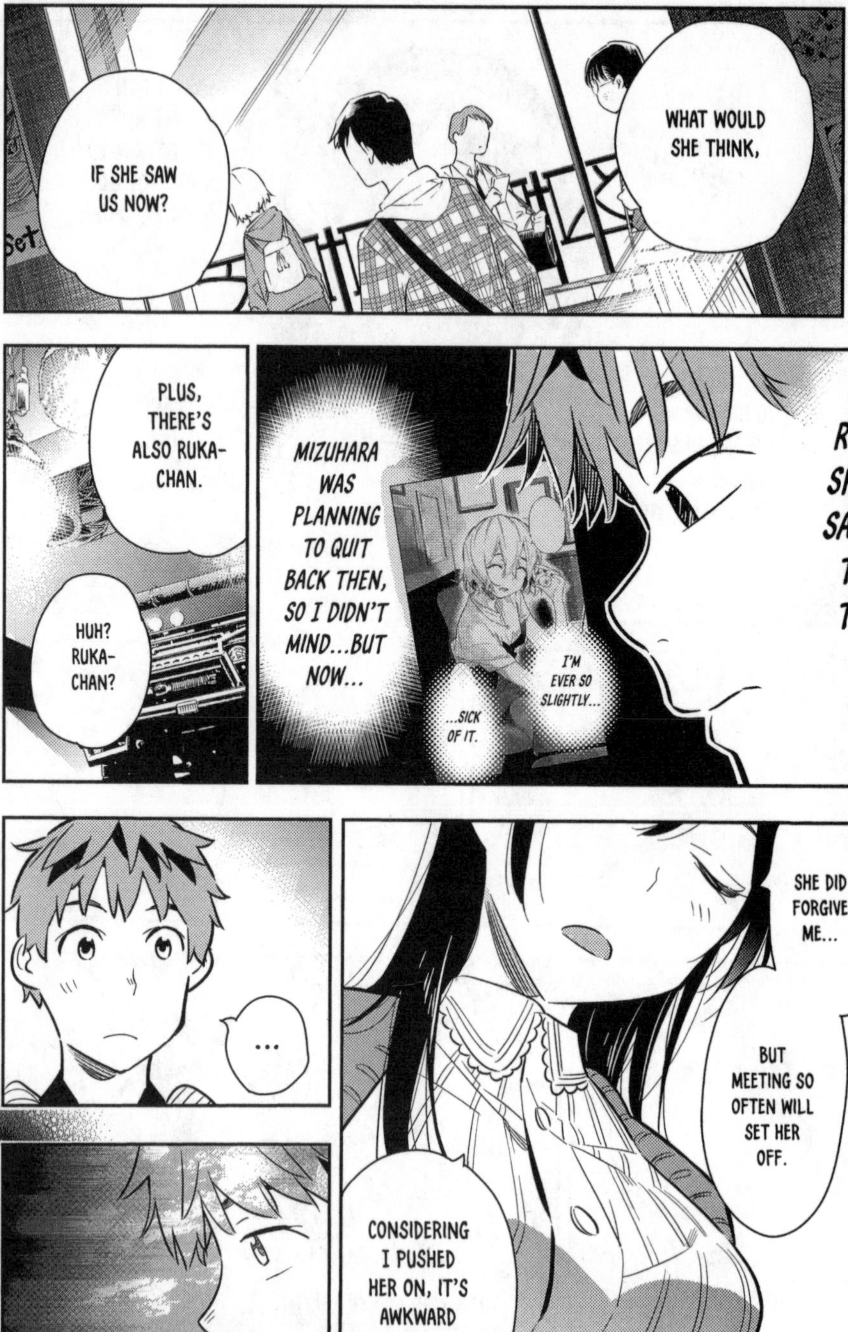
WHAT WOULD SHE THINK,
IF SHE SAW US NOW?
OH, RIGHT, SHE DID SAY NOT TO DO THAT.
MIZUHARA WAS PLANNING TO QUIT BACK THEN, SO I DIDN'T MIND...BUT NOW...
I'M EVER SO SLIGHTLY...
...SICK OF IT.
PLUS, THERE'S ALSO RUKA-CHAN.
HUH? RUKA-CHAN?
SHE DID FORGIVE ME...
BUT MEETING SO OFTEN WILL SET HER OFF.
CONSIDERING I PUSHED HER ON, IT'S AWKWARD FOR ME.
...

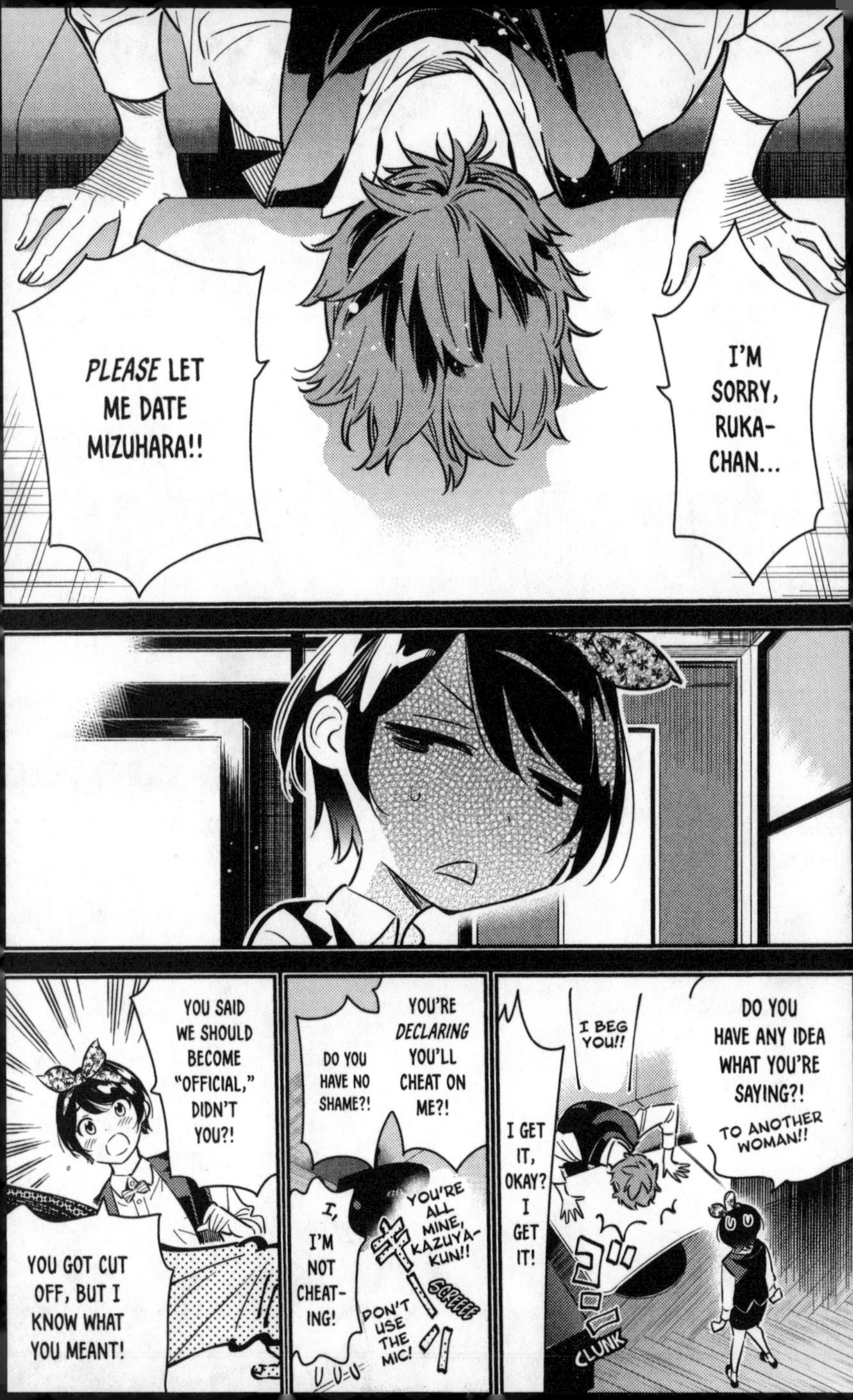
I'M SORRY, RUKA-CHAN...
PLEASE LET ME DATE MIZUHARA!!
DO YOU HAVE ANY IDEA WHAT YOU'RE SAYING?!
TO ANOTHER WOMAN!!
I BEG YOU!!
I GET IT, OKAY? I GET IT!
CLUNK
YOU'RE *DECLARING* YOU'LL CHEAT ON ME?!
DO YOU HAVE NO SHAME?!
YOU'RE ALL MINE, KAZUYA-KUN!!
I, I'M NOT CHEATING!
DON'T USE THE MIC!
YOU SAID WE SHOULD BECOME "OFFICIAL," DIDN'T YOU?!
YOU GOT CUT OFF, BUT I KNOW WHAT YOU MEANT!

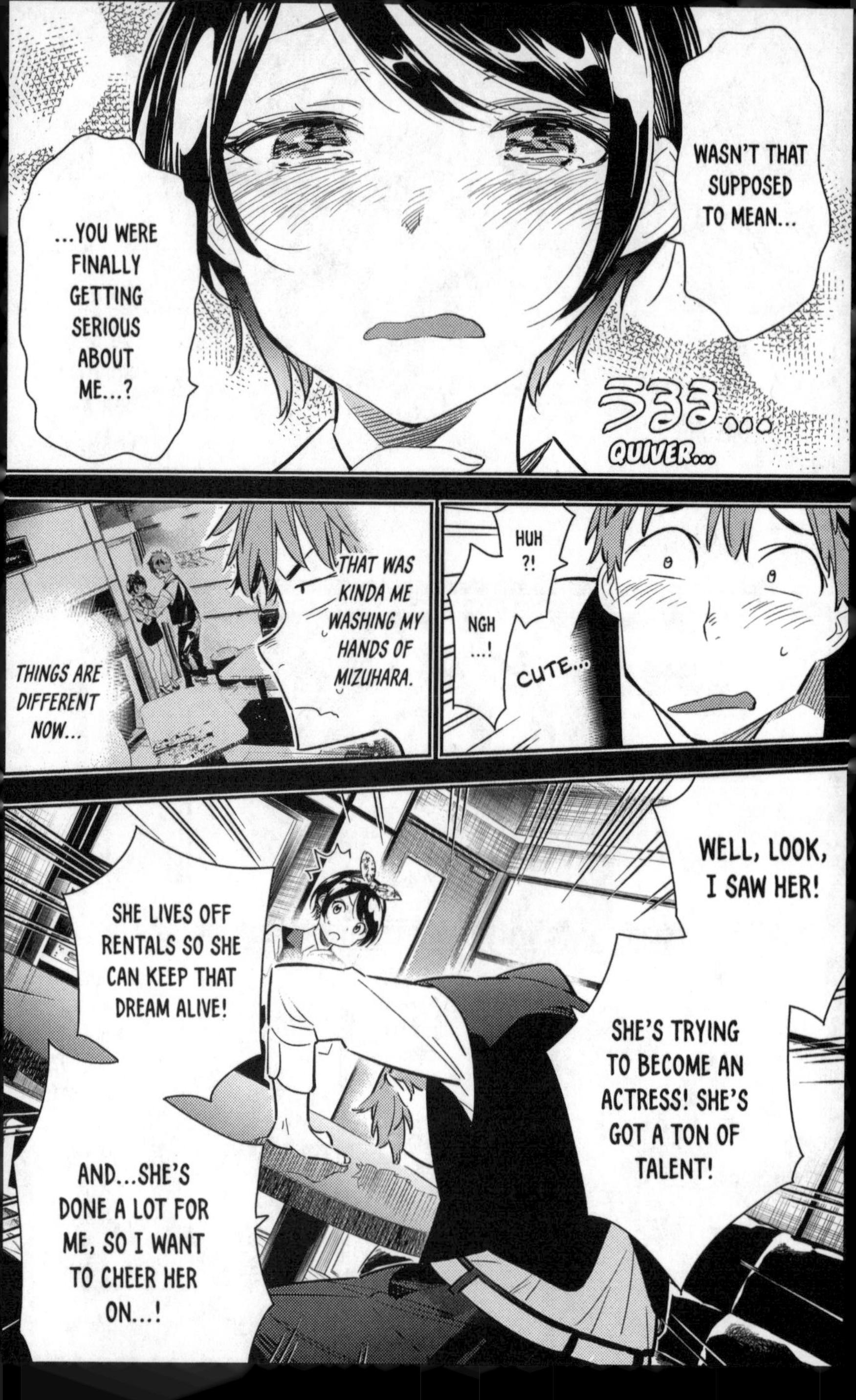
WASN'T THAT SUPPOSED TO MEAN...
...YOU WERE FINALLY GETTING SERIOUS ABOUT ME...?
うるる…
QUIVER...
HUH?!
NGH...!
CUTE...
THAT WAS KINDA ME WASHING MY HANDS OF MIZUHARA.
THINGS ARE DIFFERENT NOW...
WELL, LOOK, I SAW HER!
SHE'S TRYING TO BECOME AN ACTRESS! SHE'S GOT A TON OF TALENT!
SHE LIVES OFF RENTALS SO SHE CAN KEEP THAT DREAM ALIVE!
AND...SHE'S DONE A LOT FOR ME, SO I WANT TO CHEER HER ON...!

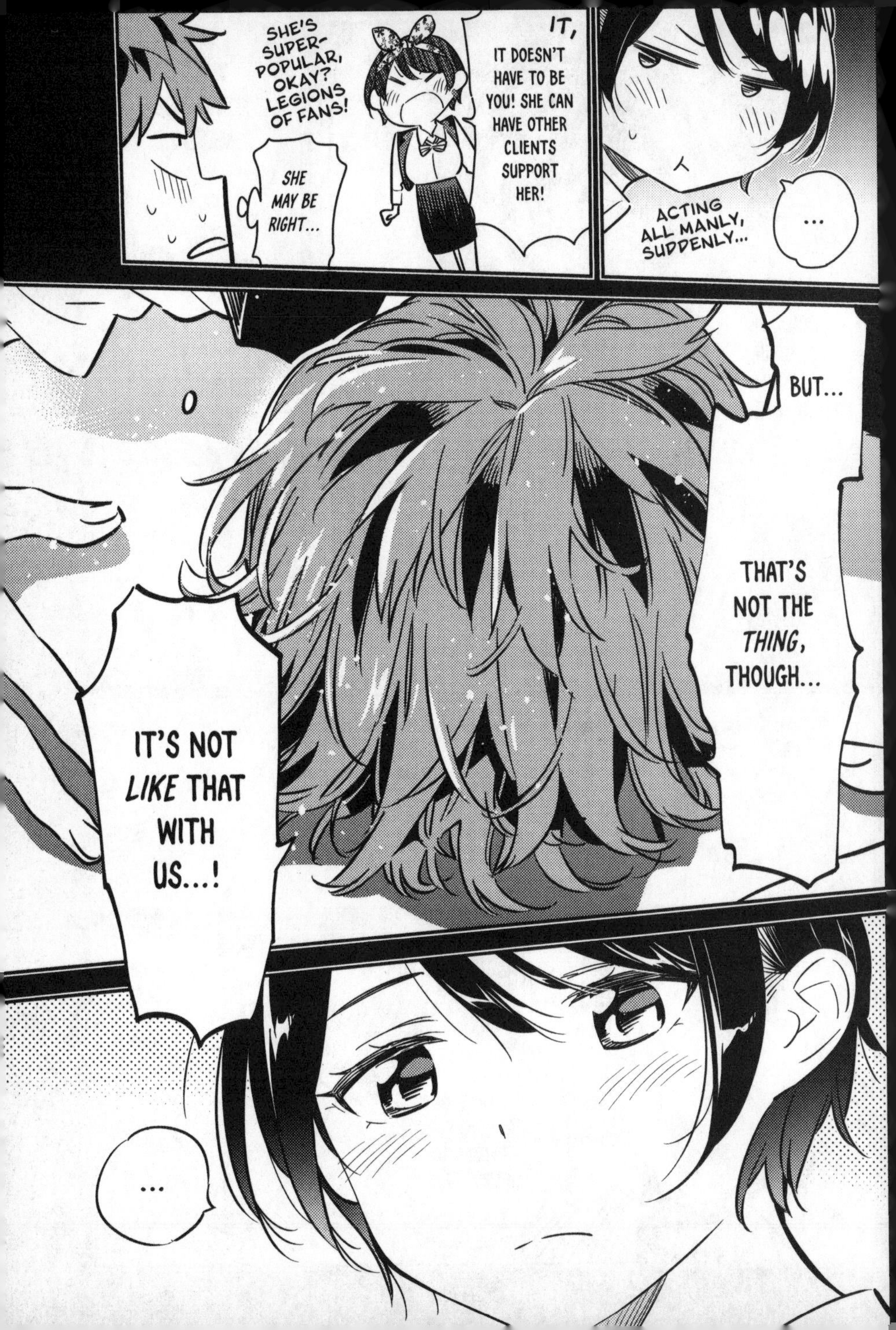
...
ACTING ALL MANLY, SUDDENLY...
IT, IT DOESN'T HAVE TO BE YOU! SHE CAN HAVE OTHER CLIENTS SUPPORT HER!
SHE'S SUPER-POPULAR, OKAY? LEGIONS OF FANS!
SHE MAY BE RIGHT...
BUT...
THAT'S NOT THE *THING*, THOUGH...
IT'S NOT *LIKE* THAT WITH US...!
...

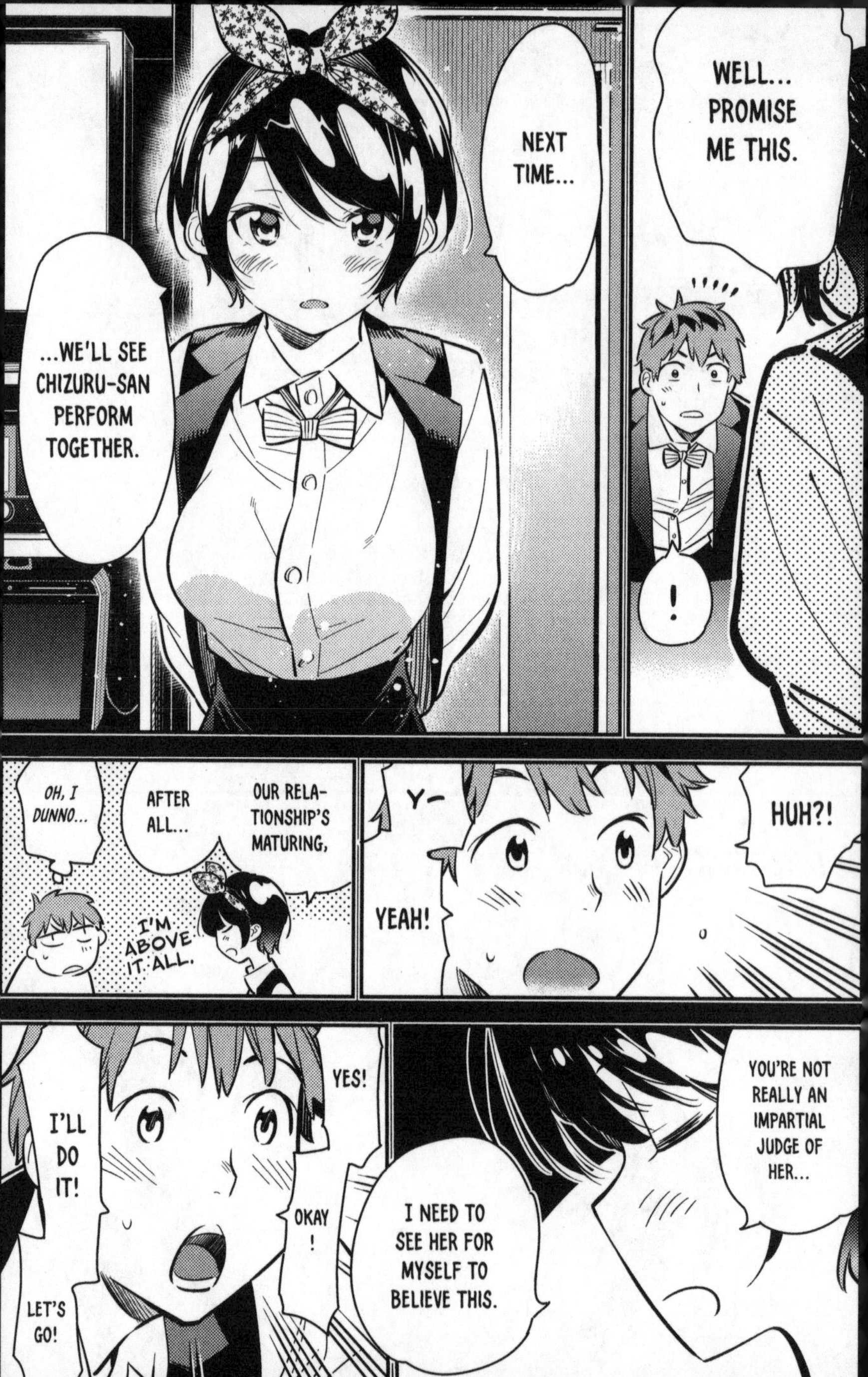

WELL... PROMISE ME THIS.
!
NEXT TIME...
...WE'LL SEE CHIZURU-SAN PERFORM TOGETHER.
HUH?!
Y-
YEAH!
OUR RELA-TIONSHIP'S MATURING,
AFTER ALL...
OH, I DUNNO...
I'M ABOVE IT ALL.
YOU'RE NOT REALLY AN IMPARTIAL JUDGE OF HER...
I NEED TO SEE HER FOR MYSELF TO BELIEVE THIS.
YES!
OKAY!
I'LL DO IT!
LET'S GO!

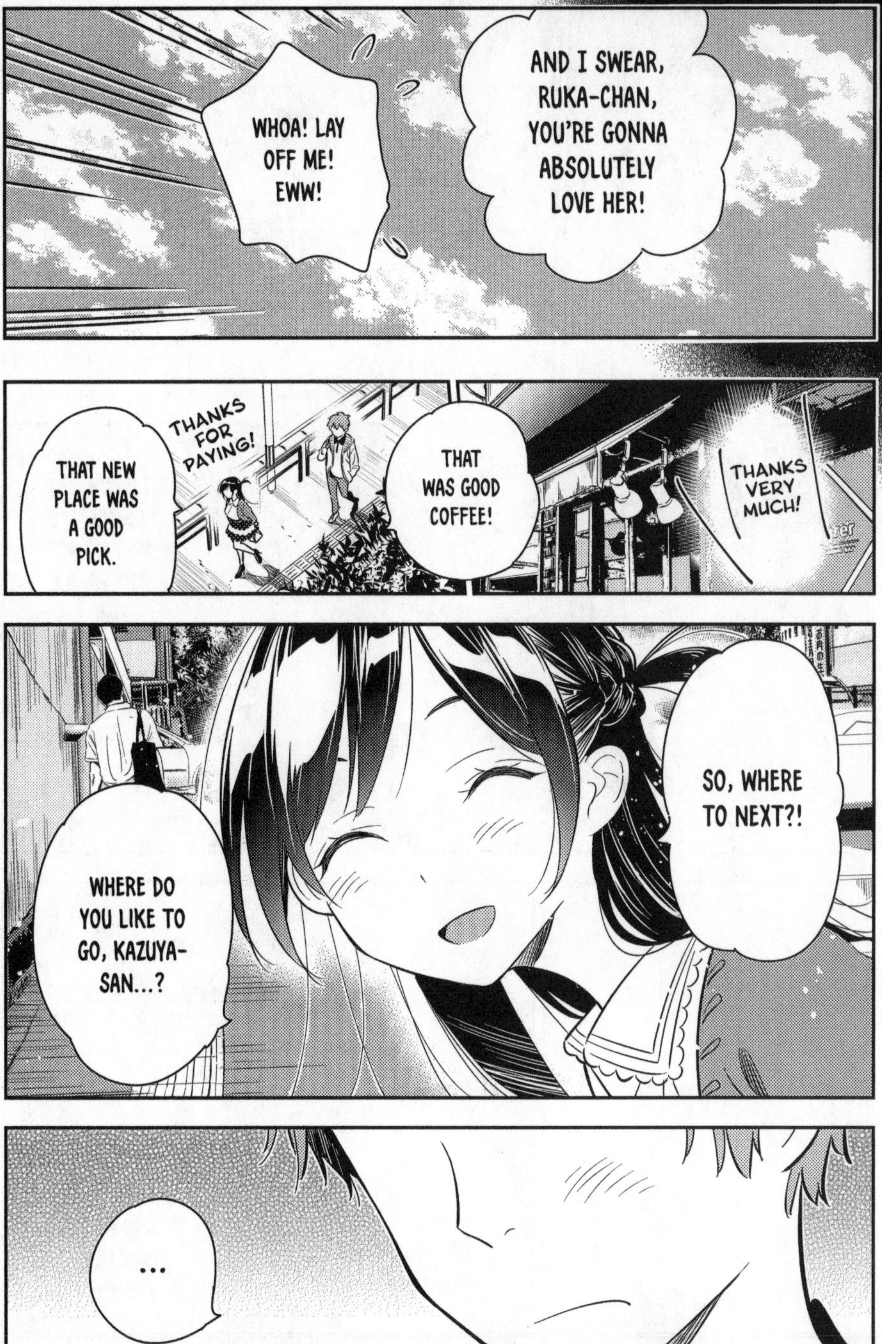
AND I SWEAR, RUKA-CHAN, YOU'RE GONNA ABSOLUTELY LOVE HER!
WHOA! LAY OFF ME! EWW!
THANKS VERY MUCH!
THAT WAS GOOD COFFEE!
THANKS FOR PAYING!
THAT NEW PLACE WAS A GOOD PICK.
SO, WHERE TO NEXT?!
WHERE DO YOU LIKE TO GO, KAZUYA-SAN...?
...

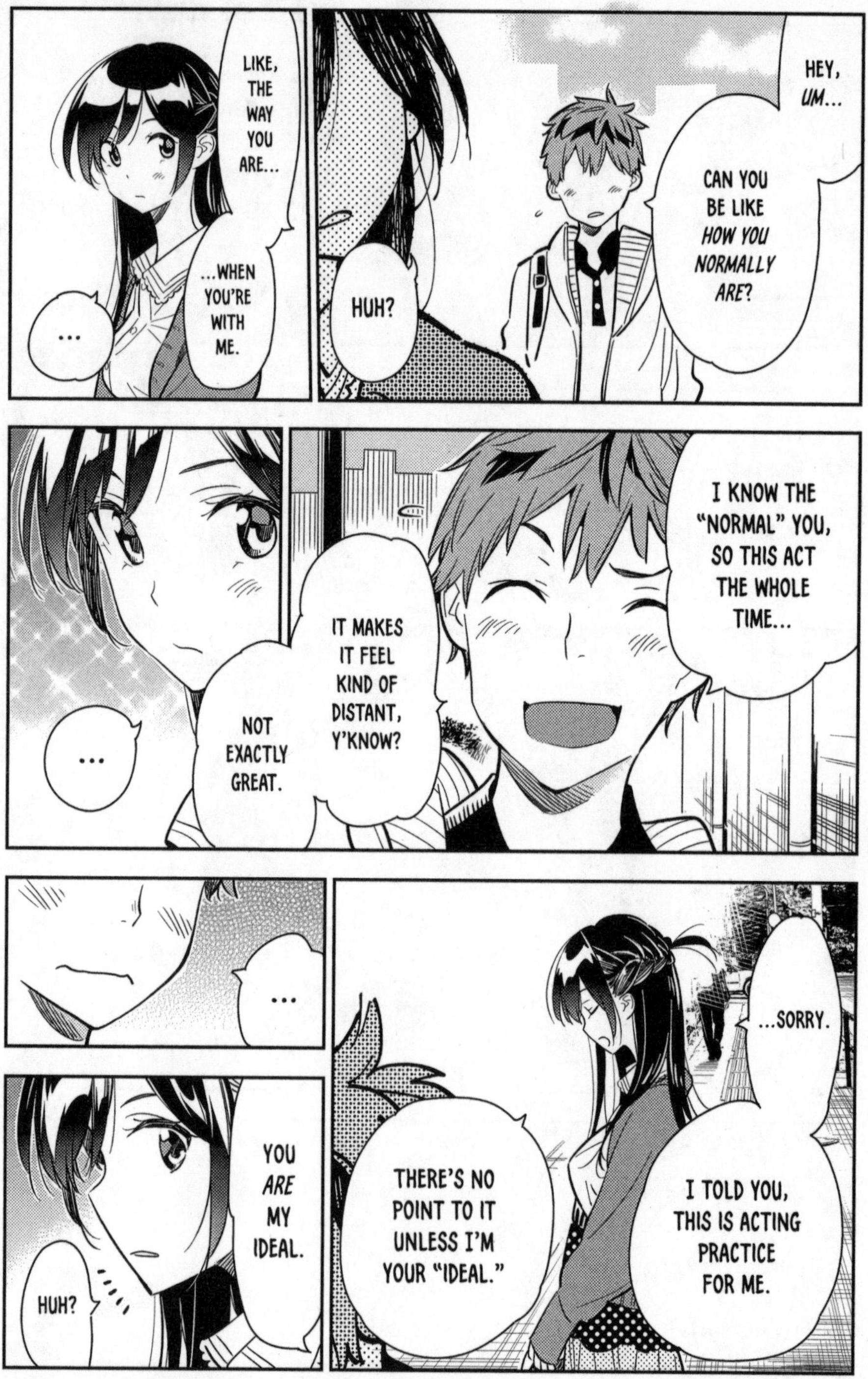
HEY, *UM*...
CAN YOU BE LIKE *HOW YOU NORMALLY ARE*?
HUH?
LIKE, THE WAY YOU ARE...
...WHEN YOU'RE WITH ME.
...
I KNOW THE "NORMAL" YOU, SO THIS ACT THE WHOLE TIME...
IT MAKES IT FEEL KIND OF DISTANT, Y'KNOW?
NOT EXACTLY GREAT.
...
...SORRY.
I TOLD YOU, THIS IS ACTING PRACTICE FOR ME.
THERE'S NO POINT TO IT UNLESS I'M YOUR "IDEAL."
...
YOU *ARE* MY IDEAL.
HUH?

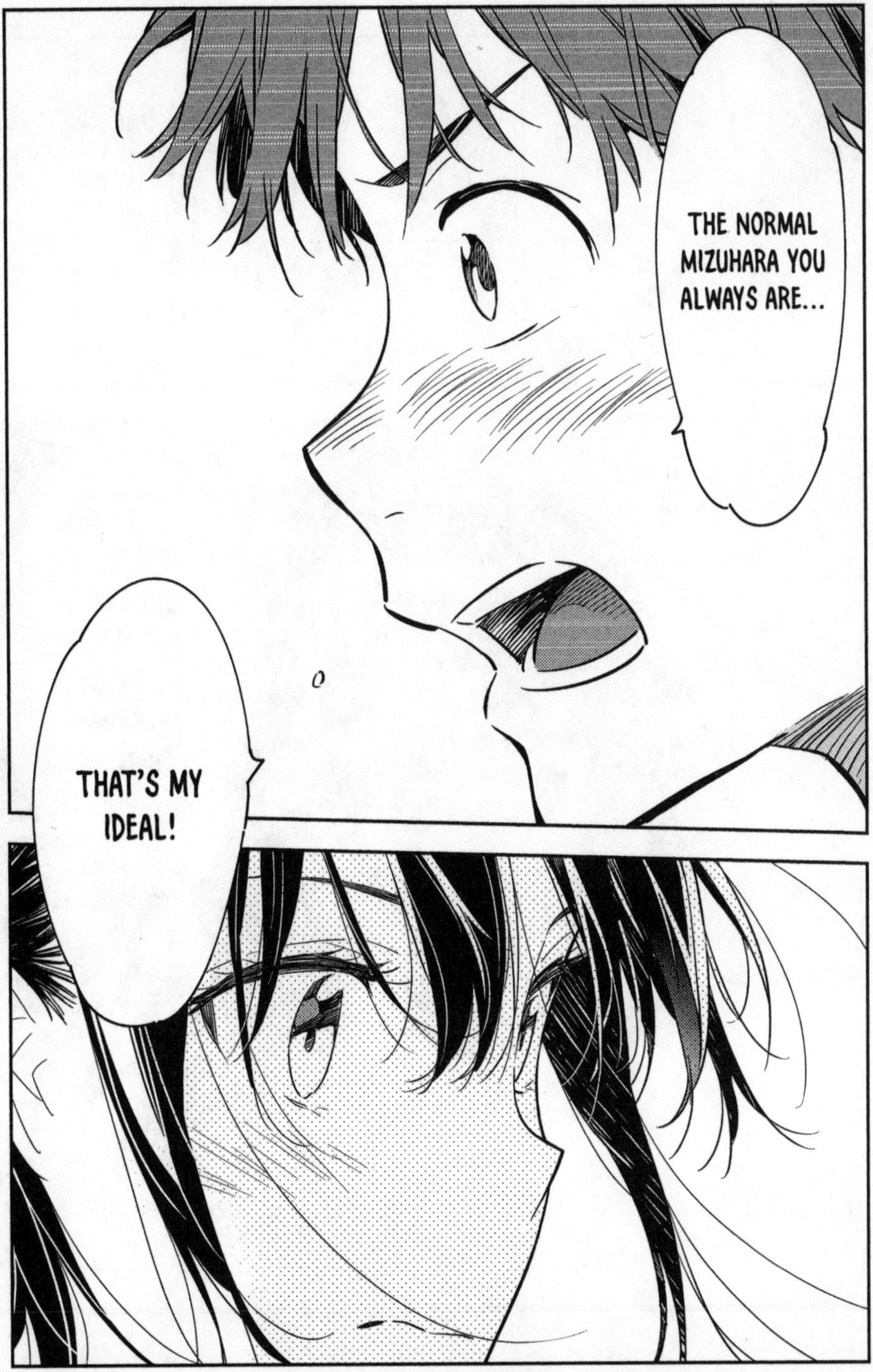
THE NORMAL MIZUHARA YOU ALWAYS ARE...
THAT'S MY IDEAL!

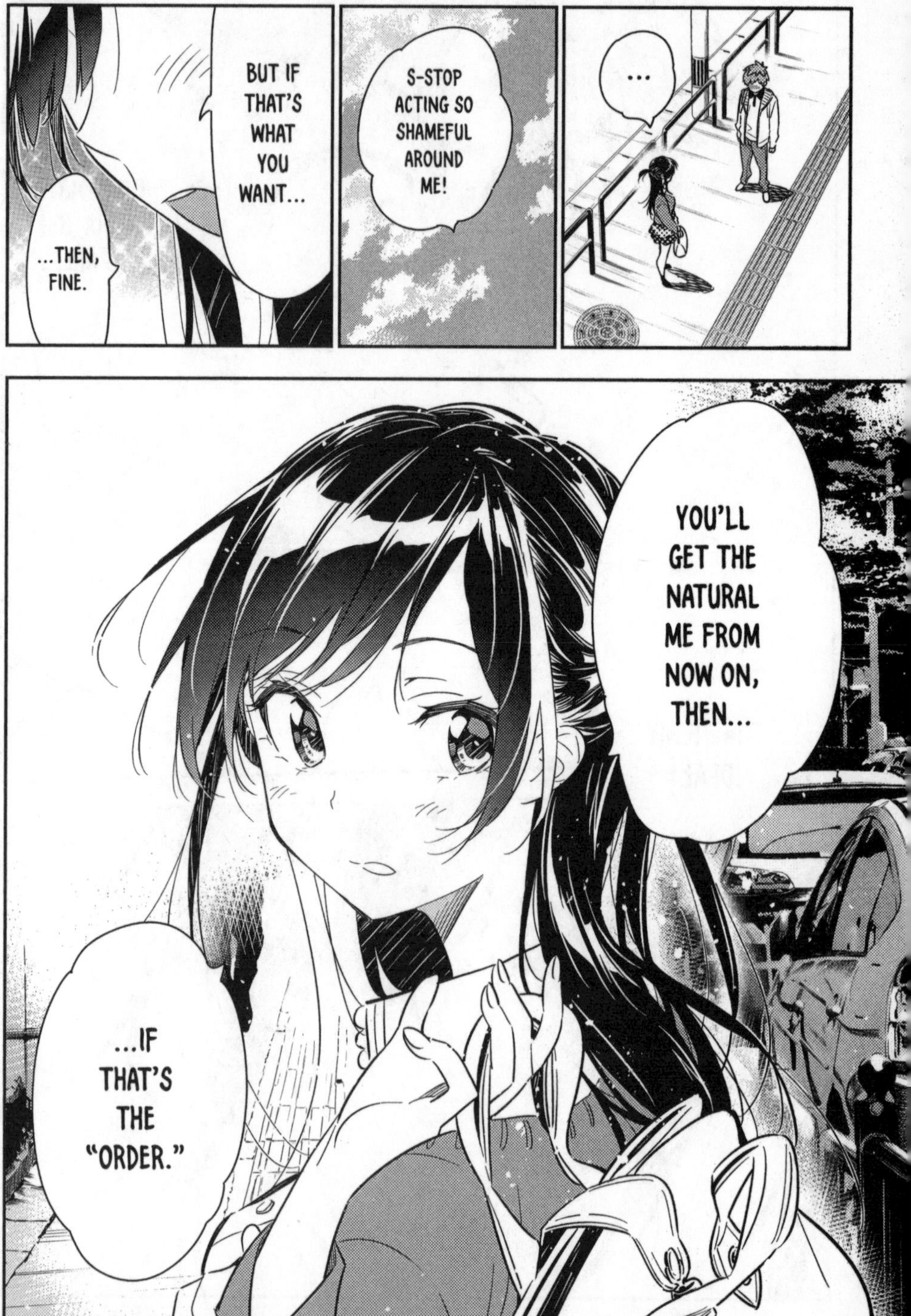
...
S-STOP ACTING SO SHAMEFUL AROUND ME!
BUT IF THAT'S WHAT YOU WANT...
...THEN, FINE.
YOU'LL GET THE NATURAL ME FROM NOW ON, THEN...
...IF THAT'S THE "ORDER."

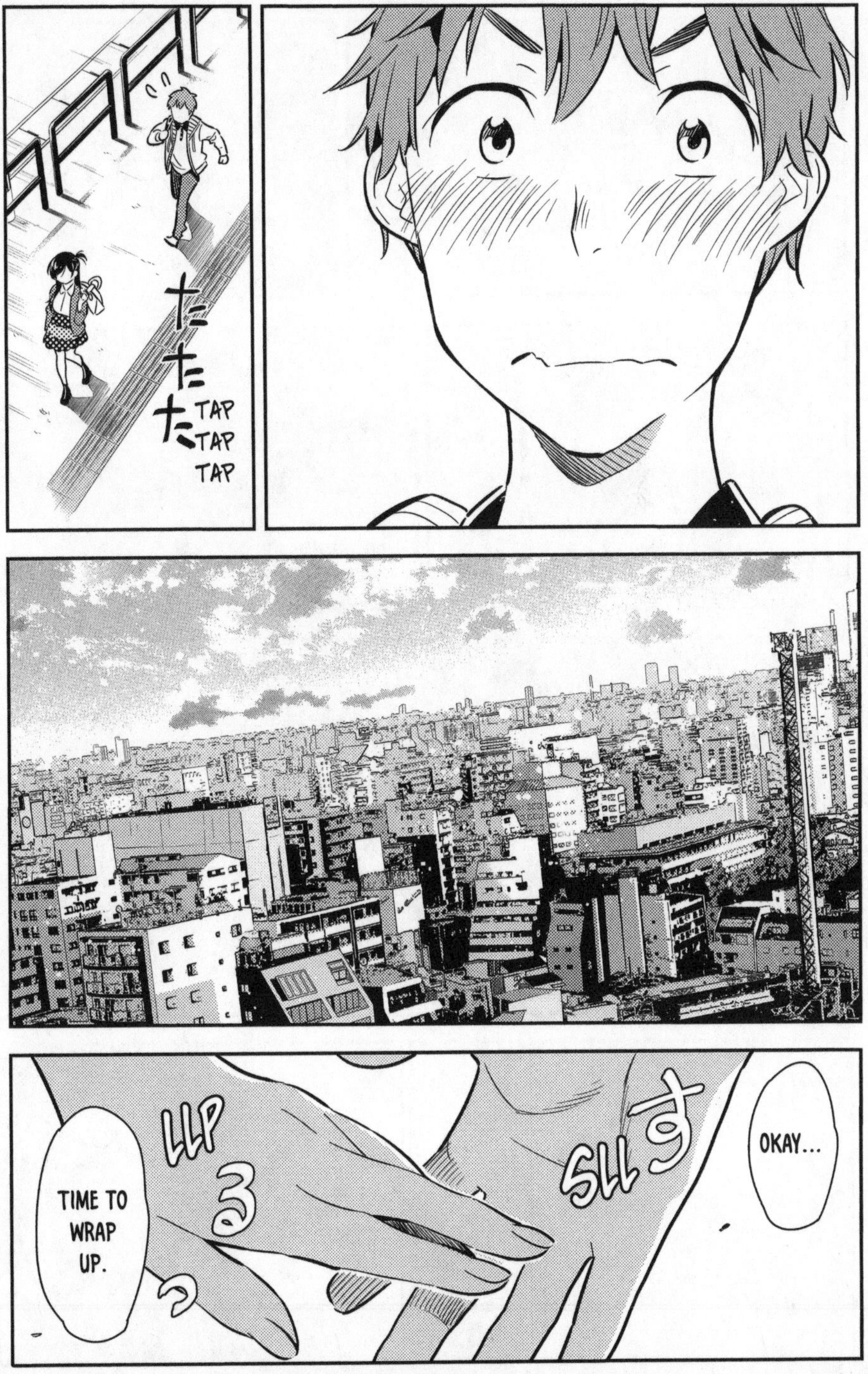
たたた
TAP TAP TAP
OKAY...
すSLI
るLLP
っ
TIME TO WRAP UP.

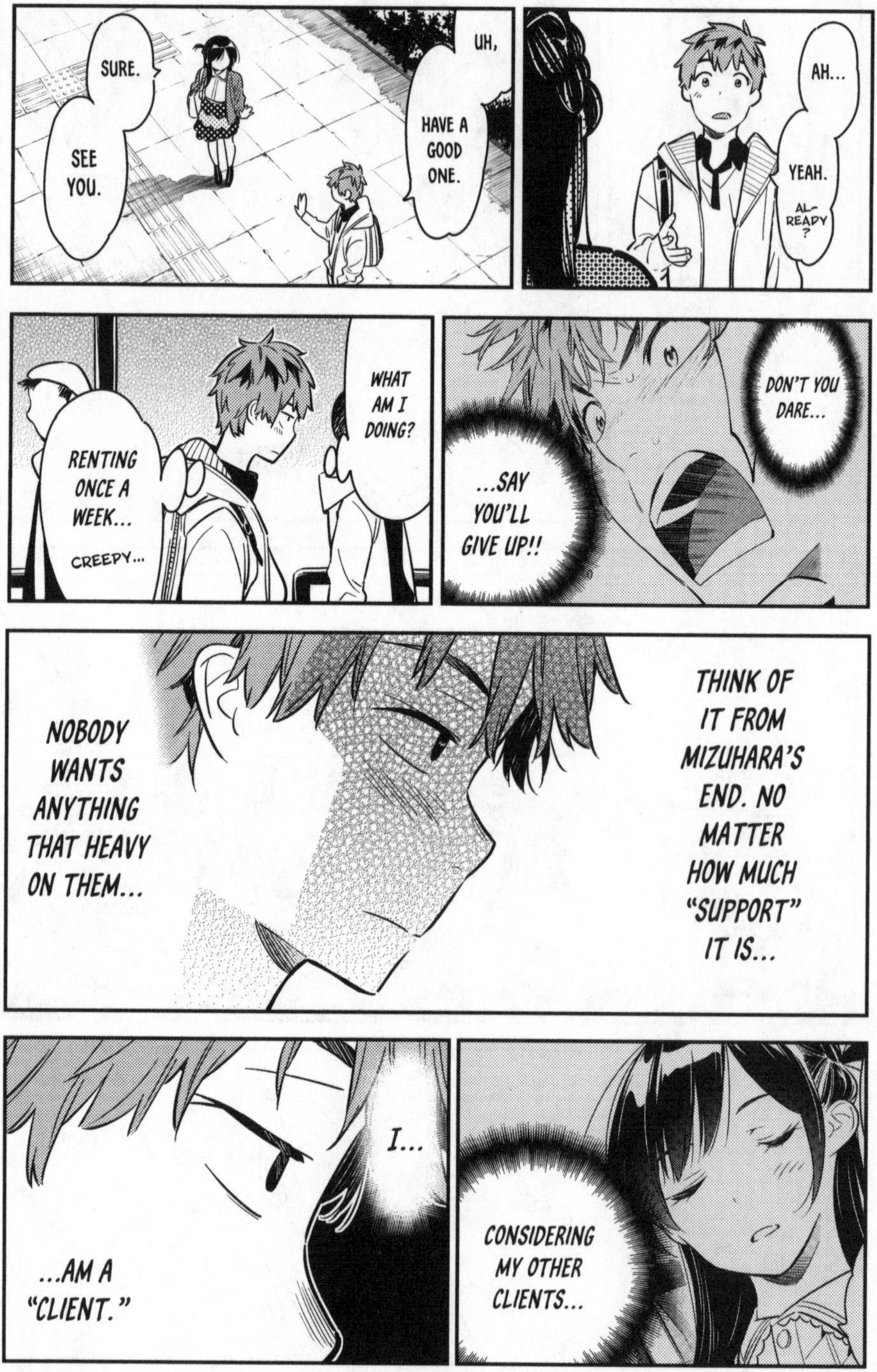
AH...
YEAH.
AL-READY?
UH,
HAVE A GOOD ONE.
SURE.
SEE YOU.
DON'T YOU DARE...
...SAY YOU'LL GIVE UP!!
WHAT AM I DOING?
RENTING ONCE A WEEK...
CREEPY...
THINK OF IT FROM MIZUHARA'S END. NO MATTER HOW MUCH "SUPPORT" IT IS...
NOBODY WANTS ANYTHING THAT HEAVY ON THEM...
CONSIDERING MY OTHER CLIENTS...
I...
...AM A "CLIENT."

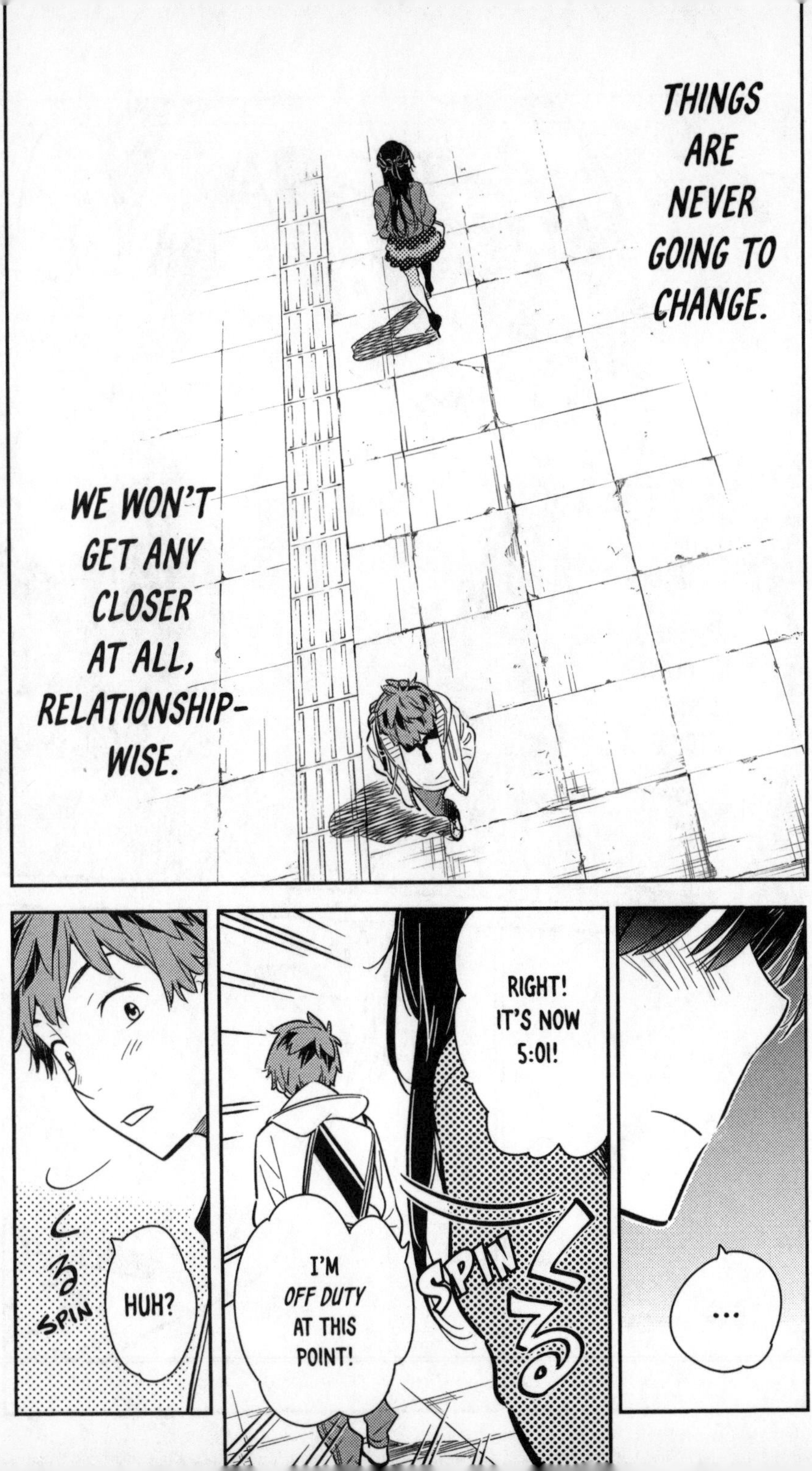
THINGS ARE NEVER GOING TO CHANGE.
WE WON'T GET ANY CLOSER AT ALL, RELATIONSHIP-WISE.
...
RIGHT! IT'S NOW 5:01!
SPIN
I'M OFF DUTY AT THIS POINT!
SPIN
HUH?

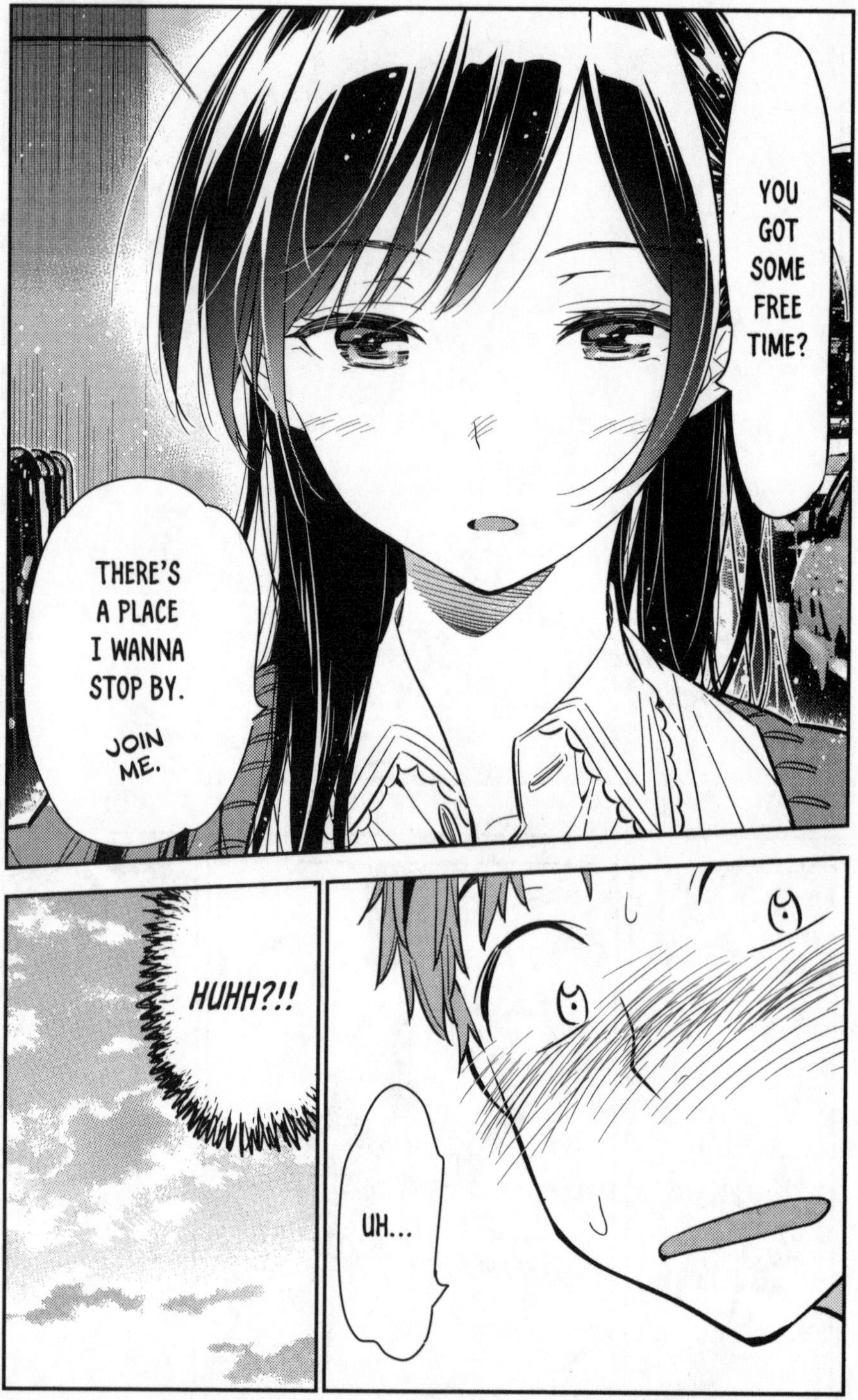
YOU GOT SOME FREE TIME?
THERE'S A PLACE I WANNA STOP BY.
JOIN ME.
UH...
HUHH?!!

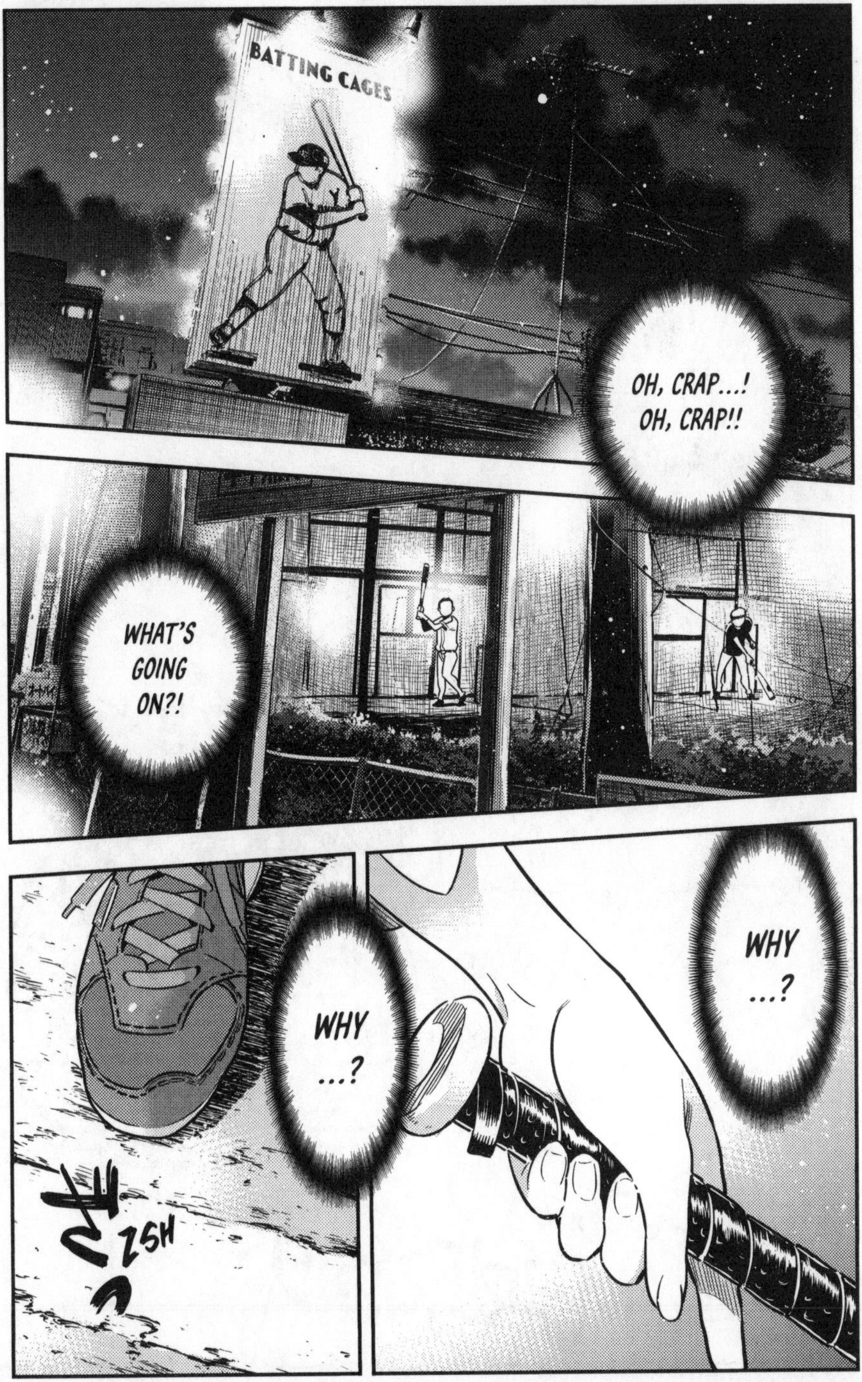
BATTING CAGES
OH, CRAP...! OH, CRAP!!
WHAT'S GOING ON?!
WHY ...?
WHY ...?

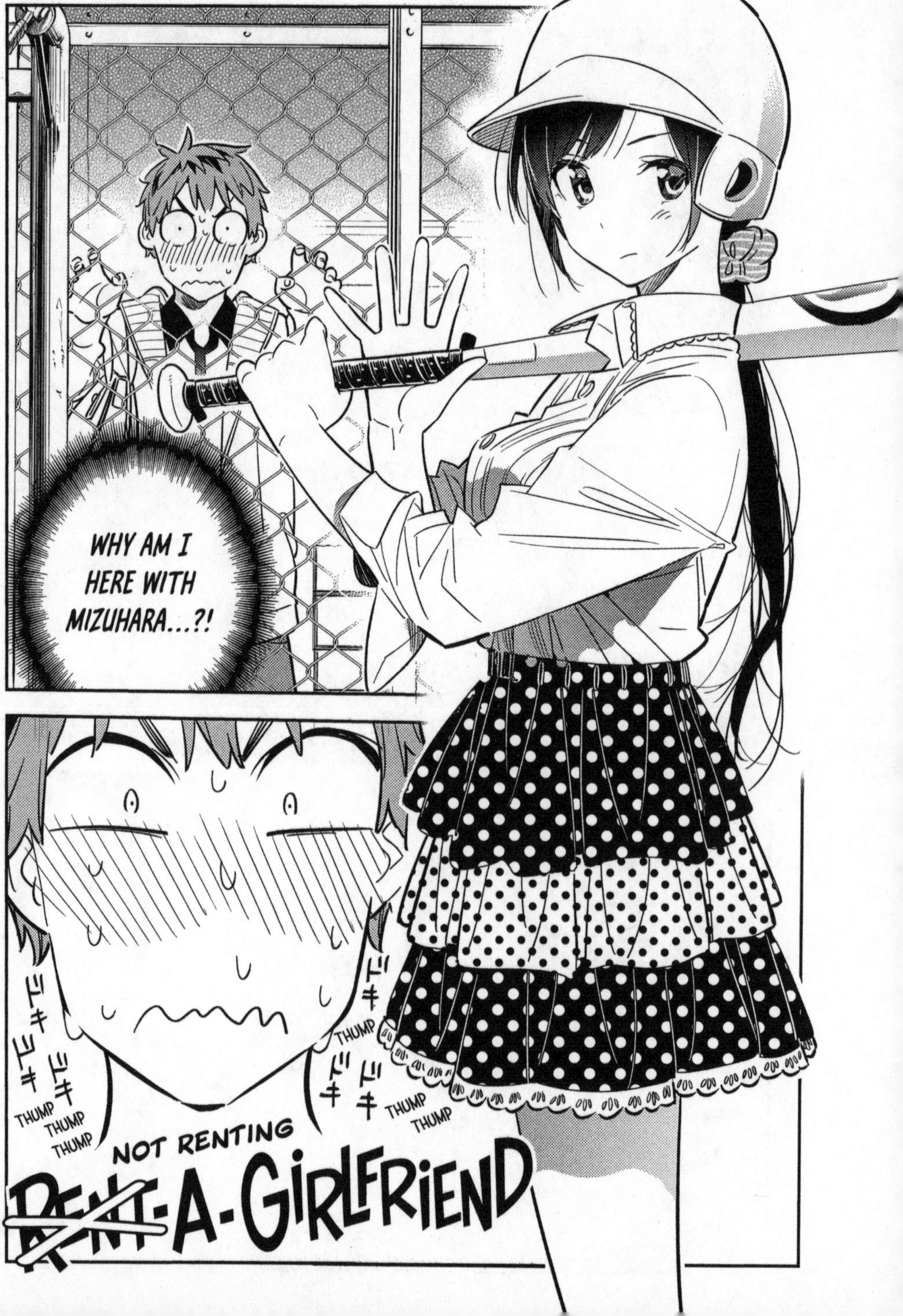
WHY AM I HERE WITH MIZUHARA...?!
ドキ THUMP
ドキ ドキ
THUMP THUMP
ドキ ドキ ドキ
THUMP THUMP THUMP
NOT RENTING
RENT-A-GIRLFRIEND

RATING 57 MY "GIRLFRIEND," CHIZURU ICHINOSE 2

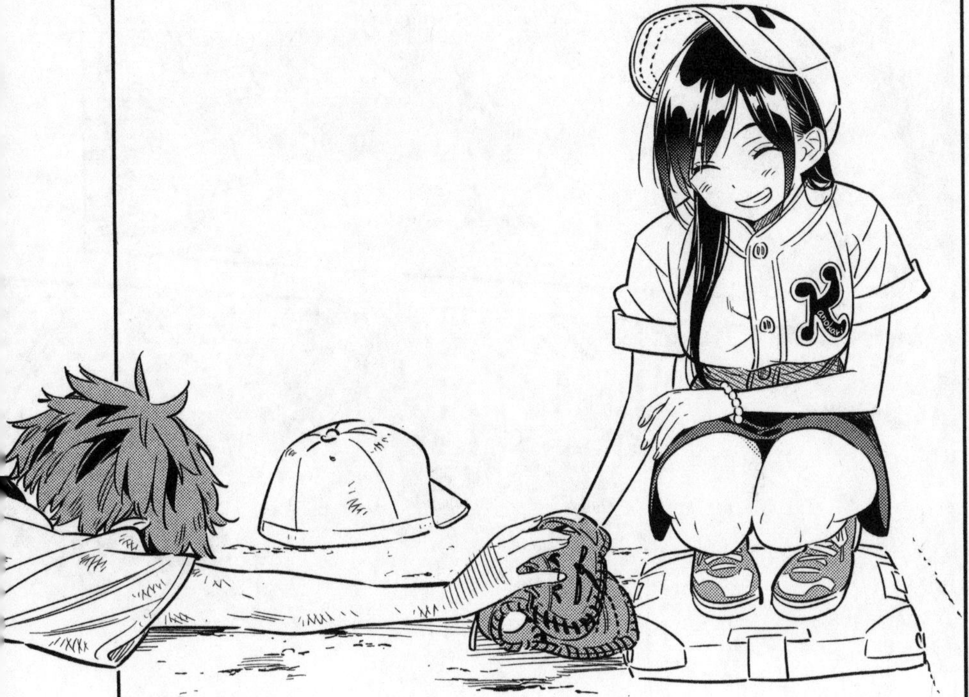

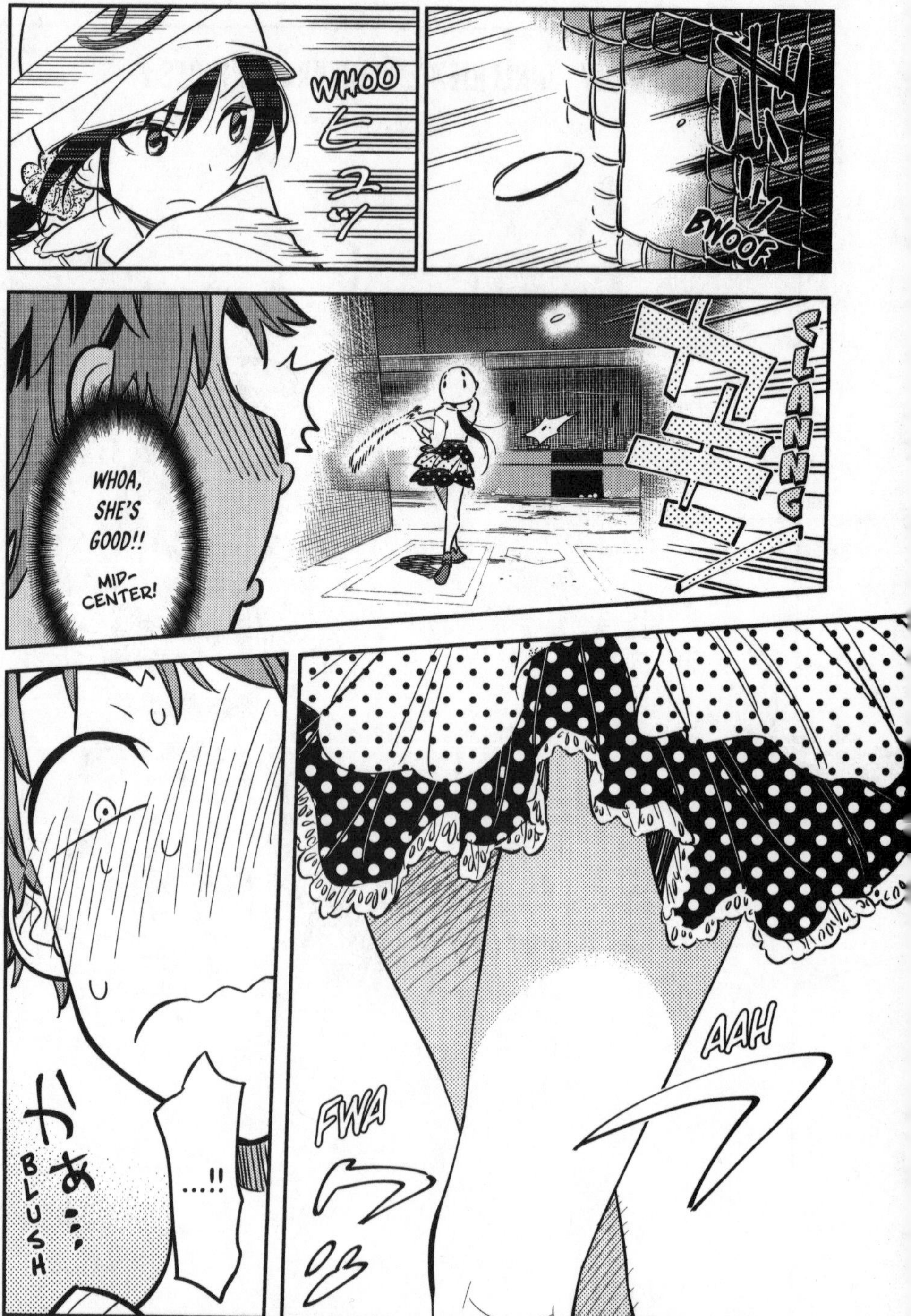
BWOOF
WHOO
ヒュッ
CLANNG
WHOA, SHE'S GOOD!!
MID-CENTER!
AAH
FWA
...!!
かぁ…
BLUSH

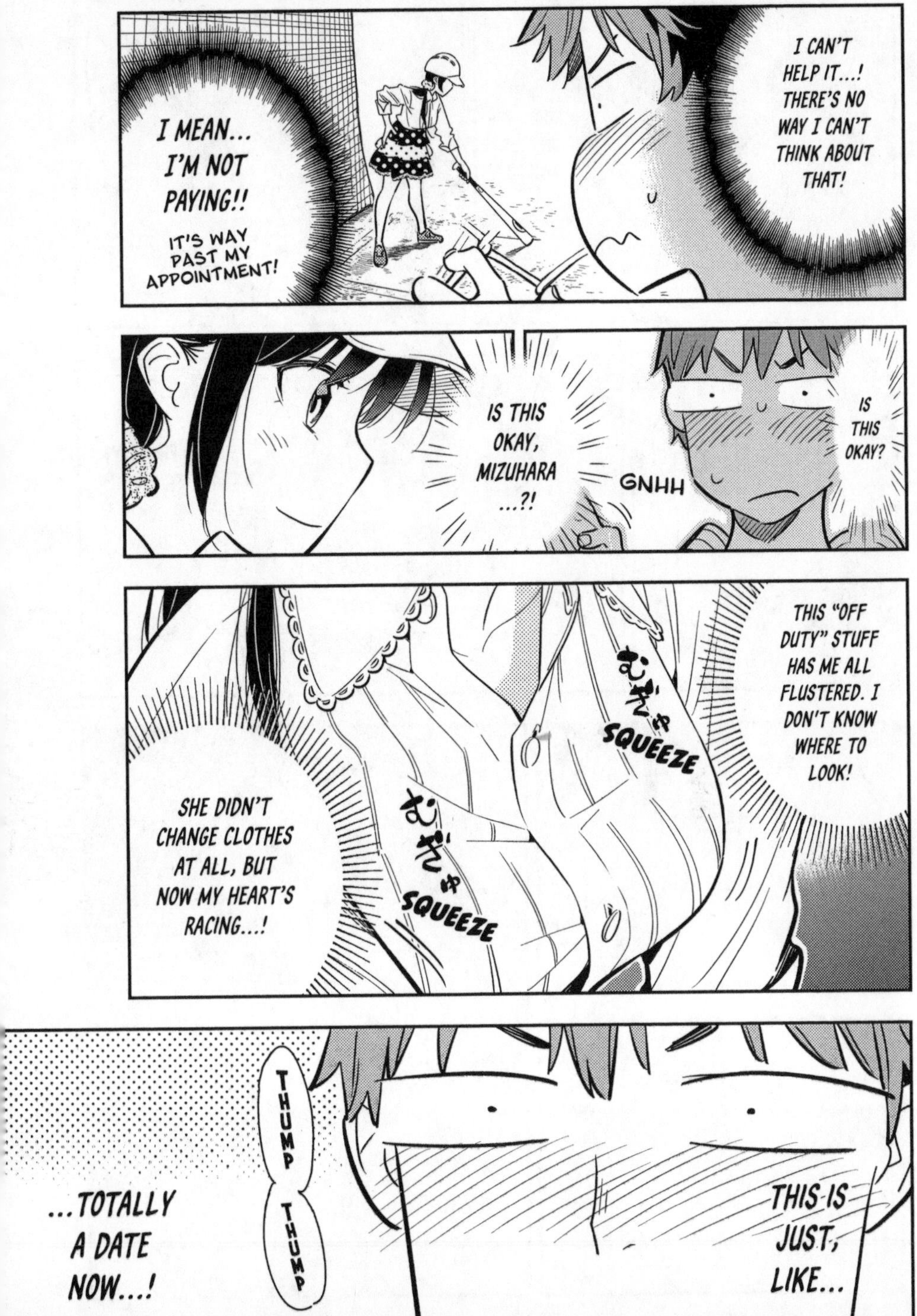
I CAN'T HELP IT...! THERE'S NO WAY I CAN'T THINK ABOUT THAT!
I MEAN... I'M NOT PAYING!!
IT'S WAY PAST MY APPOINTMENT!
IS THIS OKAY?
GNHH
IS THIS OKAY, MIZUHARA ...?!
THIS "OFF DUTY" STUFF HAS ME ALL FLUSTERED. I DON'T KNOW WHERE TO LOOK!
むぎゅ SQUEEZE
むぎゅ SQUEEZE
SHE DIDN'T CHANGE CLOTHES AT ALL, BUT NOW MY HEART'S RACING...!
THIS IS JUST, LIKE...
THUMP THUMP
...TOTALLY A DATE NOW...!

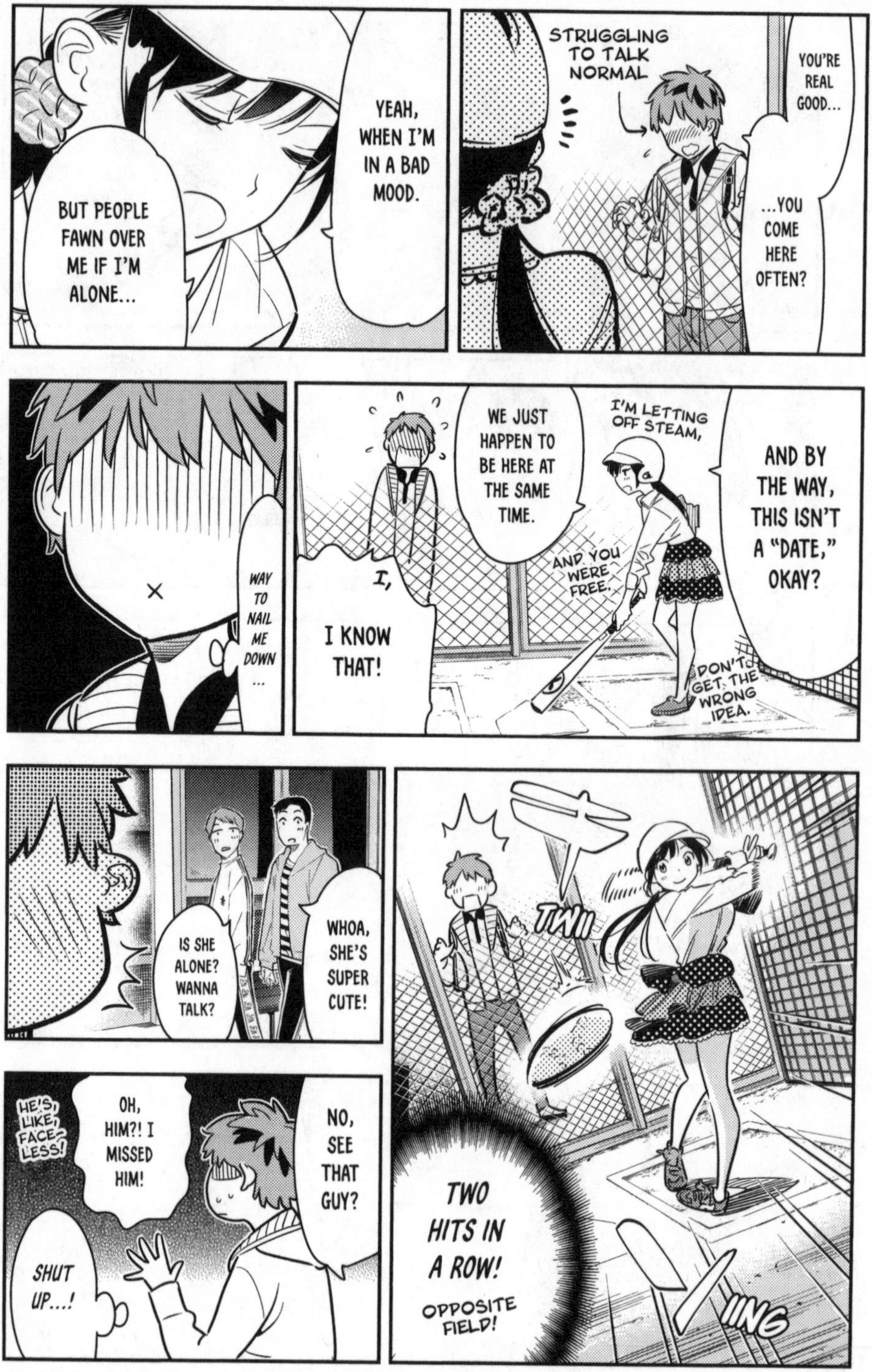
YOU'RE REAL GOOD...
STRUGGLING TO TALK NORMAL
...YOU COME HERE OFTEN?
YEAH, WHEN I'M IN A BAD MOOD.
BUT PEOPLE FAWN OVER ME IF I'M ALONE...
AND BY THE WAY, THIS ISN'T A "DATE," OKAY?
I'M LETTING OFF STEAM,
AND YOU WERE FREE.
DON'T GET THE WRONG IDEA.
WE JUST HAPPEN TO BE HERE AT THE SAME TIME.
I,
I KNOW THAT!
WAY TO NAIL ME DOWN...
TWII
TWO HITS IN A ROW!
OPPOSITE FIELD!
IING
WHOA, SHE'S SUPER CUTE!
IS SHE ALONE? WANNA TALK?
NO, SEE THAT GUY?
OH, HIM?! I MISSED HIM!
HE'S, LIKE, FACELESS!
SHUT UP...!

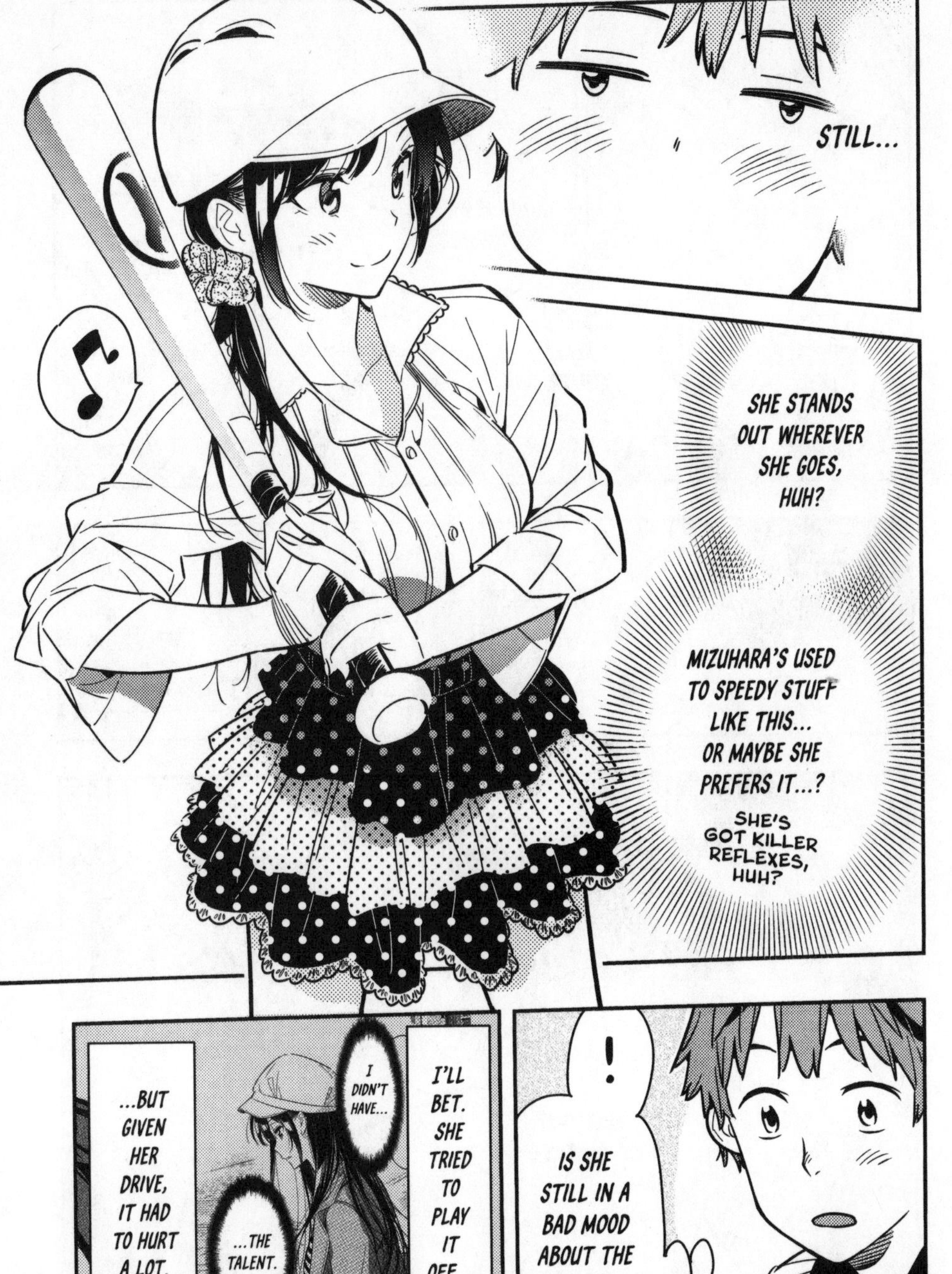
STILL...
SHE STANDS OUT WHEREVER SHE GOES, HUH?
MIZUHARA'S USED TO SPEEDY STUFF LIKE THIS... OR MAYBE SHE PREFERS IT...?
SHE'S GOT KILLER REFLEXES, HUH?
!
IS SHE STILL IN A BAD MOOD ABOUT THE PLAY?
I'LL BET. SHE TRIED TO PLAY IT OFF...
I DIDN'T HAVE...
...THE TALENT.
...BUT GIVEN HER DRIVE, IT HAD TO HURT A LOT.

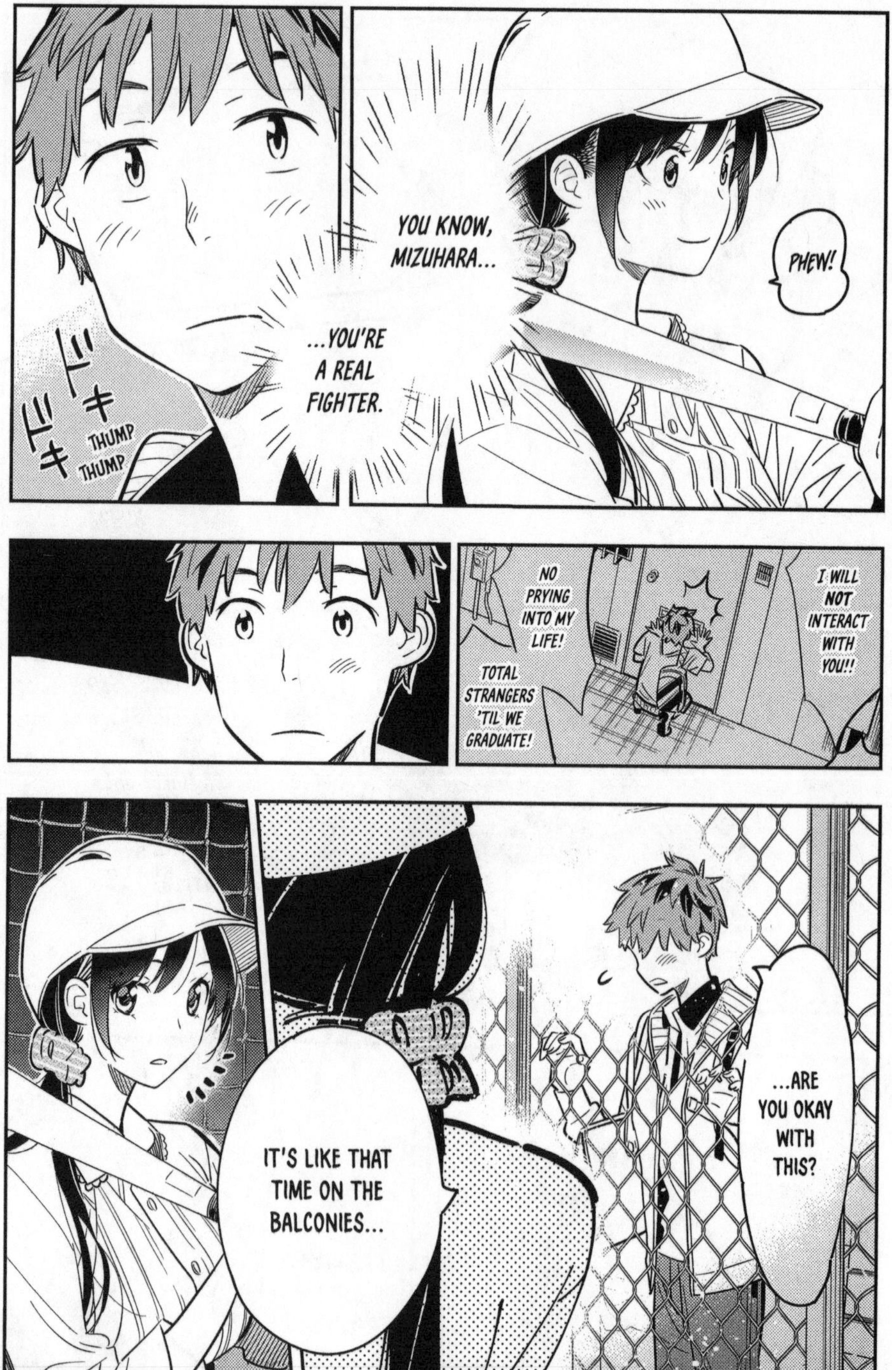
PHEW!
YOU KNOW, MIZUHARA...
...YOU'RE A REAL FIGHTER.
ドキドキ
THUMP THUMP
I WILL NOT INTERACT WITH YOU!!
NO PRYING INTO MY LIFE!
TOTAL STRANGERS 'TIL WE GRADUATE!
...ARE YOU OKAY WITH THIS?
IT'S LIKE THAT TIME ON THE BALCONIES...

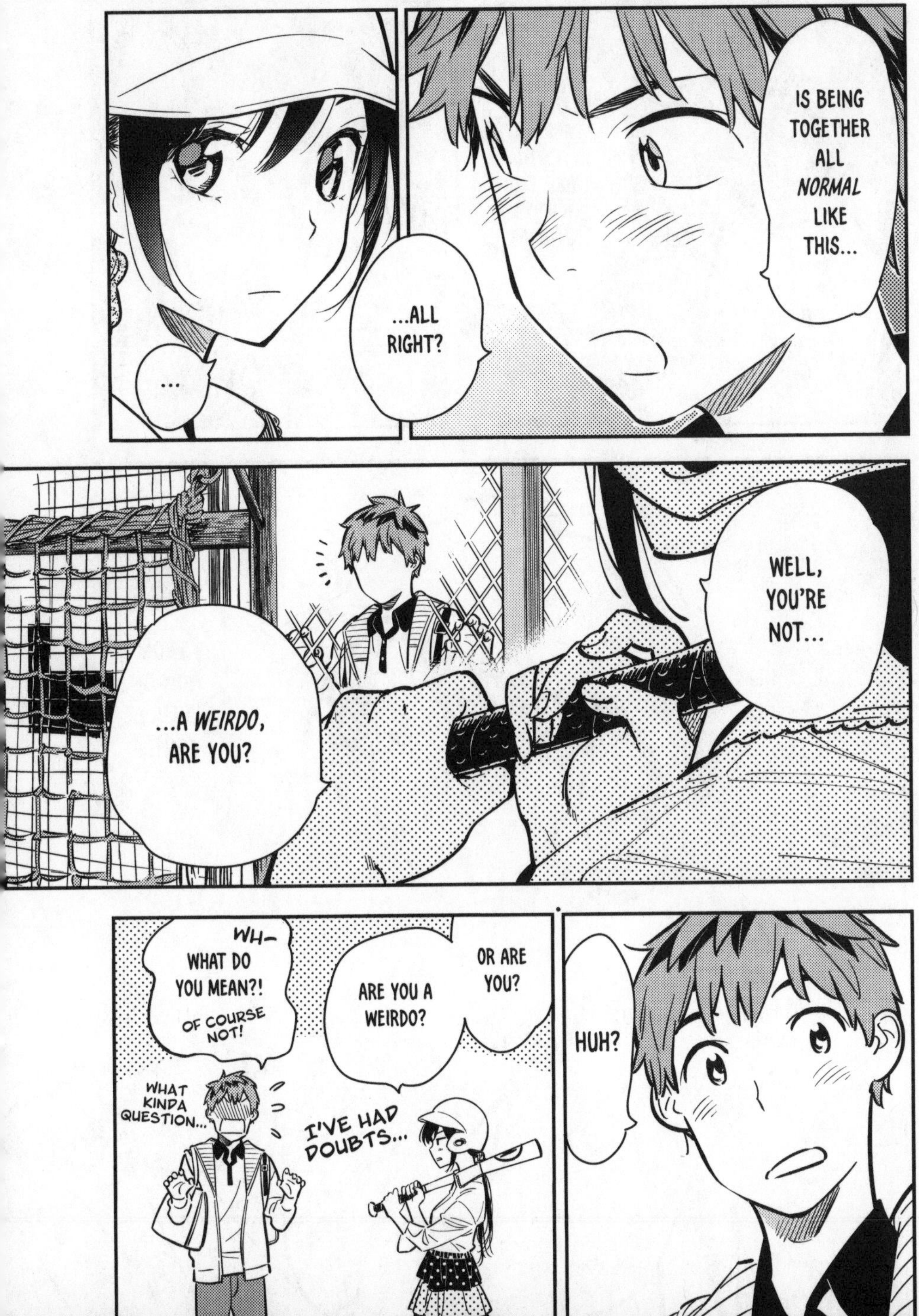
IS BEING TOGETHER ALL *NORMAL* LIKE THIS...
...ALL RIGHT?
...
WELL, YOU'RE NOT...
...A *WEIRDO*, ARE YOU?
HUH?
OR ARE YOU?
ARE YOU A WEIRDO?
WH- WHAT DO YOU MEAN?! OF COURSE NOT!
I'VE HAD DOUBTS...
WHAT KINDA QUESTION...

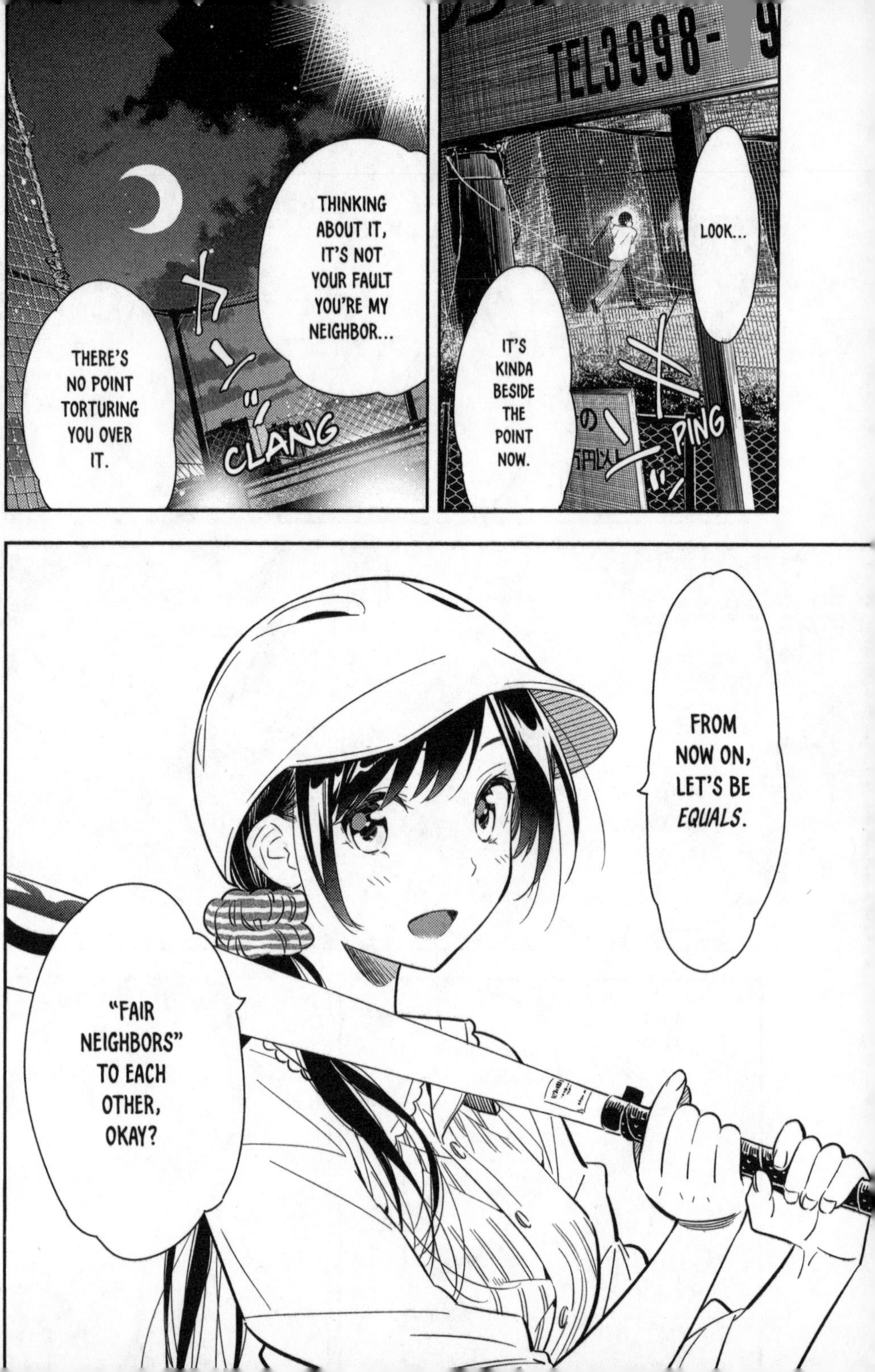
LOOK...
IT'S KINDA BESIDE THE POINT NOW.
PING
THINKING ABOUT IT, IT'S NOT YOUR FAULT YOU'RE MY NEIGHBOR...
THERE'S NO POINT TORTURING YOU OVER IT.
CLANG
FROM NOW ON, LET'S BE *EQUALS*.
"FAIR NEIGHBORS" TO EACH OTHER, OKAY?

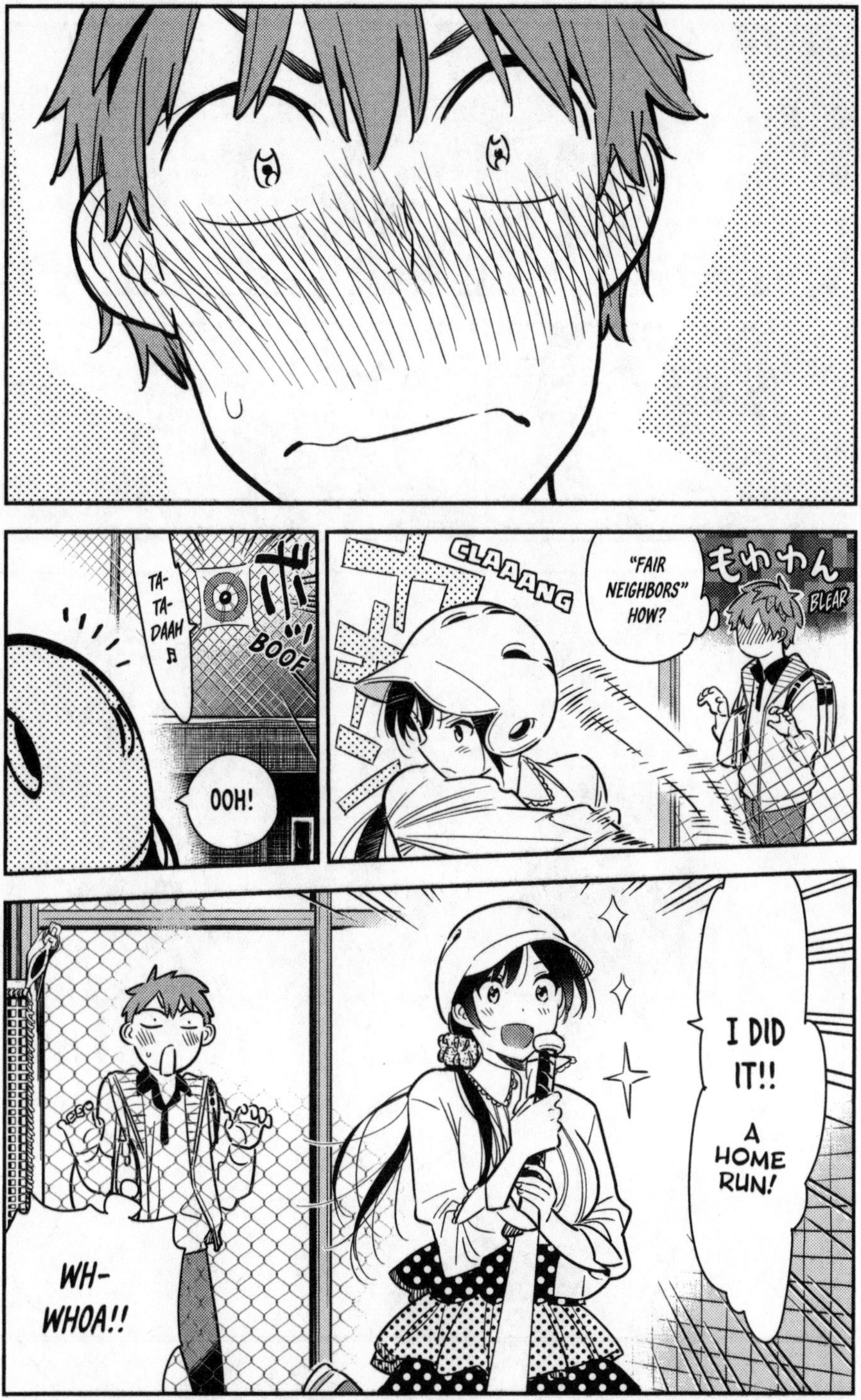
BLEAR
"FAIR NEIGHBORS" HOW?
CLAAAANG
BOOF
TA-TA-DAAH ♪
OOH!
I DID IT!!
A HOME RUN!
WH-WHOA!!

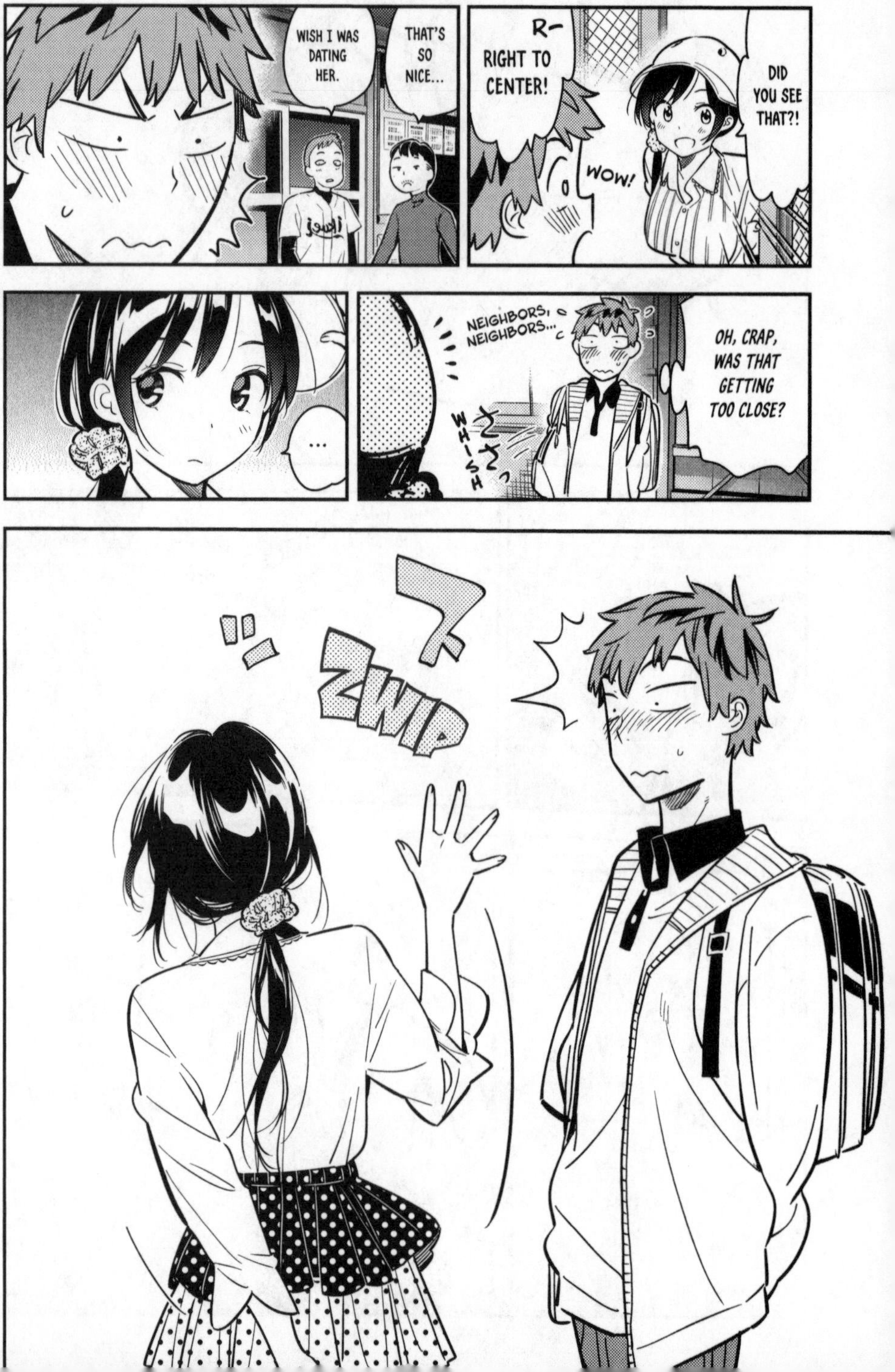
DID YOU SEE THAT?!
R– RIGHT TO CENTER!
WOW!
THAT'S SO NICE...
WISH I WAS DATING HER.
OH, CRAP, WAS THAT GETTING TOO CLOSE?
NEIGHBORS, NEIGHBORS...
WHISH
...
ZWIP

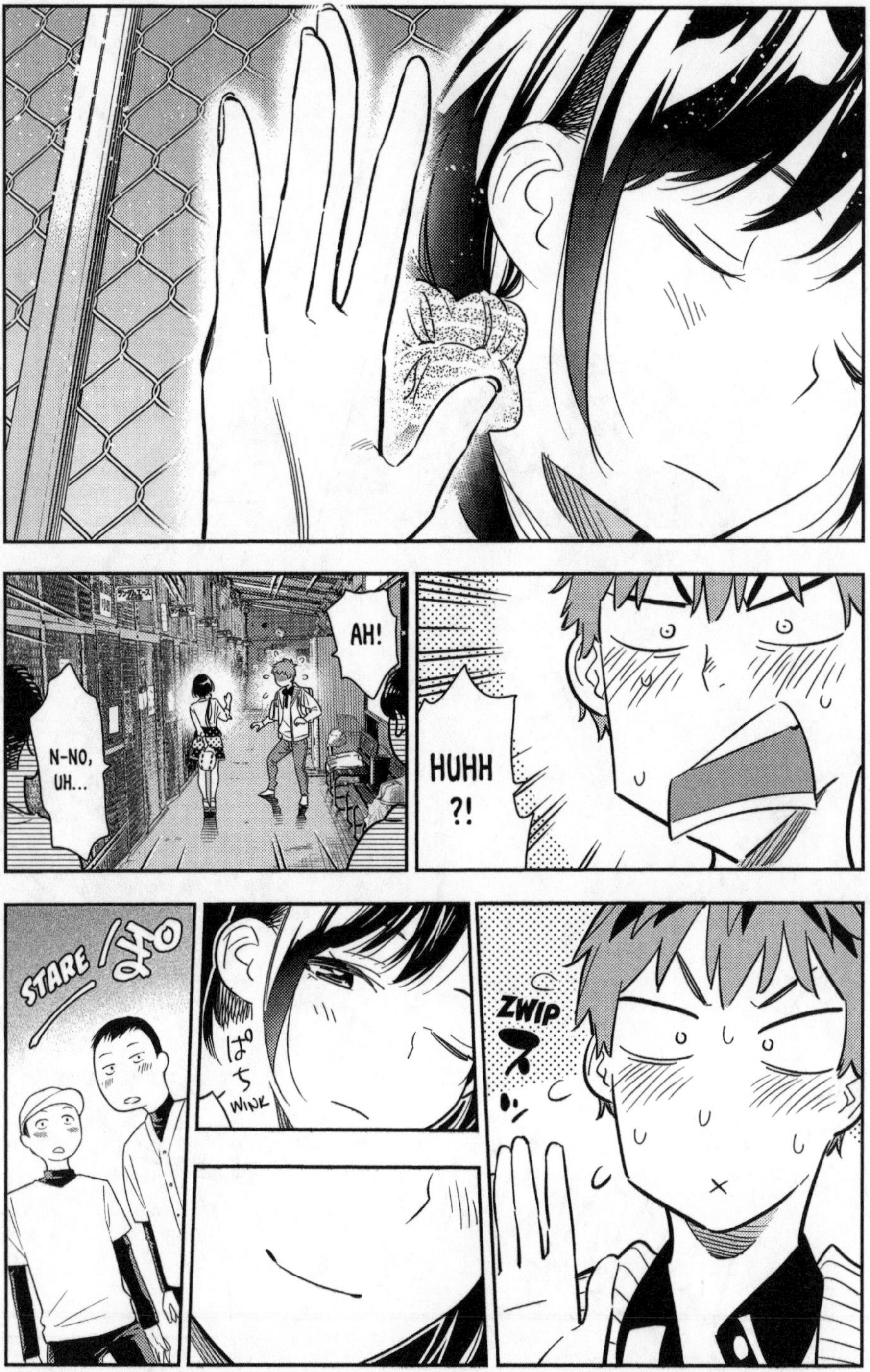
HUHH ?!
AH!
N-NO, UH...
ZWIP
スッ
ぱち
WINK
STARE

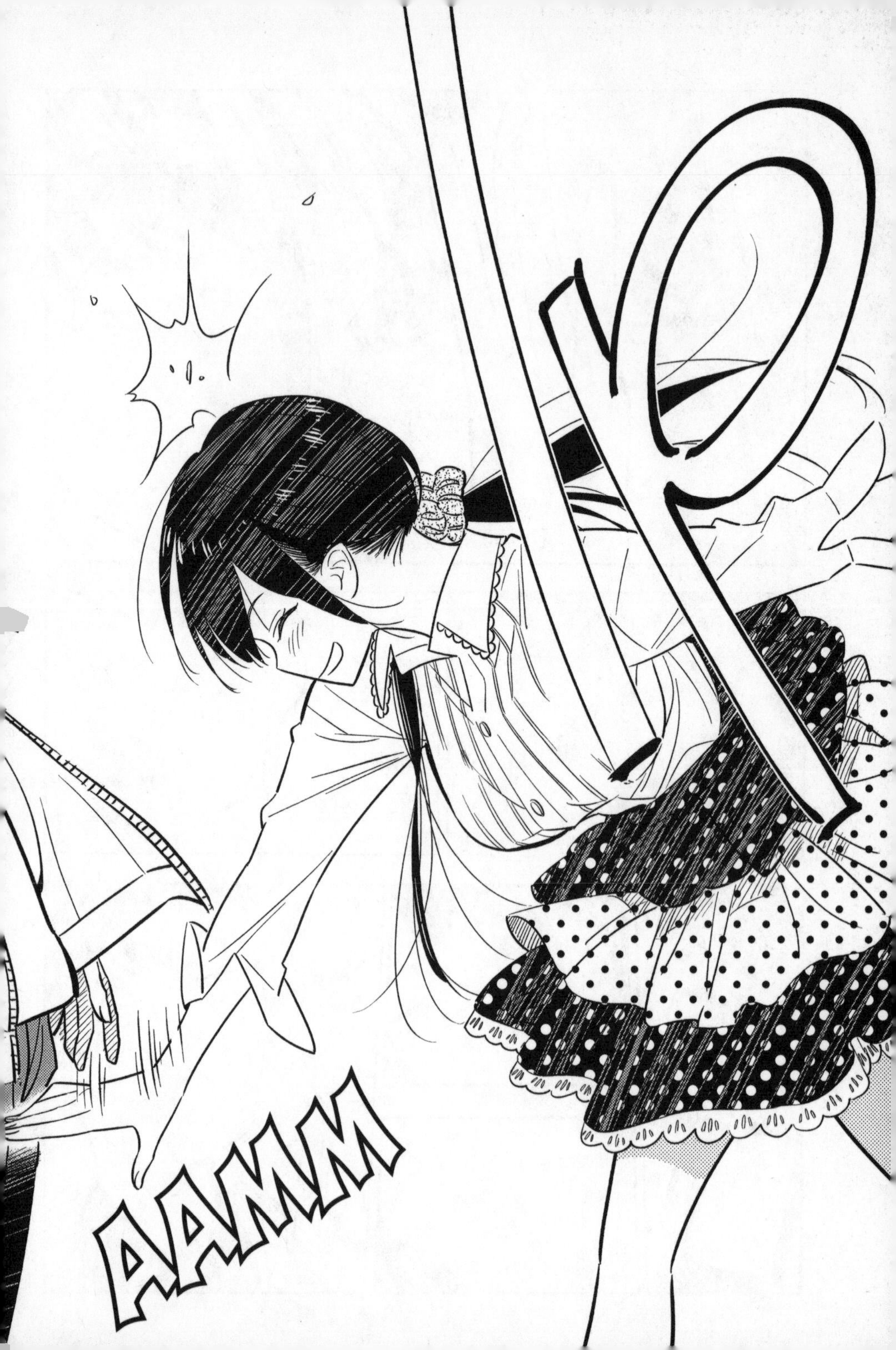
AAMM

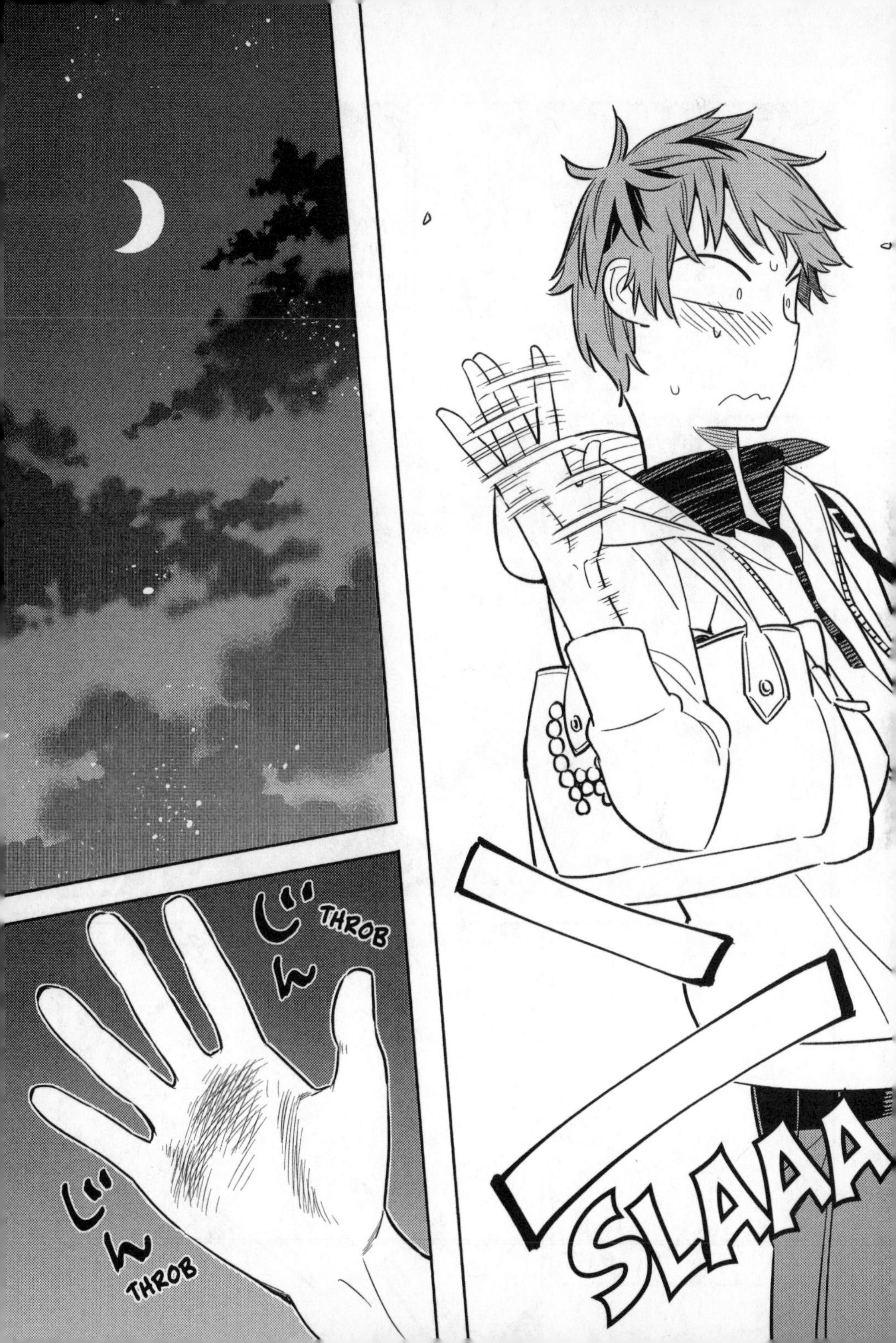
SLAAA
じん
THROB
じん
THROB

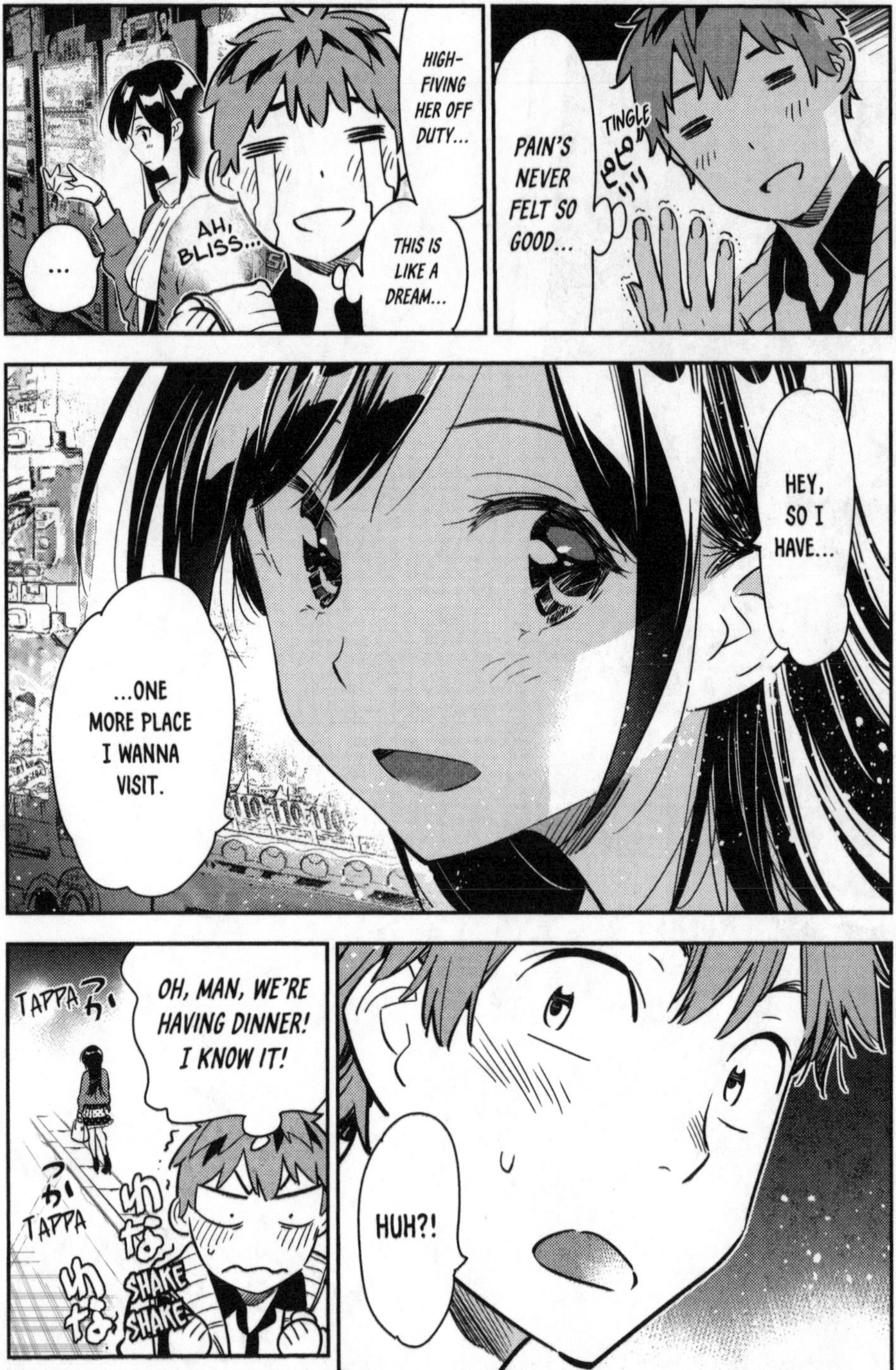
TINGLE
PAIN'S NEVER FELT SO GOOD...
HIGH-FIVING HER OFF DUTY...
THIS IS LIKE A DREAM...
AH, BLISS...
...
HEY, SO I HAVE...
...ONE MORE PLACE I WANNA VISIT.
HUH?!
OH, MAN, WE'RE HAVING DINNER! I KNOW IT!
TAPPA
TAPPA
SHAKE SHAKE

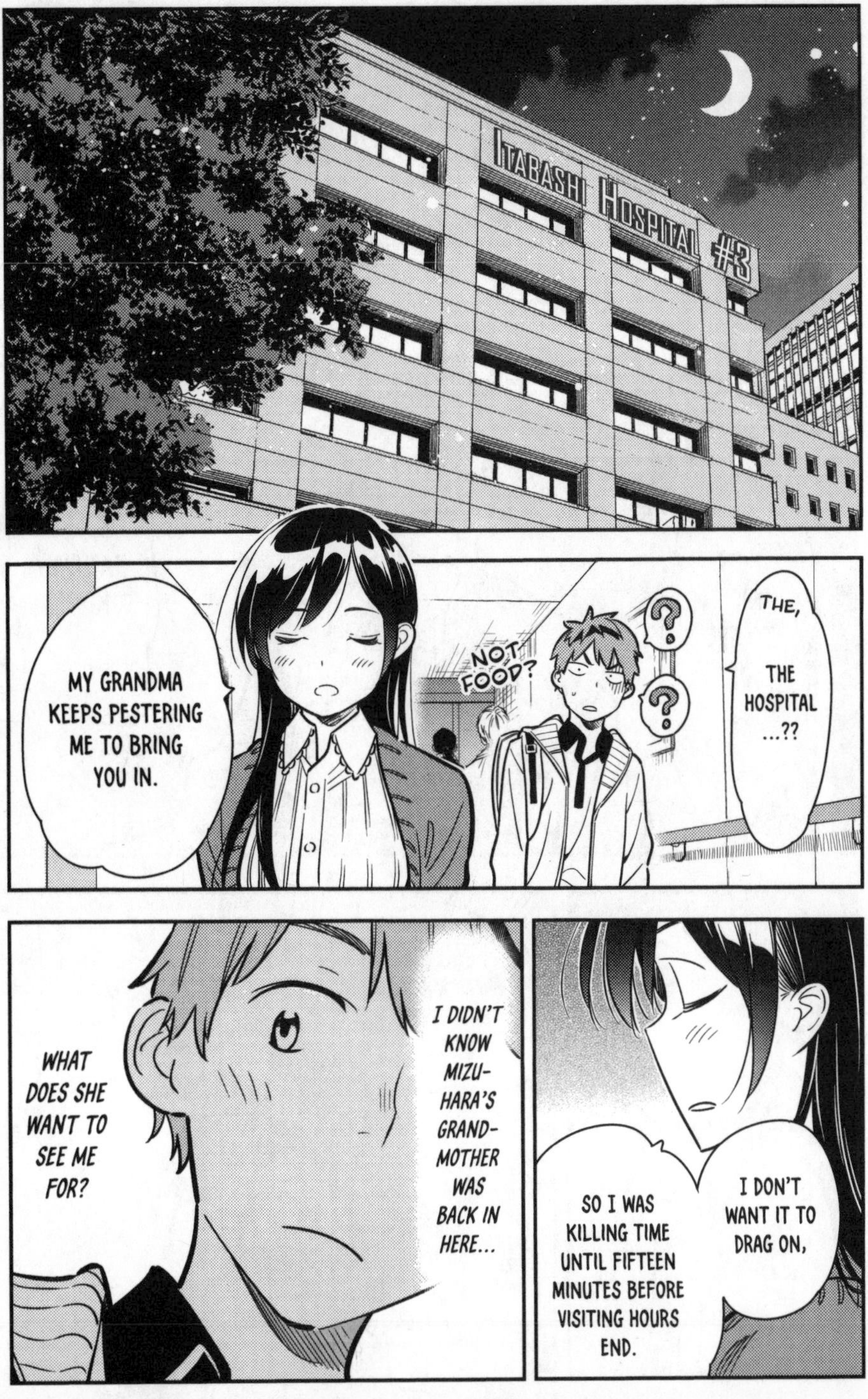
ITABASHI HOSPITAL #3
THE, THE HOSPITAL ...??
NOT FOOD?
MY GRANDMA KEEPS PESTERING ME TO BRING YOU IN.
I DON'T WANT IT TO DRAG ON,
SO I WAS KILLING TIME UNTIL FIFTEEN MINUTES BEFORE VISITING HOURS END.
I DIDN'T KNOW MIZUHARA'S GRANDMOTHER WAS BACK IN HERE...
WHAT DOES SHE WANT TO SEE ME FOR?

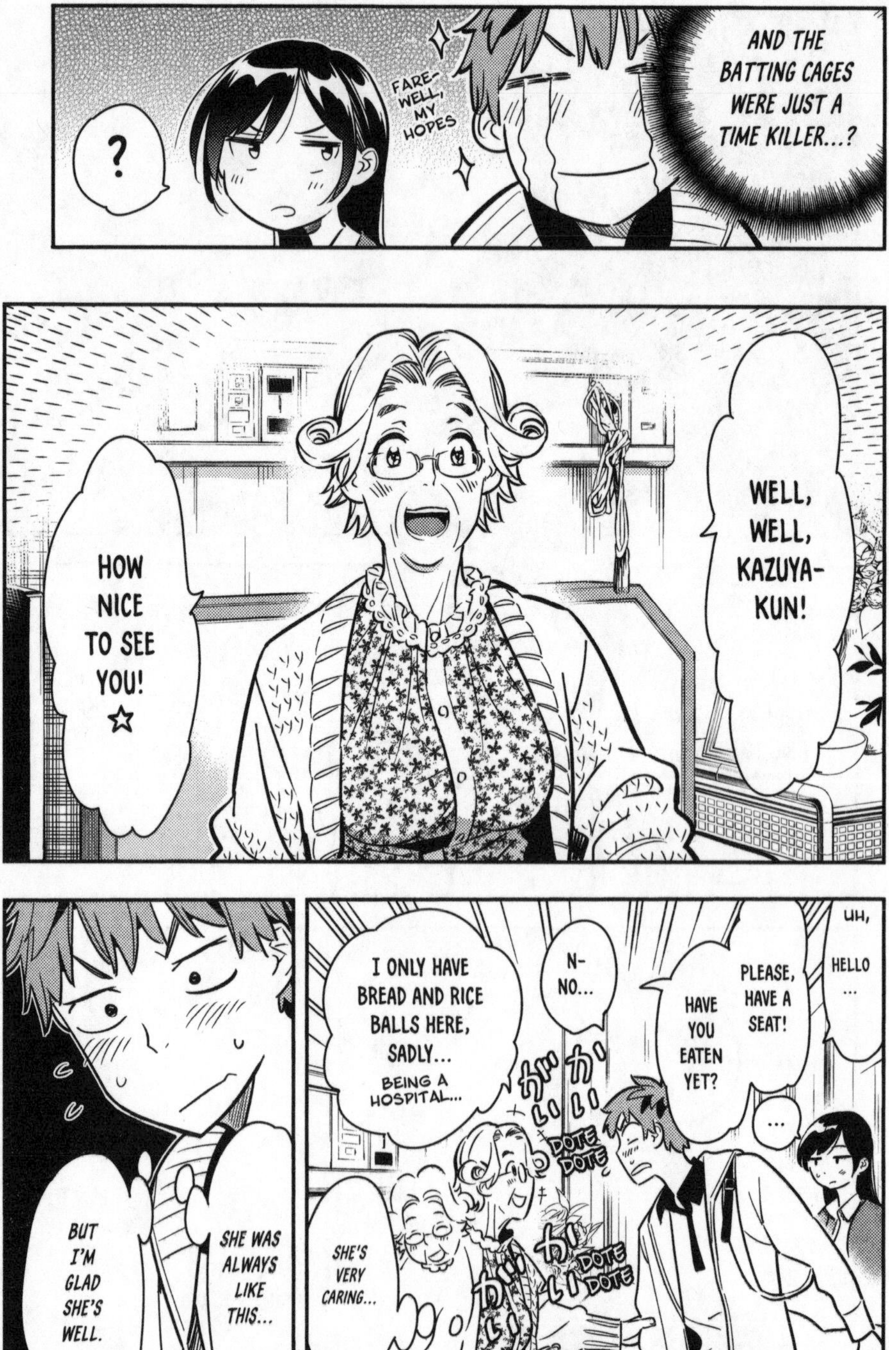
AND THE BATTING CAGES WERE JUST A TIME KILLER...?
FARE-WELL, MY HOPES
?
WELL, WELL, KAZUYA-KUN!
HOW NICE TO SEE YOU! ☆
UH, HELLO...
PLEASE, HAVE A SEAT!
HAVE YOU EATEN YET?
N-NO...
I ONLY HAVE BREAD AND RICE BALLS HERE, SADLY... BEING A HOSPITAL...
...
DOTE DOTE
DOTE DOTE
SHE'S VERY CARING...
SHE WAS ALWAYS LIKE THIS...
BUT I'M GLAD SHE'S WELL.

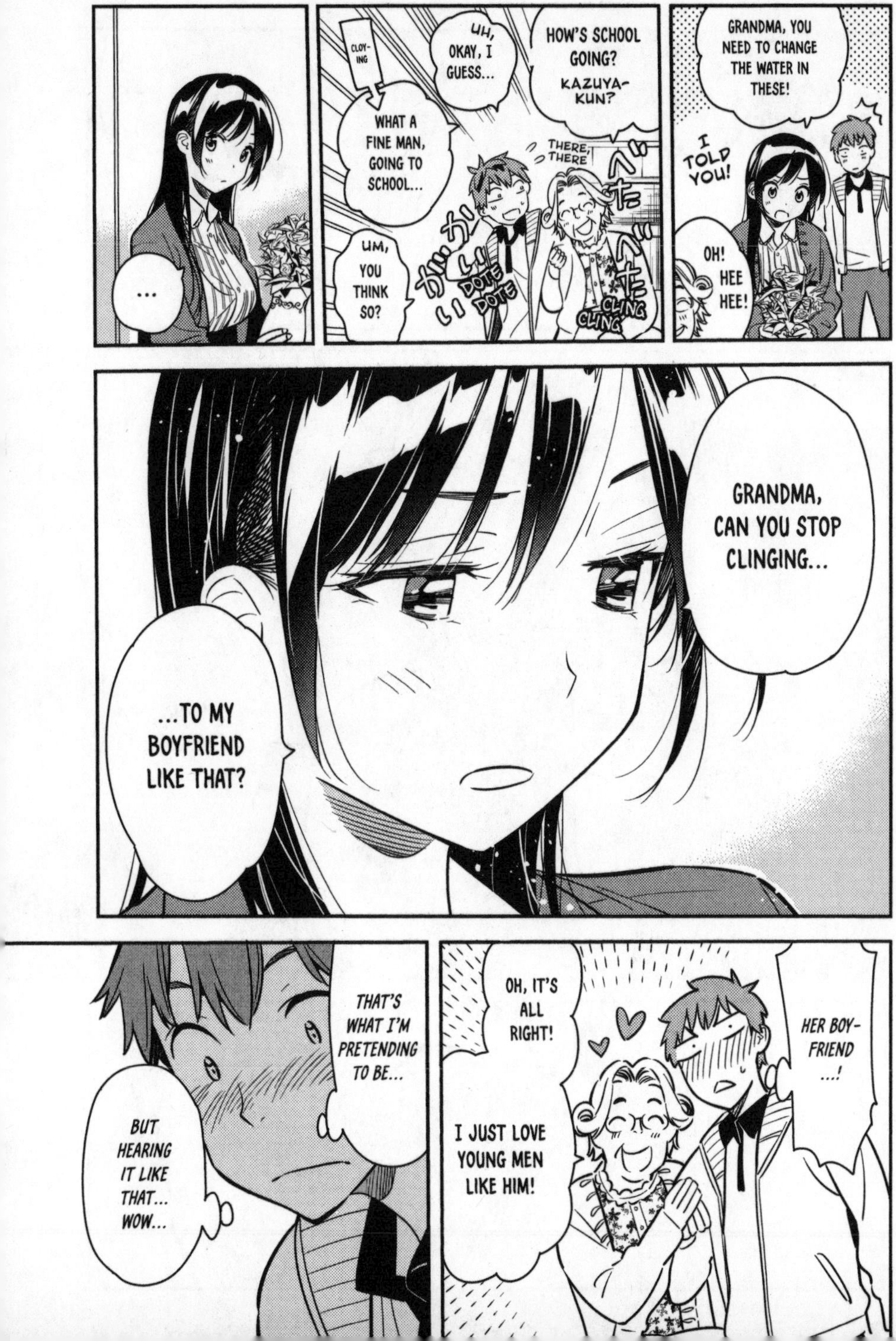
GRANDMA, YOU NEED TO CHANGE THE WATER IN THESE!
I TOLD YOU!
OH! HEE HEE!
HOW'S SCHOOL GOING?
KAZUYA-KUN?
UH, OKAY, I GUESS...
CLOYING
WHAT A FINE MAN, GOING TO SCHOOL...
THERE, THERE
UM, YOU THINK SO?
DOTE DOTE
CLING CLING
...
GRANDMA, CAN YOU STOP CLINGING...
...TO MY BOYFRIEND LIKE THAT?
HER BOY-FRIEND ...!
OH, IT'S ALL RIGHT!
I JUST LOVE YOUNG MEN LIKE HIM!
THAT'S WHAT I'M PRETENDING TO BE...
BUT HEARING IT LIKE THAT... WOW...

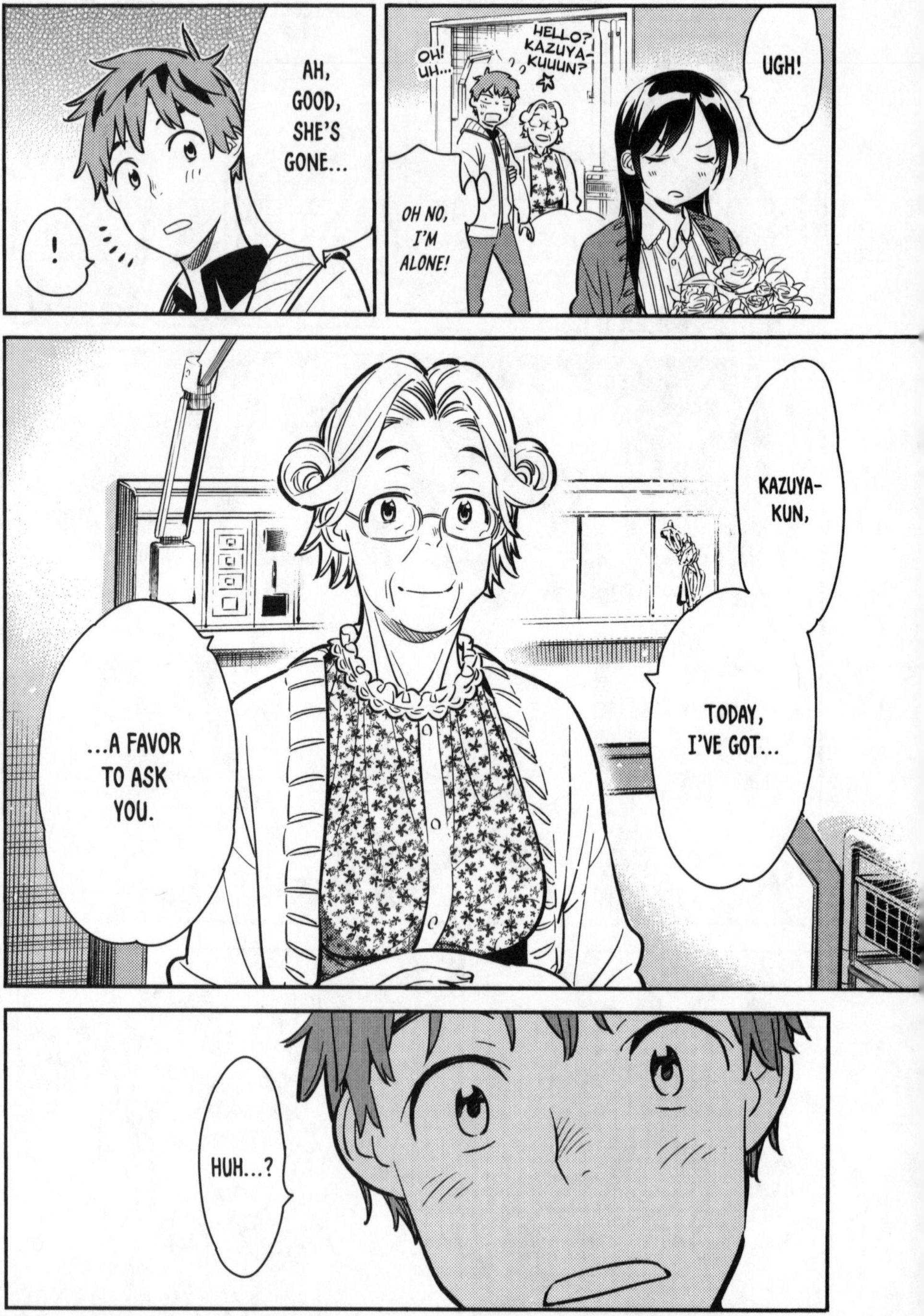
UGH!
HELLO? KAZUYA-KUUUN?
OH! UH...
OH NO, I'M ALONE!
AH, GOOD, SHE'S GONE...
!
KAZUYA-KUN,
TODAY, I'VE GOT...
...A FAVOR TO ASK YOU.
HUH...?

RATING 58
MY "GIRLFRIEND," CHIZURU ICHINOSE 3

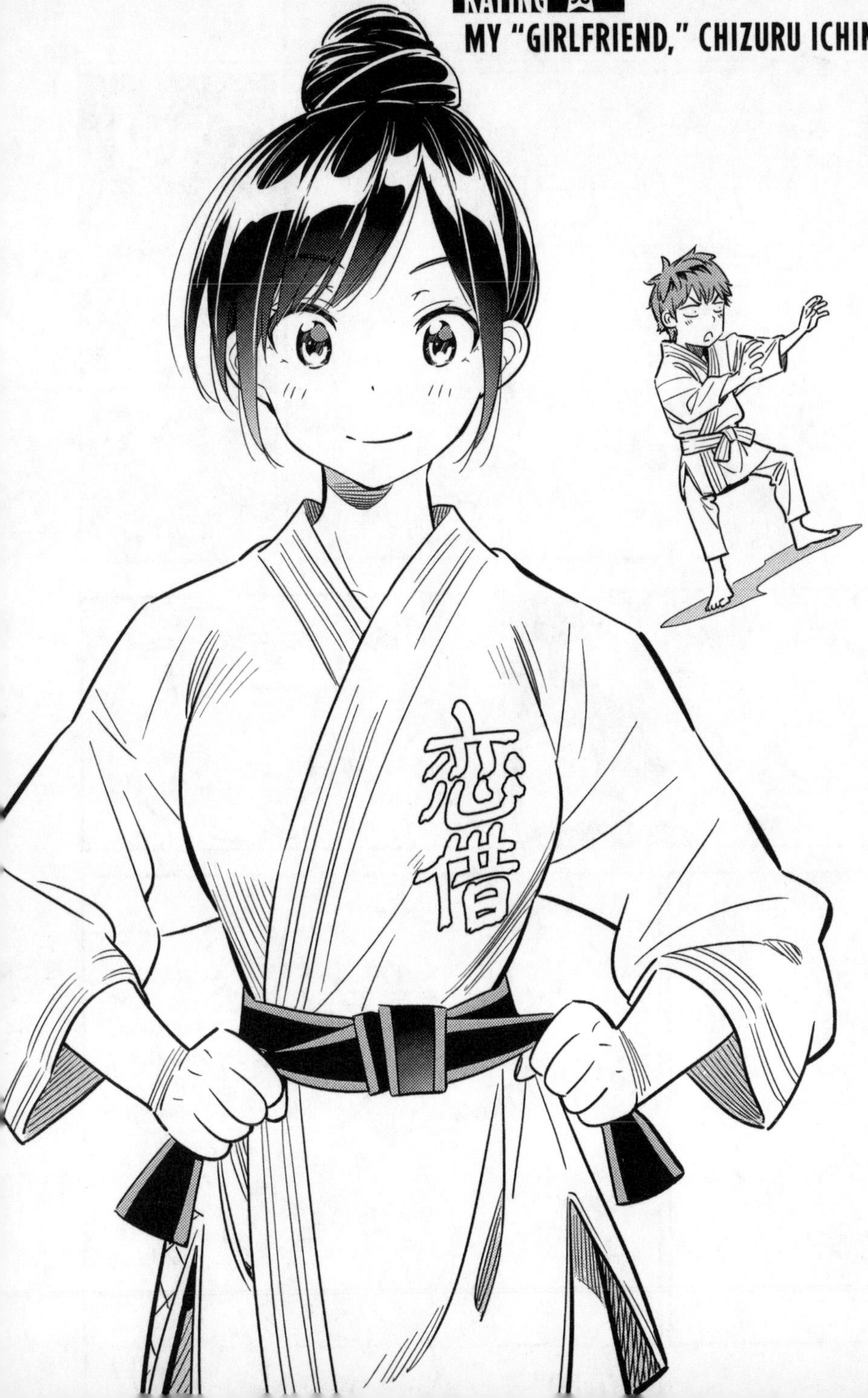
恋借

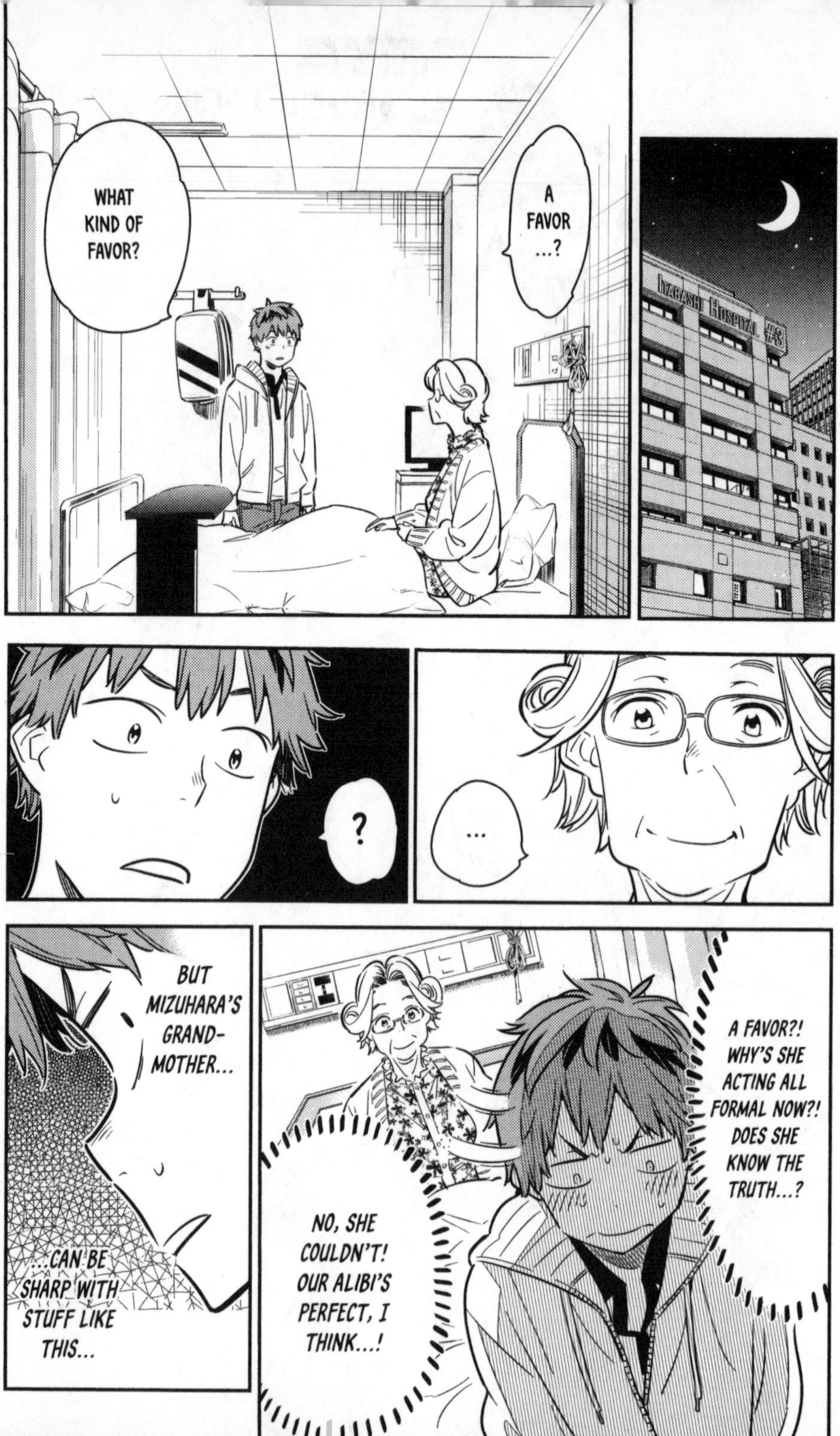
A FAVOR ...?
WHAT KIND OF FAVOR?
...
?
A FAVOR?! WHY'S SHE ACTING ALL FORMAL NOW?! DOES SHE KNOW THE TRUTH...?
NO, SHE COULDN'T! OUR ALIBI'S PERFECT, I THINK...!
BUT MIZUHARA'S GRAND-MOTHER...
...CAN BE SHARP WITH STUFF LIKE THIS...

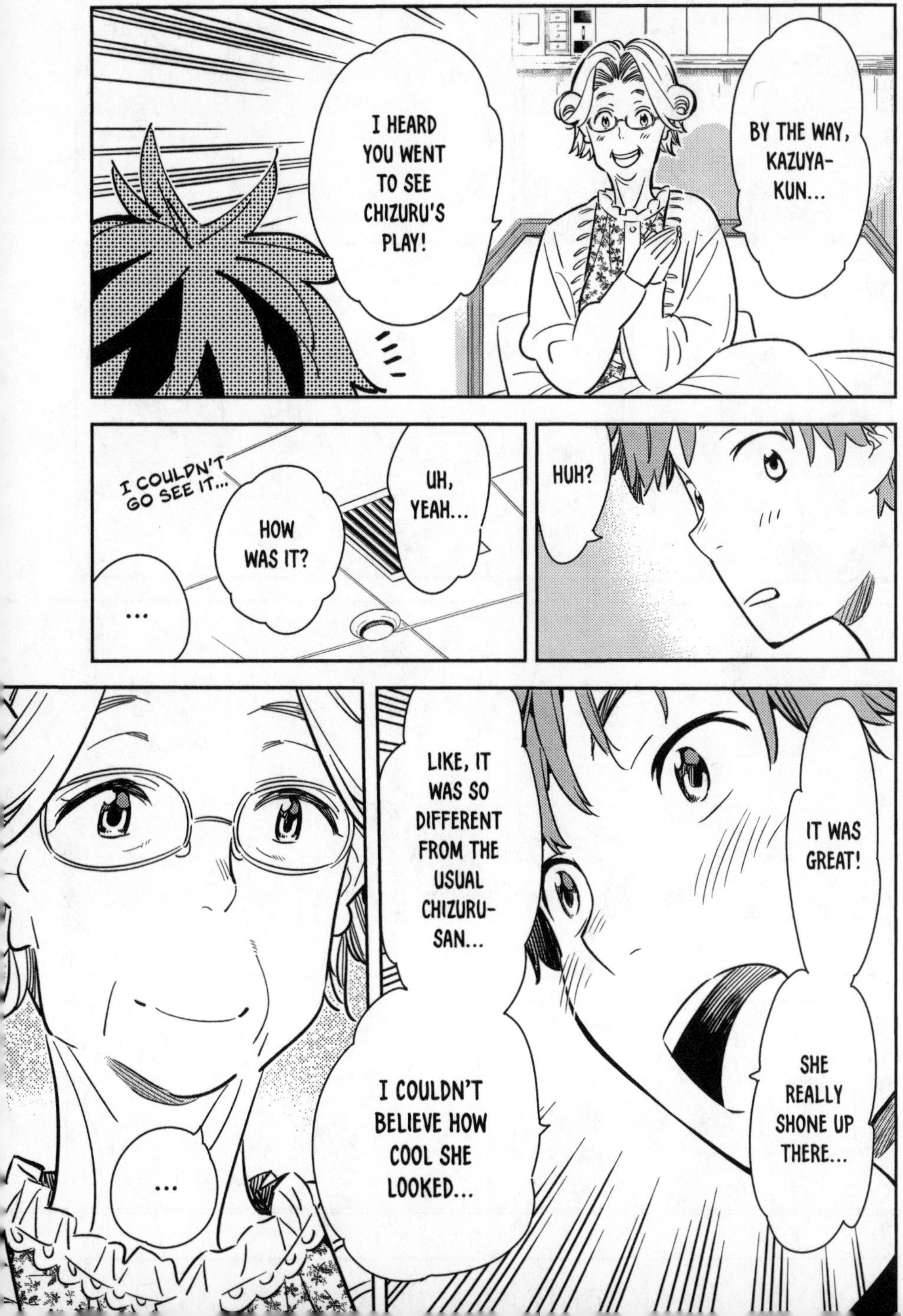
BY THE WAY, KAZUYA-KUN...
I HEARD YOU WENT TO SEE CHIZURU'S PLAY!
HUH?
UH, YEAH...
HOW WAS IT?
I COULDN'T GO SEE IT...
...
IT WAS GREAT!
LIKE, IT WAS SO DIFFERENT FROM THE USUAL CHIZURU-SAN...
SHE REALLY SHONE UP THERE...
I COULDN'T BELIEVE HOW COOL SHE LOOKED...
...

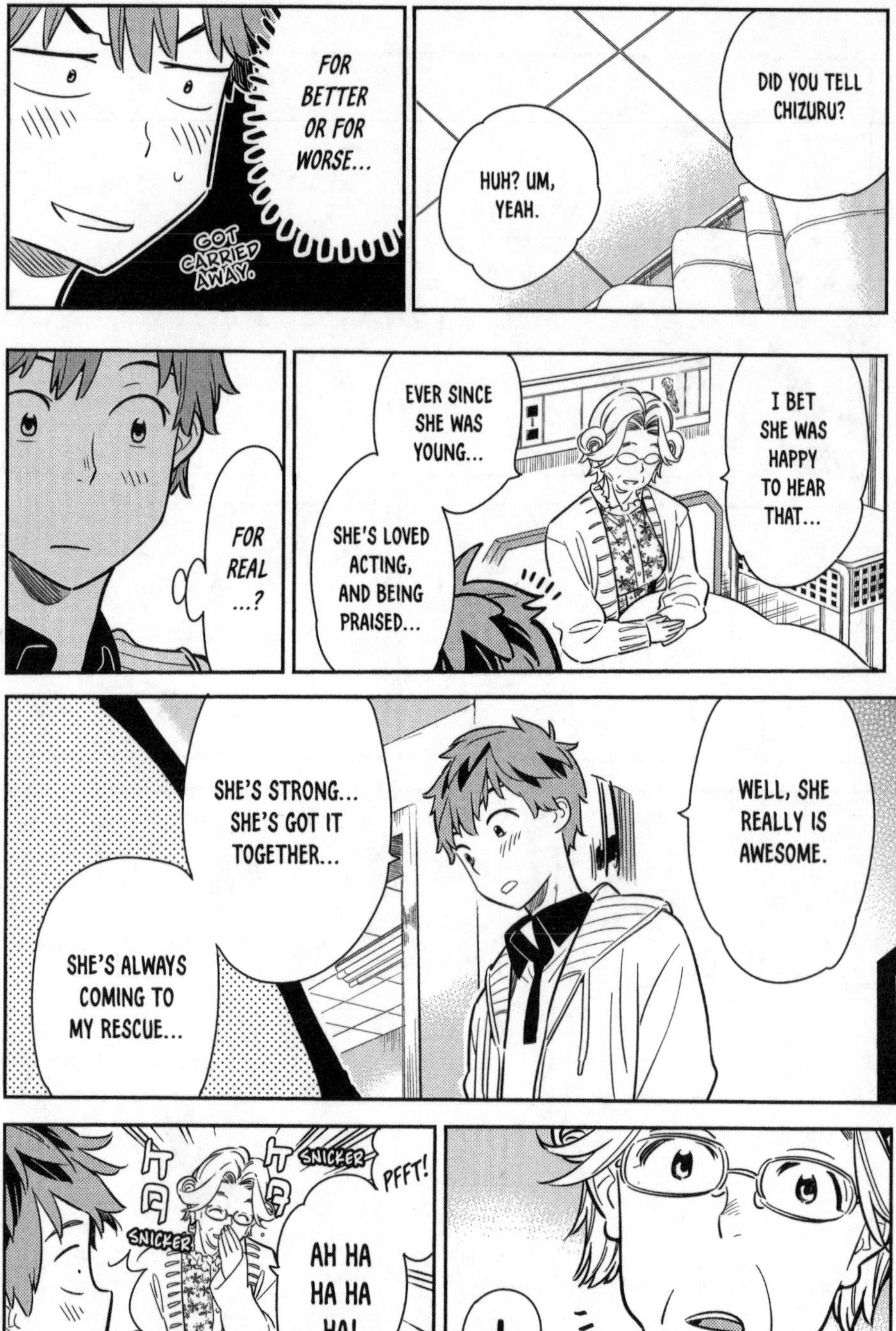
DID YOU TELL CHIZURU?
HUH? UM, YEAH.
FOR BETTER OR FOR WORSE...
GOT CARRIED AWAY.
I BET SHE WAS HAPPY TO HEAR THAT...
EVER SINCE SHE WAS YOUNG...
SHE'S LOVED ACTING, AND BEING PRAISED...
FOR REAL ...?
WELL, SHE REALLY IS AWESOME.
SHE'S STRONG... SHE'S GOT IT TOGETHER...
SHE'S ALWAYS COMING TO MY RESCUE...
!
PFFT!
SNICKER
AH HA HA HA HA!
SNICKER

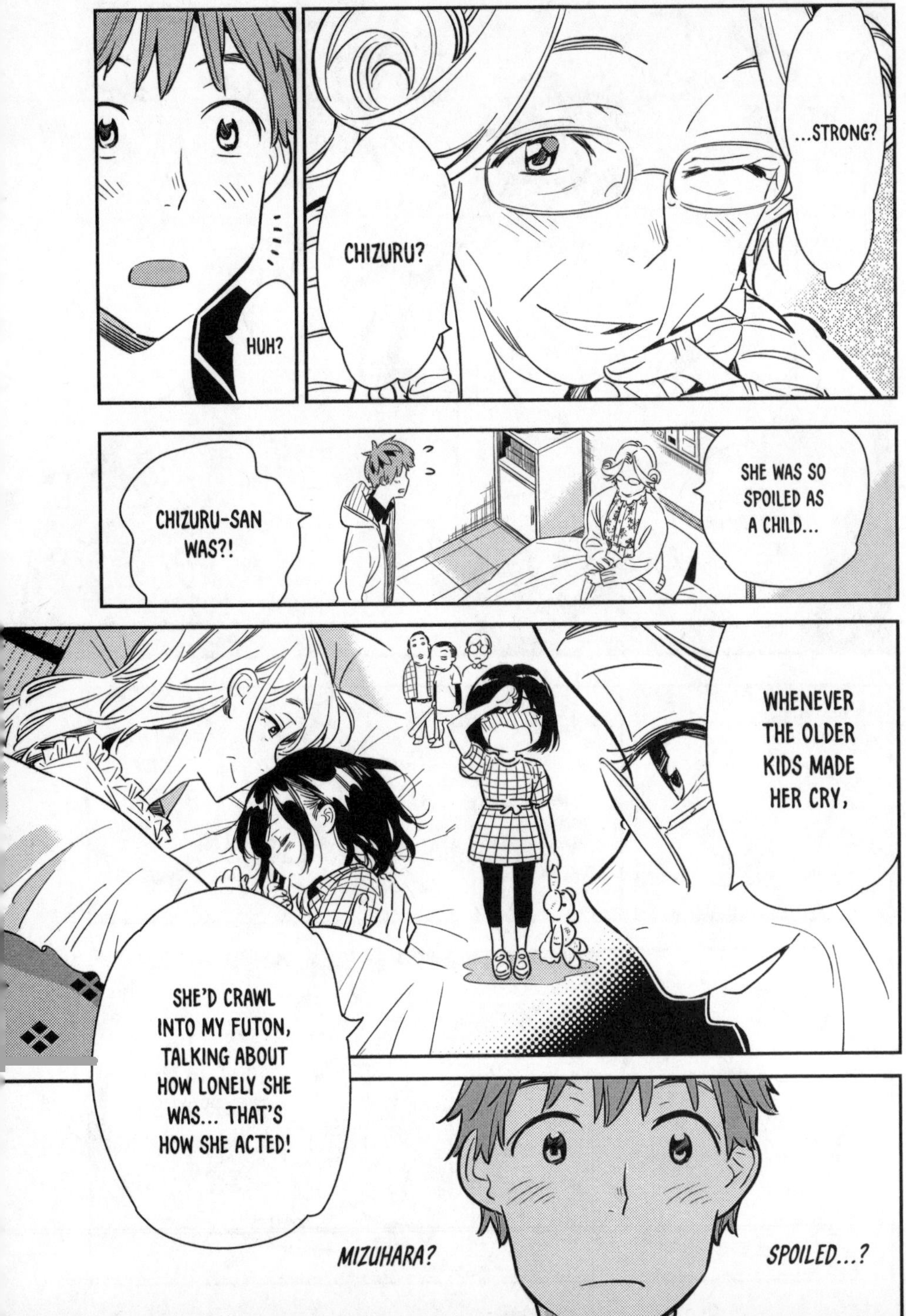
...STRONG?
CHIZURU?
HUH?
SHE WAS SO SPOILED AS A CHILD...
CHIZURU-SAN WAS?!
WHENEVER THE OLDER KIDS MADE HER CRY,
SHE'D CRAWL INTO MY FUTON, TALKING ABOUT HOW LONELY SHE WAS... THAT'S HOW SHE ACTED!
SPOILED...?
MIZUHARA?

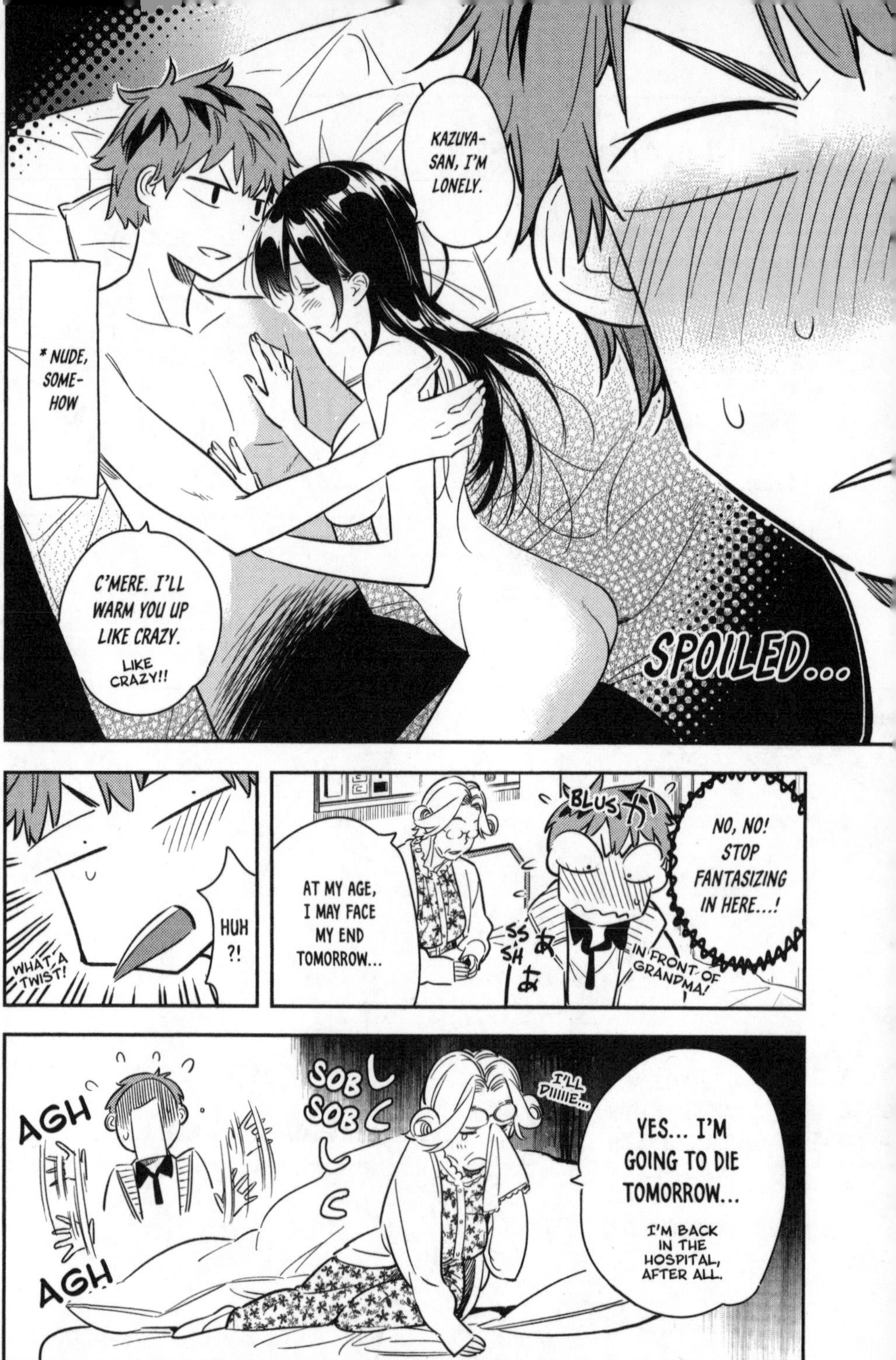
KAZUYA-SAN, I'M LONELY.
SPOILED...
* NUDE, SOMEHOW
C'MERE. I'LL WARM YOU UP LIKE CRAZY.
LIKE CRAZY!!
NO, NO! STOP FANTASIZING IN HERE...!
IN FRONT OF GRANDMA!
SSSH
AT MY AGE, I MAY FACE MY END TOMORROW...
HUH?!
WHAT A TWIST!
YES... I'M GOING TO DIE TOMORROW...
I'M BACK IN THE HOSPITAL, AFTER ALL.
I'LL DIIIIIE...
SOB SOB
AGH
AGH

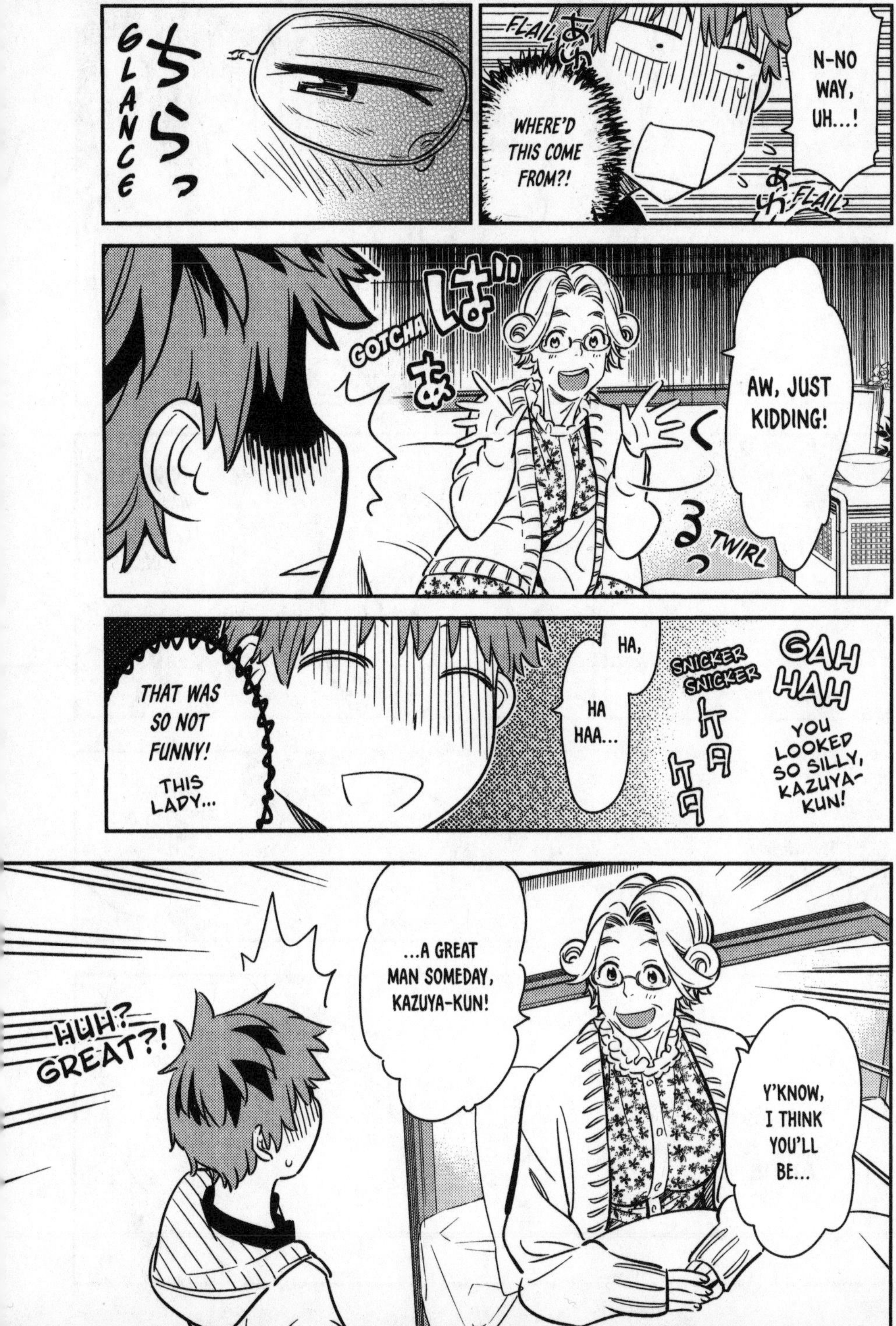
N-NO WAY, UH...!
FLAIL
WHERE'D THIS COME FROM?!
FLAIL
GLANCE
AW, JUST KIDDING!
TWIRL
GOTCHA
GAH HAH
YOU LOOKED SO SILLY, KAZUYA-KUN!
SNICKER SNICKER
HA,
HA HAA...
THAT WAS SO NOT FUNNY!
THIS LADY...
Y'KNOW, I THINK YOU'LL BE...
...A GREAT MAN SOMEDAY, KAZUYA-KUN!
HUH? GREAT?!

NAH...
I DUNNO IF I CAN DO THAT...
SNIF
NOT A WIMP LIKE ME...
OHH? DON'T BE SILLY! I KNOW YOU CAN DO IT, KAZUYA-KUN!
OH? UH, YOU THINK ...?
I'M CERTAIN OF IT!!
BOY, MAYBE YOU'RE RIGHT...
GOOD AT FLATTERY
SIMPLETON
AND THE WAY I SEE IT, KAZUYA-KUN...
YOU'RE A *LOT STRONGER* THAN HER!
HUH?
NOBODY'S PERFECT OUT THERE.
WE LOSE OUR WAY...
...WE MAKE MISTAKES.
WE REALIZE HOW WEAK AND FRAGILE WE ARE, WE FALL TO OUR KNEES...
BUT EVERY TIME, WE STAND BACK UP, STRIVING FOR HAPPINESS.
THAT'S WHAT ALL OF US CALL "LIFE."

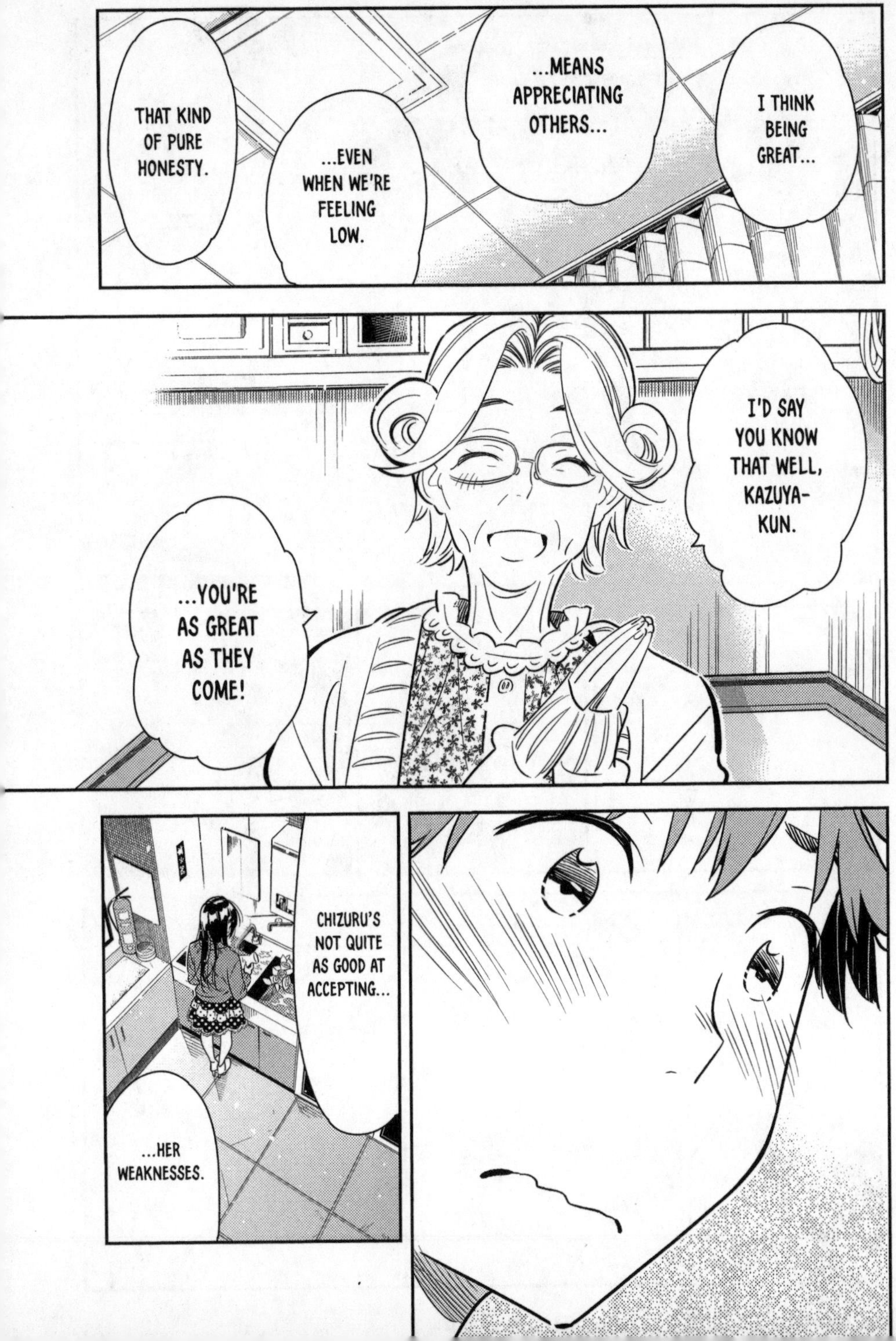
I THINK BEING GREAT...
...MEANS APPRECIATING OTHERS...
...EVEN WHEN WE'RE FEELING LOW.
THAT KIND OF PURE HONESTY.
I'D SAY YOU KNOW THAT WELL, KAZUYA-KUN.
...YOU'RE AS GREAT AS THEY COME!
CHIZURU'S NOT QUITE AS GOOD AT ACCEPTING...
...HER WEAKNESSES.

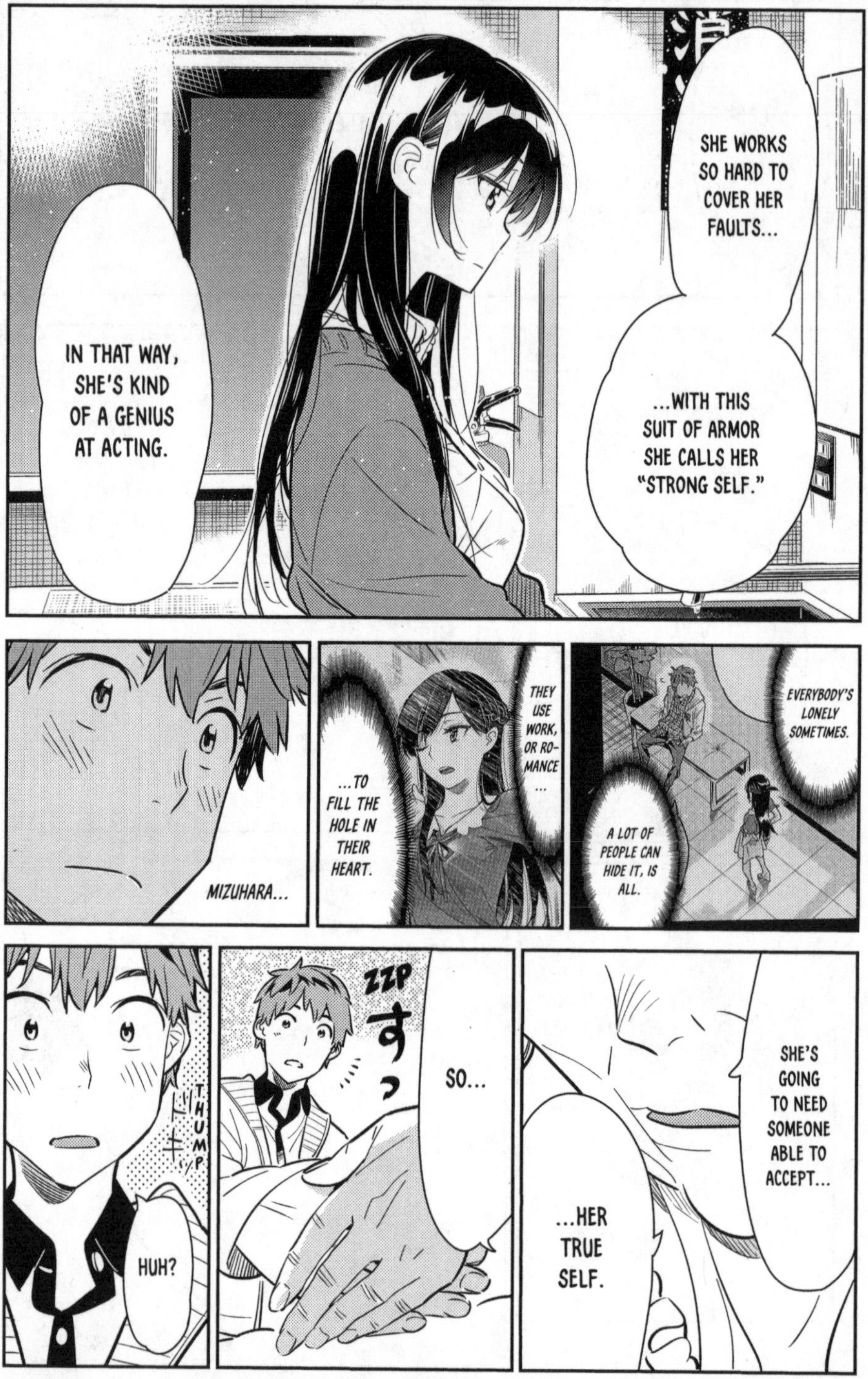
SHE WORKS SO HARD TO COVER HER FAULTS...
...WITH THIS SUIT OF ARMOR SHE CALLS HER "STRONG SELF."
IN THAT WAY, SHE'S KIND OF A GENIUS AT ACTING.
EVERYBODY'S LONELY SOMETIMES.
A LOT OF PEOPLE CAN HIDE IT, IS ALL.
THEY USE WORK, OR ROMANCE...
...TO FILL THE HOLE IN THEIR HEART.
MIZUHARA...
SHE'S GOING TO NEED SOMEONE ABLE TO ACCEPT...
...HER TRUE SELF.
SO...
ZZP
すっ
...
THUMP
HUH?

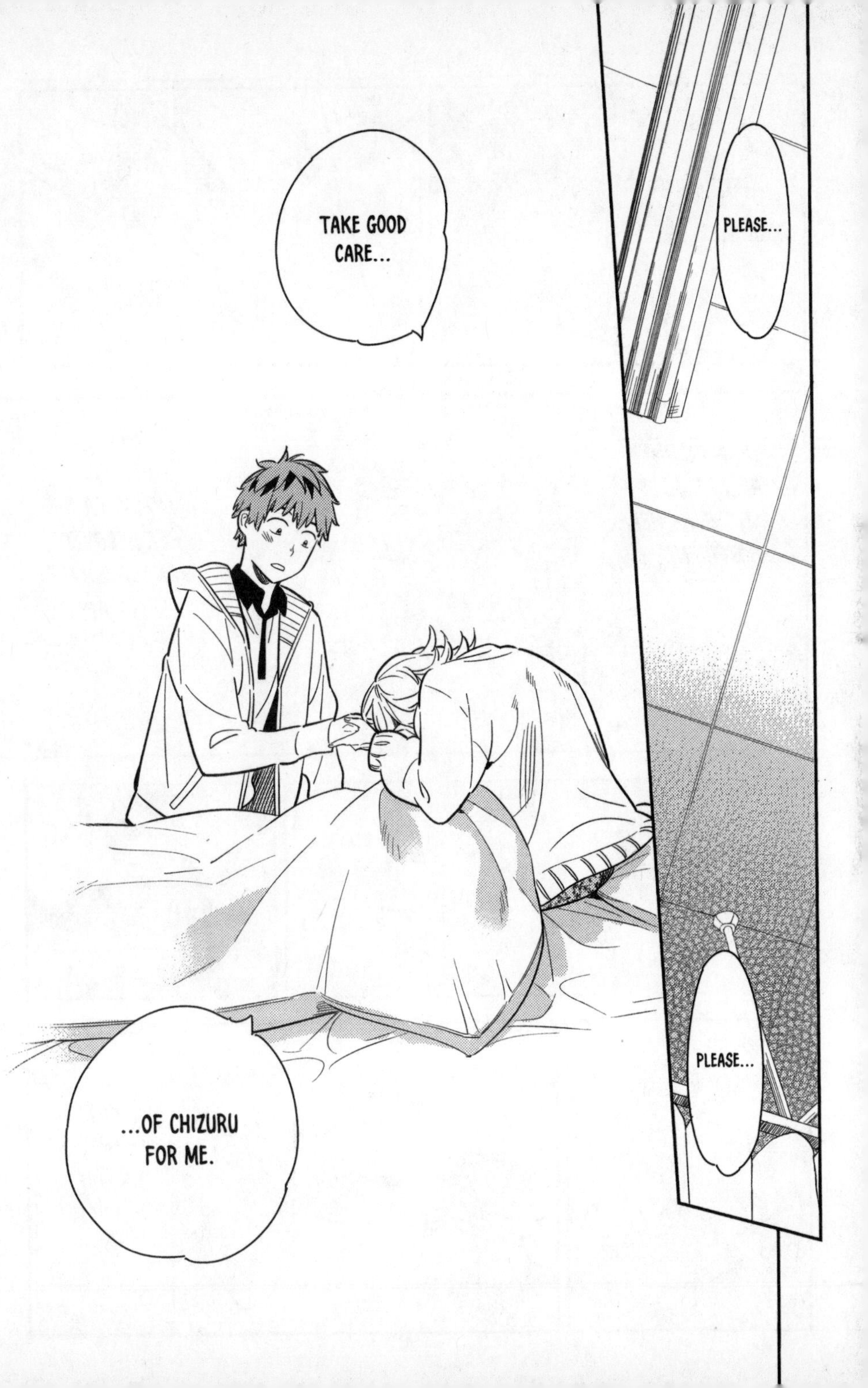
PLEASE...
PLEASE...
TAKE GOOD CARE...
...OF CHIZURU FOR ME.

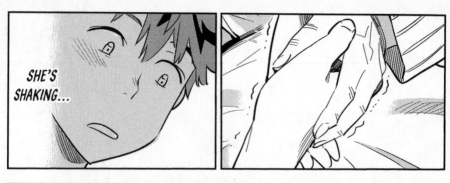

SHE'S SHAKING...
YEAH... I GET IT... MIZUHARA'S HER BELOVED GRANDDAUGHTER, AFTER ALL.
SHE WOULDN'T ACCEPT JUST ANYONE AS HER BOYFRIEND...
YOU'RE...
...KAZUYA-KUN, RIGHT?
I CAN'T BE RECKLESS.
I CAN'T PROMISE...
...TO BE THERE FOR HER MY WHOLE LIFE.
BUT WHAT I CAN SAY IS...
...I LOVE HER.
OH?

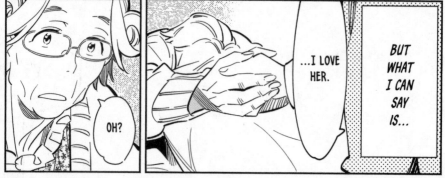

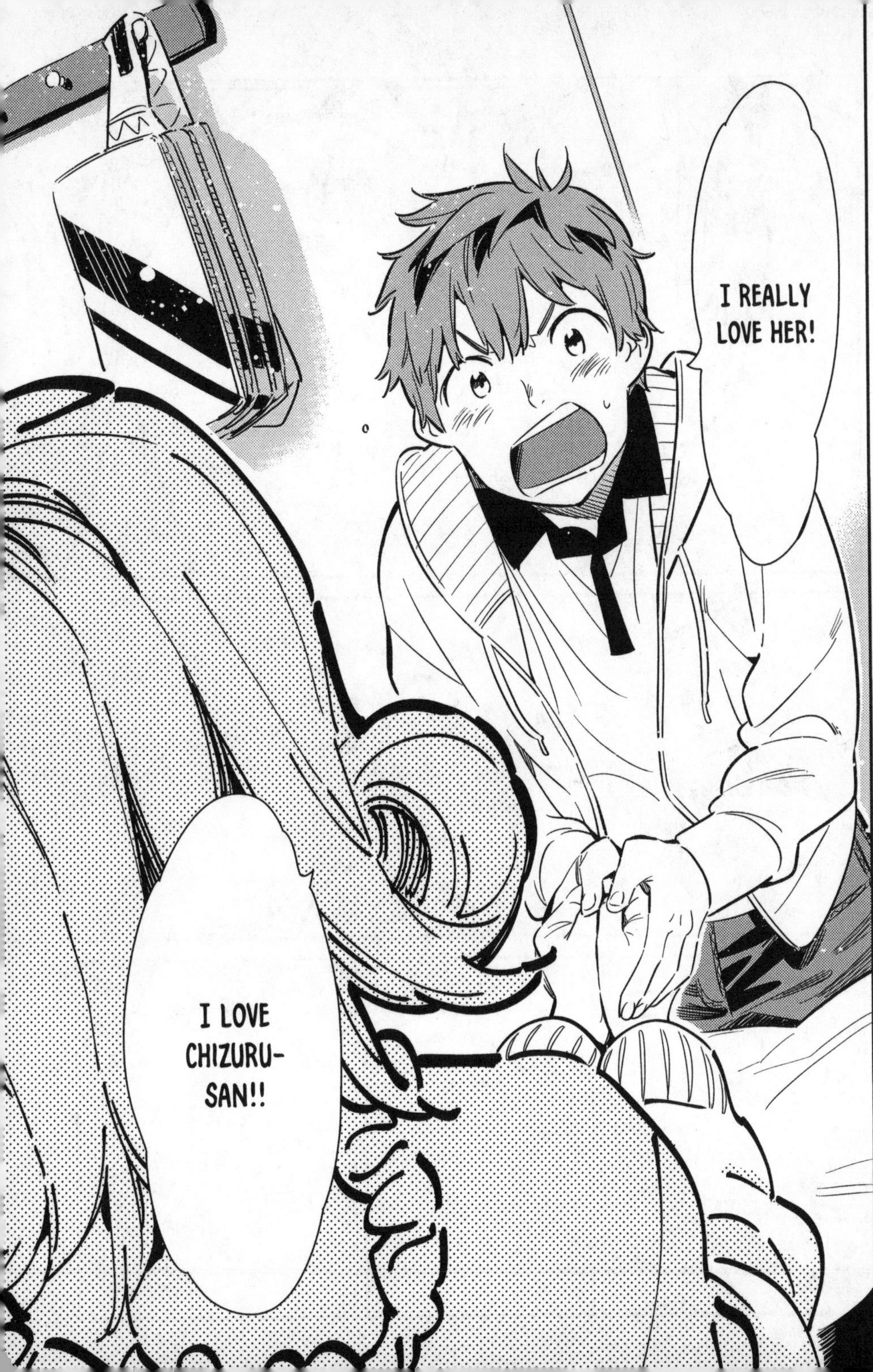
I REALLY LOVE HER!
I LOVE CHIZURU-SAN!!

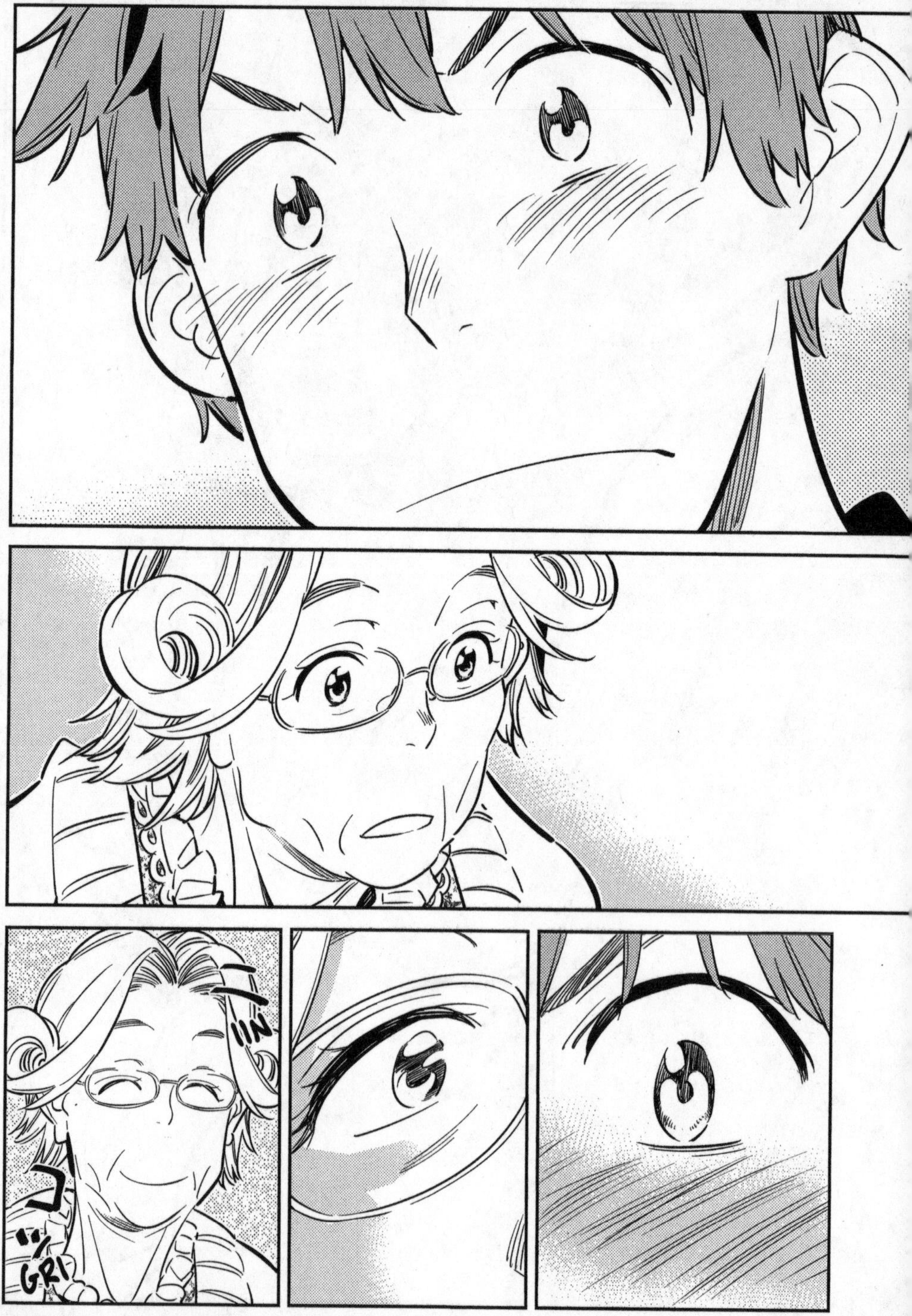
GRI
IIN

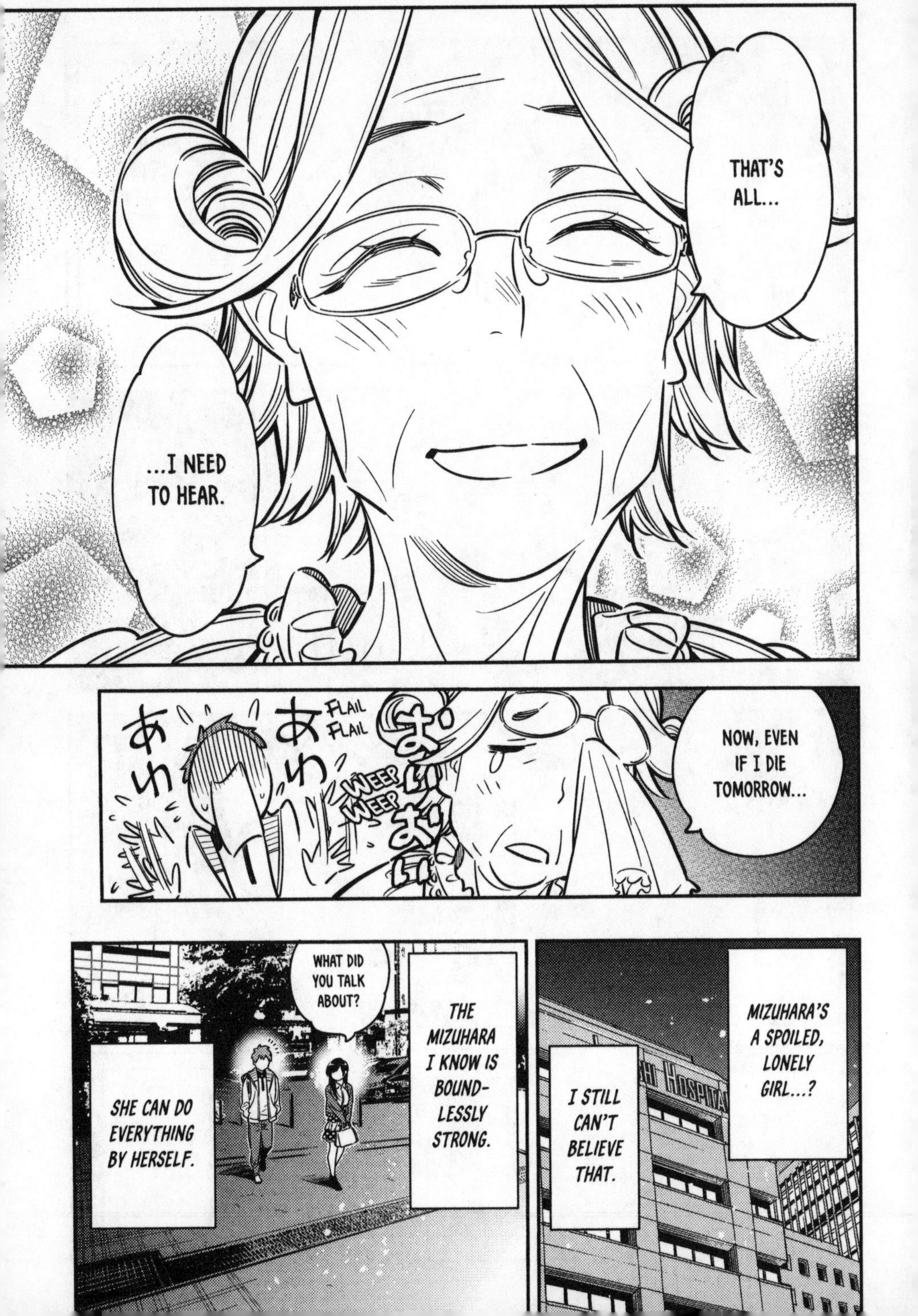
THAT'S ALL...
...I NEED TO HEAR.
NOW, EVEN IF I DIE TOMORROW...
おいおい
WEEP WEEP
あわあわ
FLAIL FLAIL
MIZUHARA'S A SPOILED, LONELY GIRL...?
I STILL CAN'T BELIEVE THAT.
THE MIZUHARA I KNOW IS BOUND-LESSLY STRONG.
WHAT DID YOU TALK ABOUT?
SHE CAN DO EVERYTHING BY HERSELF.

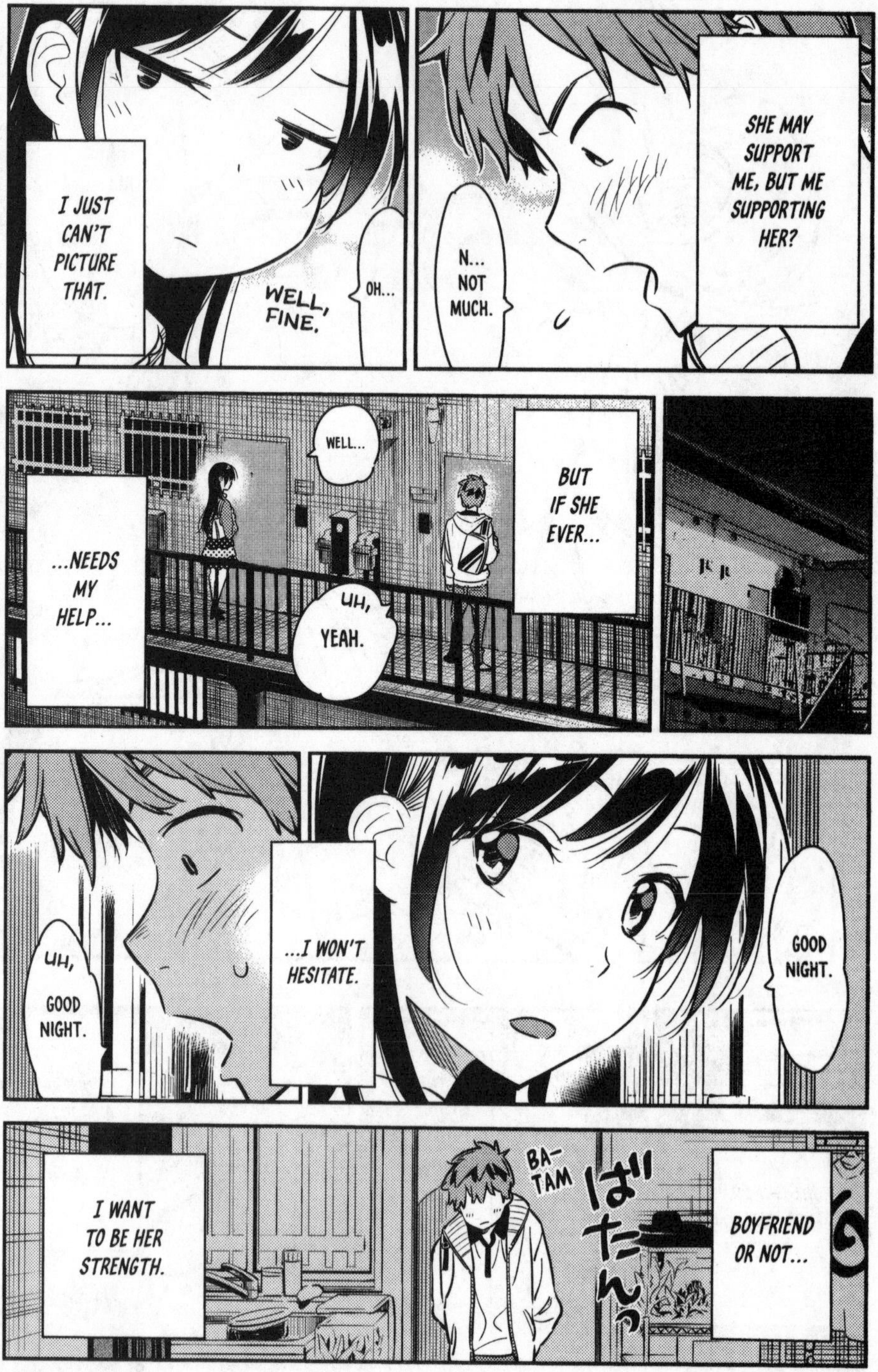
SHE MAY SUPPORT ME, BUT ME SUPPORTING HER?
N... NOT MUCH.
OH...
WELL, FINE.
I JUST CAN'T PICTURE THAT.
BUT IF SHE EVER...
WELL...
UH, YEAH.
...NEEDS MY HELP...
GOOD NIGHT.
...I WON'T HESITATE.
UH, GOOD NIGHT.
BOYFRIEND OR NOT...
ばたんっ
BA-TAM
I WANT TO BE HER STRENGTH.

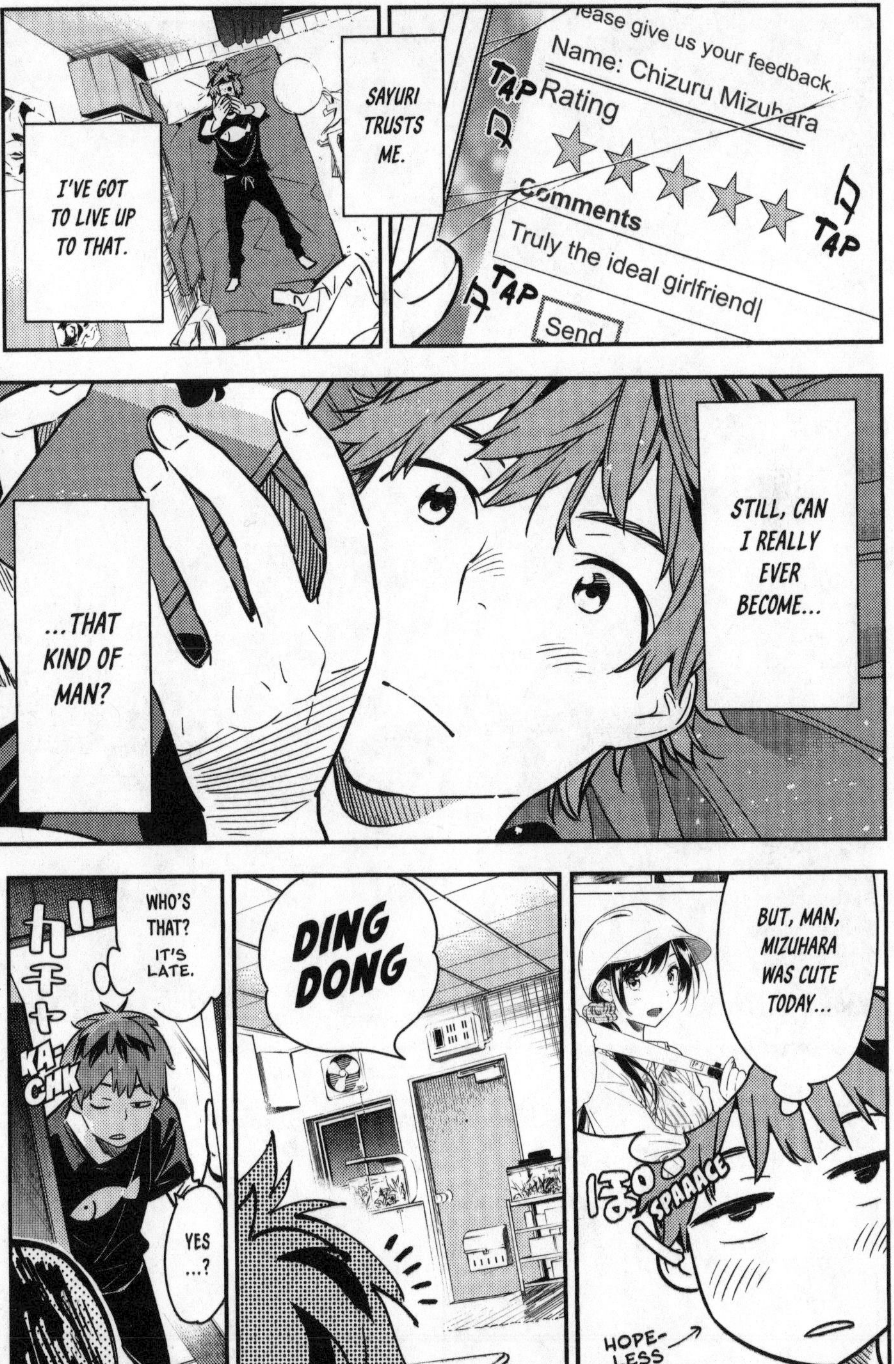
lease give us your feedback.
Name: Chizuru Mizuhara
Rating
Comments
Truly the ideal girlfriend|
Send
TAP
TAP
TAP
SAYURI TRUSTS ME.
I'VE GOT TO LIVE UP TO THAT.
STILL, CAN I REALLY EVER BECOME...
...THAT KIND OF MAN?
BUT, MAN, MIZUHARA WAS CUTE TODAY...
SPAAACE
HOPE-LESS
DING DONG
WHO'S THAT? IT'S LATE.
KA-CHK
YES ...?

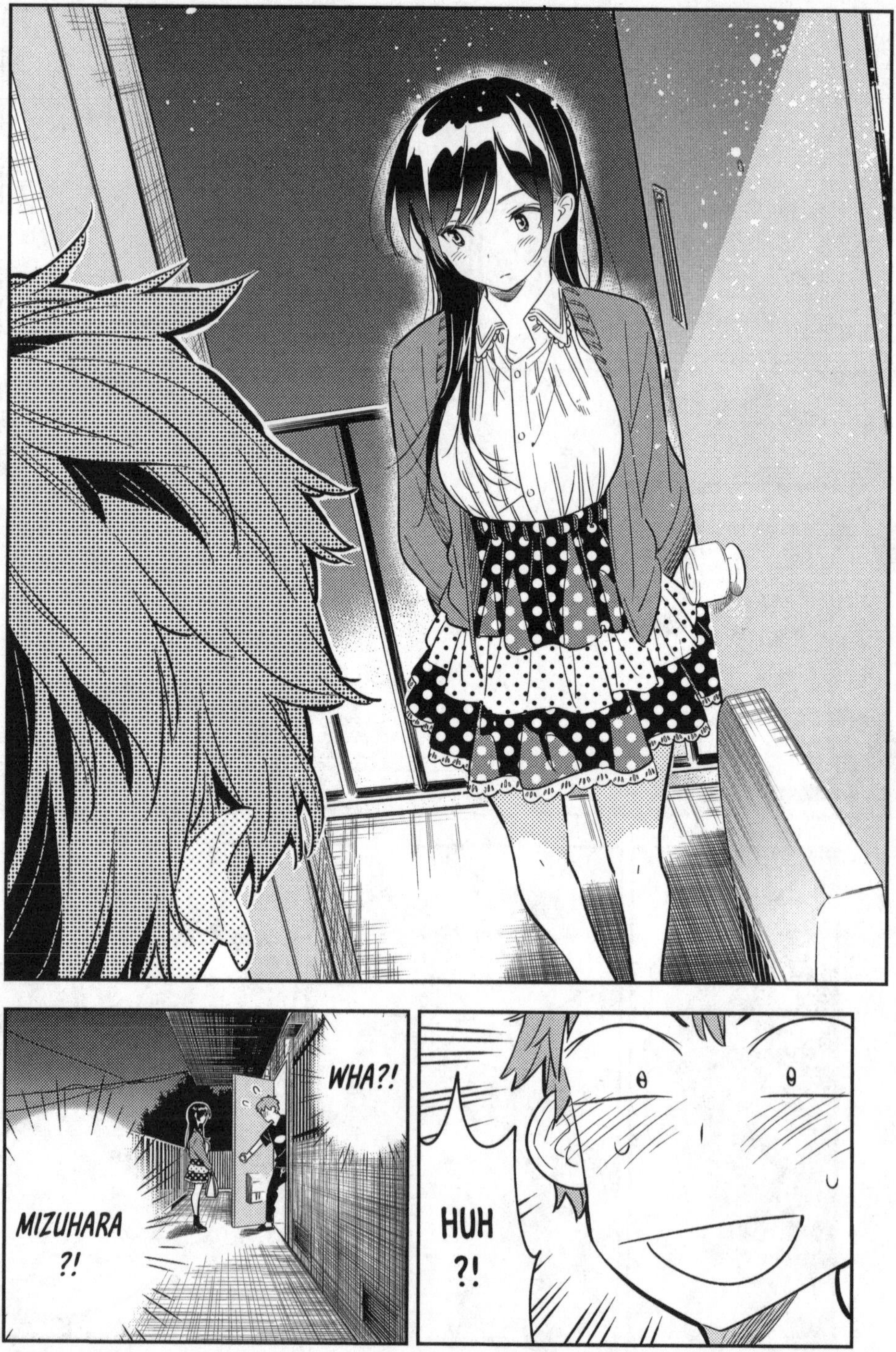
HUH ?!
WHA?!
MIZUHARA ?!

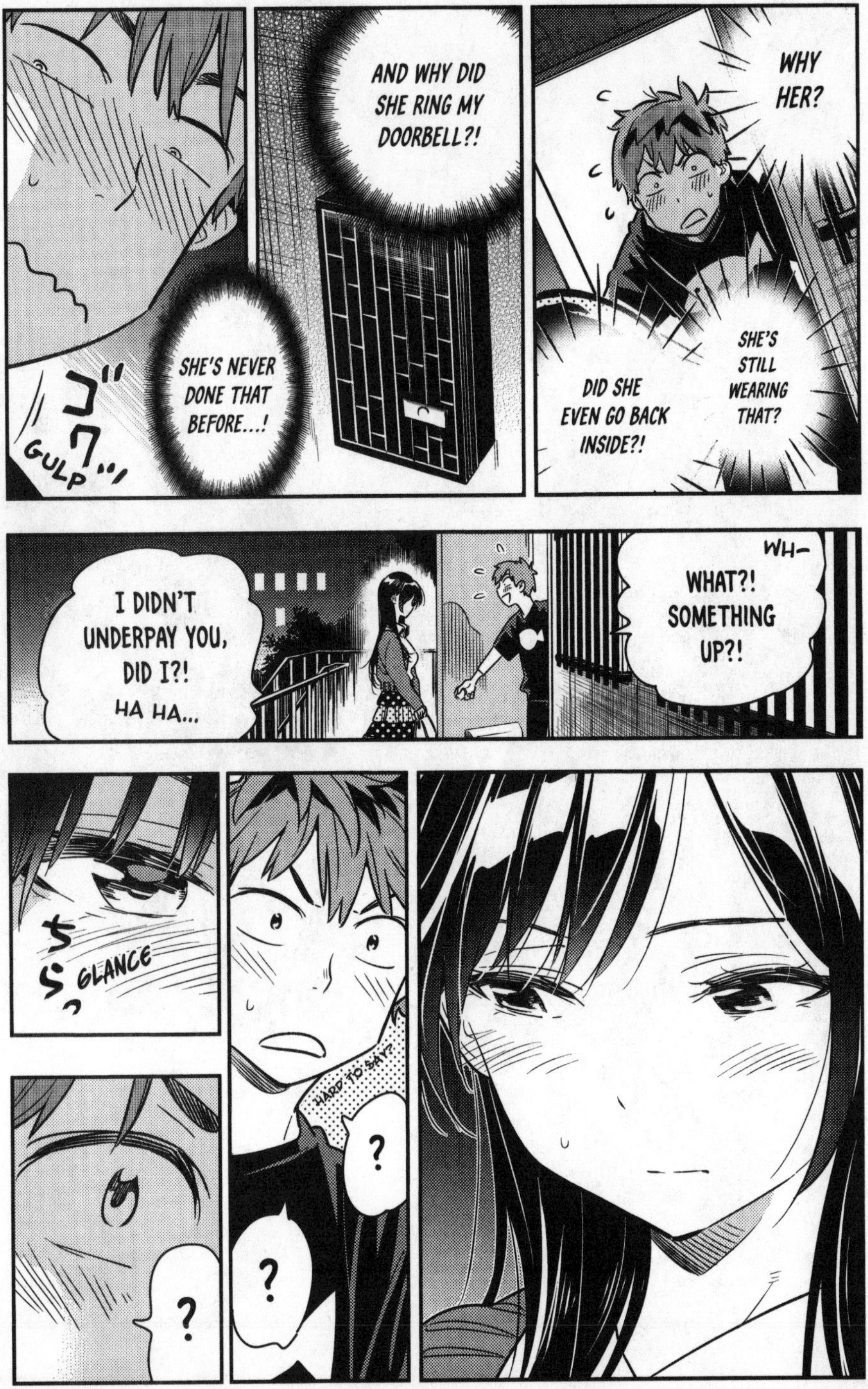
WHY HER?
SHE'S STILL WEARING THAT?
DID SHE EVEN GO BACK INSIDE?!
AND WHY DID SHE RING MY DOORBELL?!
SHE'S NEVER DONE THAT BEFORE...!
ゴクッ
GULP
WH- WHAT?! SOMETHING UP?!
I DIDN'T UNDERPAY YOU, DID I?!
HA HA...
HARD TO SAY?
?
?
ちらっ
GLANCE
?

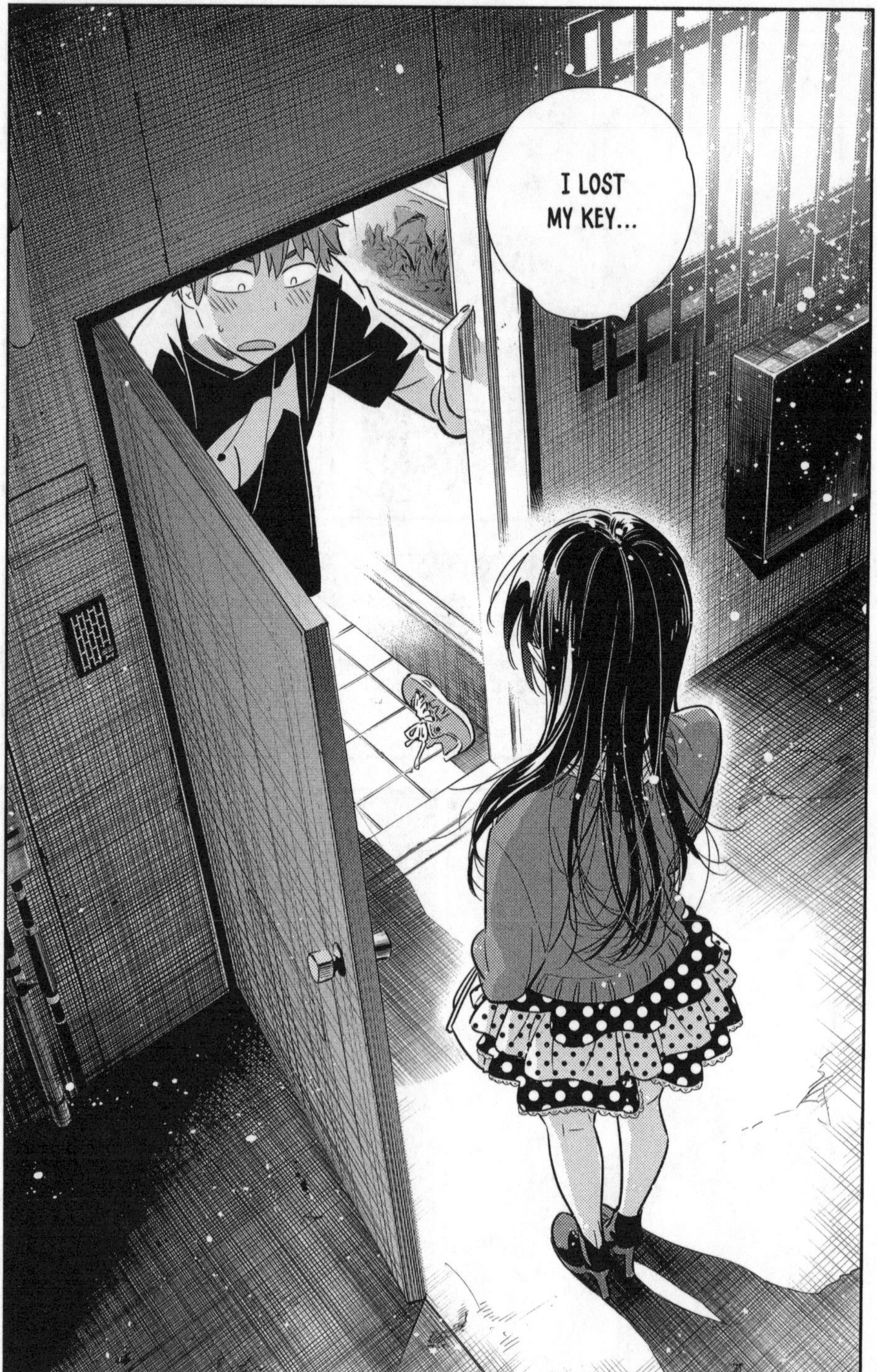
I LOST MY KEY...

I SAID IT'D NEVER BE BACK, BUT THE BONUS PAGE RETURNS FOR AN APOLOGY.

THANK YOU FOR PURCHASING VOLUME 7!

BOY, THIS VOLUME SURE ENDED DRAMATICALLY. SORRY! LET'S GO BACK TO PAGE 153 FOR A MOMENT. AS I SAID IN THE LAST BOOK, I WAS NO HIGH SCHOOL BASEBALL WHIZ, BUT I PLAYED IT FOR NINE YEARS THROUGH MIDDLE AND ELEMENTARY SCHOOL, SO IT'S FUN FOR ME TO DRAW BASEBALL SCENES (THE POSING, THE "OOH, IT'S CUTE FOR A GIRL TO CARRY A BAT THIS WAY" STUFF, ETC.) SO CHAPTER 57, AND ALL ITS CONTENT FOR BASEBALL (AND BASEBALL PROP) MANIACS, WAS REALLY EXCITING FOR US ALL, I THINK. THE END RESULT: I THOUGHT THE TITLE PAGE WAS A HOME RUN! THE POSE NIMBLY ENCAPSULATES THE COUPLE'S RELATIONSHIP, YOU KNOW?
BUT TAKE ANOTHER LOOK, AND...WELL...
I MADE MIZUHARA LEFT-HANDED.
SO AWFUL. WHAT DID I EVEN SPEND NINE YEARS DOING? (SERIOUSLY, IF I DIDN'T MESS UP SO MUCH BACK THEN... SORRY, TEAMMATES...) I THOUGHT ABOUT DRAWING IT OVER AGAIN, OF COURSE...BUT...I DON'T KNOW... MIZUHARA... DOESN'T SHE LOOK CUTE? THAT'S RIGHT. SADLY, I JUST DREW HER TOO DARN ADORABLE!
THAT KILLER SMILE...
IT HAS THE PERFECT "JUST RIGHT" FEEL!
I SHOULD REALLY DO IT OVER AGAIN, BUT OH WELL!
AND SO, INSTEAD OF REDRAWING IT, I'M BORROWING THIS PAGE TO PUT TOGETHER A (VERY CONTRIVED) SCENE THAT EXPLAINS THE IMAGE. OF COURSE, I WANT TO APOLOGIZE TO EVERYONE FOR A LOT OF OTHER THINGS, TOO... BUT I'LL HAVE TO GET TO THOSE SOME OTHER TIME.

THANKS FOR READING...!!
MIYAJIMA

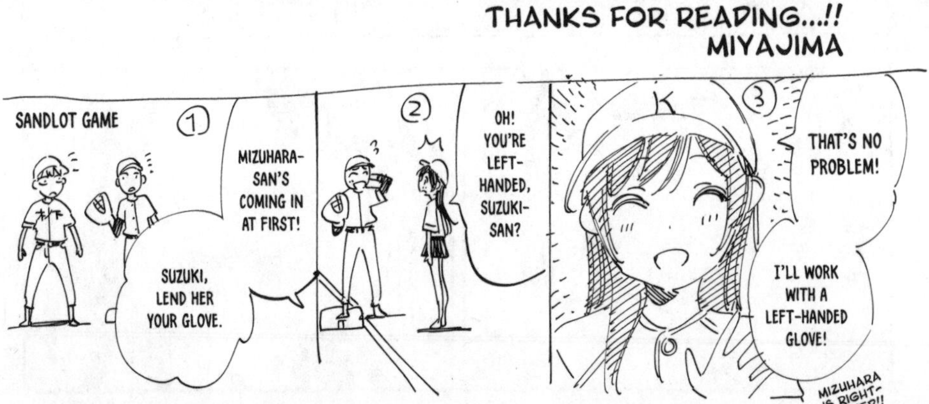
SANDLOT GAME
1
MIZUHARA-SAN'S COMING IN AT FIRST!
SUZUKI, LEND HER YOUR GLOVE.
2
OH! YOU'RE LEFT-HANDED, SUZUKI-SAN?
3
THAT'S NO PROBLEM!
I'LL WORK WITH A LEFT-HANDED GLOVE!
MIZUHARA IS RIGHT-HANDED!!

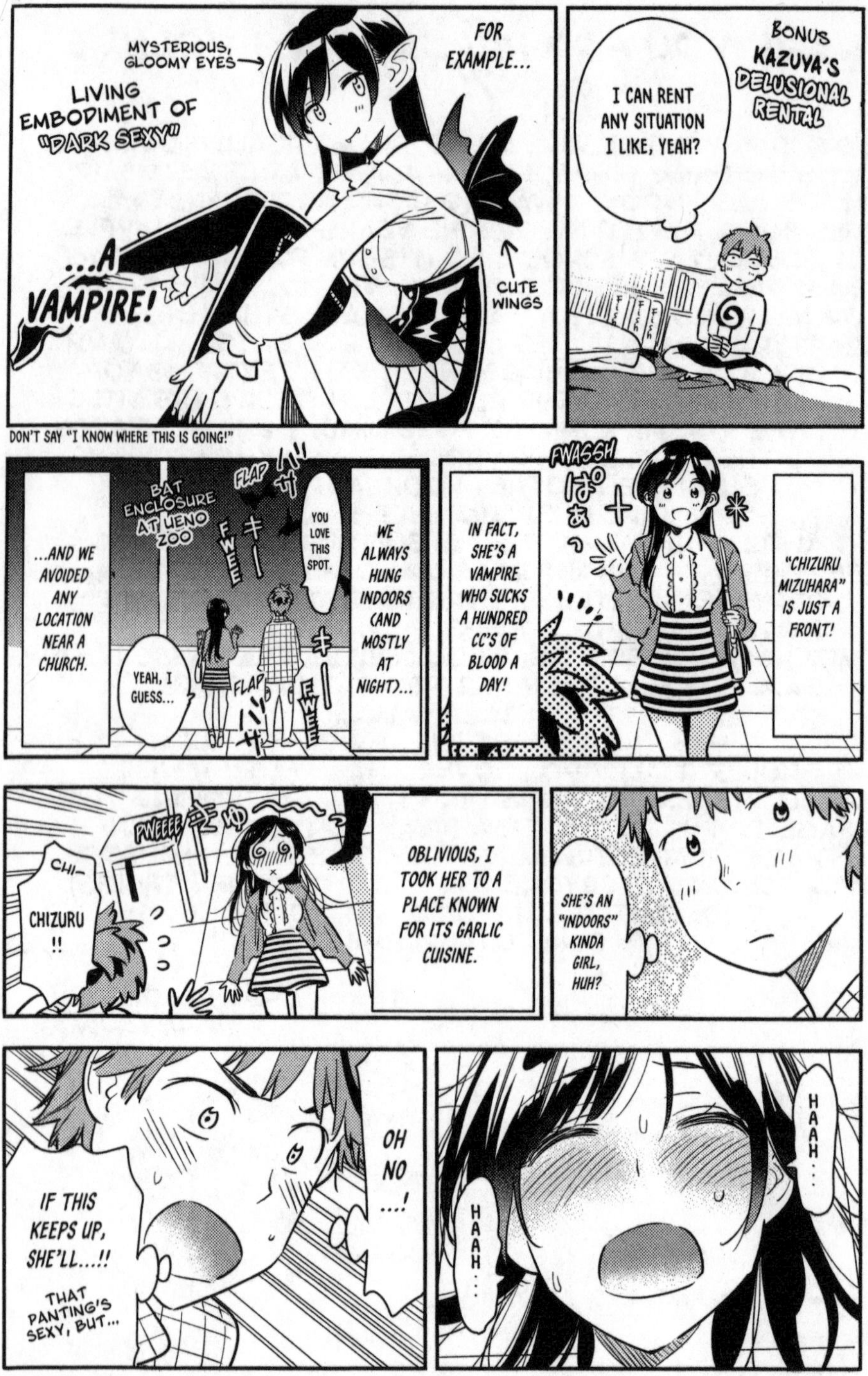
BONUS KAZUYA'S DELUSIONAL RENTAL
I CAN RENT ANY SITUATION I LIKE, YEAH?
FOR EXAMPLE...
MYSTERIOUS, GLOOMY EYES
LIVING EMBODIMENT OF "DARK SEXY"
CUTE WINGS
...A VAMPIRE!
DON'T SAY "I KNOW WHERE THIS IS GOING!"
"CHIZURU MIZUHARA" IS JUST A FRONT!
FWASSH ぱぁっ
IN FACT, SHE'S A VAMPIRE WHO SUCKS A HUNDRED CC'S OF BLOOD A DAY!
WE ALWAYS HUNG INDOORS (AND MOSTLY AT NIGHT)...
YOU LOVE THIS SPOT.
FLAP バサ
BAT ENCLOSURE AT UENO ZOO
FWEE キー
FWEE キー
FLAP バサ
YEAH, I GUESS...
...AND WE AVOIDED ANY LOCATION NEAR A CHURCH.
SHE'S AN "INDOORS" KINDA GIRL, HUH?
OBLIVIOUS, I TOOK HER TO A PLACE KNOWN FOR ITS GARLIC CUISINE.
PWEEEE きゅ〜〜
CHI- CHIZURU!!
HAAH...
HAAH...
OH NO...!
IF THIS KEEPS UP, SHE'LL...!!
THAT PANTING'S SEXY, BUT...

RENT-A-GIRLFRIEND STAFF: A, IROHKI, TEMAENO, KUSUMI, MITSUKI, MINATO

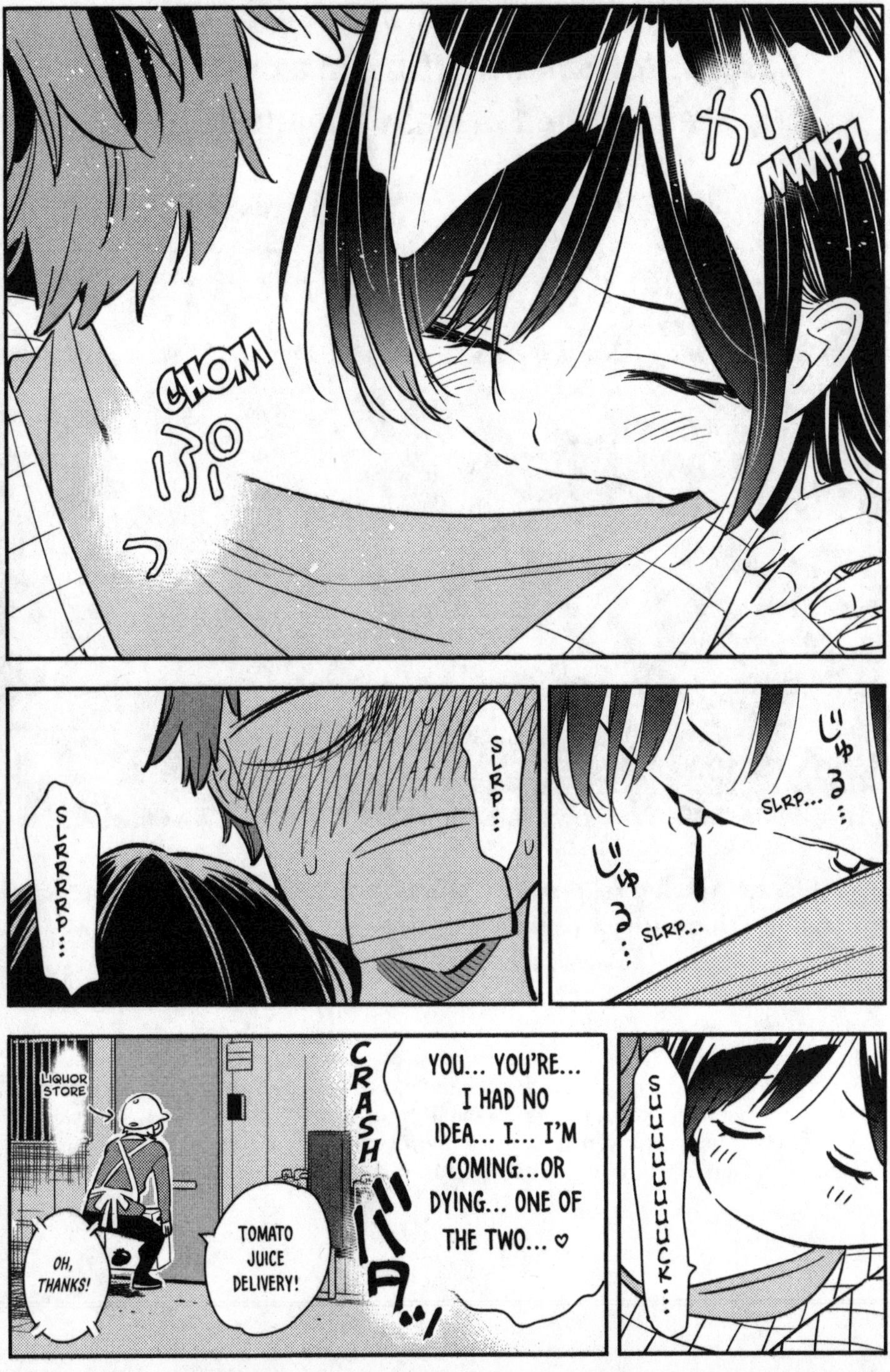
MMP!
CHOM
じゅる…
SLRP…
じゅる…
SLRP…
SLRP…
SLRRRRP…
SUUUUUUUCK…
YOU… YOU'RE… I HAD NO IDEA… I… I'M COMING…OR DYING… ONE OF THE TWO… ♡
CRASH
TOMATO JUICE DELIVERY!
OH, THANKS!
LIQUOR STORE

EDITORS: HIRAOKA-SAN, HIRATSUKA-SAN, HARA-SAN, CHOKAI-SAN. ALSO THANKS TO EVERYBODY WHO PICKED UP THIS BOOK!! SEE YOU SOON! ♡

The beloved characters from *Cardcaptor Sakura* return in a brand new, reimagined fantasy adventure!

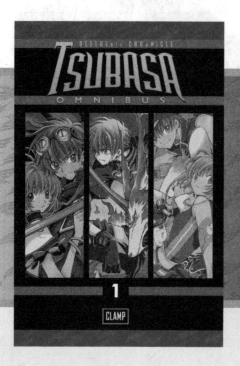

"[*Tsubasa*] takes readers on a fantastic ride that only gets more exhilarating with each successive chapter." —Anime News Network

In the Kingdom of Clow, an archaeological dig unleashes an incredible power, causing Princess Sakura to lose her memories. To save her, her childhood friend Syaoran must follow the orders of the Dimension Witch and travel alongside Kurogane, an unrivaled warrior; Fai, a powerful magician; and Mokona, a curiously strange creature, to retrieve Sakura's dispersed memories!

The art-deco cyberpunk classic from the creators of *xxxHOLiC* and *Cardcaptor Sakura!*

"Starred Review.
This experimental
sci-fi work from
CLAMP reads like a
romantic version of
AKIRA."
—Publishers Weekly

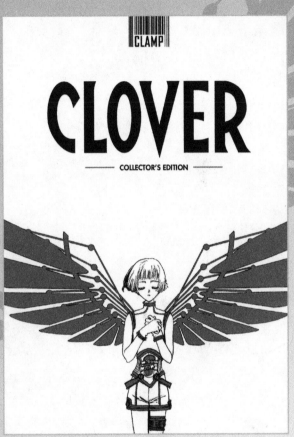

CLOVER © CLAMP-ShigatsuTsuitachi CO.,LTD./Kodansha Ltd.

Su was born into a bleak future, where the government keeps
tight control over children with magical powers—codenamed
"Clovers." With Su being the only "four-leaf" Clover in the
world, she has been kept isolated nearly her whole life. Can
ex-military agent Kazuhiko deliver her to the happiness she
seeks? Experience the complete series in this hardcover
edition, which also includes over twenty pages of ravishing
color art!

The adorable new odd-couple cat comedy manga from the creator of the beloved *Chi's Sweet Home*, in full color!

Praise for Chi's Sweet Home

"Nearly impossible to turn away... a true all-ages title that anyone, young or old, cat lover or not, will enjoy. The stories will bring a smile to your face and warm your heart."

—School Library Journal

Sue & Tai-chan

Konami Kanata

Sue is an aging housecat who's looking forward to living out her life in peace... but her plans change when the mischievous black tomcat Tai-chan enters the picture! Hey! Sue never signed up to be a catsitter! *Sue & Tai-chan* is the latest from the reigning meow-narch of cute kitty comics, Konami Kanata.

KC
KODANSHA
COMICS

THE WORLD OF CLAMP!

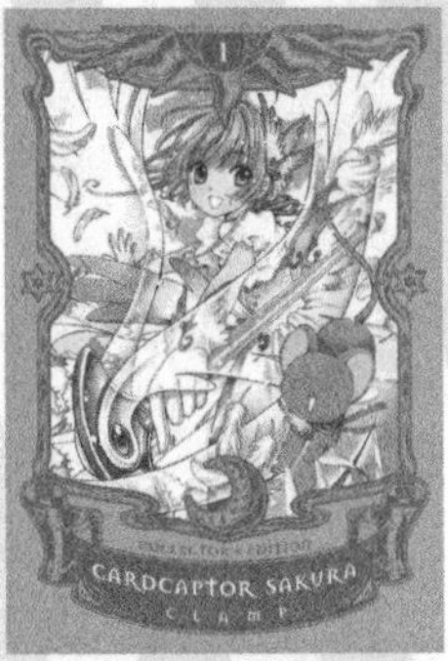
1
CARDCAPTOR SAKURA
CLAMP

Cardcaptor Sakura
Collector's Edition

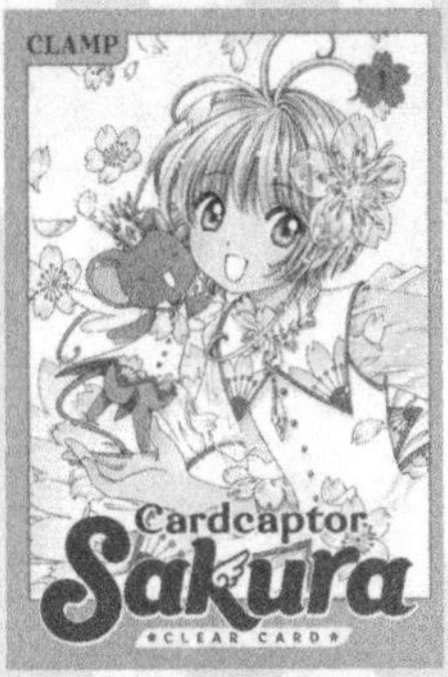
CLAMP
Cardcaptor
Sakura
CLEAR CARD

Cardcaptor Sakura:
Clear Card

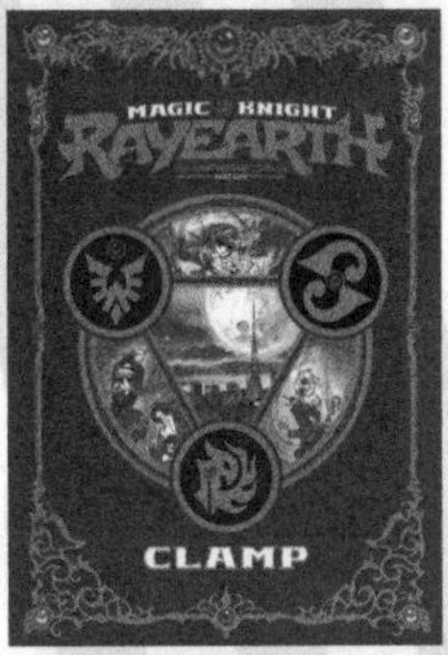
MAGIC KNIGHT
RAYEARTH
CLAMP

Magic Knight Rayearth
25th Anniversary Box Set

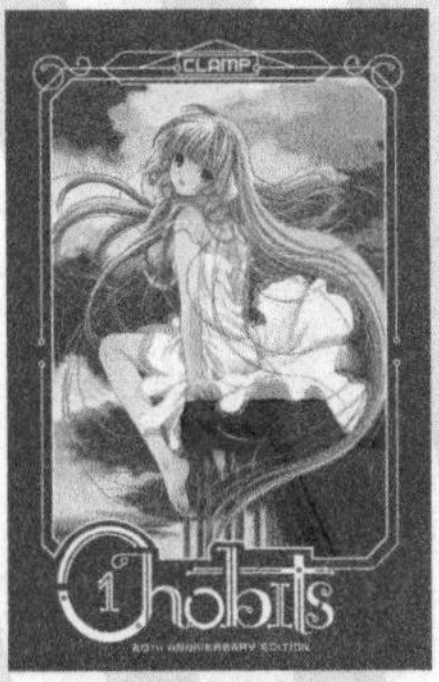
CLAMP
1
Chobits

Chobits

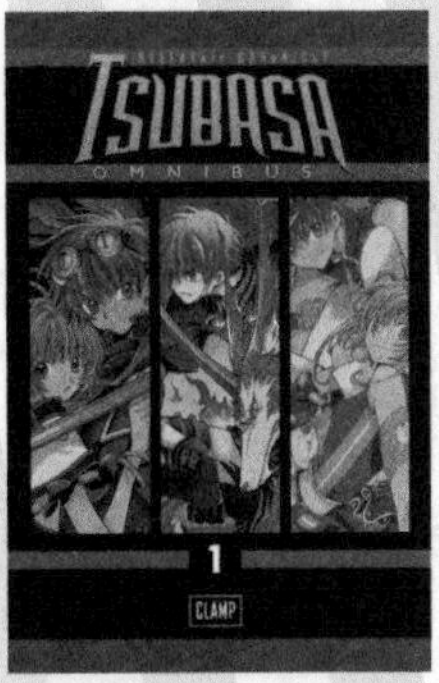
TSUBASA
OMNIBUS
1
CLAMP

TSUBASA Omnibus

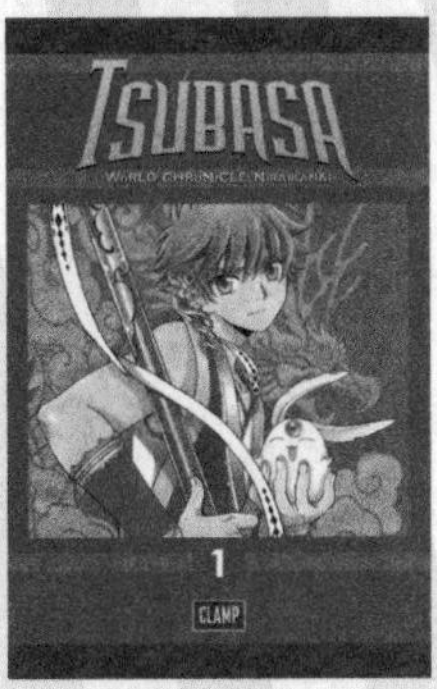
TSUBASA
1
CLAMP

TSUBASA WoRLD CHRoNiCLE

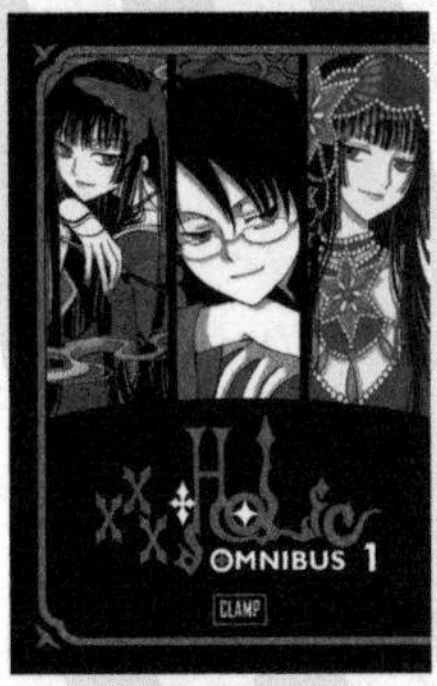
xxxHOLiC
OMNIBUS 1
CLAMP

xxxHOLiC Omnibus

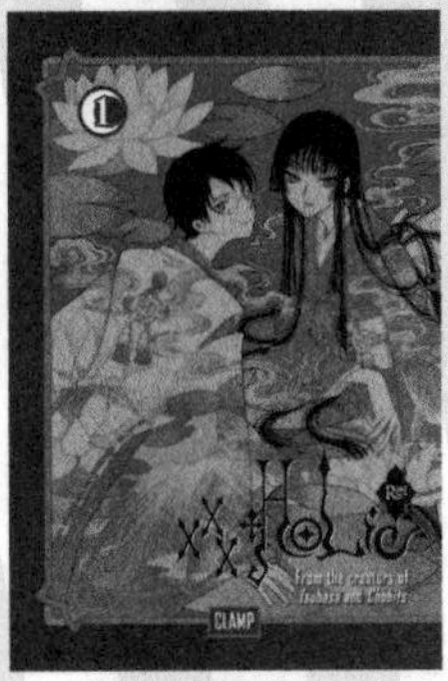
1
xxxHOLiC
CLAMP

xxxHOLiC Rei

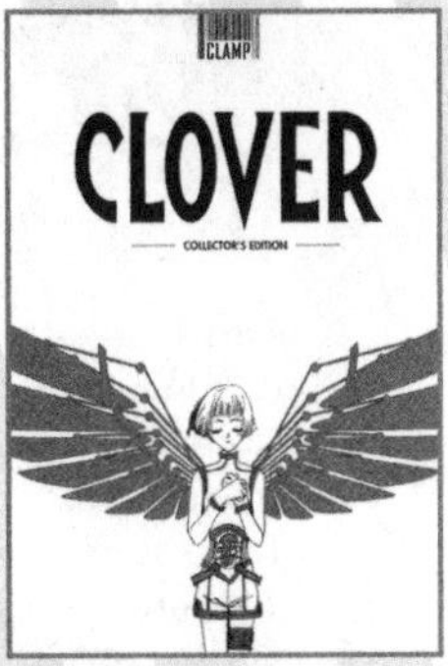
CLAMP
CLOVER
COLLECTOR'S EDITION

CLOVER Collector's Edition

KC KODANSHA COMICS

Kodansha Comics welcomes you to explore the expansive world of CLAMP, the all-female artist collective that has produced some of the most acclaimed manga of the century. Our growing catalog includes icons like *Cardcaptor Sakura* and *Magic Knight Rayearth*, each crafted with CLAMP's one-of-a-kind style and characters!

THE SWEET SCENT OF LOVE IS IN THE AIR! FOR FANS OF OFFBEAT ROMANCES LIKE *WOTAKOI*

Sweat and Soap © Kintetsu Yamada / Kodansha Ltd.

In an office romance, there's a fine line between sexy and awkward... and that line is where Asako — a woman who sweats copiously — meets Koutarou — a perfume developer who can't get enough of Asako's, er, scent. Don't miss a romcom manga like no other!

KC
KODANSHA
COMICS

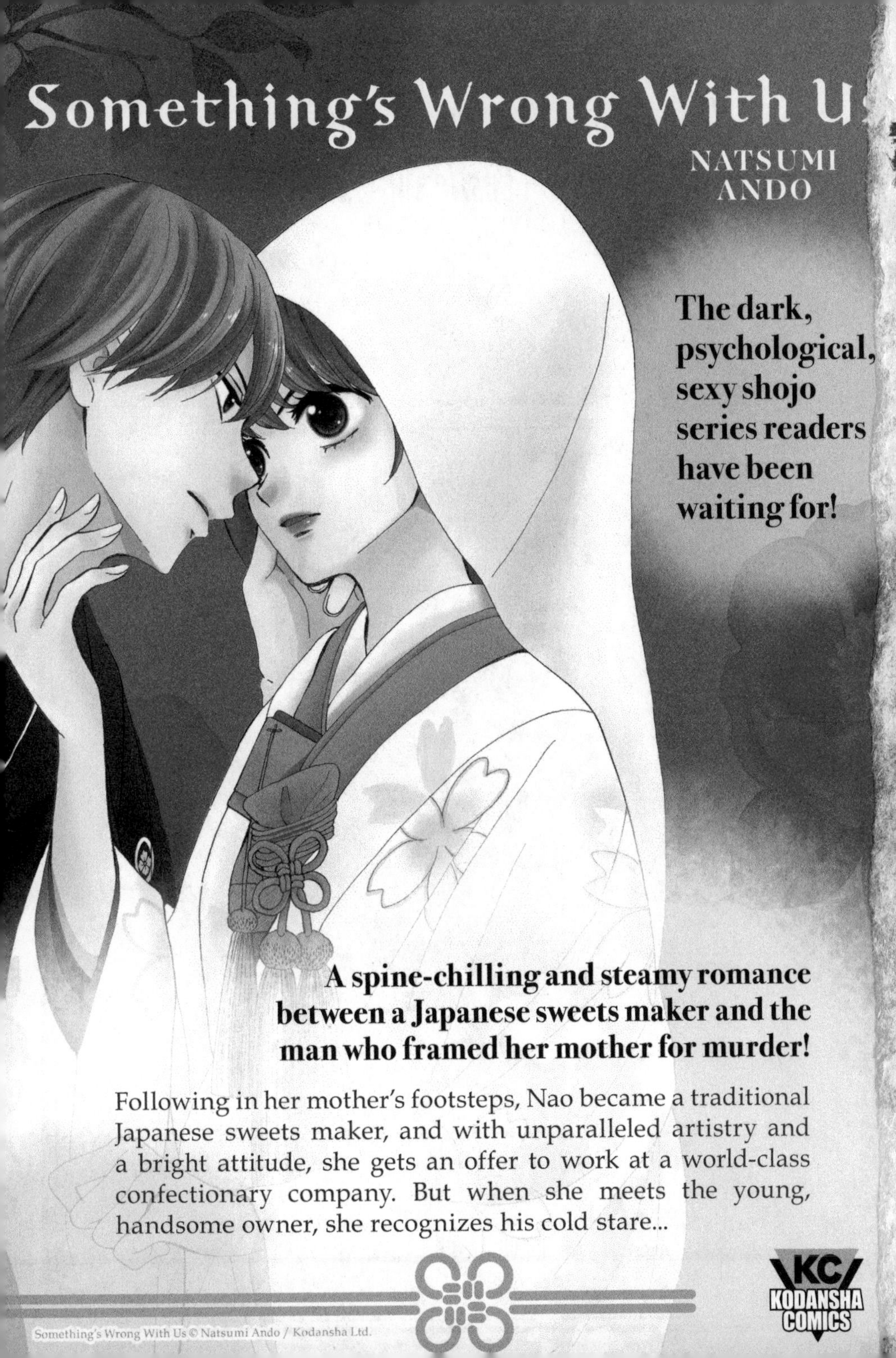
Something's Wrong With Us
NATSUMI ANDO
The dark, psychological, sexy shojo series readers have been waiting for!
A spine-chilling and steamy romance between a Japanese sweets maker and the man who framed her mother for murder!
Following in her mother's footsteps, Nao became a traditional Japanese sweets maker, and with unparalleled artistry and a bright attitude, she gets an offer to work at a world-class confectionary company. But when she meets the young, handsome owner, she recognizes his cold stare...
KC KODANSHA COMICS
Something's Wrong With Us © Natsumi Ando / Kodansha Ltd.

Young characters and steampunk setting, like *Howl's Moving Castle* and *Battle Angel Alita*

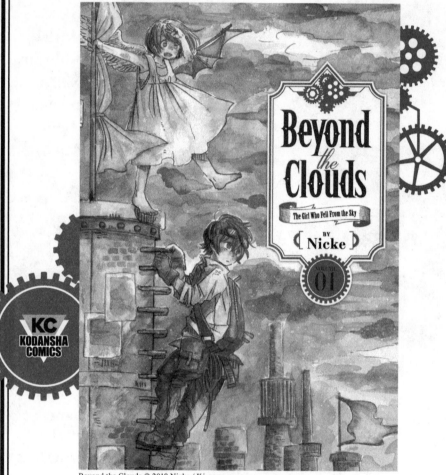

Beyond the Clouds © 2018 Nicke / Ki-oon

A boy with a talent for machines and a mysterious girl whose wings he's fixed will take you beyond the clouds! In the tradition of the high-flying, resonant adventure stories of Studio Ghibli comes a gorgeous tale about the longing of young hearts for adventure and friendship!

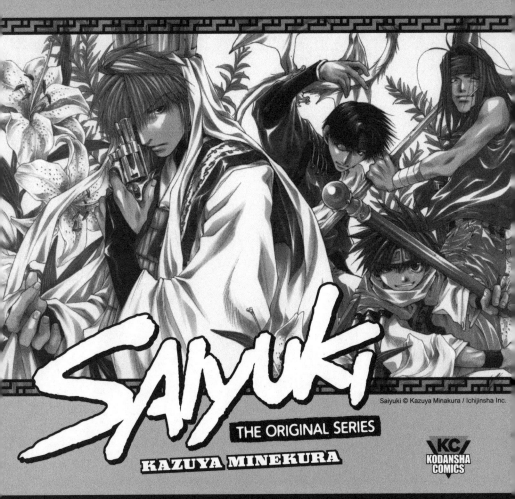

PERFECT WORLD

Rie Aruga

A TOUCHING
NEW SERIES
ABOUT LOVE AND
COPING WITH
DISABILITY

An office party reunites Tsugumi with her high school crush Itsuki. He's realized his dream of becoming an architect, but along the way, he experienced a spinal injury that put him in a wheelchair. Now Tsugumi's rekindled feelings will butt up against prejudices she never considered — and Itsuki will have to decide if he's ready to let someone into his heart...

"Depicts with great delicacy and courage the difficulties some with disabilities experience getting involved in romantic relationships... Rie Aruga refuses to romanticize, pushing her heroine to face the reality of disability. She invites her readers to the same tasks of empathy, knowledge and recognition."
—Slate.fr

"An important entry [in manga romance]... The emotional core of both plot and characters indicates thoughtfulness... [Aruga's] research is readily apparent in the text and artwork, making this feel like a real story."
—Anime News Network

KC
KODANSHA
COMICS

A SMART, NEW ROMANTIC COMEDY FOR FANS OF *SHORTCAKE CAKE* AND *TERRACE HOUSE*!

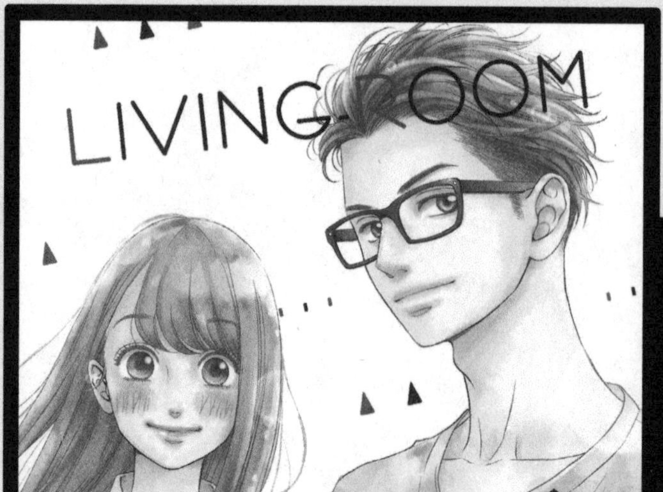
LIVING-ROOM
1
Keiko Iwashita
MATSUNAGA-SAN

A romance manga starring high school girl Meeko, who learns to live on her own in a boarding house whose living room is home to the odd (but handsome) Matsunaga-san. She begins to adjust to her new life away from her parents, but Meeko soon learns that no matter how far away from home she is, she's still a young girl at heart — especially when she finds herself falling for Matsunaga-san.

A Kodansha Comics Trade Paperback Original
Rent-A-Girlfriend 7 copyright © 2018 Reiji Miyajima
English translation copyright © 2021 Reiji Miyajima

Published in the United States by Kodansha Comics, an imprint of Kodansha USA Publishing, LLC, New York.

Publication rights for this English edition arranged through Kodansha Ltd., Tokyo.

First published in Japan in 2018 by Kodansha Ltd., Tokyo as Kanojo, okarishimasu, volume 7.

ISBN 978-1-64651-091-7

Original cover design by Kohei Nawata Design Office

Printed in the United States of America.

www.kodansha.us

9 8 7 6 5 4 3 2
Translation: Kevin Gifford
Lettering: Paige Pumphrey
Editing: Jordan Blanco
Kodansha Comics edition cover design by Phil Balsman

Publisher: Kiichiro Sugawara

Director of publishing services: Ben Applegate
Associate director of operations: Stephen Pakula
Publishing services managing editors: Alanna Ruse, Madison Salters
Production managers: Emi Lotto, Angela Zurlo
Logo and character art ©Kodansha USA Publishing, LLC